MURMURS OF DOUBT

REBECCA FOX

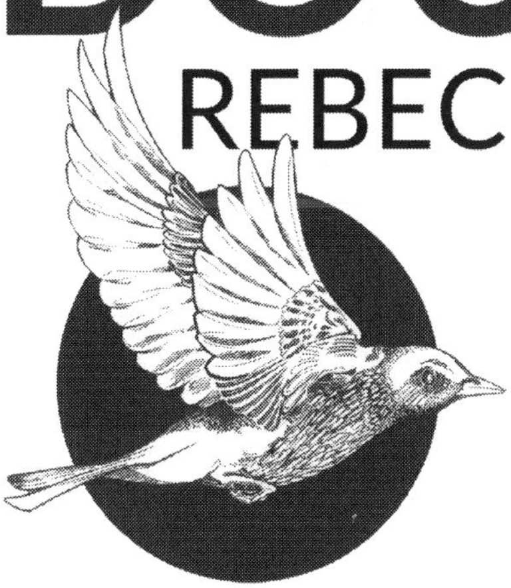

Published by Ockham Publishing in the United Kingdom

ISBN 978-1-910780-14-5

Cover design by Rebecca Fox

www.ockham-publishing.com

MURMURS OF DOUBT

CONTENTS

INTRODUCTION
BY ROBIN INCE

I AM FORTUNATE TO HAVE NEVER HAD A FERVENT BELIEF. I was brought up a Christian, but in a church where its grasp and the hell of dogma was not so overpowering, and the community not so brutal or accusatory that I couldn't just slip away. I have never had to brutalise my mind in an attempt to separate myself from a childhood indoctrination. I've still held silly beliefs and argued furiously for them, but the timeline from closely held to turn-to-dust belief is usually days not years. I am sure I hold some pretty daft beliefs now, but I don't think they rule my life. I attempt to be a utilitarian and hold to the belief of Kurt Vonnegut —God damn it, you've got to be kind—and the belief of Carl Sagan that looking up at the planets and stars and questioning why they are as they are is a humbling experience.

In recent times, there seems to have been an outburst of groups keen to claw back their bigotries. The accepted belief that the vast majority were marching happily towards tolerance has started to teeter. The optimism that came with the easy access to vast libraries of information via the internet didn't take into account the new speed that misinformation and disinformation could travel at. Rather than increasing pragmatic doubt, the wealth of accessible information has flooded our brains and made people cocksure and triumphant even when all the reliable evidence is against them. At the time of writing, there is a grotesque and vain baby-man in charge of the White House and his first week has not gone well.

Across the scientific community, in many different disciplines, there is a vast quantity of evidence powerfully suggesting that the actions of humans are causing the climate to change at a dangerous speed. Despite this, a large number of politicians and their constituents consider it all to be piffle. The human genome has now been sequenced, we are seeing magnificent possibilities of combating and preventing disease using cutting edge genetic innovation, and yet in the most recent surveys, belief in evolution as a theory of life on Earth is decreasing.

In a world where many people rely, on a minute-by-minute basis, on the creations of the scientific and technological mind, they have been persuaded to be highly suspicious of scientists and their work. While feeding off the comforts brought to us by curiosity and experiment, we mock the scientists as an out of touch "elite".

Is this retrograde step a blip in progress, or are we facing a long haul backwards, traveling back to a world of burning the old and unwed for crop failure and blaming those who are not as us for unruly weather and catastrophes? Sadly, we've never quite managed to progress forward enough to entirely rid our system of politicians who blame floods on the happiness of same sex couples. Apparently, the water gods don't like happy lesbians.

Why are we still struggling to embrace evidence-based thinking when it has given us so much? Why are our primal and primeval fears still so vivid when we have the tools to combat them? "You can prove anything with facts", as the comedian Stewart Lee was once told by someone both fact-less and certain. The power of anecdote still trumps the power of statistics. However good the graph is, it doesn't stick in the mind as powerfully as "I had a friend who told me that her mum...something something...and then after she died, it turned out she had loads of spiders living in her brain". Communicating ideas means that we have to make them alluring.

I have been fortunate to spend the last decade working with scientists and trying to find the best ways to convey information so that it stays 'sticky'. One of the most liberating discoveries was the importance of doubt. Here we were in a probabilistic universe, where physicists were engaged in a pursuit with no end in sight, and where all ideas and theories should be treated with differing levels of doubt. We are a creature demanding certainty and finding it very difficult to get used to the idea that it is not at hand.

There are those in politics and the media that wish to believe that their "voting herd" are simple-minded people after simple pleasures, that a desire to look at the night sky through a telescope or look at great art is an exclusive pursuit for the pampered and pretentious. Having played in shows around the world, at outdoor rock festivals and indoor chapels, in breweries and in barns, I know this is bullshit. People delight in being curious. They want to question things and they like knowing how to pick things apart pragmatically. Skepticism is a very necessary tool when we have so much information around us. When you are offered so many truths on an hourly basis, you need the mental equipment to work out what is most likely to be right, or at least most likely to be least wrong. This is not just about the scientific; it is about the political and the social. If we are to survive, we must arm ourselves with critical thinking and learn how to make our stories both accurate and attractive. There is much money and power to be gained by those who effectively mislead, turning the innocents into pariahs and outcasts for their own gain.

Whilst there has been an increase in the dehumanising of groups in the last decade, Rebecca's work rehumanises those who some wish to turn into outcasts. She gives a voice to the marginalised and those who the mainstream may wish to declare do not or cannot belong.

Mark Twain wrote, "it is easier to fool people than convince them that they have been fooled". Once you have publicly declared even a lightly held belief, the natural human position seems to be to hold onto it with a tight grip in the face of opposition. How do we coax people from these brutal beliefs, self punishing credo and damaging wrong-headedness?

Rebecca's work is a good start; her storytelling and art work together to double the potency of her point. Each chapter is persuasive because it is human. Human empathy is two-pronged. It is empathy that allows a torturer to work out the most effective treatment to destroy, but it is empathy that makes us act when we see others suffering in a way we would not wish to ourselves. Rebecca places us in other people's lives, and for a few pages we see through their eyes and we are steered towards questioning justice and action. Days later, we realise how 'sticky' these tales have been; they are still with us, gleaming in the physical events around us that reflect her storytelling. They are a call to avoid being complacent in our thinking and passive in our actions. They remind us that we must keep rethinking why we believe what we believe and why we act as we do.

Robin Ince, January 2017

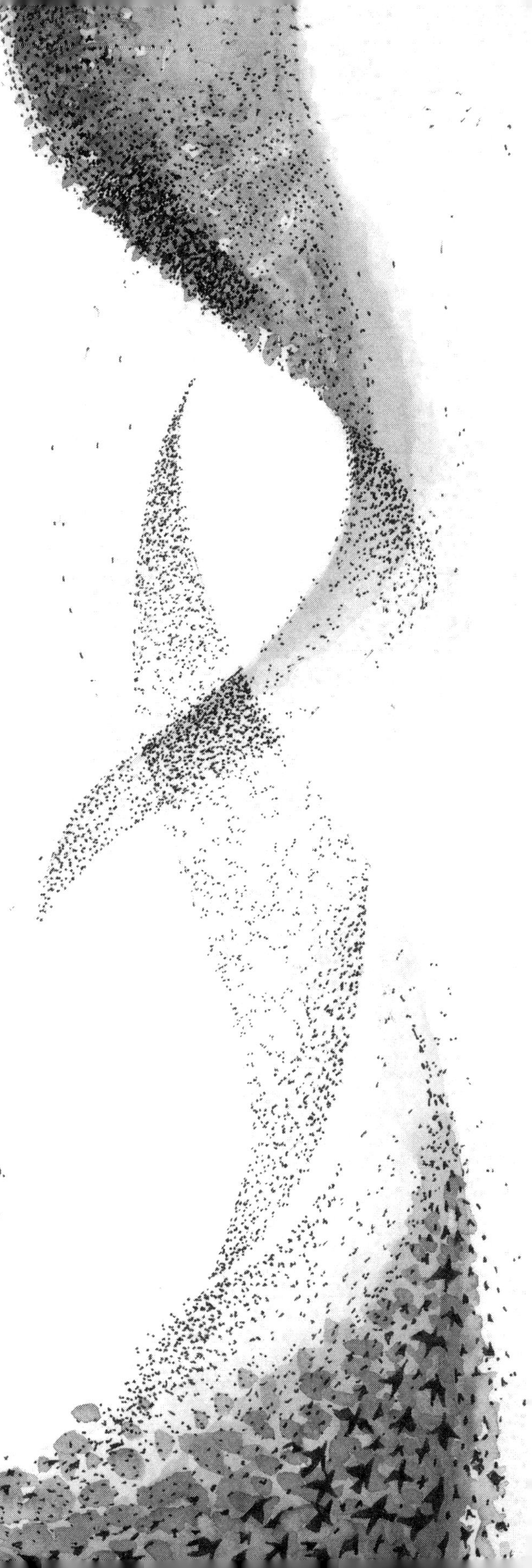

PRIVILEGED TO BE
DHARAMSALA, NORTHERN INDIA

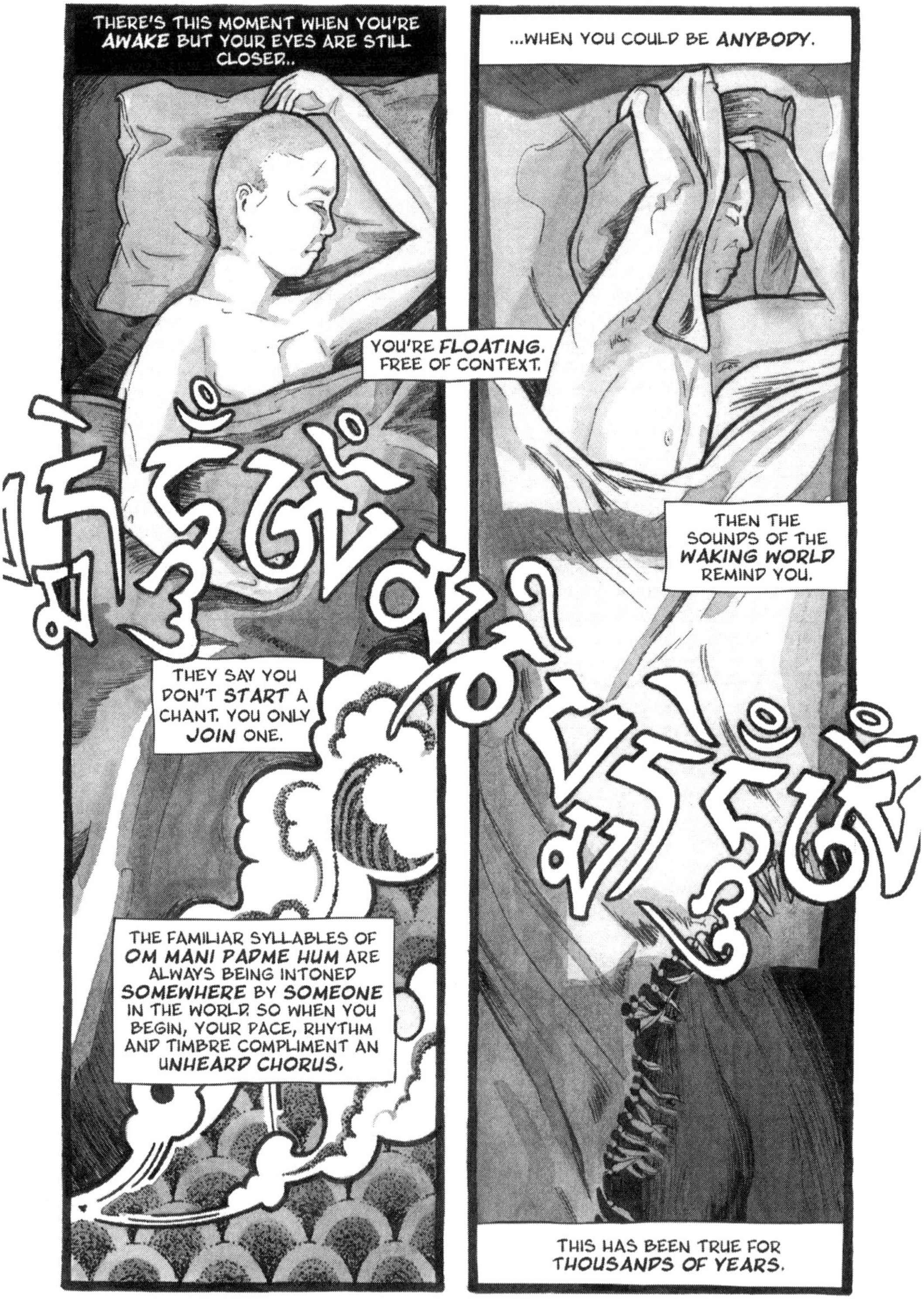
THERE'S THIS MOMENT WHEN YOU'RE AWAKE BUT YOUR EYES ARE STILL CLOSED...
...WHEN YOU COULD BE ANYBODY.
YOU'RE FLOATING. FREE OF CONTEXT.
THEN THE SOUNDS OF THE WAKING WORLD REMIND YOU.
THEY SAY YOU DON'T START A CHANT. YOU ONLY JOIN ONE.
THE FAMILIAR SYLLABLES OF OM MANI PADME HUM ARE ALWAYS BEING INTONED SOMEWHERE BY SOMEONE IN THE WORLD. SO WHEN YOU BEGIN, YOUR PACE, RHYTHM AND TIMBRE COMPLIMENT AN UNHEARD CHORUS.
THIS HAS BEEN TRUE FOR THOUSANDS OF YEARS.

WE *REJOIN* THE WORLD

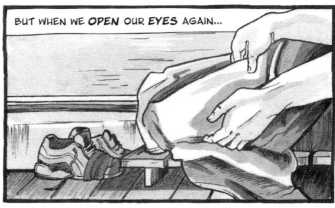

BUT WHEN WE *OPEN* OUR *EYES* AGAIN...

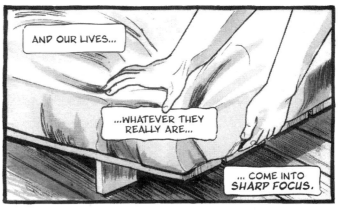

AND OUR LIVES...

...WHATEVER THEY REALLY ARE...

... COME INTO *SHARP FOCUS.*

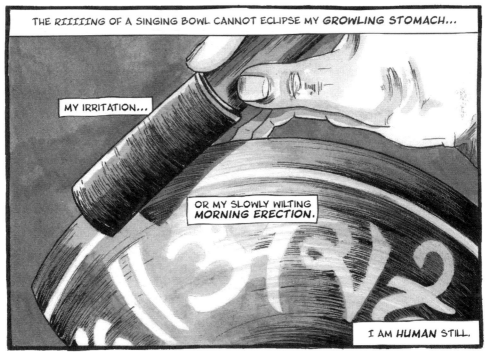

THE *RIIIIING* OF A SINGING BOWL CANNOT ECLIPSE MY *GROWLING STOMACH...*

MY IRRITATION...

OR MY SLOWLY WILTING *MORNING ERECTION.*

I AM *HUMAN* STILL.

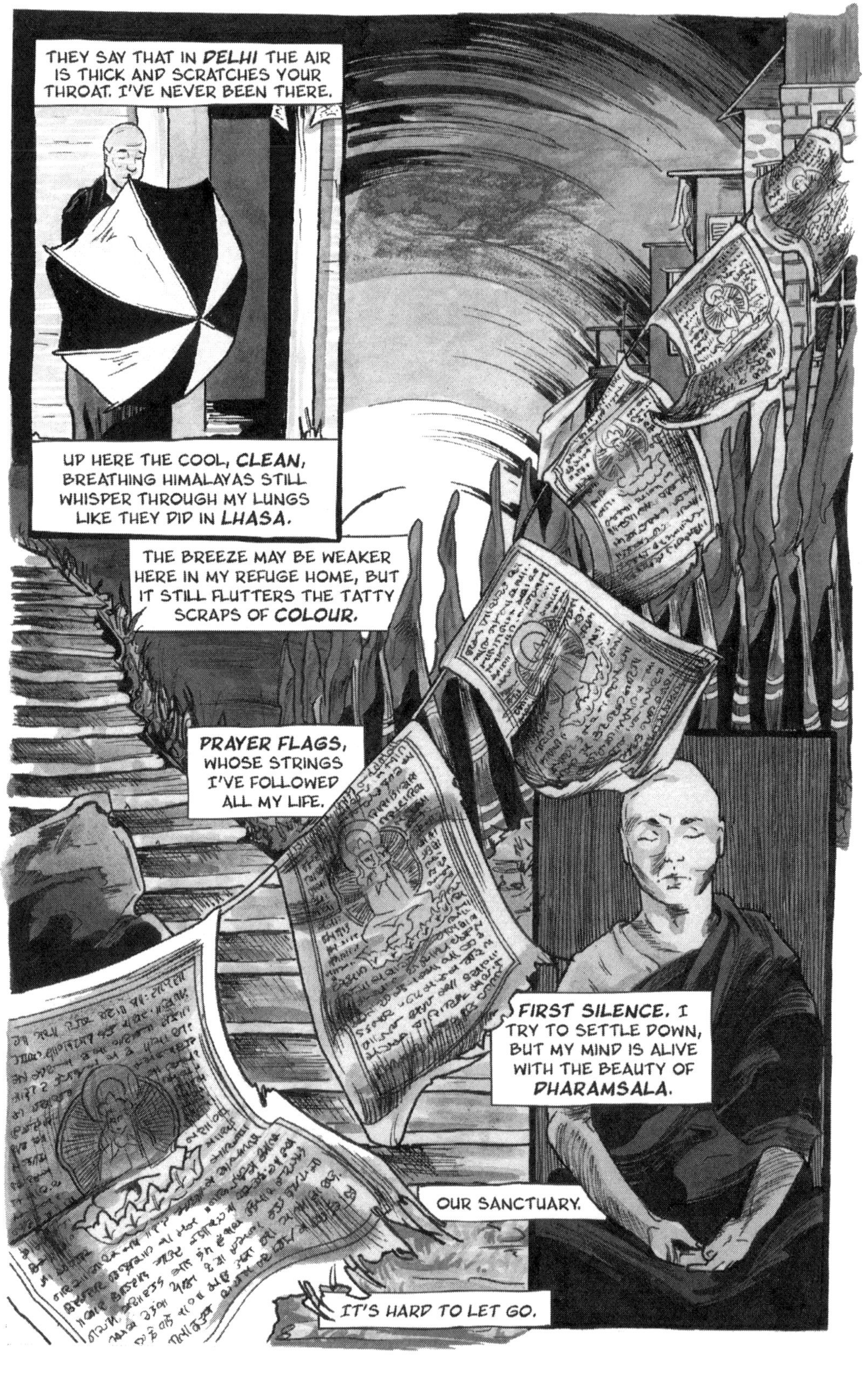
THEY SAY THAT IN DELHI THE AIR IS THICK AND SCRATCHES YOUR THROAT. I'VE NEVER BEEN THERE.
UP HERE THE COOL, CLEAN, BREATHING HIMALAYAS STILL WHISPER THROUGH MY LUNGS LIKE THEY DID IN LHASA.
THE BREEZE MAY BE WEAKER HERE IN MY REFUGE HOME, BUT IT STILL FLUTTERS THE TATTY SCRAPS OF COLOUR.
PRAYER FLAGS, WHOSE STRINGS I'VE FOLLOWED ALL MY LIFE.
FIRST SILENCE. I TRY TO SETTLE DOWN, BUT MY MIND IS ALIVE WITH THE BEAUTY OF DHARAMSALA.
OUR SANCTUARY.
IT'S HARD TO LET GO.

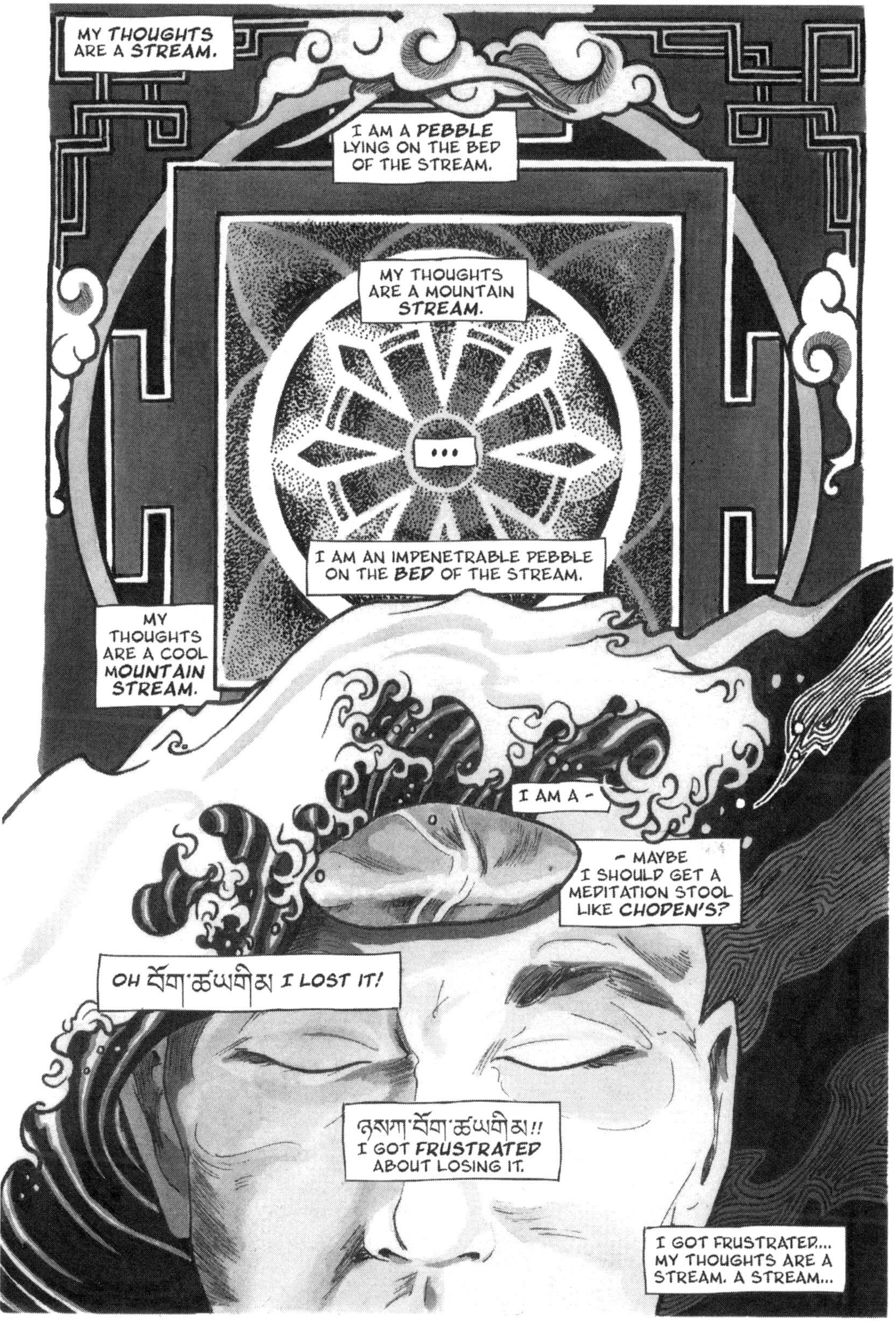
MY THOUGHTS ARE A STREAM.
I AM A PEBBLE LYING ON THE BED OF THE STREAM.
MY THOUGHTS ARE A MOUNTAIN STREAM.
...
I AM AN IMPENETRABLE PEBBLE ON THE BED OF THE STREAM.
MY THOUGHTS ARE A COOL MOUNTAIN STREAM.
I AM A -
- MAYBE I SHOULD GET A MEDITATION STOOL LIKE CHODEN'S?
OH བོག་ཚཡགིམ I LOST IT!
ཉམག་བོག་ཚཡགིམ!! I GOT FRUSTRATED ABOUT LOSING IT.
I GOT FRUSTRATED... MY THOUGHTS ARE A STREAM. A STREAM...

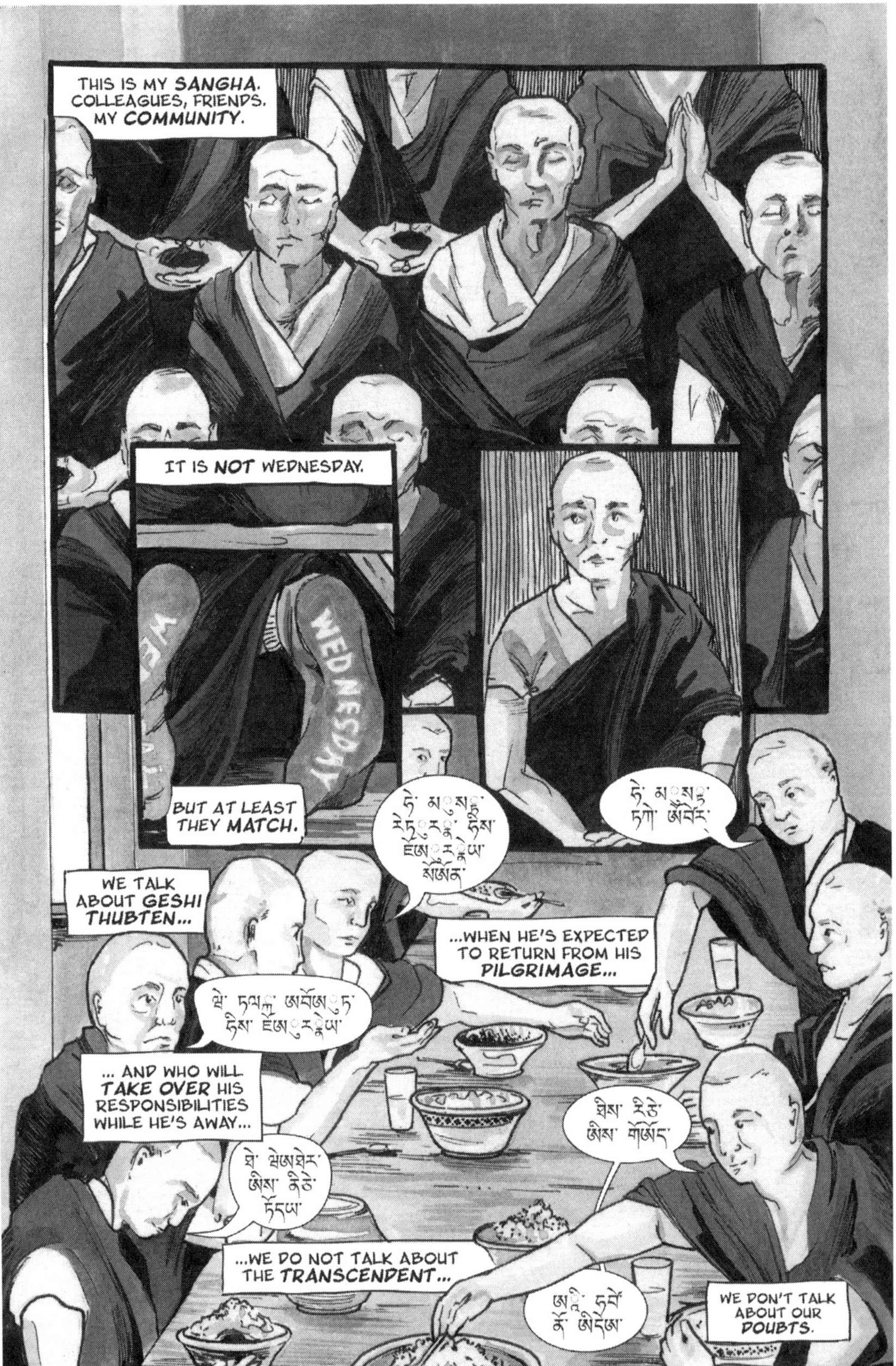
THIS IS MY SANGHA. COLLEAGUES, FRIENDS. MY COMMUNITY.
IT IS NOT WEDNESDAY.
WEDNESDAY
BUT AT LEAST THEY MATCH.
WE TALK ABOUT GESHI THUBTEN...
...WHEN HE'S EXPECTED TO RETURN FROM HIS PILGRIMAGE...
... AND WHO WILL TAKE OVER HIS RESPONSIBILITIES WHILE HE'S AWAY...
...WE DO NOT TALK ABOUT THE TRANSCENDENT...
WE DON'T TALK ABOUT OUR DOUBTS.

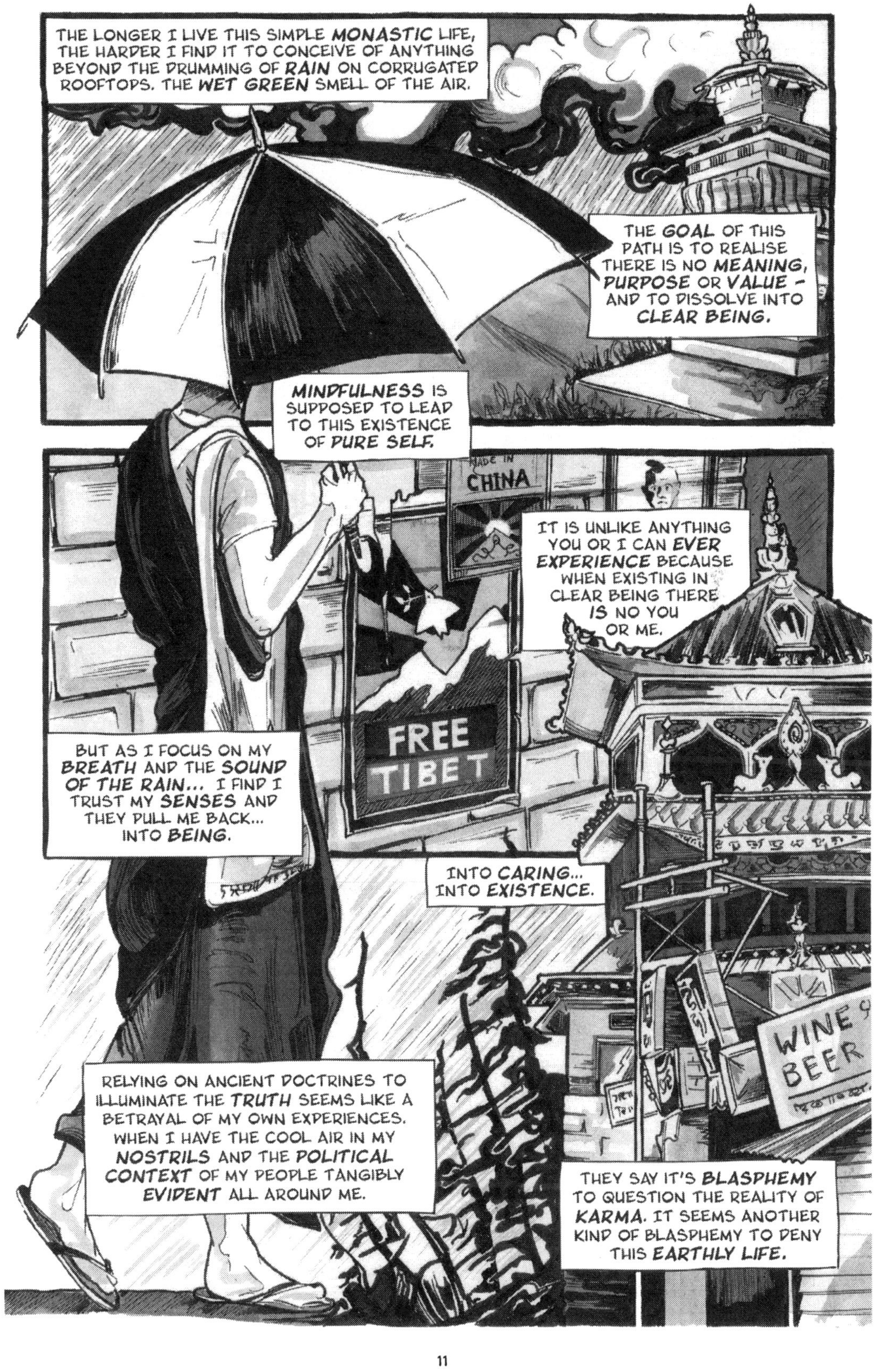
THE LONGER I LIVE THIS SIMPLE MONASTIC LIFE, THE HARDER I FIND IT TO CONCEIVE OF ANYTHING BEYOND THE DRUMMING OF RAIN ON CORRUGATED ROOFTOPS. THE WET GREEN SMELL OF THE AIR.
THE GOAL OF THIS PATH IS TO REALISE THERE IS NO MEANING, PURPOSE OR VALUE – AND TO DISSOLVE INTO CLEAR BEING.
MINDFULNESS IS SUPPOSED TO LEAD TO THIS EXISTENCE OF PURE SELF.
MADE IN CHINA
IT IS UNLIKE ANYTHING YOU OR I CAN EVER EXPERIENCE BECAUSE WHEN EXISTING IN CLEAR BEING THERE IS NO YOU OR ME.
FREE TIBET
BUT AS I FOCUS ON MY BREATH AND THE SOUND OF THE RAIN... I FIND I TRUST MY SENSES AND THEY PULL ME BACK... INTO BEING.
INTO CARING... INTO EXISTENCE.
WINE BEER
RELYING ON ANCIENT DOCTRINES TO ILLUMINATE THE TRUTH SEEMS LIKE A BETRAYAL OF MY OWN EXPERIENCES. WHEN I HAVE THE COOL AIR IN MY NOSTRILS AND THE POLITICAL CONTEXT OF MY PEOPLE TANGIBLY EVIDENT ALL AROUND ME.
THEY SAY IT'S BLASPHEMY TO QUESTION THE REALITY OF KARMA. IT SEEMS ANOTHER KIND OF BLASPHEMY TO DENY THIS EARTHLY LIFE.

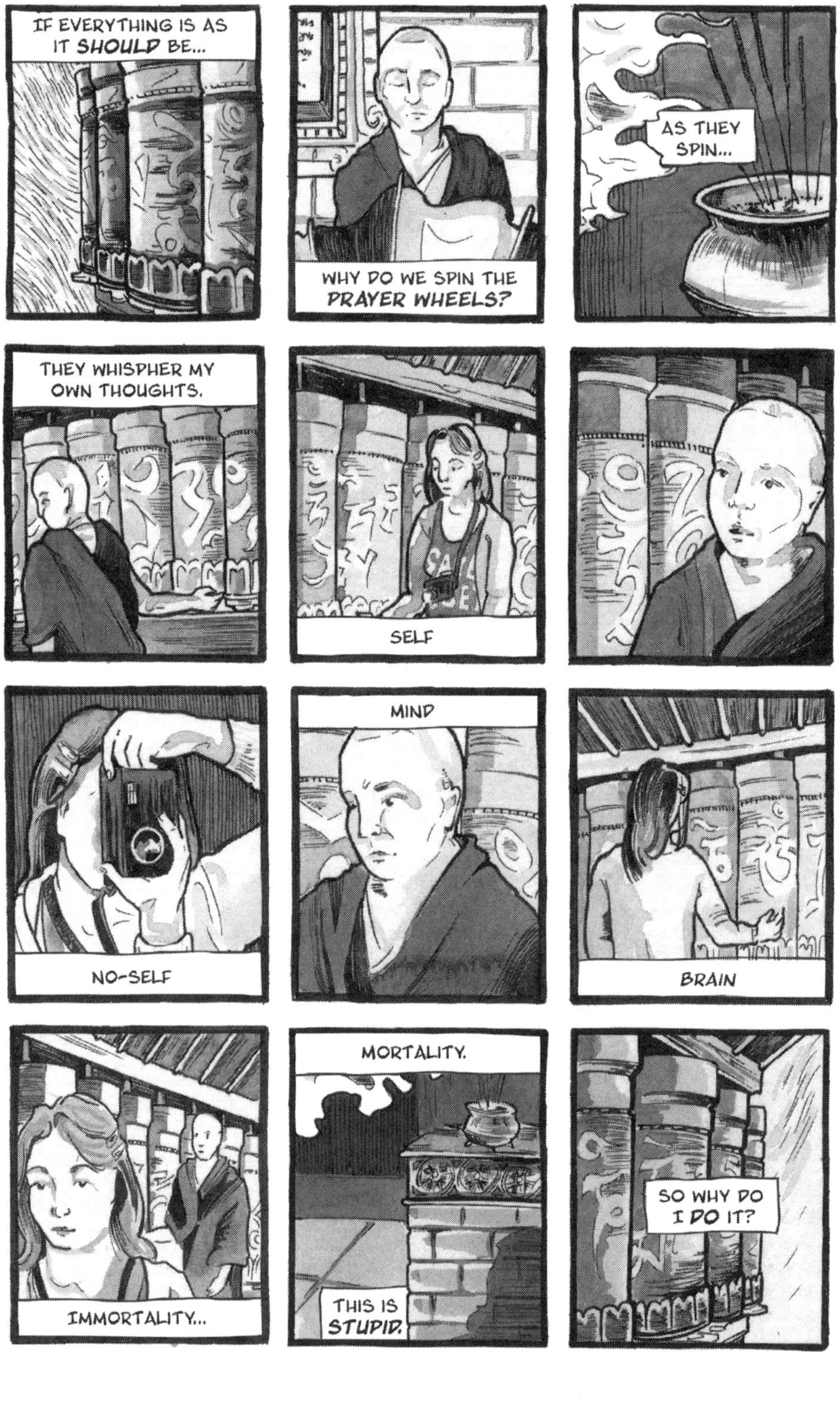
IF EVERYTHING IS AS IT SHOULD BE...
WHY DO WE SPIN THE PRAYER WHEELS?
AS THEY SPIN...
THEY WHISPHER MY OWN THOUGHTS.
SELF
NO-SELF
MIND
BRAIN
IMMORTALITY...
MORTALITY.
THIS IS STUPID.
SO WHY DO I DO IT?

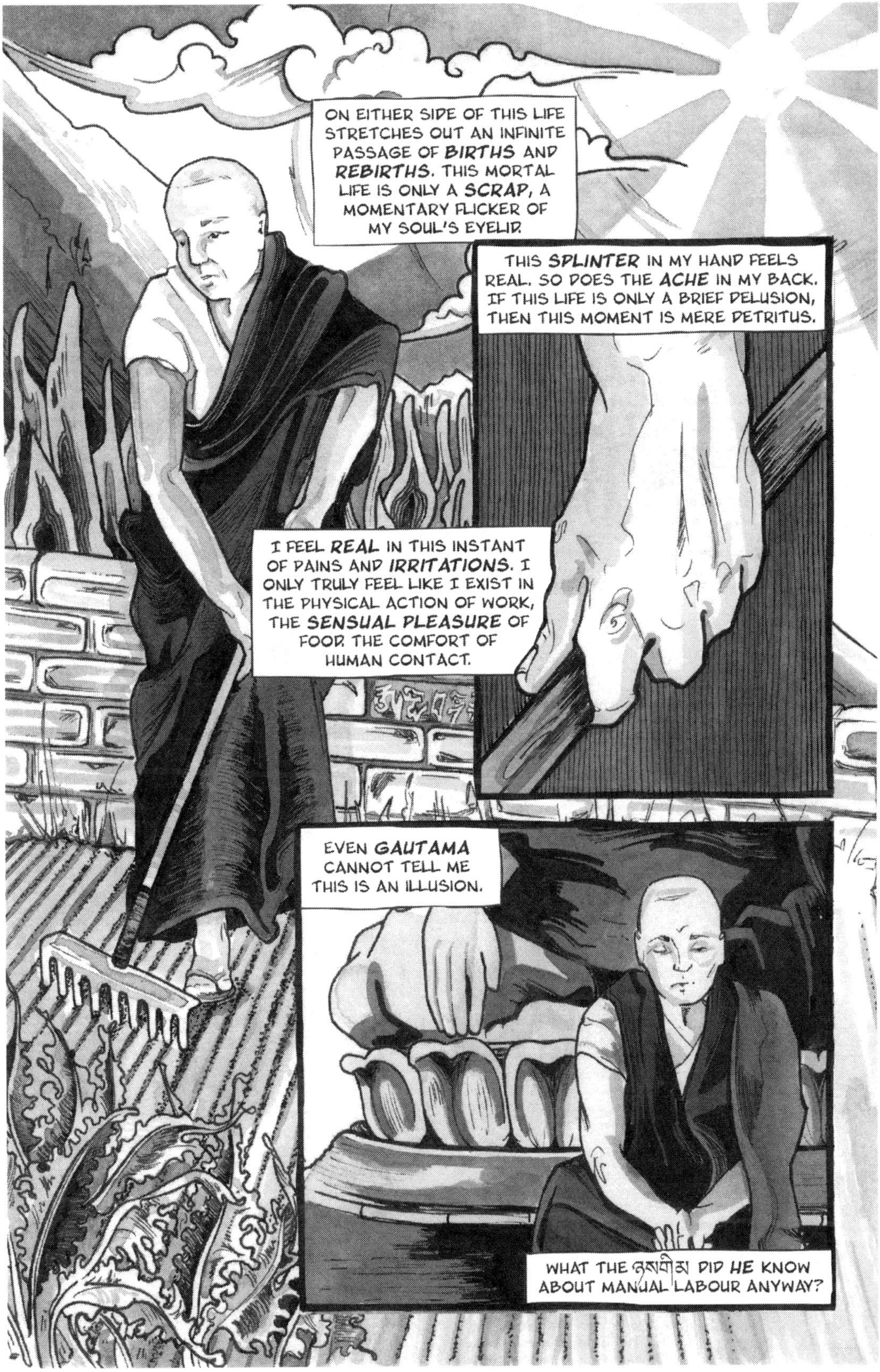
ON EITHER SIDE OF THIS LIFE STRETCHES OUT AN INFINITE PASSAGE OF **BIRTHS** AND **REBIRTHS**. THIS MORTAL LIFE IS ONLY A **SCRAP**, A MOMENTARY FLICKER OF MY SOUL'S EYELID.
THIS **SPLINTER** IN MY HAND FEELS REAL. SO DOES THE **ACHE** IN MY BACK. IF THIS LIFE IS ONLY A BRIEF DELUSION, THEN THIS MOMENT IS MERE DETRITUS.
I FEEL **REAL** IN THIS INSTANT OF PAINS AND **IRRITATIONS**. I ONLY TRULY FEEL LIKE I EXIST IN THE PHYSICAL ACTION OF WORK, THE **SENSUAL PLEASURE** OF FOOD. THE COMFORT OF HUMAN CONTACT.
EVEN **GAUTAMA** CANNOT TELL ME THIS IS AN ILLUSION.
WHAT THE ཉུསབིམ DID **HE** KNOW ABOUT MANUAL LABOUR ANYWAY?

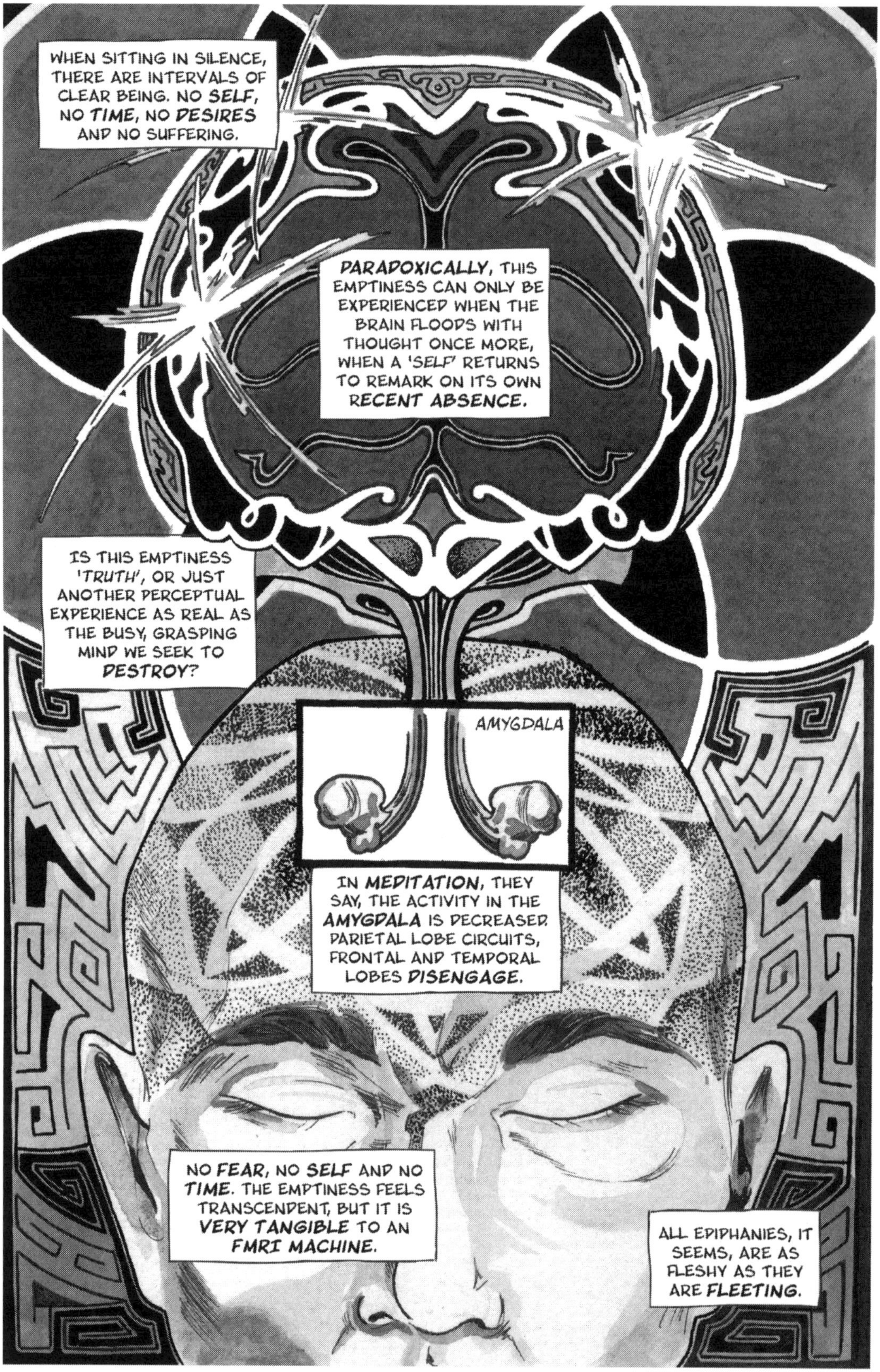
WHEN SITTING IN SILENCE, THERE ARE INTERVALS OF CLEAR BEING. NO SELF, NO TIME, NO DESIRES AND NO SUFFERING.
PARADOXICALLY, THIS EMPTINESS CAN ONLY BE EXPERIENCED WHEN THE BRAIN FLOODS WITH THOUGHT ONCE MORE, WHEN A 'SELF' RETURNS TO REMARK ON ITS OWN RECENT ABSENCE.
IS THIS EMPTINESS 'TRUTH', OR JUST ANOTHER PERCEPTUAL EXPERIENCE AS REAL AS THE BUSY, GRASPING MIND WE SEEK TO DESTROY?
AMYGDALA
IN MEDITATION, THEY SAY, THE ACTIVITY IN THE AMYGDALA IS DECREASED. PARIETAL LOBE CIRCUITS, FRONTAL AND TEMPORAL LOBES DISENGAGE.
NO FEAR, NO SELF AND NO TIME. THE EMPTINESS FEELS TRANSCENDENT, BUT IT IS VERY TANGIBLE TO AN FMRI MACHINE.
ALL EPIPHANIES, IT SEEMS, ARE AS FLESHY AS THEY ARE FLEETING.

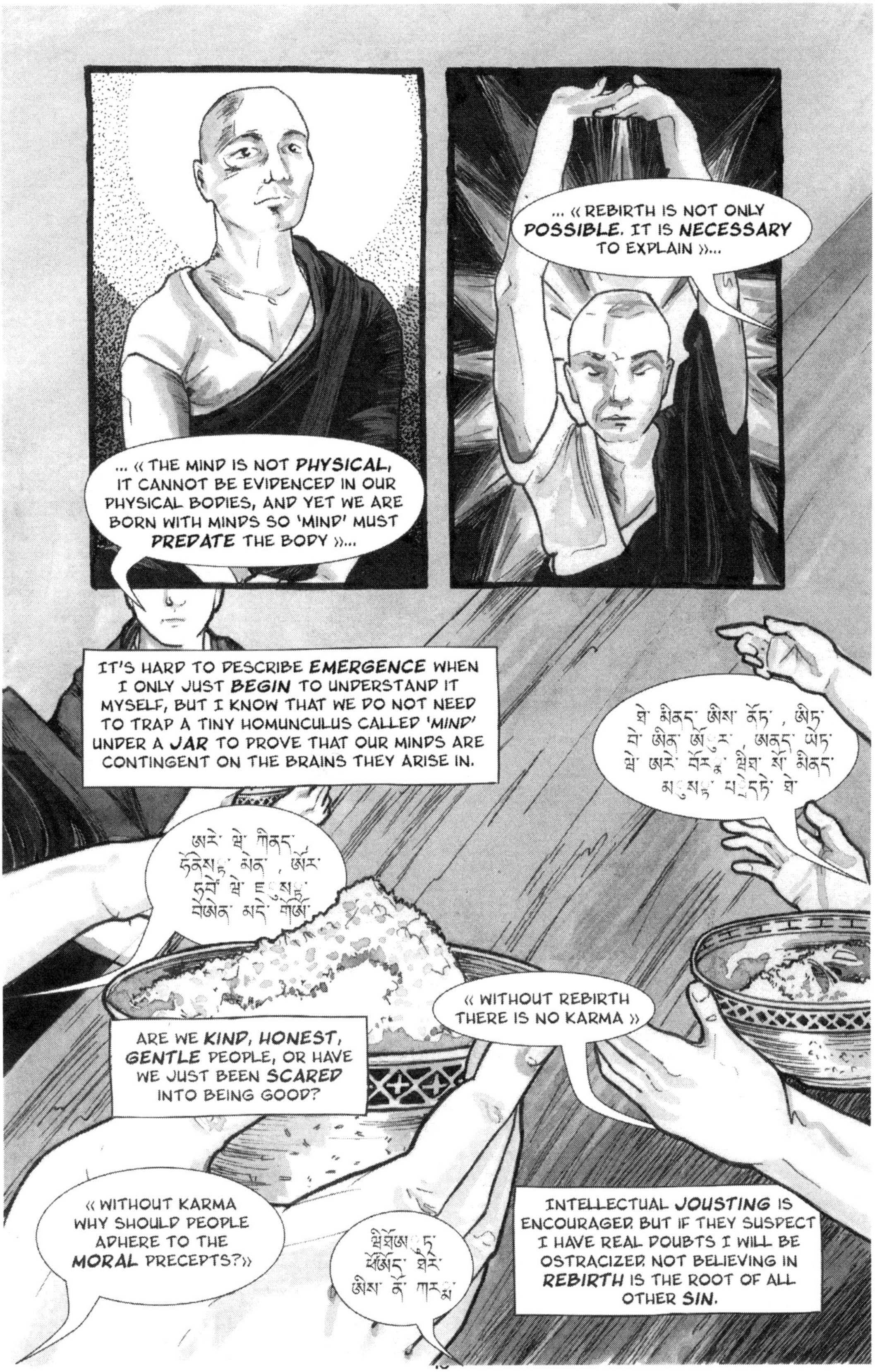
... « THE MIND IS NOT PHYSICAL, IT CANNOT BE EVIDENCED IN OUR PHYSICAL BODIES, AND YET WE ARE BORN WITH MINDS SO 'MIND' MUST PREDATE THE BODY »...
... « REBIRTH IS NOT ONLY POSSIBLE. IT IS NECESSARY TO EXPLAIN »...
IT'S HARD TO DESCRIBE EMERGENCE WHEN I ONLY JUST BEGIN TO UNDERSTAND IT MYSELF, BUT I KNOW THAT WE DO NOT NEED TO TRAP A TINY HOMUNCULUS CALLED 'MIND' UNDER A JAR TO PROVE THAT OUR MINDS ARE CONTINGENT ON THE BRAINS THEY ARISE IN.
« WITHOUT REBIRTH THERE IS NO KARMA »
ARE WE KIND, HONEST, GENTLE PEOPLE, OR HAVE WE JUST BEEN SCARED INTO BEING GOOD?
« WITHOUT KARMA WHY SHOULD PEOPLE ADHERE TO THE MORAL PRECEPTS?»
INTELLECTUAL JOUSTING IS ENCOURAGED BUT IF THEY SUSPECT I HAVE REAL DOUBTS I WILL BE OSTRACIZED. NOT BELIEVING IN REBIRTH IS THE ROOT OF ALL OTHER SIN.

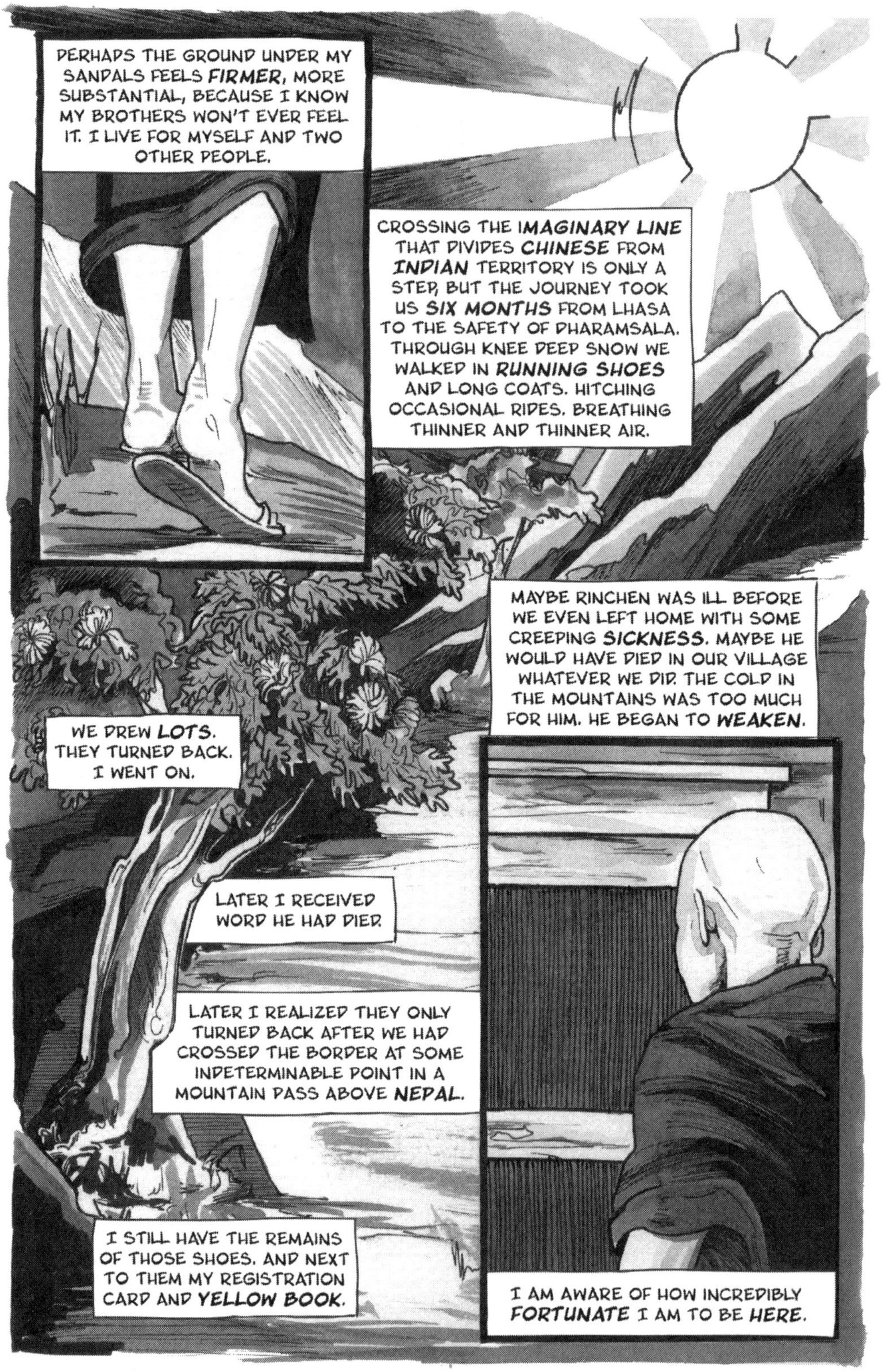
PERHAPS THE GROUND UNDER MY SANDALS FEELS FIRMER, MORE SUBSTANTIAL, BECAUSE I KNOW MY BROTHERS WON'T EVER FEEL IT. I LIVE FOR MYSELF AND TWO OTHER PEOPLE.
CROSSING THE IMAGINARY LINE THAT DIVIDES CHINESE FROM INDIAN TERRITORY IS ONLY A STEP, BUT THE JOURNEY TOOK US SIX MONTHS FROM LHASA TO THE SAFETY OF DHARAMSALA. THROUGH KNEE DEEP SNOW WE WALKED IN RUNNING SHOES AND LONG COATS. HITCHING OCCASIONAL RIDES. BREATHING THINNER AND THINNER AIR.
MAYBE RINCHEN WAS ILL BEFORE WE EVEN LEFT HOME WITH SOME CREEPING SICKNESS. MAYBE HE WOULD HAVE DIED IN OUR VILLAGE WHATEVER WE DID. THE COLD IN THE MOUNTAINS WAS TOO MUCH FOR HIM. HE BEGAN TO WEAKEN.
WE DREW LOTS. THEY TURNED BACK. I WENT ON.
LATER I RECEIVED WORD HE HAD DIED.
LATER I REALIZED THEY ONLY TURNED BACK AFTER WE HAD CROSSED THE BORDER AT SOME INDETERMINABLE POINT IN A MOUNTAIN PASS ABOVE NEPAL.
I STILL HAVE THE REMAINS OF THOSE SHOES. AND NEXT TO THEM MY REGISTRATION CARD AND YELLOW BOOK.
I AM AWARE OF HOW INCREDIBLY FORTUNATE I AM TO BE HERE.

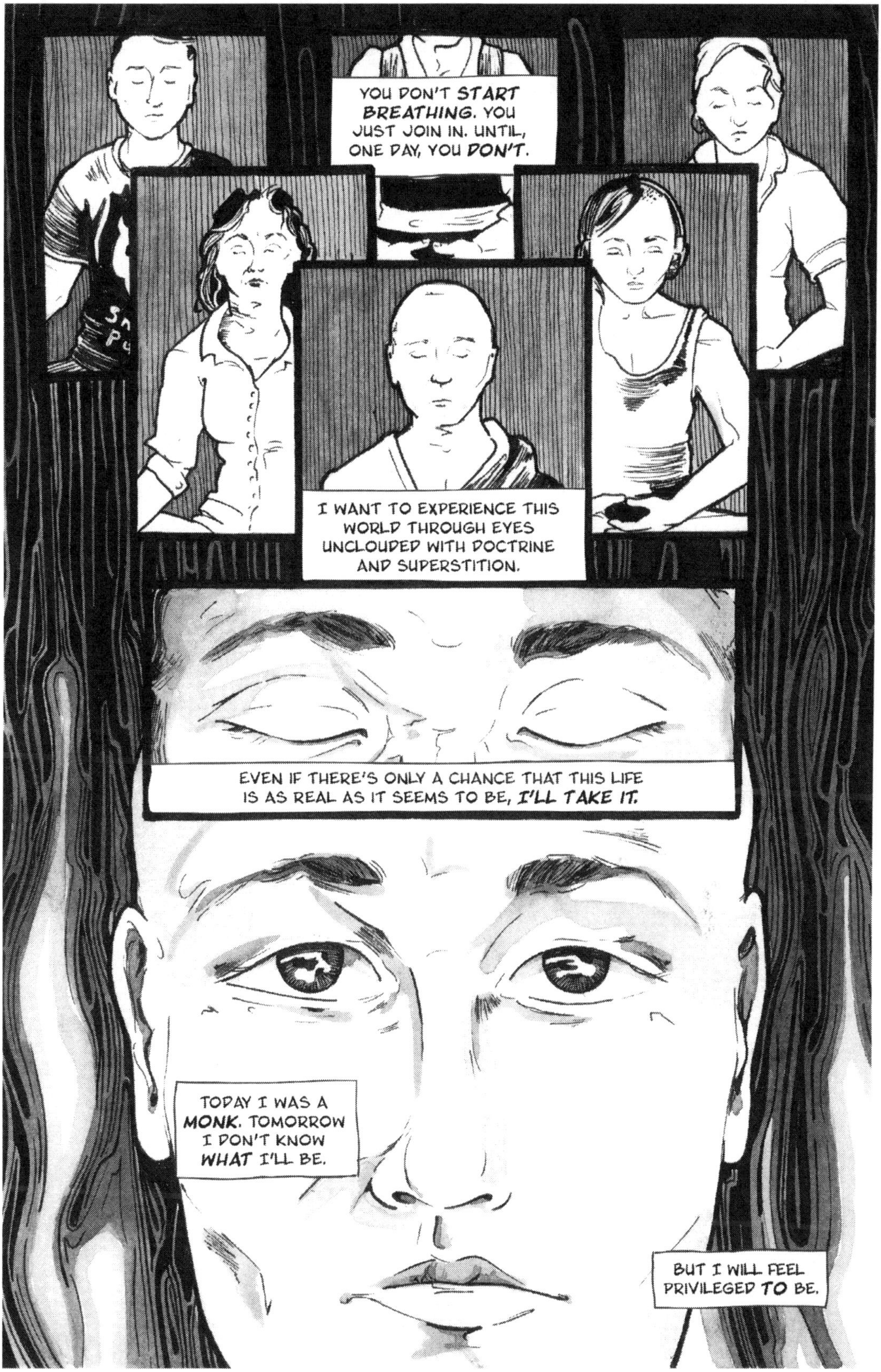
YOU DON'T START BREATHING. YOU JUST JOIN IN. UNTIL, ONE DAY, YOU DON'T.
I WANT TO EXPERIENCE THIS WORLD THROUGH EYES UNCLOUDED WITH DOCTRINE AND SUPERSTITION.
EVEN IF THERE'S ONLY A CHANCE THAT THIS LIFE IS AS REAL AS IT SEEMS TO BE, I'LL TAKE IT.
TODAY I WAS A MONK. TOMORROW I DON'T KNOW WHAT I'LL BE.
BUT I WILL FEEL PRIVILEGED TO BE.

When I first met a Buddhist monk I was surprised to find he was human. The refugee Tibetan monks living in exile in Northern India may be hardened by their gruelling journey across the Himalayas from Tibet and transformed by a lifetime of introspection, but they still have a lot more in common with the rest of humanity than they do with the wizards, sages and saints of mythology.

I don't think I was alone in my misconception. The Western perception of Buddhism is that of a philosophical tradition whose adepts transcend earthly concerns. It's treated as an ancient version of the new age spirituality of the 1970s and often used by proponents of new age ideas as support for their own dubious authenticity.

In Dharamsala, I witnessed the new age vision of Buddhism jostling uneasily with the traditional religious practices of the Tibetan Buddhists who live there. Catering to the spiritual tourists (like my then-self) there were meditation and yoga classes and bootlegged copies of the movie *What the Bleep do we Know?* While monks in maroon and saffron robes, with matching umbrellas, continued their apparently simple contemplative lives.

My new age vision of Buddhism couldn't be sustained when wandering around the medieval style Mahayana temples. It seems everyone but western Buddhists know that the Dalai Lama's favourite food is Ferrero Rocher. Mountains of them surrounded pictures of him. In his monastery Tsuglagkhang, they glisten under electric lights. Their gold wrappers match the ostentatious decor.

Like any other religion Buddhism is fraught with contradictions. In the book *Confessions of a Buddhist Atheist*, former monk Stephen Batchelor recounts his frustrations with the religion. Buddhism, in texts like the Kalama Sutta, encourages free inquiry. But as Batchelor found, on the question of the doctrine of rebirth, those who doubt are damned as guilty of thoughtcrime.

Disallowing doubt is dangerous. Our brains are a ramshackle network of systems which worked well enough to keep our ancestors alive long enough to reproduce. When we are working with such clumsy organs, prone to biases, misperceptions and mistakes, it is important to have humility about our conclusions. Doubt is the motivation we need to sift through our convictions, it is the impetus to turn to our friends and colleagues and ask, *Does this make sense?*

If an idea is not exposed to rigorous, structured scrutiny it can grow into something absurd; and then, beautiful or monstrous, its effects on the world are unpredictable and often destructive.

We all have some of these unchecked ideas lumbering around in our heads. Of course it's easier to spot other people's than our own, which is why doubt should be a communal activity, something we do out of respect and affection for our friends and out of duty to the wider world.

To doubt a body of ideas is to show its adherents the respect they deserve, to treat their claims seriously and subject them to the same standards as you should your own. Doubt opens a window of possibility that doesn't and can't exist in closed belief systems – the possibility for epiphany.

Epiphanies, in this sense, are a glimpse of the world as it really is. They can be mundane or life changing, sometimes seen only from the corner of an eye, other times inescapable. The only thing all epiphanies have in common, no matter how revelatory, is that they must all come from—and be subjected to—doubt.

I've changed my mind about a lot of things in my life as I've broadened my experience and honed my (originally very sloppy) critical thinking skills. I am now a different person to the one who wondered at the spiritual beauty of Tsuglagkhang, but I still have a lot in common with the person who wondered, *What's with all these Ferrero Rocher?*

More information, discussion and links at
doubtcomic.com/privileged-to-be

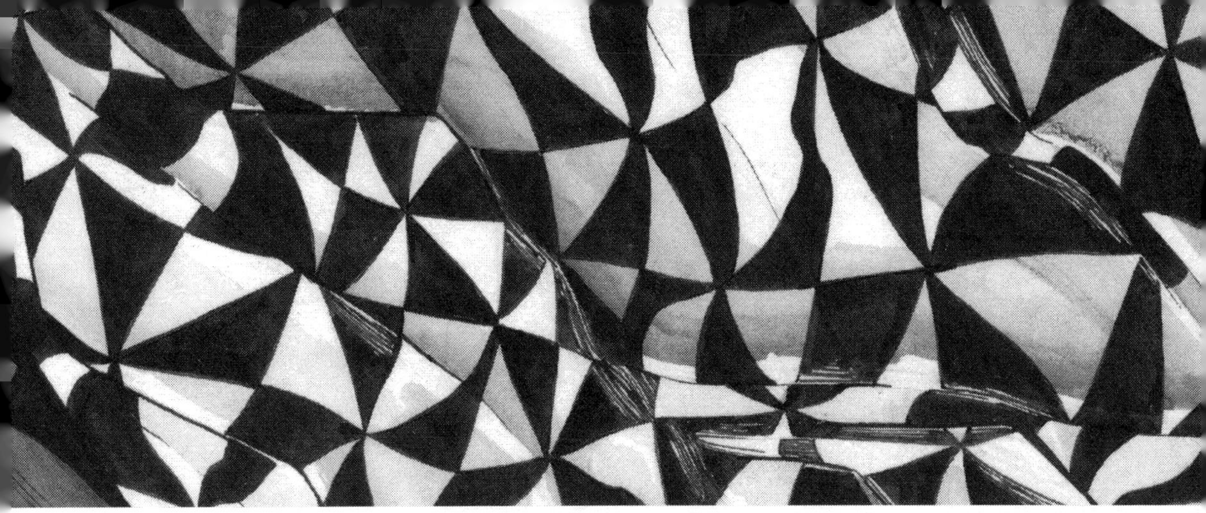

PILLOW TALK

A bedroom, New York City

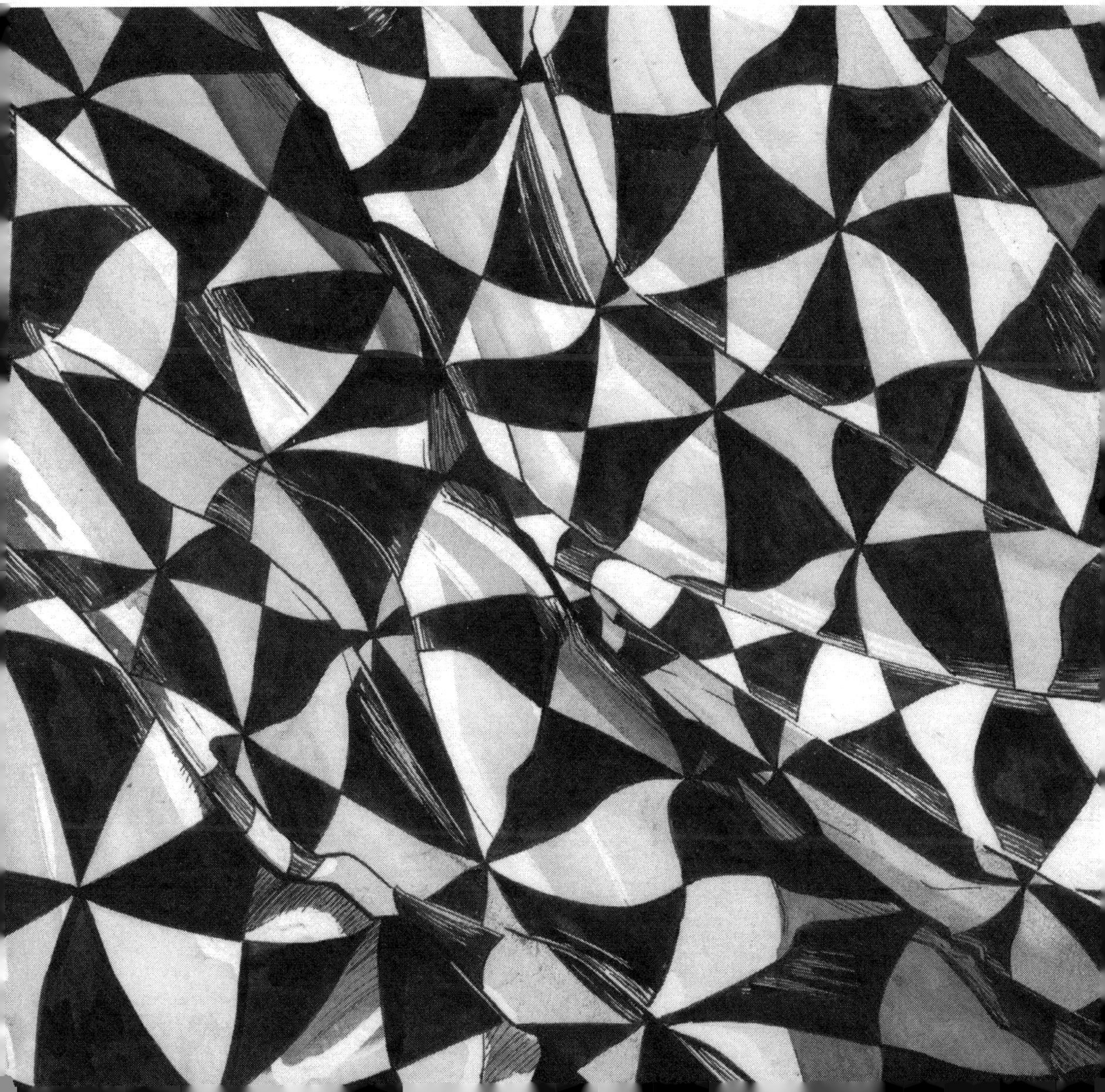

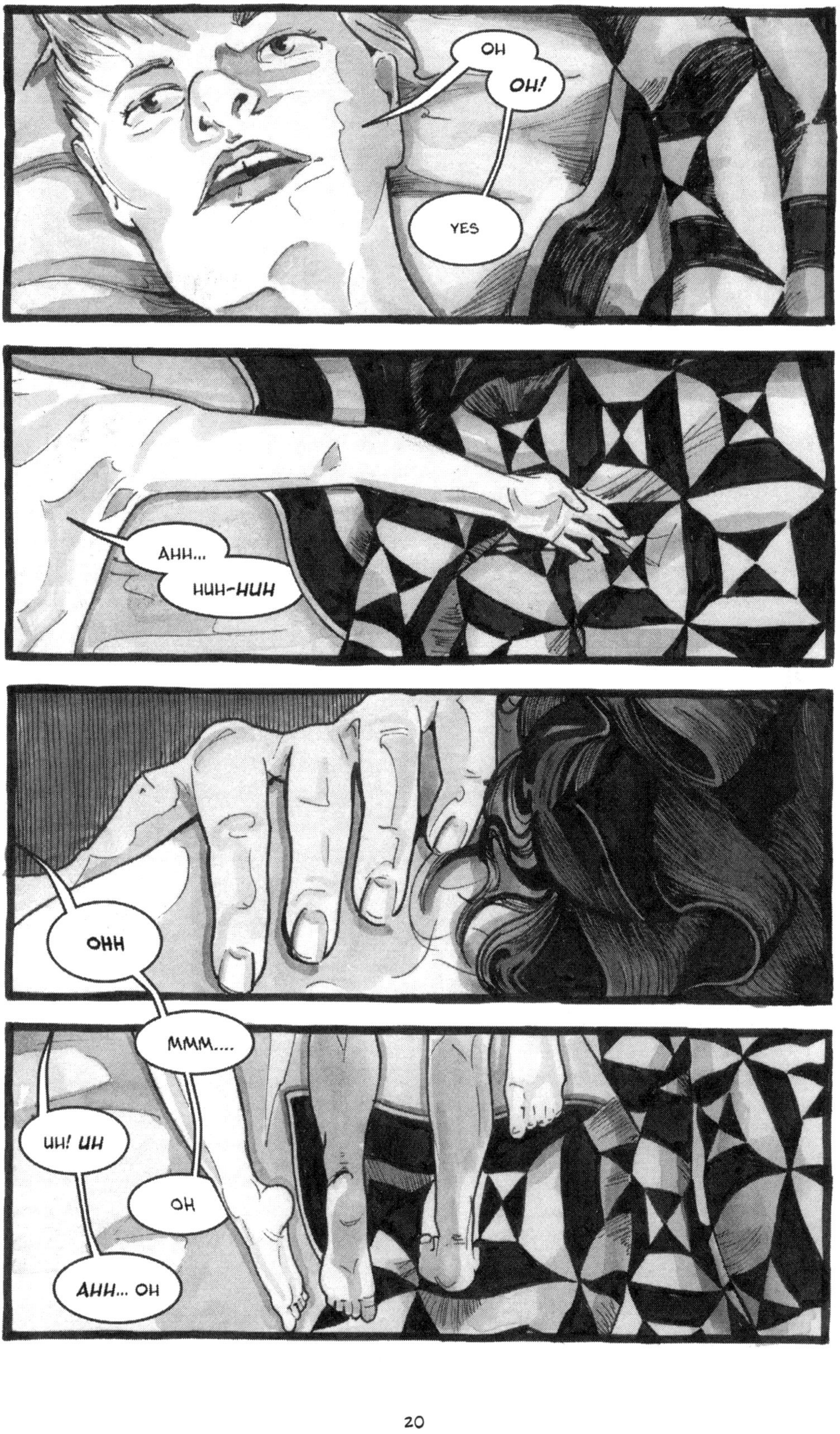
OH
OH!
YES
AHH...
HUH-HUH
OHH
MMM....
UH! UH
OH
AHH... OH

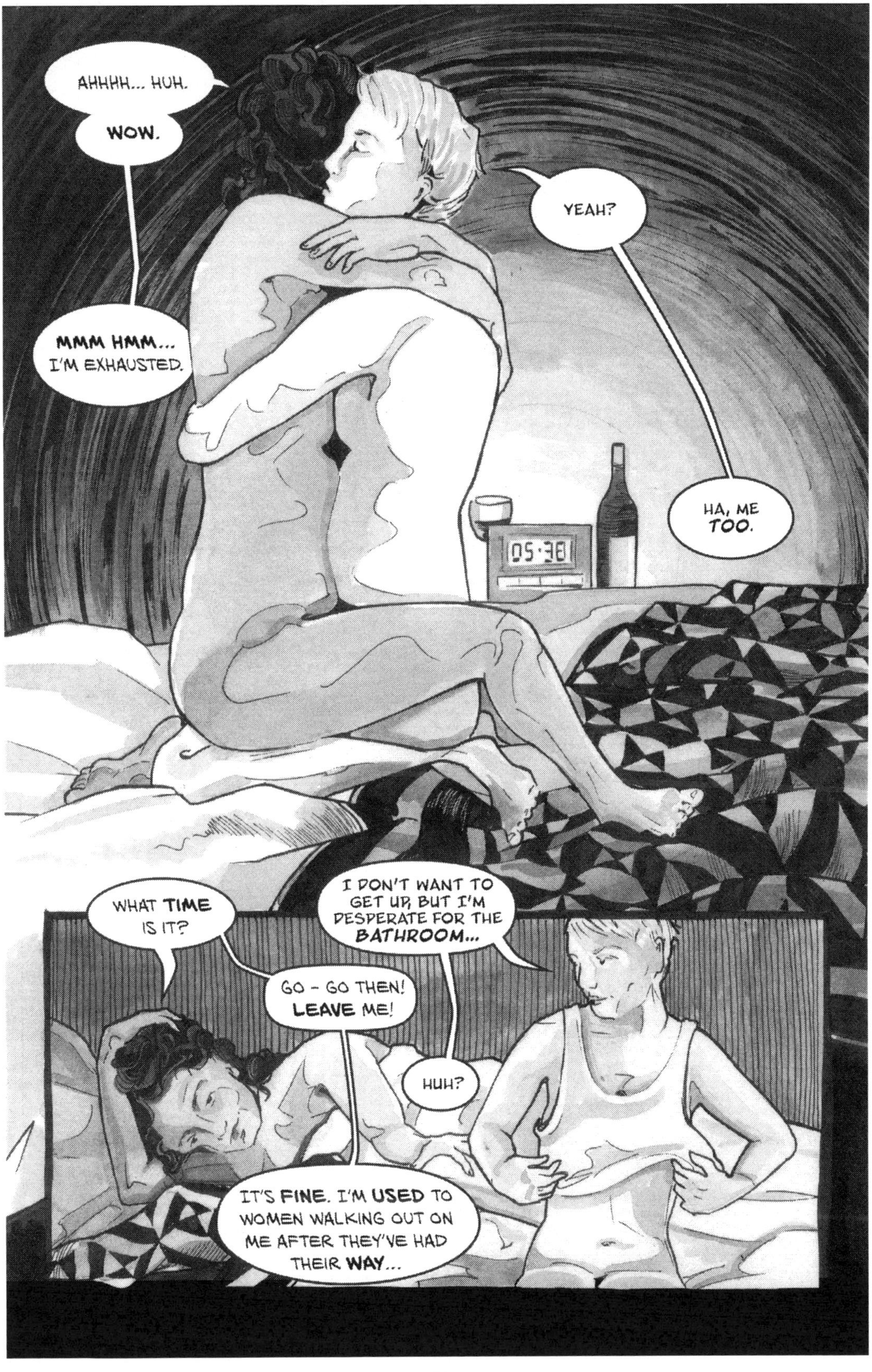
AHHHH... HUH.
WOW.
YEAH?
MMM HMM... I'M EXHAUSTED.
HA, ME TOO.
05:38
WHAT TIME IS IT?
I DON'T WANT TO GET UP, BUT I'M DESPERATE FOR THE BATHROOM...
GO - GO THEN! LEAVE ME!
HUH?
IT'S FINE. I'M USED TO WOMEN WALKING OUT ON ME AFTER THEY'VE HAD THEIR WAY...

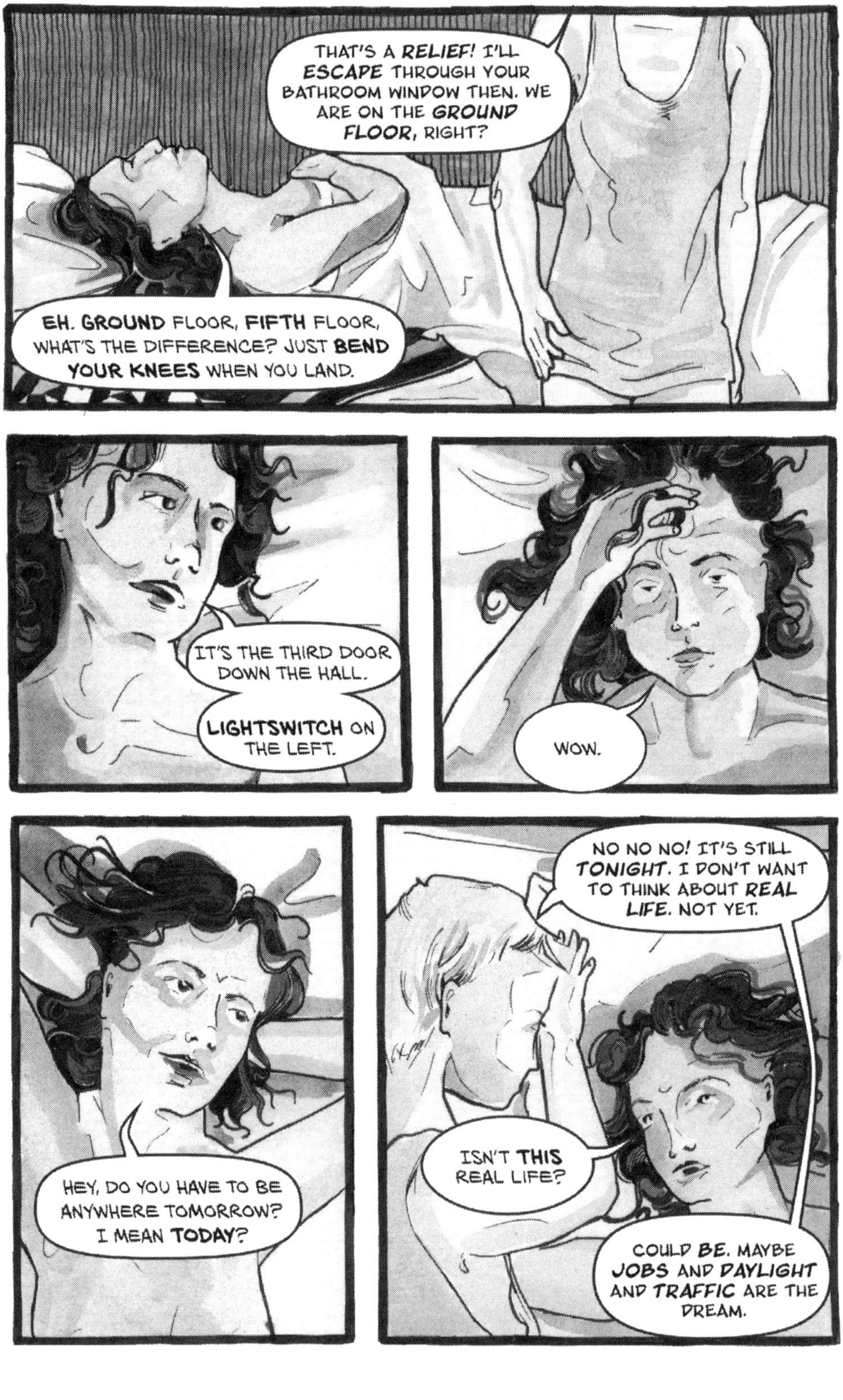
THAT'S A RELIEF! I'LL ESCAPE THROUGH YOUR BATHROOM WINDOW THEN. WE ARE ON THE GROUND FLOOR, RIGHT?
EH. GROUND FLOOR, FIFTH FLOOR, WHAT'S THE DIFFERENCE? JUST BEND YOUR KNEES WHEN YOU LAND.
IT'S THE THIRD DOOR DOWN THE HALL.
LIGHTSWITCH ON THE LEFT.
WOW.
HEY, DO YOU HAVE TO BE ANYWHERE TOMORROW? I MEAN TODAY?
NO NO NO! IT'S STILL TONIGHT. I DON'T WANT TO THINK ABOUT REAL LIFE. NOT YET.
ISN'T THIS REAL LIFE?
COULD BE. MAYBE JOBS AND DAYLIGHT AND TRAFFIC ARE THE DREAM.

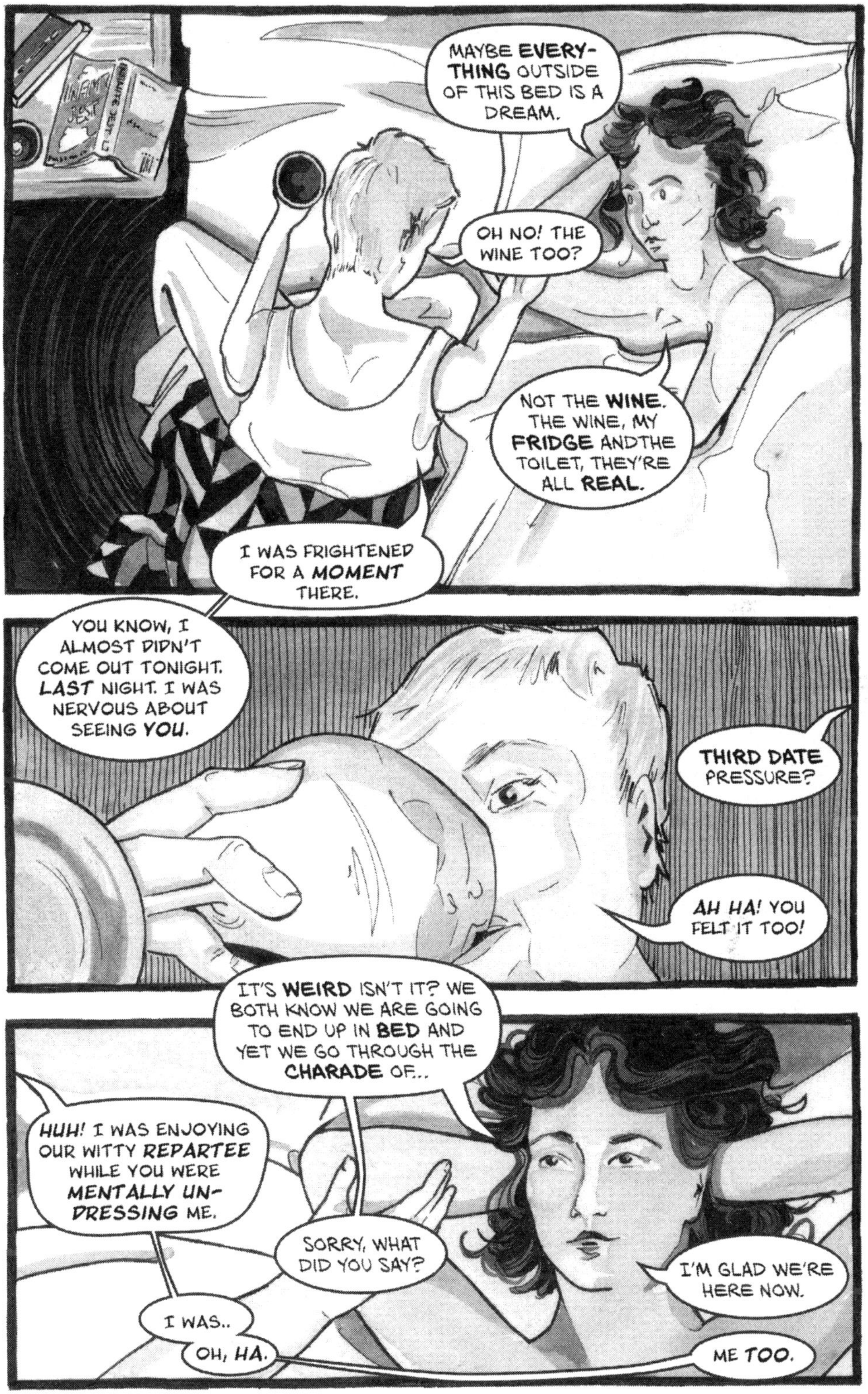

MAYBE EVERY-THING OUTSIDE OF THIS BED IS A DREAM.
OH NO! THE WINE TOO?
NOT THE WINE. THE WINE, MY FRIDGE AND THE TOILET, THEY'RE ALL REAL.
I WAS FRIGHTENED FOR A MOMENT THERE.
YOU KNOW, I ALMOST DIDN'T COME OUT TONIGHT. LAST NIGHT. I WAS NERVOUS ABOUT SEEING YOU.
THIRD DATE PRESSURE?
AH HA! YOU FELT IT TOO!
IT'S WEIRD ISN'T IT? WE BOTH KNOW WE ARE GOING TO END UP IN BED AND YET WE GO THROUGH THE CHARADE OF...
HUH! I WAS ENJOYING OUR WITTY REPARTEE WHILE YOU WERE MENTALLY UN-DRESSING ME.
SORRY, WHAT DID YOU SAY?
I WAS..
OH, HA.
I'M GLAD WE'RE HERE NOW.
ME TOO.

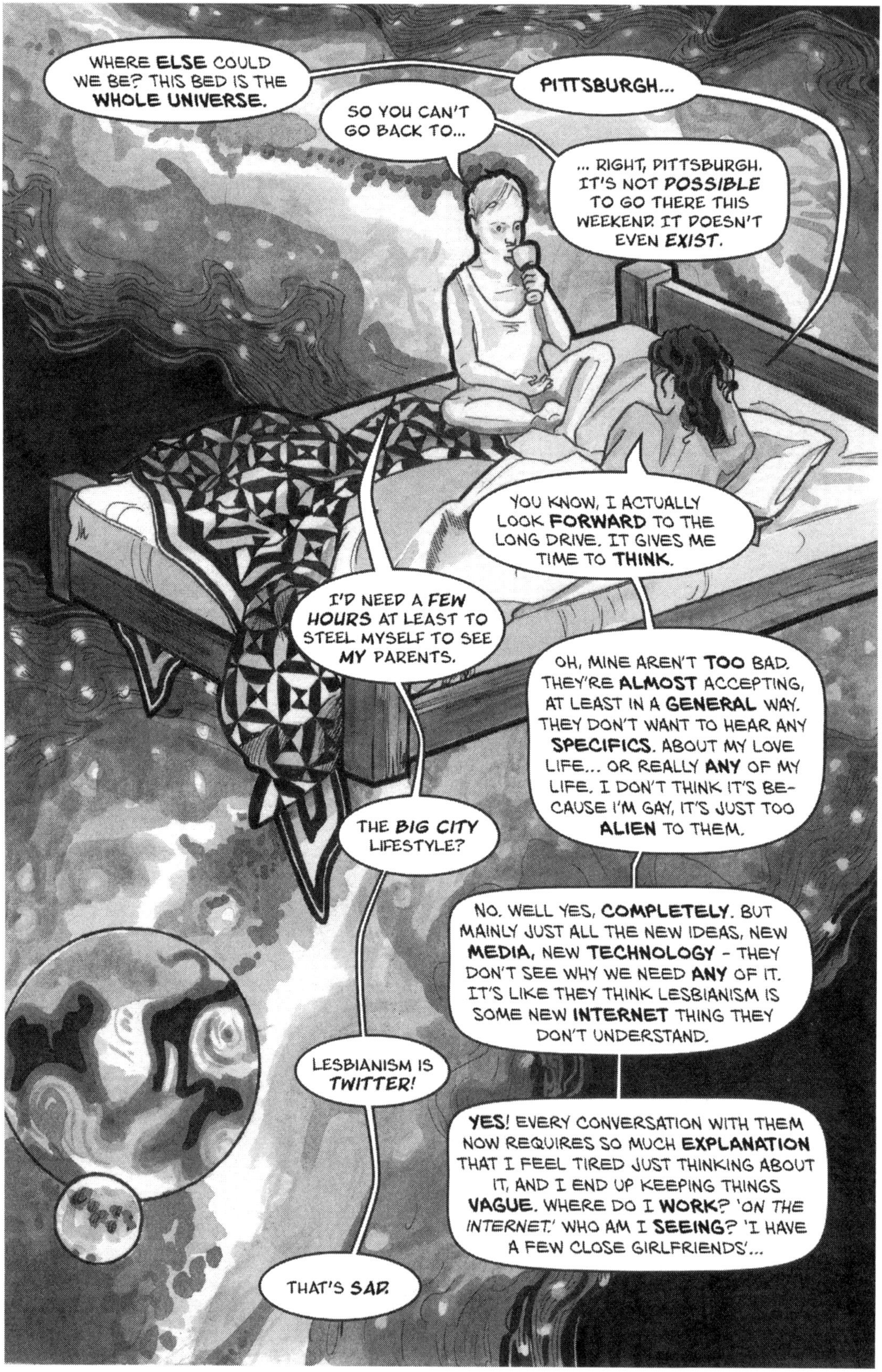
WHERE ELSE COULD WE BE? THIS BED IS THE WHOLE UNIVERSE.
PITTSBURGH...
SO YOU CAN'T GO BACK TO...
... RIGHT, PITTSBURGH. IT'S NOT POSSIBLE TO GO THERE THIS WEEKEND. IT DOESN'T EVEN EXIST.
YOU KNOW, I ACTUALLY LOOK FORWARD TO THE LONG DRIVE. IT GIVES ME TIME TO THINK.
I'D NEED A FEW HOURS AT LEAST TO STEEL MYSELF TO SEE MY PARENTS.
OH, MINE AREN'T TOO BAD. THEY'RE ALMOST ACCEPTING, AT LEAST IN A GENERAL WAY. THEY DON'T WANT TO HEAR ANY SPECIFICS. ABOUT MY LOVE LIFE... OR REALLY ANY OF MY LIFE. I DON'T THINK IT'S BE-CAUSE I'M GAY, IT'S JUST TOO ALIEN TO THEM.
THE BIG CITY LIFESTYLE?
NO. WELL YES, COMPLETELY. BUT MAINLY JUST ALL THE NEW IDEAS, NEW MEDIA, NEW TECHNOLOGY - THEY DON'T SEE WHY WE NEED ANY OF IT. IT'S LIKE THEY THINK LESBIANISM IS SOME NEW INTERNET THING THEY DON'T UNDERSTAND.
LESBIANISM IS TWITTER!
YES! EVERY CONVERSATION WITH THEM NOW REQUIRES SO MUCH EXPLANATION THAT I FEEL TIRED JUST THINKING ABOUT IT, AND I END UP KEEPING THINGS VAGUE. WHERE DO I WORK? 'ON THE INTERNET.' WHO AM I SEEING? 'I HAVE A FEW CLOSE GIRLFRIENDS'...
THAT'S SAD.

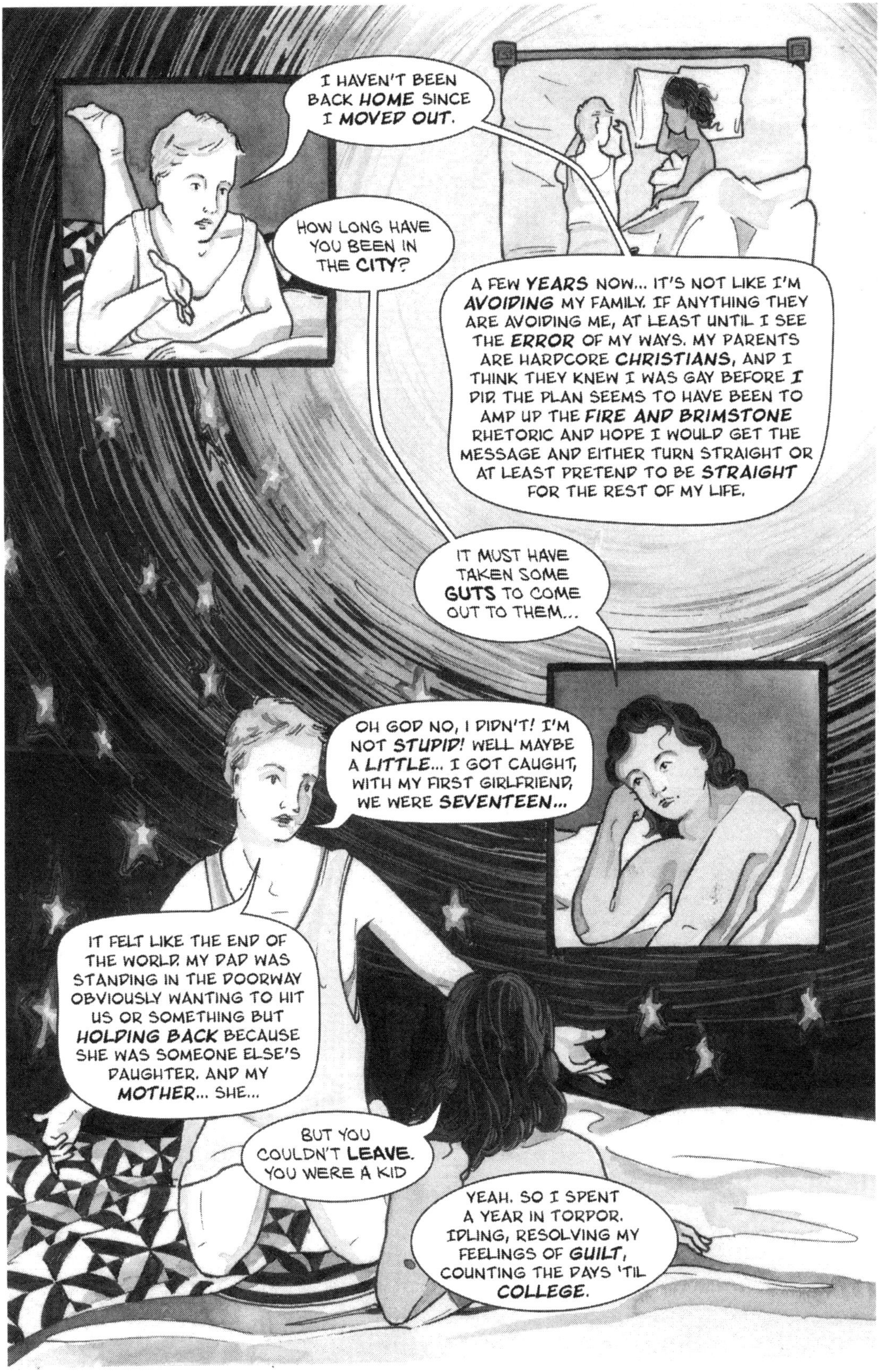
I HAVEN'T BEEN BACK HOME SINCE I MOVED OUT.
HOW LONG HAVE YOU BEEN IN THE CITY?
A FEW YEARS NOW... IT'S NOT LIKE I'M AVOIDING MY FAMILY. IF ANYTHING THEY ARE AVOIDING ME, AT LEAST UNTIL I SEE THE ERROR OF MY WAYS. MY PARENTS ARE HARDCORE CHRISTIANS, AND I THINK THEY KNEW I WAS GAY BEFORE I DID. THE PLAN SEEMS TO HAVE BEEN TO AMP UP THE FIRE AND BRIMSTONE RHETORIC AND HOPE I WOULD GET THE MESSAGE AND EITHER TURN STRAIGHT OR AT LEAST PRETEND TO BE STRAIGHT FOR THE REST OF MY LIFE.
IT MUST HAVE TAKEN SOME GUTS TO COME OUT TO THEM...
OH GOD NO, I DIDN'T! I'M NOT STUPID! WELL MAYBE A LITTLE... I GOT CAUGHT, WITH MY FIRST GIRLFRIEND, WE WERE SEVENTEEN...
IT FELT LIKE THE END OF THE WORLD. MY DAD WAS STANDING IN THE DOORWAY OBVIOUSLY WANTING TO HIT US OR SOMETHING BUT HOLDING BACK BECAUSE SHE WAS SOMEONE ELSE'S DAUGHTER. AND MY MOTHER... SHE...
BUT YOU COULDN'T LEAVE. YOU WERE A KID
YEAH. SO I SPENT A YEAR IN TORPOR. IDLING, RESOLVING MY FEELINGS OF GUILT, COUNTING THE DAYS 'TIL COLLEGE.

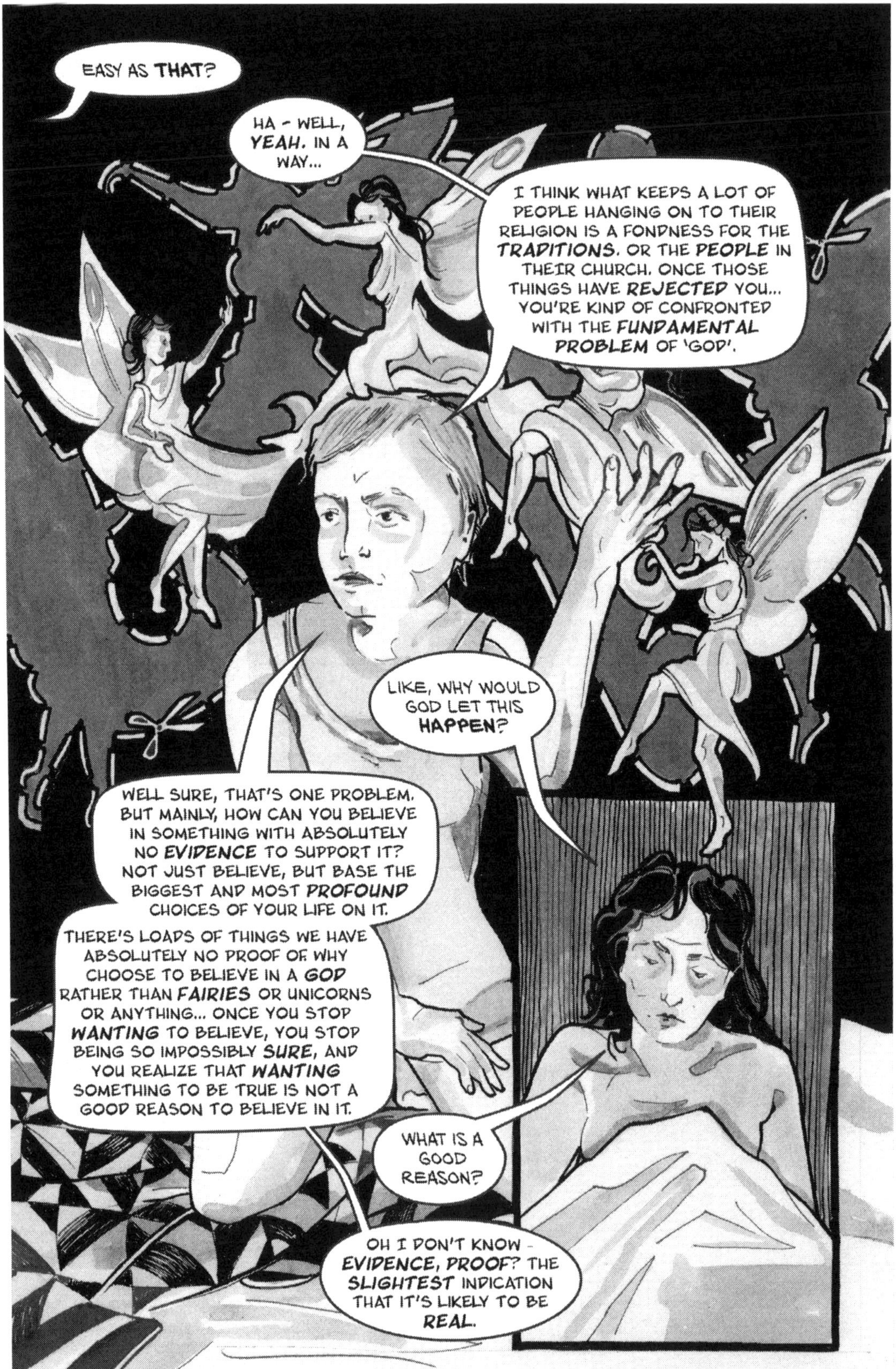
EASY AS THAT?
HA - WELL, YEAH. IN A WAY...
I THINK WHAT KEEPS A LOT OF PEOPLE HANGING ON TO THEIR RELIGION IS A FONDNESS FOR THE TRADITIONS. OR THE PEOPLE IN THEIR CHURCH. ONCE THOSE THINGS HAVE REJECTED YOU... YOU'RE KIND OF CONFRONTED WITH THE FUNDAMENTAL PROBLEM OF 'GOD'.
LIKE, WHY WOULD GOD LET THIS HAPPEN?
WELL SURE, THAT'S ONE PROBLEM. BUT MAINLY, HOW CAN YOU BELIEVE IN SOMETHING WITH ABSOLUTELY NO EVIDENCE TO SUPPORT IT? NOT JUST BELIEVE, BUT BASE THE BIGGEST AND MOST PROFOUND CHOICES OF YOUR LIFE ON IT.
THERE'S LOADS OF THINGS WE HAVE ABSOLUTELY NO PROOF OF. WHY CHOOSE TO BELIEVE IN A GOD RATHER THAN FAIRIES OR UNICORNS OR ANYTHING... ONCE YOU STOP WANTING TO BELIEVE, YOU STOP BEING SO IMPOSSIBLY SURE, AND YOU REALIZE THAT WANTING SOMETHING TO BE TRUE IS NOT A GOOD REASON TO BELIEVE IN IT.
WHAT IS A GOOD REASON?
OH I DON'T KNOW - EVIDENCE, PROOF? THE SLIGHTEST INDICATION THAT IT'S LIKELY TO BE REAL.

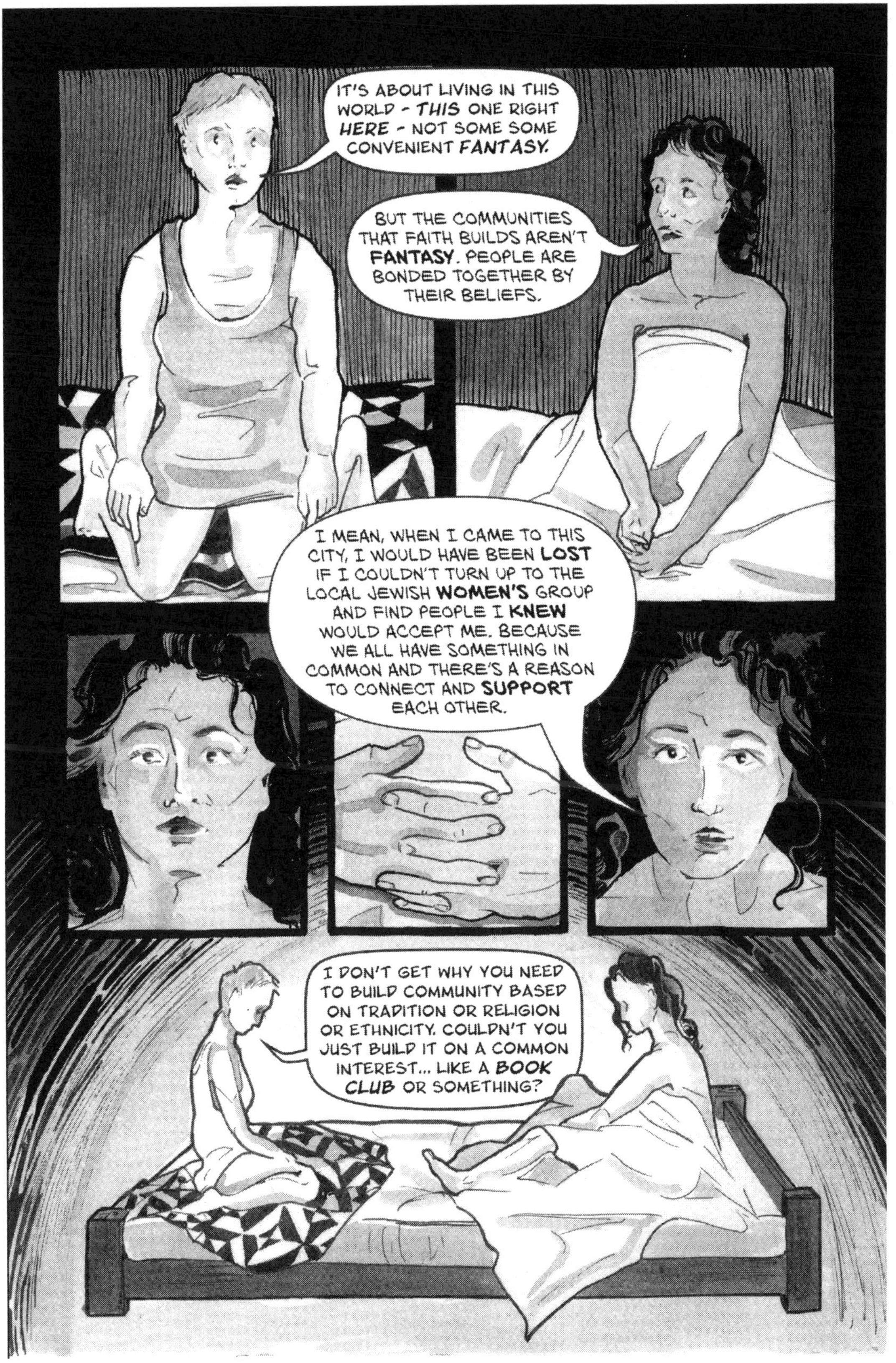
IT'S ABOUT LIVING IN THIS WORLD - THIS ONE RIGHT HERE - NOT SOME SOME CONVENIENT FANTASY.
BUT THE COMMUNITIES THAT FAITH BUILDS AREN'T FANTASY. PEOPLE ARE BONDED TOGETHER BY THEIR BELIEFS.
I MEAN, WHEN I CAME TO THIS CITY, I WOULD HAVE BEEN LOST IF I COULDN'T TURN UP TO THE LOCAL JEWISH WOMEN'S GROUP AND FIND PEOPLE I KNEW WOULD ACCEPT ME. BECAUSE WE ALL HAVE SOMETHING IN COMMON AND THERE'S A REASON TO CONNECT AND SUPPORT EACH OTHER.
I DON'T GET WHY YOU NEED TO BUILD COMMUNITY BASED ON TRADITION OR RELIGION OR ETHNICITY. COULDN'T YOU JUST BUILD IT ON A COMMON INTEREST... LIKE A BOOK CLUB OR SOMETHING?

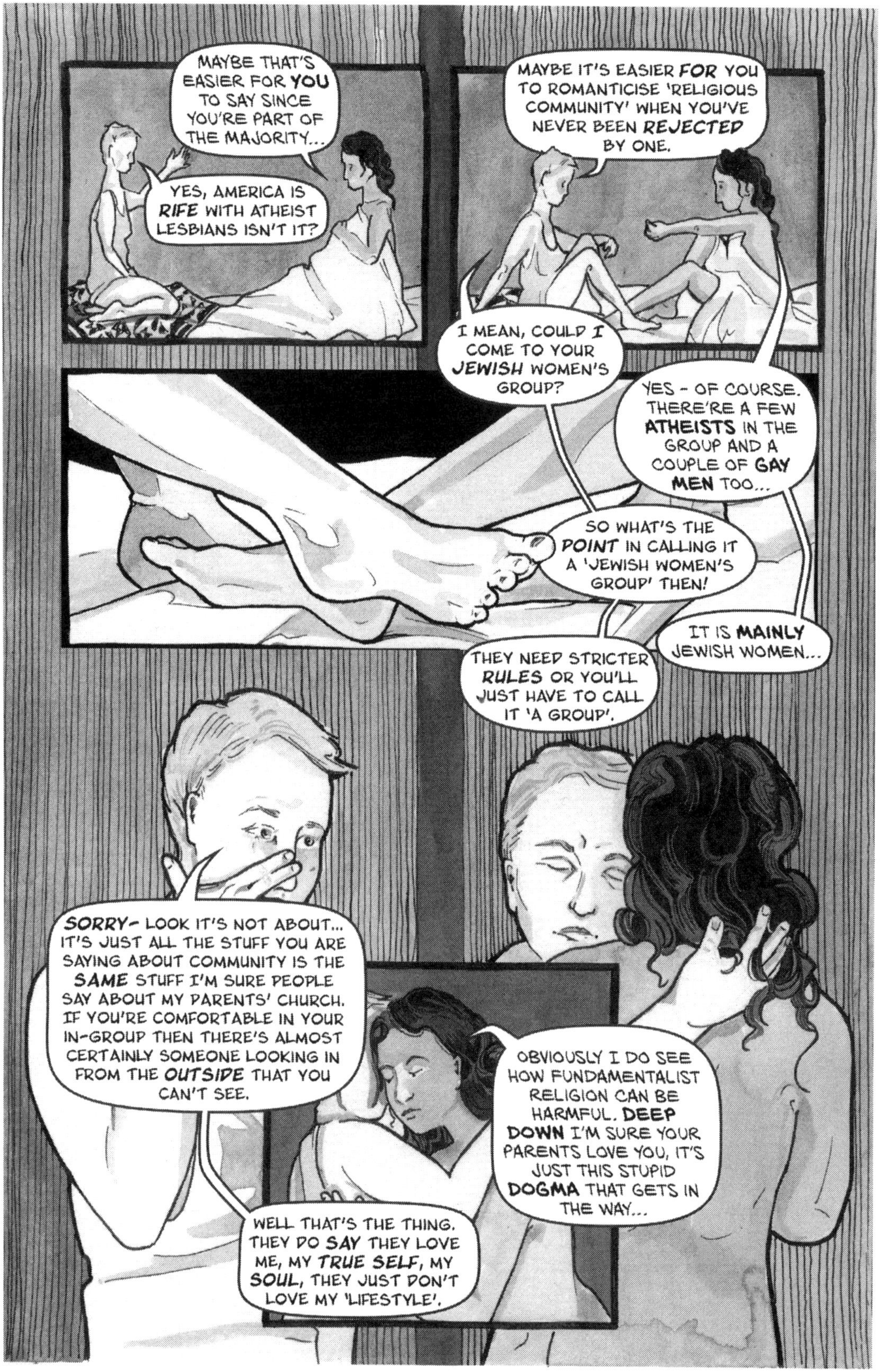
MAYBE THAT'S EASIER FOR YOU TO SAY SINCE YOU'RE PART OF THE MAJORITY...
YES, AMERICA IS RIFE WITH ATHEIST LESBIANS ISN'T IT?
MAYBE IT'S EASIER FOR YOU TO ROMANTICISE 'RELIGIOUS COMMUNITY' WHEN YOU'VE NEVER BEEN REJECTED BY ONE.
I MEAN, COULD I COME TO YOUR JEWISH WOMEN'S GROUP?
YES - OF COURSE. THERE'RE A FEW ATHEISTS IN THE GROUP AND A COUPLE OF GAY MEN TOO...
SO WHAT'S THE POINT IN CALLING IT A 'JEWISH WOMEN'S GROUP' THEN!
IT IS MAINLY JEWISH WOMEN...
THEY NEED STRICTER RULES OR YOU'LL JUST HAVE TO CALL IT 'A GROUP'.
SORRY- LOOK IT'S NOT ABOUT... IT'S JUST ALL THE STUFF YOU ARE SAYING ABOUT COMMUNITY IS THE SAME STUFF I'M SURE PEOPLE SAY ABOUT MY PARENTS' CHURCH. IF YOU'RE COMFORTABLE IN YOUR IN-GROUP THEN THERE'S ALMOST CERTAINLY SOMEONE LOOKING IN FROM THE OUTSIDE THAT YOU CAN'T SEE.
OBVIOUSLY I DO SEE HOW FUNDAMENTALIST RELIGION CAN BE HARMFUL. DEEP DOWN I'M SURE YOUR PARENTS LOVE YOU, IT'S JUST THIS STUPID DOGMA THAT GETS IN THE WAY...
WELL THAT'S THE THING. THEY DO SAY THEY LOVE ME, MY TRUE SELF, MY SOUL, THEY JUST DON'T LOVE MY 'LIFESTYLE'.

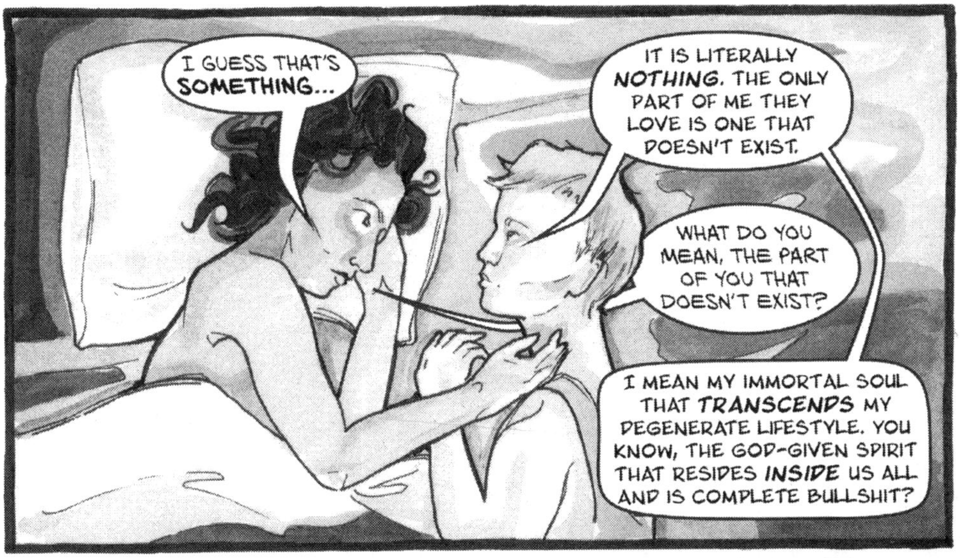
I GUESS THAT'S SOMETHING...
IT IS LITERALLY NOTHING. THE ONLY PART OF ME THEY LOVE IS ONE THAT DOESN'T EXIST.
WHAT DO YOU MEAN, THE PART OF YOU THAT DOESN'T EXIST?
I MEAN MY IMMORTAL SOUL THAT TRANSCENDS MY DEGENERATE LIFESTYLE. YOU KNOW, THE GOD-GIVEN SPIRIT THAT RESIDES INSIDE US ALL AND IS COMPLETE BULLSHIT?

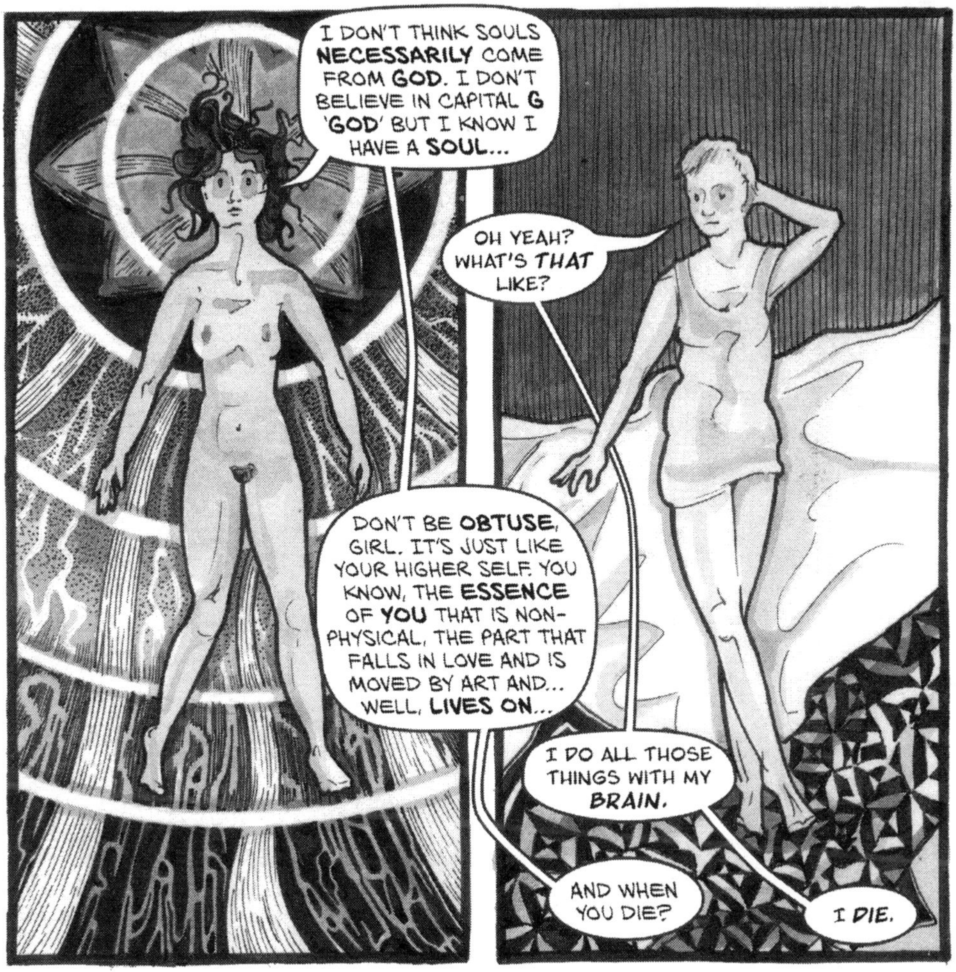
I DON'T THINK SOULS NECESSARILY COME FROM GOD. I DON'T BELIEVE IN CAPITAL G 'GOD' BUT I KNOW I HAVE A SOUL...
OH YEAH? WHAT'S THAT LIKE?
DON'T BE OBTUSE, GIRL. IT'S JUST LIKE YOUR HIGHER SELF. YOU KNOW, THE ESSENCE OF YOU THAT IS NON-PHYSICAL, THE PART THAT FALLS IN LOVE AND IS MOVED BY ART AND... WELL, LIVES ON...
I DO ALL THOSE THINGS WITH MY BRAIN.
AND WHEN YOU DIE?
I DIE.

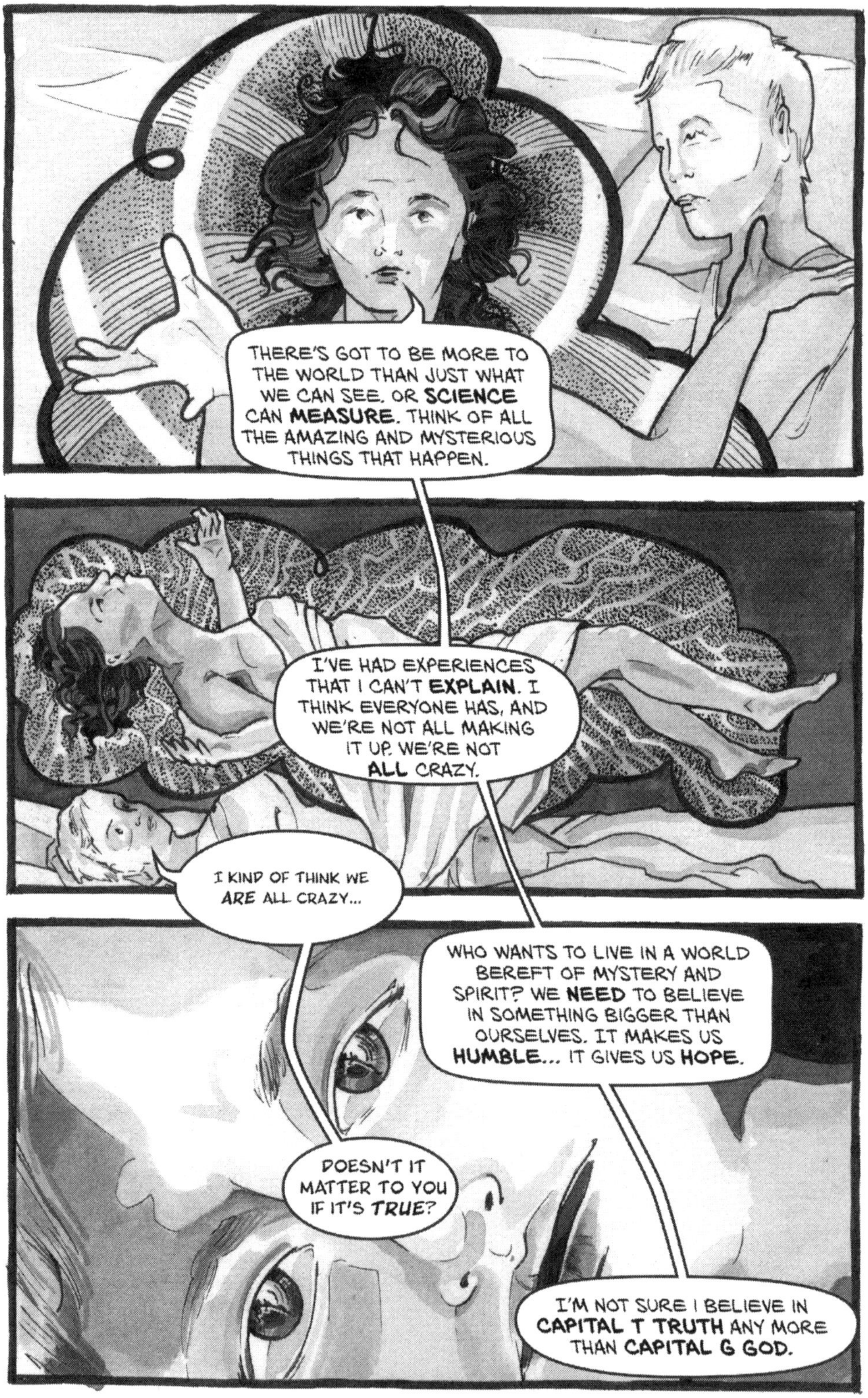
THERE'S GOT TO BE MORE TO THE WORLD THAN JUST WHAT WE CAN SEE. OR **SCIENCE** CAN **MEASURE.** THINK OF ALL THE AMAZING AND MYSTERIOUS THINGS THAT HAPPEN.
I'VE HAD EXPERIENCES THAT I CAN'T **EXPLAIN.** I THINK EVERYONE HAS, AND WE'RE NOT ALL MAKING IT UP. WE'RE NOT **ALL** CRAZY.
I KIND OF THINK WE *ARE* ALL CRAZY...
WHO WANTS TO LIVE IN A WORLD BEREFT OF MYSTERY AND SPIRIT? WE **NEED** TO BELIEVE IN SOMETHING BIGGER THAN OURSELVES. IT MAKES US **HUMBLE...** IT GIVES US **HOPE.**
DOESN'T IT MATTER TO YOU IF IT'S ***TRUE?***
I'M NOT SURE I BELIEVE IN **CAPITAL T TRUTH** ANY MORE THAN **CAPITAL G GOD.**

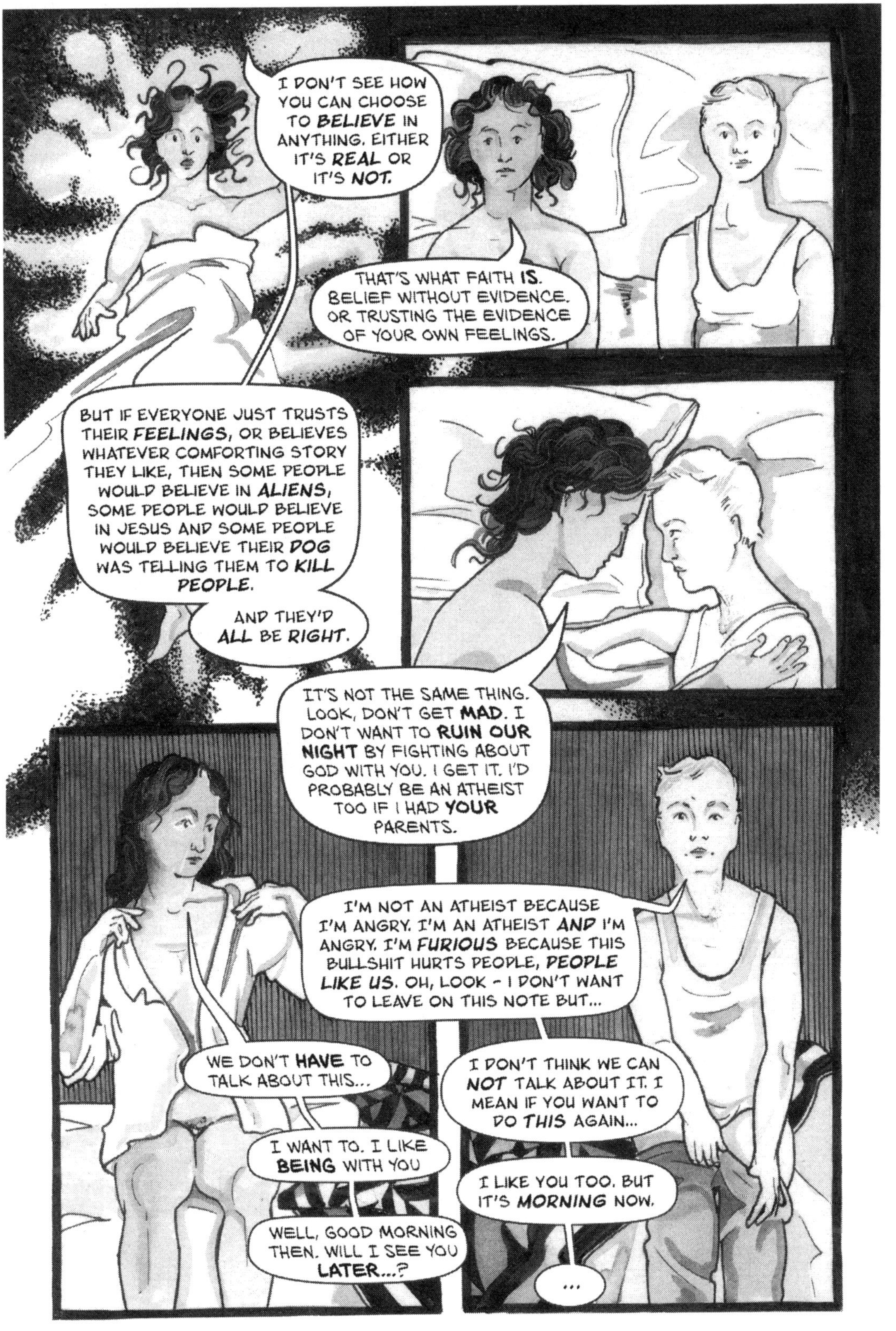
I DON'T SEE HOW YOU CAN CHOOSE TO **BELIEVE** IN ANYTHING. EITHER IT'S **REAL** OR IT'S **NOT.**
THAT'S WHAT FAITH **IS.** BELIEF WITHOUT EVIDENCE. OR TRUSTING THE EVIDENCE OF YOUR OWN FEELINGS.
BUT IF EVERYONE JUST TRUSTS THEIR **FEELINGS**, OR BELIEVES WHATEVER COMFORTING STORY THEY LIKE, THEN SOME PEOPLE WOULD BELIEVE IN **ALIENS**, SOME PEOPLE WOULD BELIEVE IN JESUS AND SOME PEOPLE WOULD BELIEVE THEIR **DOG** WAS TELLING THEM TO **KILL PEOPLE.**
AND THEY'D **ALL** BE **RIGHT**.
IT'S NOT THE SAME THING. LOOK, DON'T GET **MAD**. I DON'T WANT TO **RUIN OUR NIGHT** BY FIGHTING ABOUT GOD WITH YOU. I GET IT. I'D PROBABLY BE AN ATHEIST TOO IF I HAD **YOUR** PARENTS.
I'M NOT AN ATHEIST BECAUSE I'M ANGRY. I'M AN ATHEIST **AND** I'M ANGRY. I'M **FURIOUS** BECAUSE THIS BULLSHIT HURTS PEOPLE, **PEOPLE LIKE US**. OH, LOOK - I DON'T WANT TO LEAVE ON THIS NOTE BUT...
WE DON'T **HAVE** TO TALK ABOUT THIS...
I DON'T THINK WE CAN **NOT** TALK ABOUT IT. I MEAN IF YOU WANT TO DO **THIS** AGAIN...
I WANT TO. I LIKE **BEING** WITH YOU
I LIKE YOU TOO. BUT IT'S **MORNING** NOW.
WELL, GOOD MORNING THEN. WILL I SEE YOU **LATER...?**
...

This, well not *exactly* this, happens to me all the time.

I think I'm having a conversation about the possibility of extraterrestrial life, or the efficacy of a herbal remedy or some supernatural claim... and then I realise that I've been playing by different rules than the person I'm disagreeing with. The conflict isn't over the content of our beliefs, it is caused by differences in our epistemology.

Epistemology is the study of knowledge: what it is and how it's formed. It underlies all discourse but becomes particularly evident when you make the mistake of assuming that the person you are talking to has taken the same route to reach their beliefs as you have to reach yours.

'Knowledge' is often defined as 'justified, true beliefs.' When I am at my rational, calm, serious best I like to think I reach knowledge satisfying that definition. I come up with an idea based on other good ideas and reliable observations, and then then I look for confirming or disconfirming evidence. Once I've found enough evidential support I upgrade my idea to a *belief*, which means I provisionally accept it as part of my knowledge base—at least until some idea that better fits the evidence (or more disconfirming evidence) turns up.

I don't bother to go through this process for questions like *which make and model of car is the most fuel efficient?* I'm not interested in that, so I remain agnostic. I also don't bother to do it for issues such as *who is the best recording artist of all time?* I let emotion and aesthetic preferences lead me to a psychological conviction on that issue that, though strident, cannot be called 'knowledge'.

Faith claims are knowledge claims. When someone says 'God created the world in seven days' they mean 'I think it is true that God created the world in seven days'. But their belief is not reached by the same epistemological method I outlined above.

In his essay *Religious Credence is not Factual Belief*, Neil Van Leeuwen describes two methods of forming beliefs. 'Factual Beliefs' meet the philosophical prerequisites for knowledge, whereas 'religious credence' often falter on the 'justified' and 'true' criteria. What Van Leeuwen defines as *religious credence*, I might be tempted to label more broadly as 'intuitive beliefs' to include the common non-religious beliefs in the supernatural and emotional and aesthetic convictions.

When I've debated theists in the past, I have assumed that the beliefs they are expounding are reached using the same epistemological method that I have employed to reach my beliefs about the existence of a deity. So I point out their incoherent, contradictory nature and the lack of evidence to support their beliefs... because that is what would convince me to change my mind on the topic at hand. Van Leeuwen's article made me realise that the reason both me and the theist I'm talking to often end up frustrated is that we are having our conversation at the wrong level. In retrospect it's ridiculous that it took me so long to figure this out, after all it is stated several times in the Bible, perhaps most clearly here:

> *Now faith is the assurance of things hoped for, the conviction of things not seen.*
> (Hebrews 11:1)

Faith is belief without evidence. No amount of reasoning will convince someone of the incorrect content of their intuitive beliefs. To have a productive conversation about someone's intuitive beliefs you need to discuss epistemology. Once you've agreed on what knowledge *is*, and how we attain it, perhaps we can get onto discussing UFOs, homeopathy and whatever prophet or saviour they favour. If you have time.

More information, discussion and links at
doubtcomic.com/pillow-talk

INDONESIAN PUNK ROCK
SUBURB OF YOGYAKARTA, INDONESIA

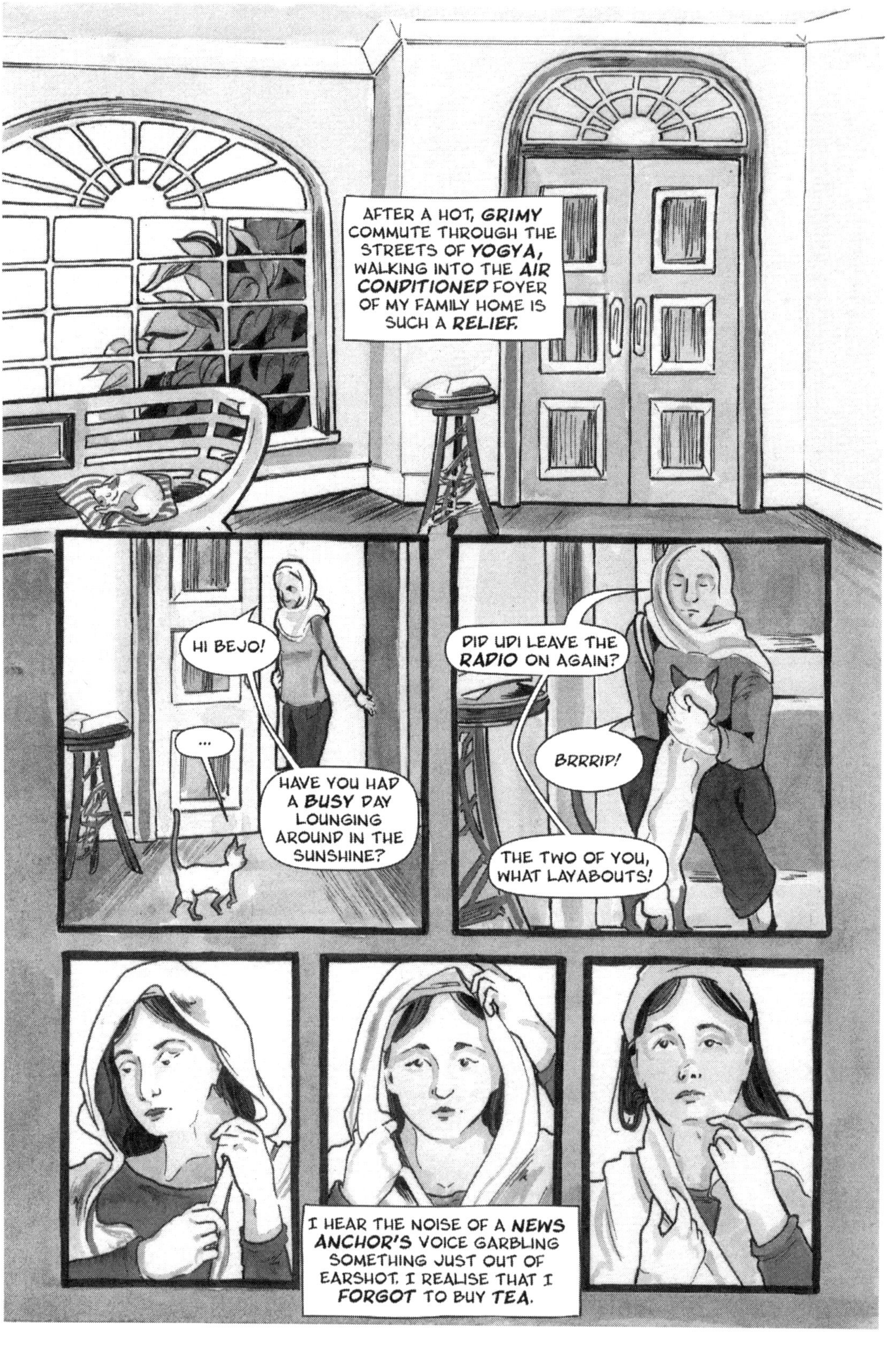
AFTER A HOT, GRIMY COMMUTE THROUGH THE STREETS OF YOGYA, WALKING INTO THE AIR CONDITIONED FOYER OF MY FAMILY HOME IS SUCH A RELIEF.
HI BEJO!
...
HAVE YOU HAD A BUSY DAY LOUNGING AROUND IN THE SUNSHINE?
DID UDI LEAVE THE RADIO ON AGAIN?
BRRRIP!
THE TWO OF YOU, WHAT LAYABOUTS!
I HEAR THE NOISE OF A NEWS ANCHOR'S VOICE GARBLING SOMETHING JUST OUT OF EARSHOT. I REALISE THAT I FORGOT TO BUY TEA.

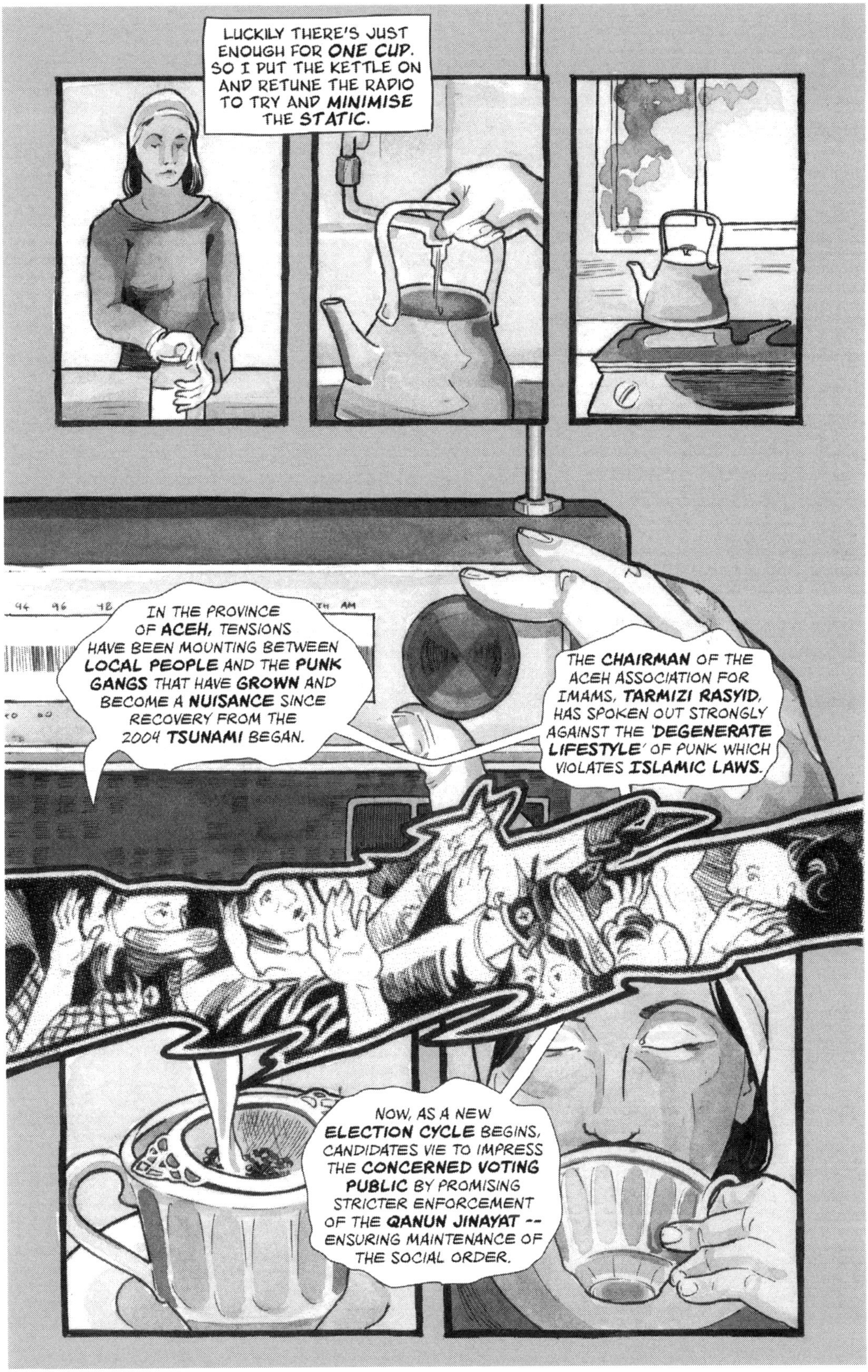
LUCKILY THERE'S JUST ENOUGH FOR ONE CUP. SO I PUT THE KETTLE ON AND RETUNE THE RADIO TO TRY AND MINIMISE THE STATIC.
IN THE PROVINCE OF ACEH, TENSIONS HAVE BEEN MOUNTING BETWEEN LOCAL PEOPLE AND THE PUNK GANGS THAT HAVE GROWN AND BECOME A NUISANCE SINCE RECOVERY FROM THE 2004 TSUNAMI BEGAN.
THE CHAIRMAN OF THE ACEH ASSOCIATION FOR IMAMS, TARMIZI RASYID, HAS SPOKEN OUT STRONGLY AGAINST THE 'DEGENERATE LIFESTYLE' OF PUNK WHICH VIOLATES ISLAMIC LAWS.
NOW, AS A NEW ELECTION CYCLE BEGINS, CANDIDATES VIE TO IMPRESS THE CONCERNED VOTING PUBLIC BY PROMISING STRICTER ENFORCEMENT OF THE QANUN JINAYAT -- ENSURING MAINTENANCE OF THE SOCIAL ORDER.

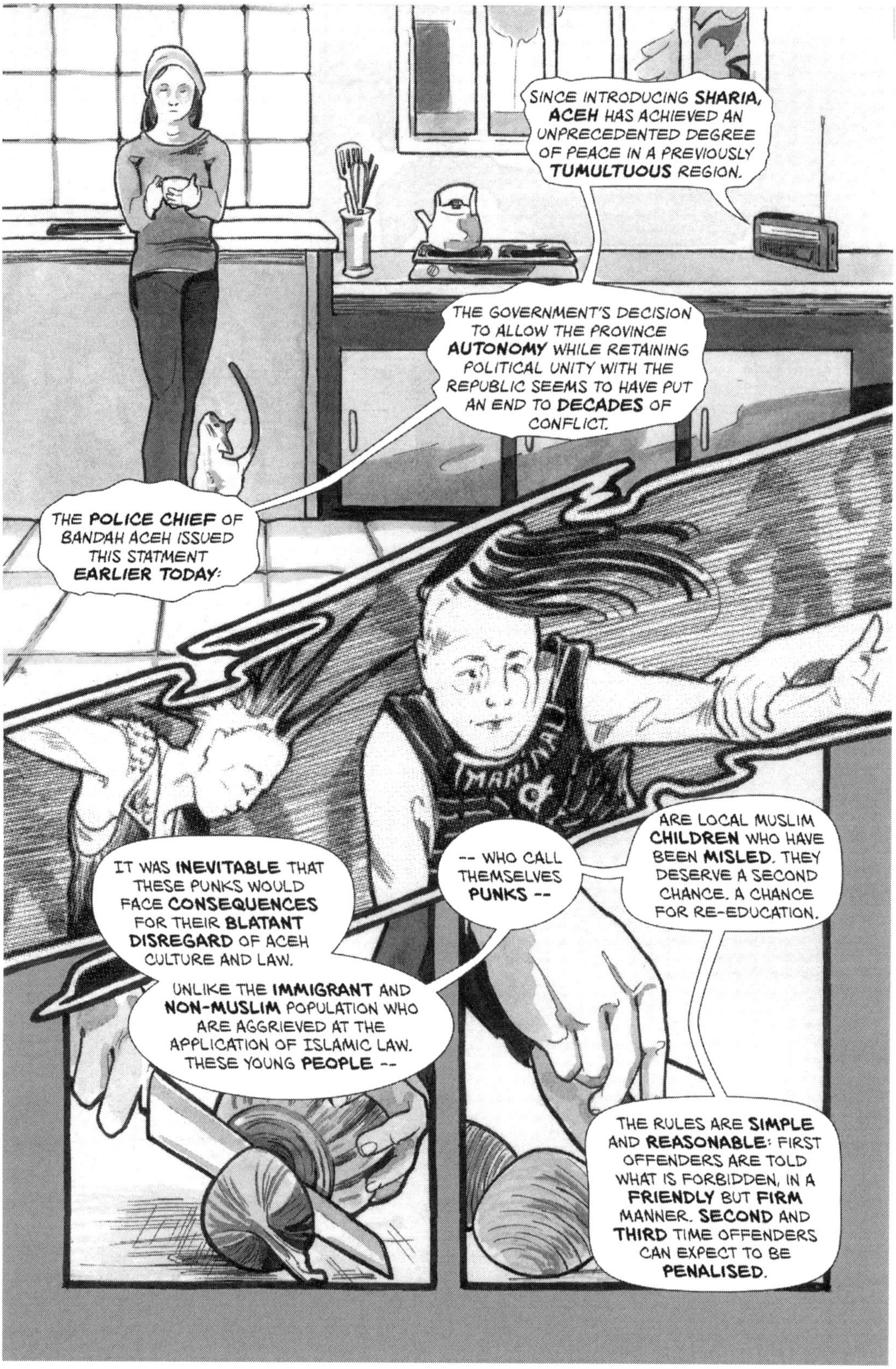

SINCE INTRODUCING **SHARIA**, **ACEH** HAS ACHIEVED AN UNPRECEDENTED DEGREE OF PEACE IN A PREVIOUSLY **TUMULTUOUS** REGION.
THE GOVERNMENT'S DECISION TO ALLOW THE PROVINCE **AUTONOMY** WHILE RETAINING POLITICAL UNITY WITH THE REPUBLIC SEEMS TO HAVE PUT AN END TO **DECADES** OF CONFLICT.
THE **POLICE CHIEF** OF BANDAH ACEH ISSUED THIS STATMENT **EARLIER TODAY**:
IT WAS **INEVITABLE** THAT THESE PUNKS WOULD FACE **CONSEQUENCES** FOR THEIR **BLATANT DISREGARD** OF ACEH CULTURE AND LAW.
UNLIKE THE **IMMIGRANT** AND **NON-MUSLIM** POPULATION WHO ARE AGGRIEVED AT THE APPLICATION OF ISLAMIC LAW. THESE YOUNG **PEOPLE** --
-- WHO CALL THEMSELVES **PUNKS** --
ARE LOCAL MUSLIM **CHILDREN** WHO HAVE BEEN **MISLED**. THEY DESERVE A SECOND CHANCE. A CHANCE FOR RE-EDUCATION.
THE RULES ARE **SIMPLE** AND **REASONABLE**: FIRST OFFENDERS ARE TOLD WHAT IS FORBIDDEN, IN A **FRIENDLY** BUT **FIRM** MANNER. **SECOND** AND **THIRD** TIME OFFENDERS CAN EXPECT TO BE **PENALISED**.

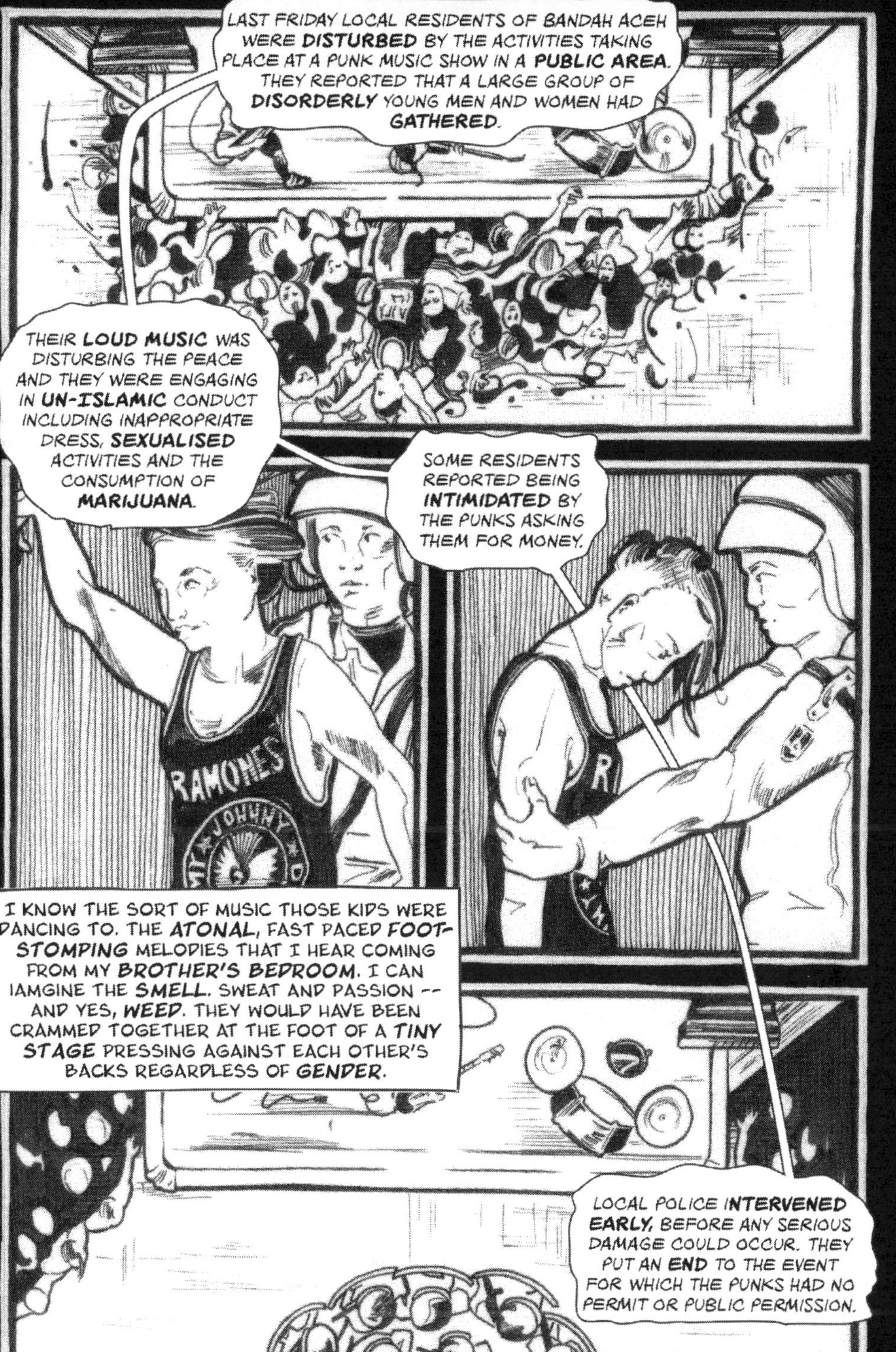
LAST FRIDAY LOCAL RESIDENTS OF BANDAH ACEH WERE DISTURBED BY THE ACTIVITIES TAKING PLACE AT A PUNK MUSIC SHOW IN A PUBLIC AREA. THEY REPORTED THAT A LARGE GROUP OF DISORDERLY YOUNG MEN AND WOMEN HAD GATHERED.
THEIR LOUD MUSIC WAS DISTURBING THE PEACE AND THEY WERE ENGAGING IN UN-ISLAMIC CONDUCT INCLUDING INAPPROPRIATE DRESS, SEXUALISED ACTIVITIES AND THE CONSUMPTION OF MARIJUANA.
SOME RESIDENTS REPORTED BEING INTIMIDATED BY THE PUNKS ASKING THEM FOR MONEY.
RAMONES
I KNOW THE SORT OF MUSIC THOSE KIDS WERE DANCING TO. THE ATONAL, FAST PACED FOOT-STOMPING MELODIES THAT I HEAR COMING FROM MY BROTHER'S BEDROOM. I CAN IAMGINE THE SMELL. SWEAT AND PASSION -- AND YES, WEED. THEY WOULD HAVE BEEN CRAMMED TOGETHER AT THE FOOT OF A TINY STAGE PRESSING AGAINST EACH OTHER'S BACKS REGARDLESS OF GENDER.
LOCAL POLICE INTERVENED EARLY, BEFORE ANY SERIOUS DAMAGE COULD OCCUR. THEY PUT AN END TO THE EVENT FOR WHICH THE PUNKS HAD NO PERMIT OR PUBLIC PERMISSION.

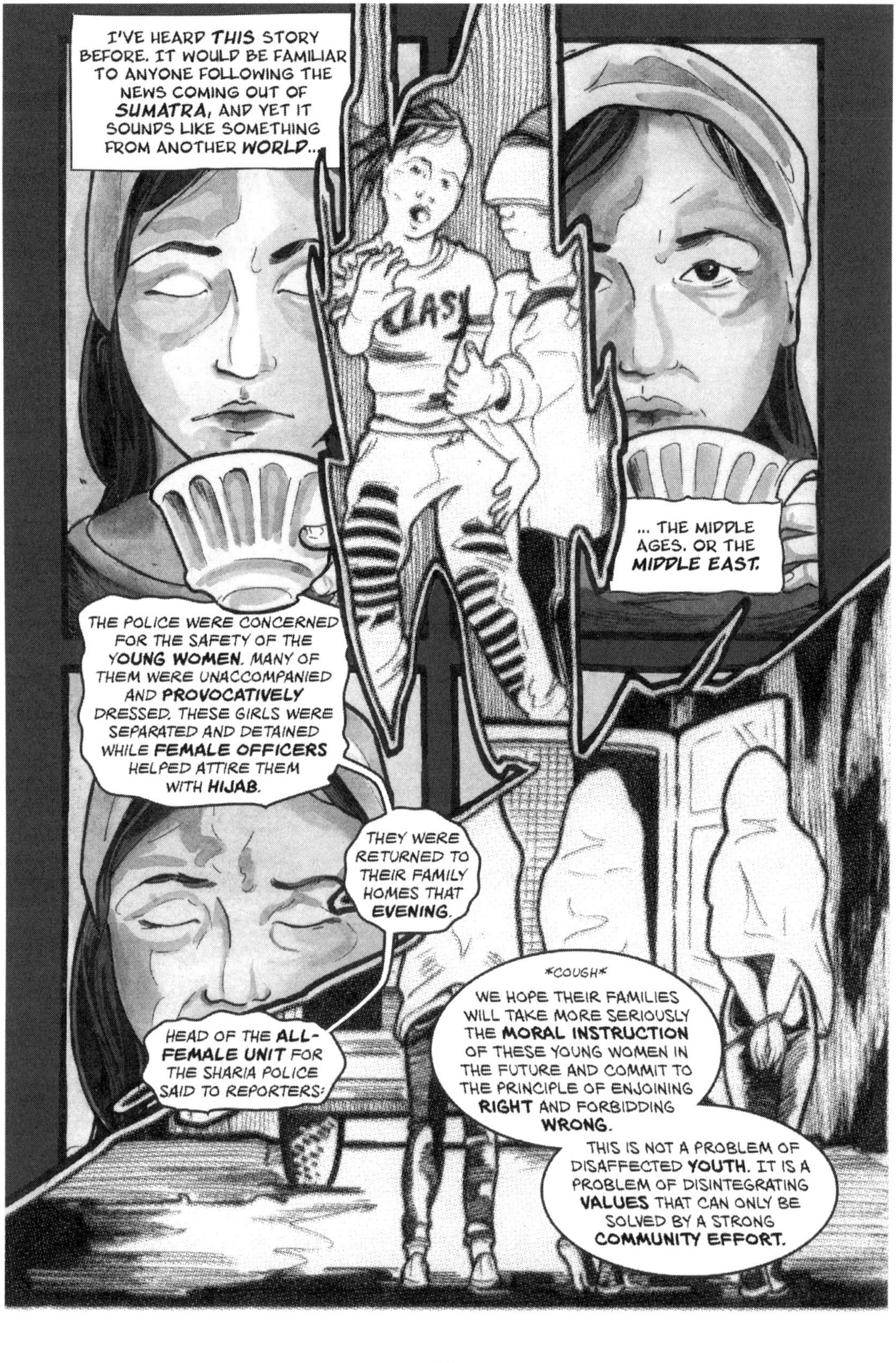
I'VE HEARD THIS STORY BEFORE. IT WOULD BE FAMILIAR TO ANYONE FOLLOWING THE NEWS COMING OUT OF SUMATRA, AND YET IT SOUNDS LIKE SOMETHING FROM ANOTHER WORLD...
... THE MIDDLE AGES. OR THE MIDDLE EAST.
THE POLICE WERE CONCERNED FOR THE SAFETY OF THE YOUNG WOMEN. MANY OF THEM WERE UNACCOMPANIED AND PROVOCATIVELY DRESSED. THESE GIRLS WERE SEPARATED AND DETAINED WHILE FEMALE OFFICERS HELPED ATTIRE THEM WITH HIJAB.
THEY WERE RETURNED TO THEIR FAMILY HOMES THAT EVENING.
HEAD OF THE ALL-FEMALE UNIT FOR THE SHARIA POLICE SAID TO REPORTERS:
COUGH
WE HOPE THEIR FAMILIES WILL TAKE MORE SERIOUSLY THE MORAL INSTRUCTION OF THESE YOUNG WOMEN IN THE FUTURE AND COMMIT TO THE PRINCIPLE OF ENJOINING RIGHT AND FORBIDDING WRONG.
THIS IS NOT A PROBLEM OF DISAFFECTED YOUTH. IT IS A PROBLEM OF DISINTEGRATING VALUES THAT CAN ONLY BE SOLVED BY A STRONG COMMUNITY EFFORT.

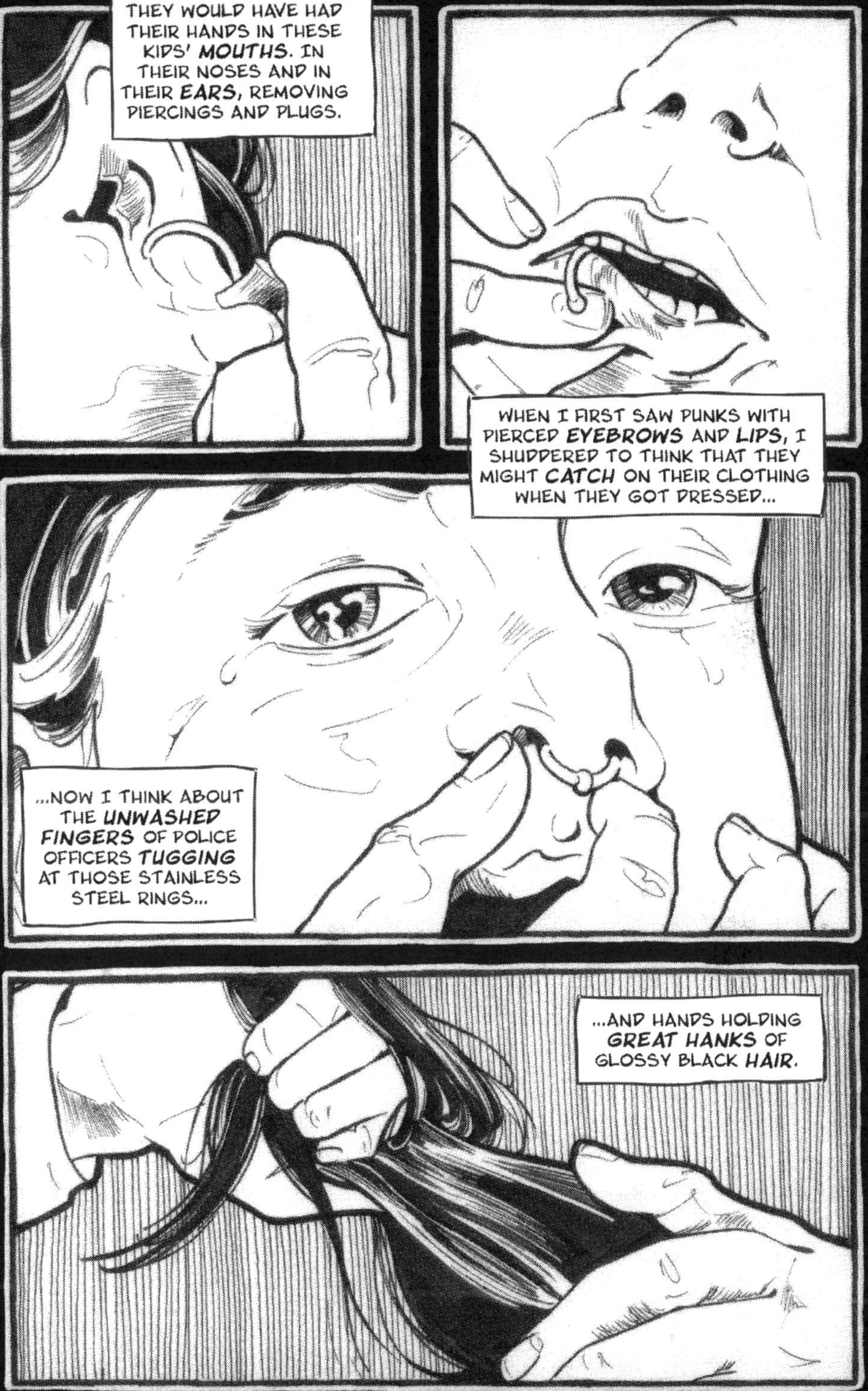
THEY WOULD HAVE HAD THEIR HANDS IN THESE KIDS' MOUTHS. IN THEIR NOSES AND IN THEIR EARS, REMOVING PIERCINGS AND PLUGS.
WHEN I FIRST SAW PUNKS WITH PIERCED EYEBROWS AND LIPS, I SHUDDERED TO THINK THAT THEY MIGHT CATCH ON THEIR CLOTHING WHEN THEY GOT DRESSED...
...NOW I THINK ABOUT THE UNWASHED FINGERS OF POLICE OFFICERS TUGGING AT THOSE STAINLESS STEEL RINGS...
...AND HANDS HOLDING GREAT HANKS OF GLOSSY BLACK HAIR.

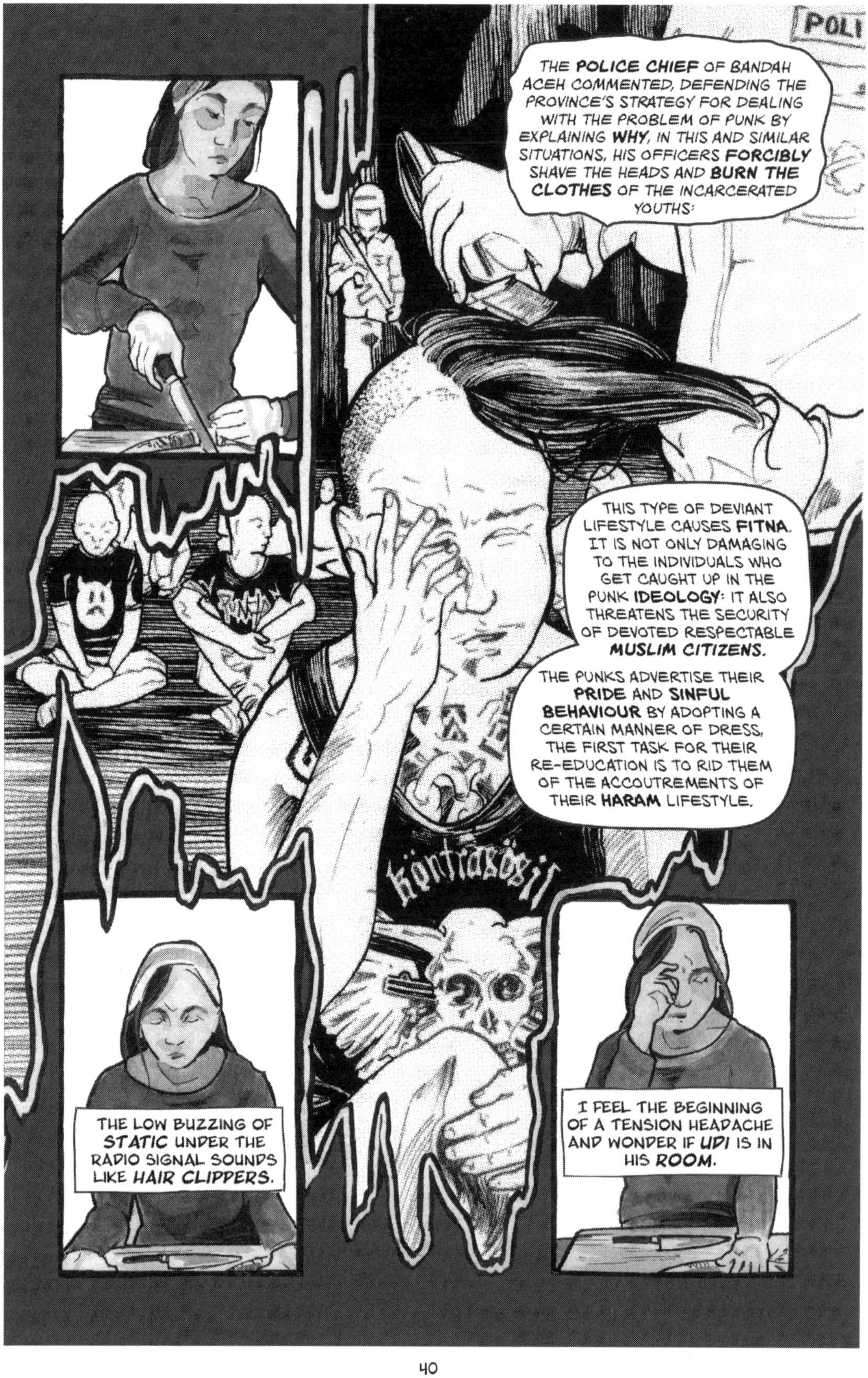
POLI
THE POLICE CHIEF OF BANDAH ACEH COMMENTED, DEFENDING THE PROVINCE'S STRATEGY FOR DEALING WITH THE PROBLEM OF PUNK BY EXPLAINING WHY, IN THIS AND SIMILAR SITUATIONS, HIS OFFICERS FORCIBLY SHAVE THE HEADS AND BURN THE CLOTHES OF THE INCARCERATED YOUTHS:
THIS TYPE OF DEVIANT LIFESTYLE CAUSES FITNA. IT IS NOT ONLY DAMAGING TO THE INDIVIDUALS WHO GET CAUGHT UP IN THE PUNK IDEOLOGY: IT ALSO THREATENS THE SECURITY OF DEVOTED RESPECTABLE MUSLIM CITIZENS.
THE PUNKS ADVERTISE THEIR PRIDE AND SINFUL BEHAVIOUR BY ADOPTING A CERTAIN MANNER OF DRESS, THE FIRST TASK FOR THEIR RE-EDUCATION IS TO RID THEM OF THE ACCOUTREMENTS OF THEIR HARAM LIFESTYLE.
Köntrasösil
THE LOW BUZZING OF STATIC UNDER THE RADIO SIGNAL SOUNDS LIKE HAIR CLIPPERS.
I FEEL THE BEGINNING OF A TENSION HEADACHE AND WONDER IF UDI IS IN HIS ROOM.

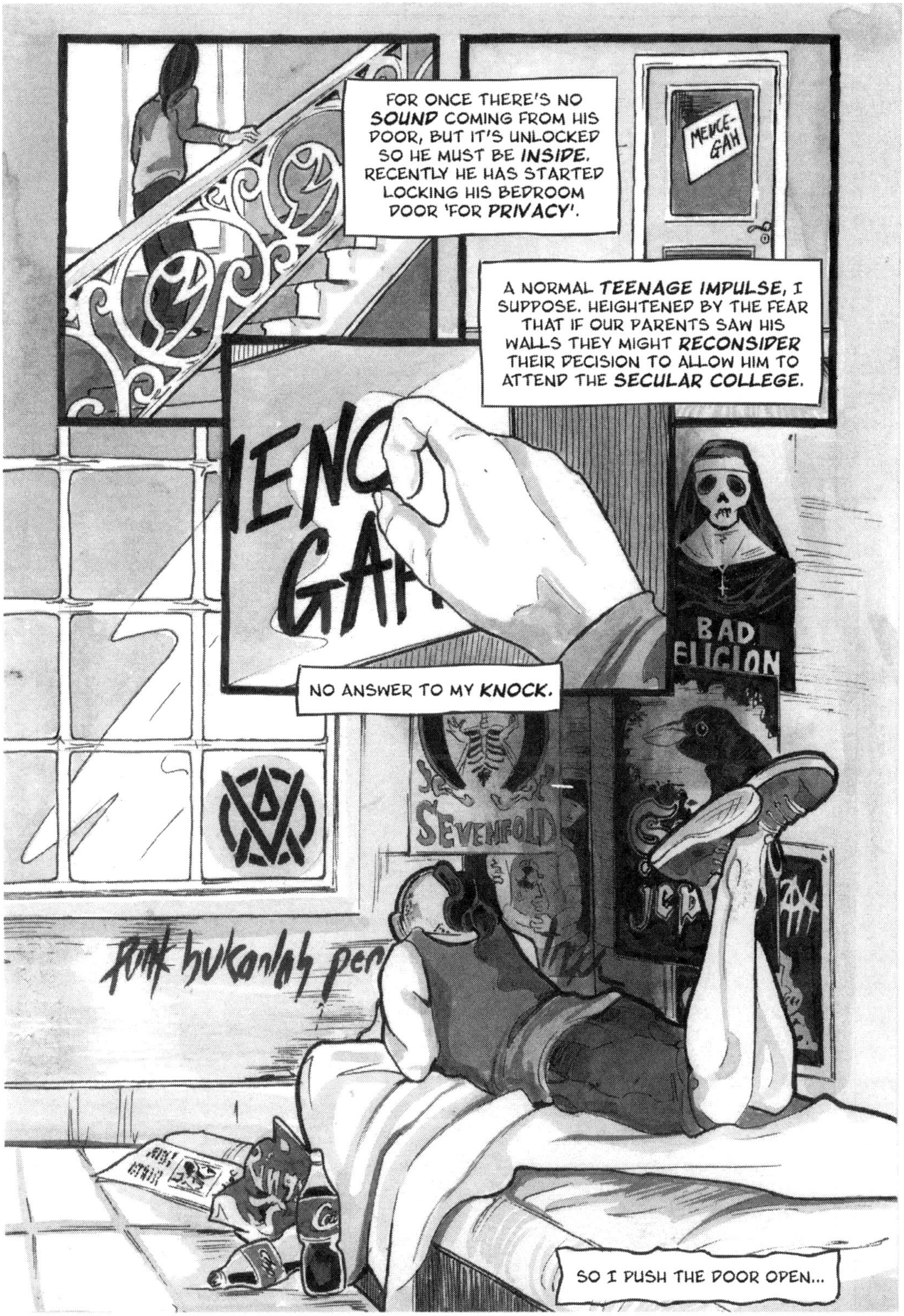
FOR ONCE THERE'S NO SOUND COMING FROM HIS DOOR, BUT IT'S UNLOCKED SO HE MUST BE INSIDE. RECENTLY HE HAS STARTED LOCKING HIS BEDROOM DOOR 'FOR PRIVACY'.
MENCE-GAH
A NORMAL TEENAGE IMPULSE, I SUPPOSE. HEIGHTENED BY THE FEAR THAT IF OUR PARENTS SAW HIS WALLS THEY MIGHT RECONSIDER THEIR DECISION TO ALLOW HIM TO ATTEND THE SECULAR COLLEGE.
NO ANSWER TO MY KNOCK.
SEVENFOLD
SO I PUSH THE DOOR OPEN...

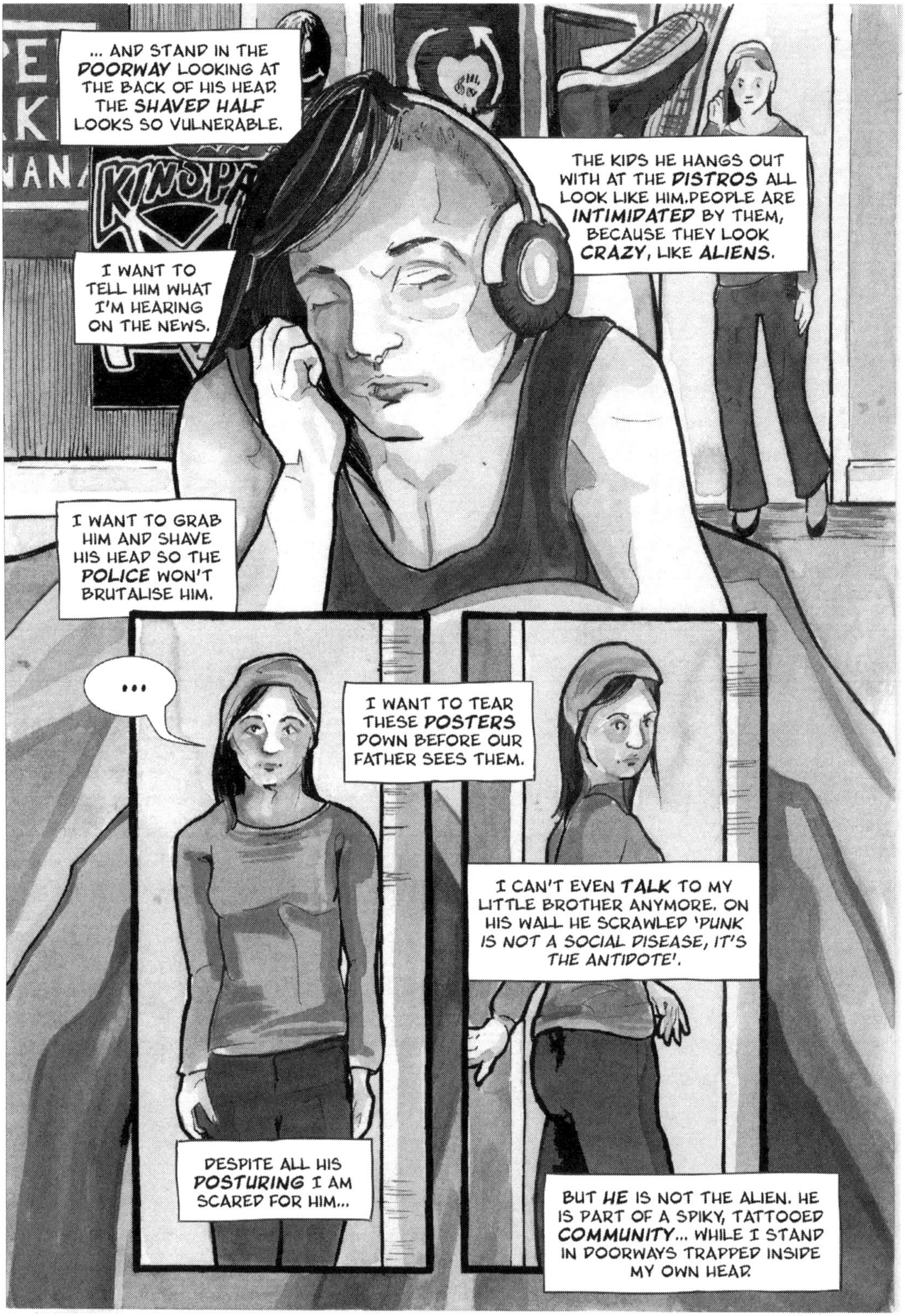
... AND STAND IN THE DOORWAY LOOKING AT THE BACK OF HIS HEAD. THE SHAVED HALF LOOKS SO VULNERABLE.
THE KIDS HE HANGS OUT WITH AT THE DISTROS ALL LOOK LIKE HIM.PEOPLE ARE INTIMIDATED BY THEM, BECAUSE THEY LOOK CRAZY, LIKE ALIENS.
I WANT TO TELL HIM WHAT I'M HEARING ON THE NEWS.
I WANT TO GRAB HIM AND SHAVE HIS HEAD SO THE POLICE WON'T BRUTALISE HIM.
...
I WANT TO TEAR THESE POSTERS DOWN BEFORE OUR FATHER SEES THEM.
DESPITE ALL HIS POSTURING I AM SCARED FOR HIM...
I CAN'T EVEN TALK TO MY LITTLE BROTHER ANYMORE. ON HIS WALL HE SCRAWLED 'PUNK IS NOT A SOCIAL DISEASE, IT'S THE ANTIDOTE'.
BUT HE IS NOT THE ALIEN. HE IS PART OF A SPIKY, TATTOOED COMMUNITY... WHILE I STAND IN DOORWAYS TRAPPED INSIDE MY OWN HEAD.

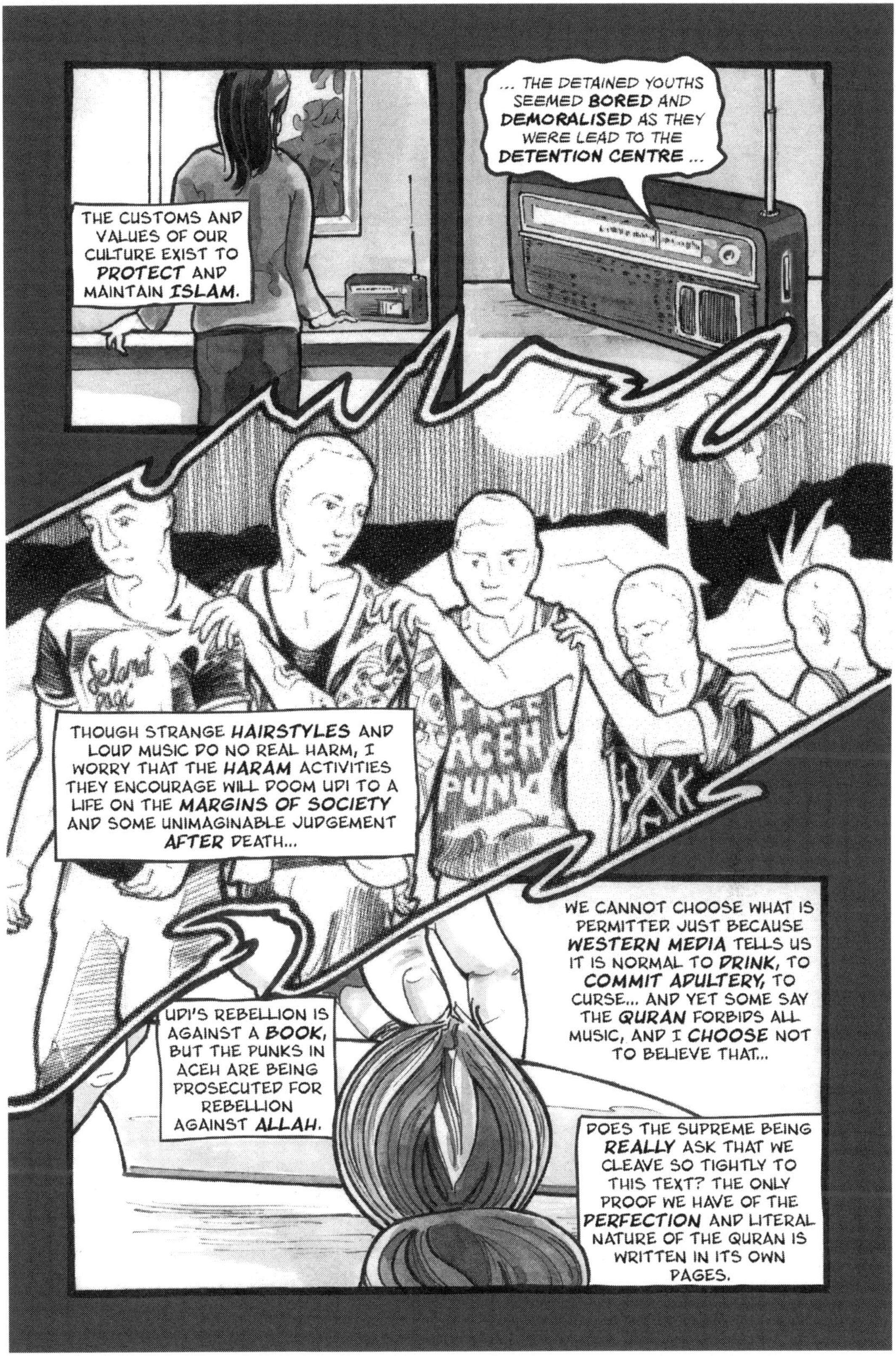
THE CUSTOMS AND VALUES OF OUR CULTURE EXIST TO PROTECT AND MAINTAIN ISLAM.
... THE DETAINED YOUTHS SEEMED BORED AND DEMORALISED AS THEY WERE LEAD TO THE DETENTION CENTRE ...
FREE ACEH PUNK
THOUGH STRANGE HAIRSTYLES AND LOUD MUSIC DO NO REAL HARM, I WORRY THAT THE HARAM ACTIVITIES THEY ENCOURAGE WILL DOOM UDI TO A LIFE ON THE MARGINS OF SOCIETY AND SOME UNIMAGINABLE JUDGEMENT AFTER DEATH...
WE CANNOT CHOOSE WHAT IS PERMITTED JUST BECAUSE WESTERN MEDIA TELLS US IT IS NORMAL TO DRINK, TO COMMIT ADULTERY, TO CURSE... AND YET SOME SAY THE QURAN FORBIDS ALL MUSIC, AND I CHOOSE NOT TO BELIEVE THAT...
UDI'S REBELLION IS AGAINST A BOOK, BUT THE PUNKS IN ACEH ARE BEING PROSECUTED FOR REBELLION AGAINST ALLAH.
DOES THE SUPREME BEING REALLY ASK THAT WE CLEAVE SO TIGHTLY TO THIS TEXT? THE ONLY PROOF WE HAVE OF THE PERFECTION AND LITERAL NATURE OF THE QURAN IS WRITTEN IN ITS OWN PAGES.

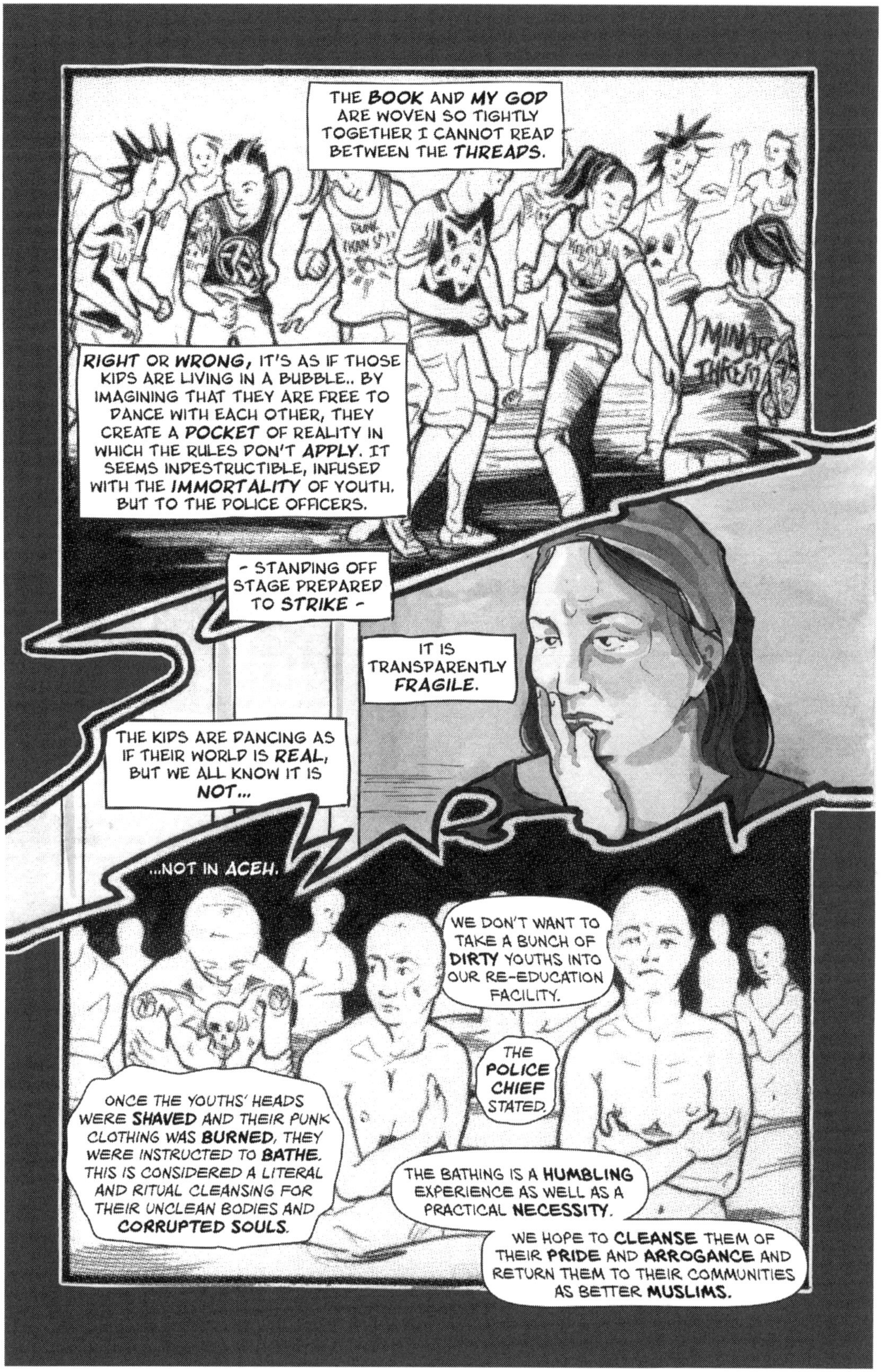
THE BOOK AND MY GOD ARE WOVEN SO TIGHTLY TOGETHER I CANNOT READ BETWEEN THE THREADS.
MINOR THREAT
RIGHT OR WRONG, IT'S AS IF THOSE KIDS ARE LIVING IN A BUBBLE.. BY IMAGINING THAT THEY ARE FREE TO DANCE WITH EACH OTHER, THEY CREATE A POCKET OF REALITY IN WHICH THE RULES DON'T APPLY. IT SEEMS INDESTRUCTIBLE, INFUSED WITH THE IMMORTALITY OF YOUTH. BUT TO THE POLICE OFFICERS.
- STANDING OFF STAGE PREPARED TO STRIKE -
IT IS TRANSPARENTLY FRAGILE.
THE KIDS ARE DANCING AS IF THEIR WORLD IS REAL, BUT WE ALL KNOW IT IS NOT...
...NOT IN ACEH.
WE DON'T WANT TO TAKE A BUNCH OF DIRTY YOUTHS INTO OUR RE-EDUCATION FACILITY.
THE POLICE CHIEF STATED.
ONCE THE YOUTHS' HEADS WERE SHAVED AND THEIR PUNK CLOTHING WAS BURNED, THEY WERE INSTRUCTED TO BATHE. THIS IS CONSIDERED A LITERAL AND RITUAL CLEANSING FOR THEIR UNCLEAN BODIES AND CORRUPTED SOULS.
THE BATHING IS A HUMBLING EXPERIENCE AS WELL AS A PRACTICAL NECESSITY.
WE HOPE TO CLEANSE THEM OF THEIR PRIDE AND ARROGANCE AND RETURN THEM TO THEIR COMMUNITIES AS BETTER MUSLIMS.

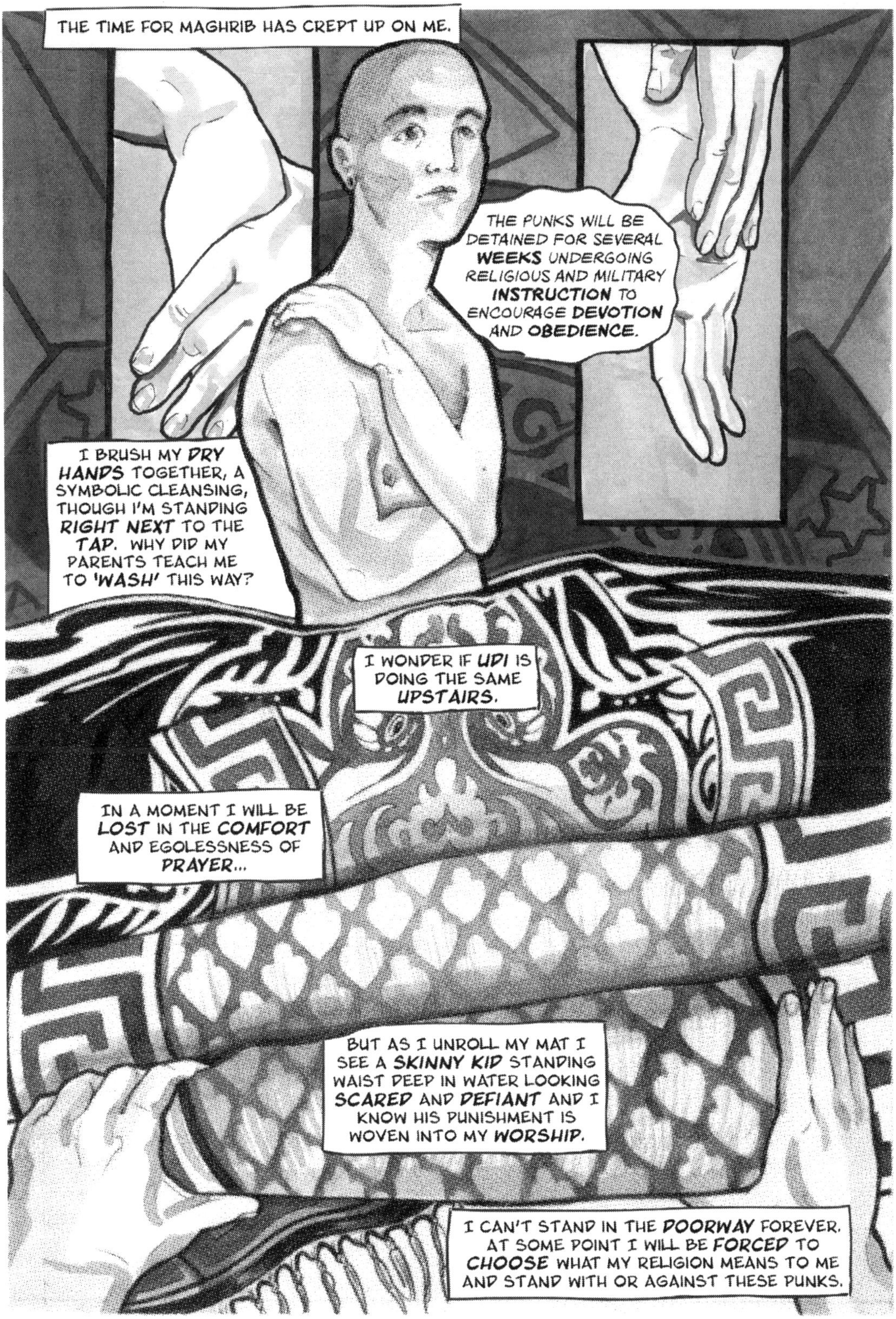
THE TIME FOR MAGHRIB HAS CREPT UP ON ME.
THE PUNKS WILL BE DETAINED FOR SEVERAL WEEKS UNDERGOING RELIGIOUS AND MILITARY INSTRUCTION TO ENCOURAGE DEVOTION AND OBEDIENCE.
I BRUSH MY DRY HANDS TOGETHER, A SYMBOLIC CLEANSING, THOUGH I'M STANDING RIGHT NEXT TO THE TAP. WHY DID MY PARENTS TEACH ME TO 'WASH' THIS WAY?
I WONDER IF UDI IS DOING THE SAME UPSTAIRS.
IN A MOMENT I WILL BE LOST IN THE COMFORT AND EGOLESSNESS OF PRAYER...
BUT AS I UNROLL MY MAT I SEE A SKINNY KID STANDING WAIST DEEP IN WATER LOOKING SCARED AND DEFIANT AND I KNOW HIS PUNISHMENT IS WOVEN INTO MY WORSHIP.
I CAN'T STAND IN THE DOORWAY FOREVER. AT SOME POINT I WILL BE FORCED TO CHOOSE WHAT MY RELIGION MEANS TO ME AND STAND WITH OR AGAINST THESE PUNKS.

Walking the streets of a small town on a small Indonesian island somewhere off the coast of Singapore, I glanced into a dark shop. It was sandwiched by a grocery stall and an auto shop vendor for the ubiquitous Indonesian moped. What had caught my eye was a poster pasted to the wall: the bat-winged skull logo of the American metalcore band Avenged Sevenfold.

That was the first, but far from the last, logo of a familiar punk or metal band I noticed on a poster, t-shirt or tattooed on someone's skin as my partner and I travelled around Indonesia. We were occasionally approached by Indonesian teenagers in tight black jeans, with studded collars and leather jackets, who commented on our tattoos or my partner's long hair. More than one teenage boy commented that he would like to grow his hair long 'if he could get away with it'. I remembered my father forbidding me as a teenager from getting my ears pierced (a rule which I semantically evaded by piercing them myself).

In a fairly conservative part of southern England, piercing your own ears a dozen times, ripping holes in the knees of your jeans and dying your hair was a way for teenagers like me to signal that we didn't belong. Like any youth subculture, our fashion and music choices were defined in opposition to our parents' values, and those of society as we saw it. It was also defined by enthusiastic moshing to the music of local punk bands and similarly enthusiastic drug and alcohol use.

We were rebels, and the risks we took were worth it for being true to our own values: freedom of expression, anti-discrimination and anti-authoritarianism.

We thought we were pretty hardcore.

The punks I met in Indonesia don't belong either. The society they are rebelling against is much more conservative than the one I grew up in and the familial, legal, religious and societal rules they transgress are much stricter.

Indonesia is the most populous Islamic nation and has long been heralded as the most tolerant and liberal face of the Muslim religion, but the interpretation of the religion is becoming increasingly fundamentalist. Hijab sales are growing, alcohol sales are plummeting. Minority religious groups, like Christians and Hindus, were once tolerated or even embraced by the culture, but are now concerned for their safety. LGBT activists are often attacked and in 2012 an atheist was arrested and jailed for two years for having the temerity to post 'God does not exist' on his Facebook wall.

In an interview for *Vice*, a street punk from the province of Aceh explained:

"We are haram, like pork meat."

He was smiling while he said it, but his words chilled me. It's not the way they dress, the music they listen to or even their activities that are considered forbidden (although they all are); they *themselves* are haram.

In the Judeo-Christian tradition that's like the distinction between labelling someone as a sinner and labelling someone as a sin.

I was horrified when, in 2011, I saw the pictures of Indonesian punks being forcibly shaved, tortured, humiliated and imprisoned for doing exactly the same things I did at their age. Listening to the same music I listen to now when I draw comics — not just the same sort of music, but the same records. I had met kids like them. I had *been* a kid like them.

More information, discussion and links at
doubtcomic.com/indonesian-punk-rock

AN OCEANIC FEELING
SMALL FISHING VILLAGE, GREECE

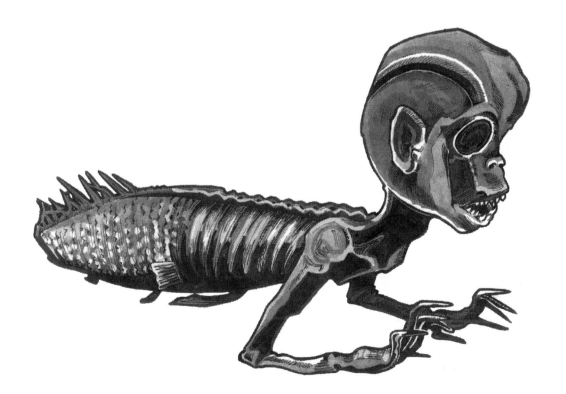

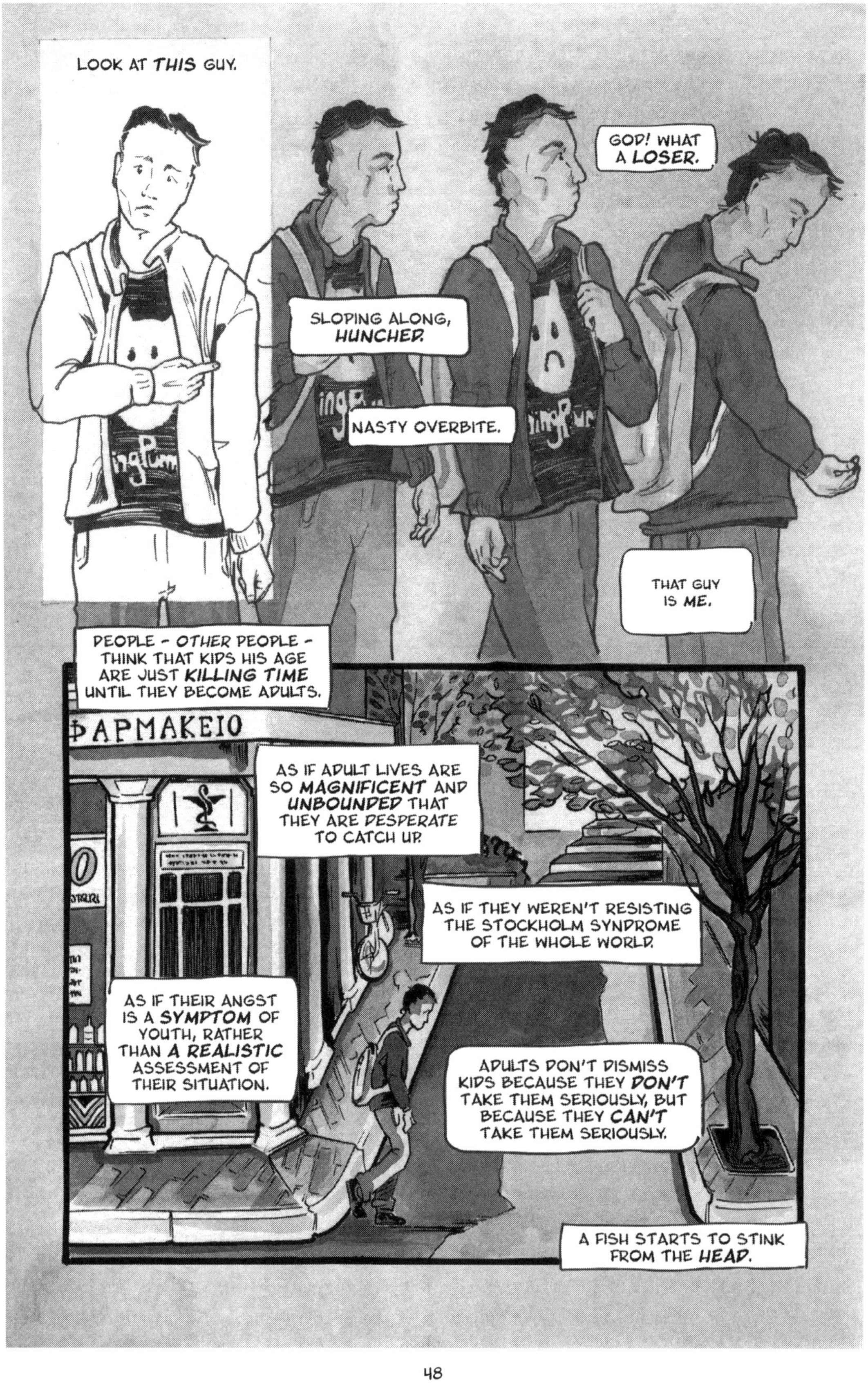
LOOK AT THIS GUY.
SLOPING ALONG, HUNCHED.
NASTY OVERBITE.
GOD! WHAT A LOSER.
THAT GUY IS ME.
PEOPLE - OTHER PEOPLE - THINK THAT KIDS HIS AGE ARE JUST KILLING TIME UNTIL THEY BECOME ADULTS.
ΦΑΡΜΑΚΕΙΟ
AS IF ADULT LIVES ARE SO MAGNIFICENT AND UNBOUNDED THAT THEY ARE DESPERATE TO CATCH UP.
AS IF THEY WEREN'T RESISTING THE STOCKHOLM SYNDROME OF THE WHOLE WORLD.
AS IF THEIR ANGST IS A SYMPTOM OF YOUTH, RATHER THAN A REALISTIC ASSESSMENT OF THEIR SITUATION.
ADULTS DON'T DISMISS KIDS BECAUSE THEY DON'T TAKE THEM SERIOUSLY, BUT BECAUSE THEY CAN'T TAKE THEM SERIOUSLY.
A FISH STARTS TO STINK FROM THE HEAD.

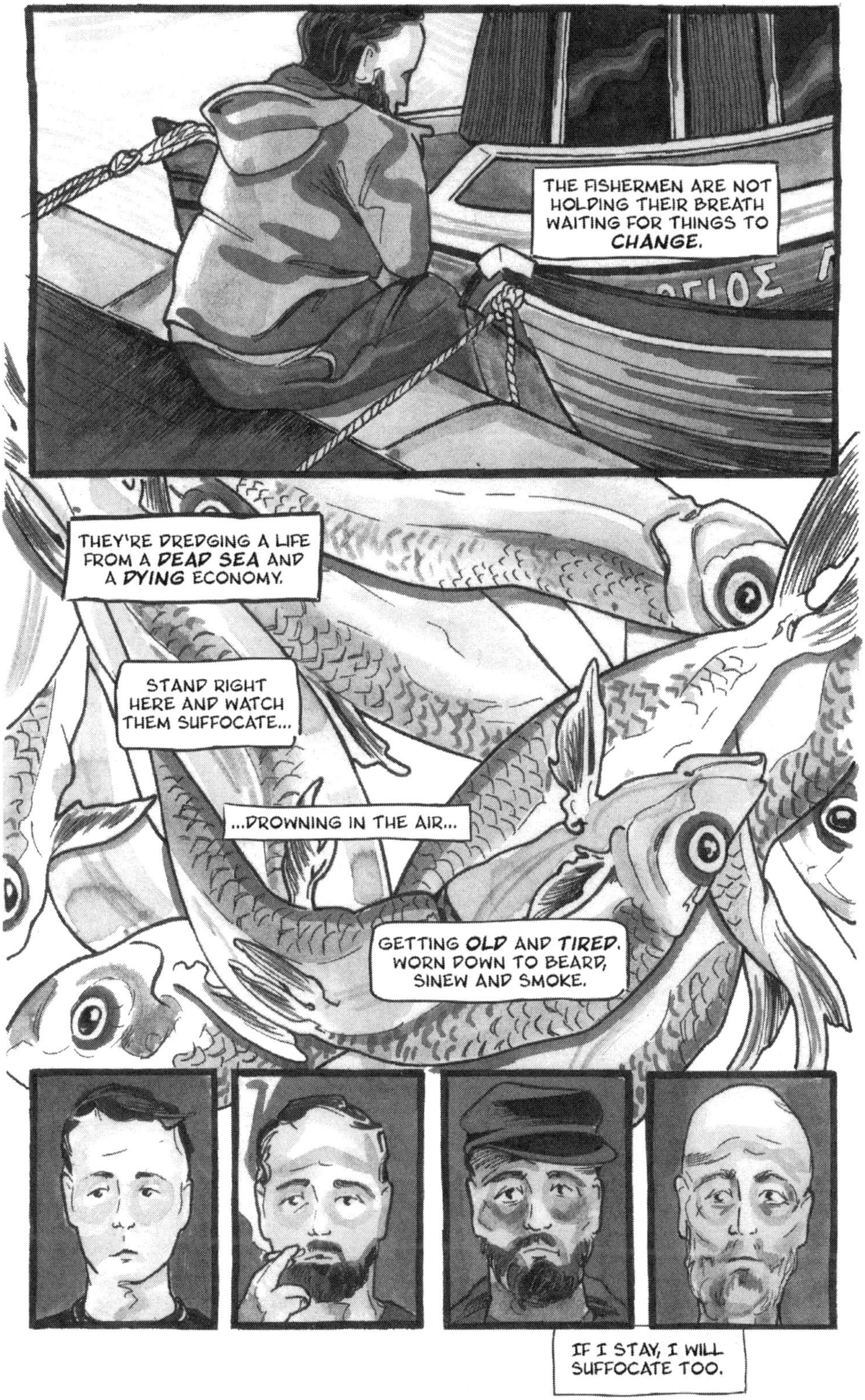
THE FISHERMEN ARE NOT HOLDING THEIR BREATH WAITING FOR THINGS TO CHANGE.
ΟΣΙΟΣ
THEY'RE DREDGING A LIFE FROM A DEAD SEA AND A DYING ECONOMY.
STAND RIGHT HERE AND WATCH THEM SUFFOCATE...
...DROWNING IN THE AIR...
GETTING OLD AND TIRED. WORN DOWN TO BEARD, SINEW AND SMOKE.
IF I STAY, I WILL SUFFOCATE TOO.

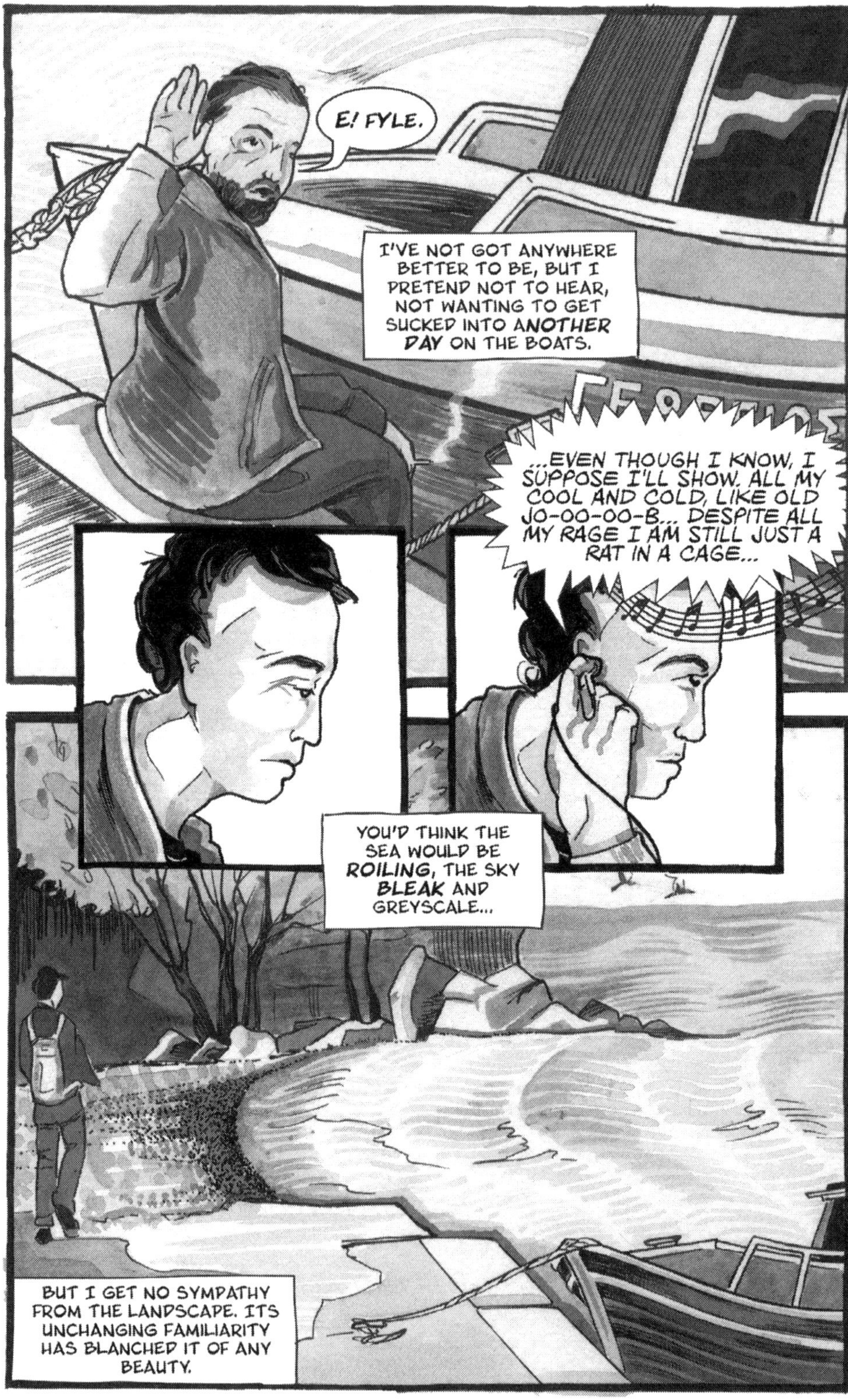
E! FYLE.
I'VE NOT GOT ANYWHERE BETTER TO BE, BUT I PRETEND NOT TO HEAR, NOT WANTING TO GET SUCKED INTO ANOTHER DAY ON THE BOATS.
...EVEN THOUGH I KNOW, I SUPPOSE I'LL SHOW. ALL MY COOL AND COLD, LIKE OLD JO-OO-OO-B... DESPITE ALL MY RAGE I AM STILL JUST A RAT IN A CAGE...
YOU'D THINK THE SEA WOULD BE ROILING, THE SKY BLEAK AND GREYSCALE...
BUT I GET NO SYMPATHY FROM THE LANDSCAPE. ITS UNCHANGING FAMILIARITY HAS BLANCHED IT OF ANY BEAUTY.

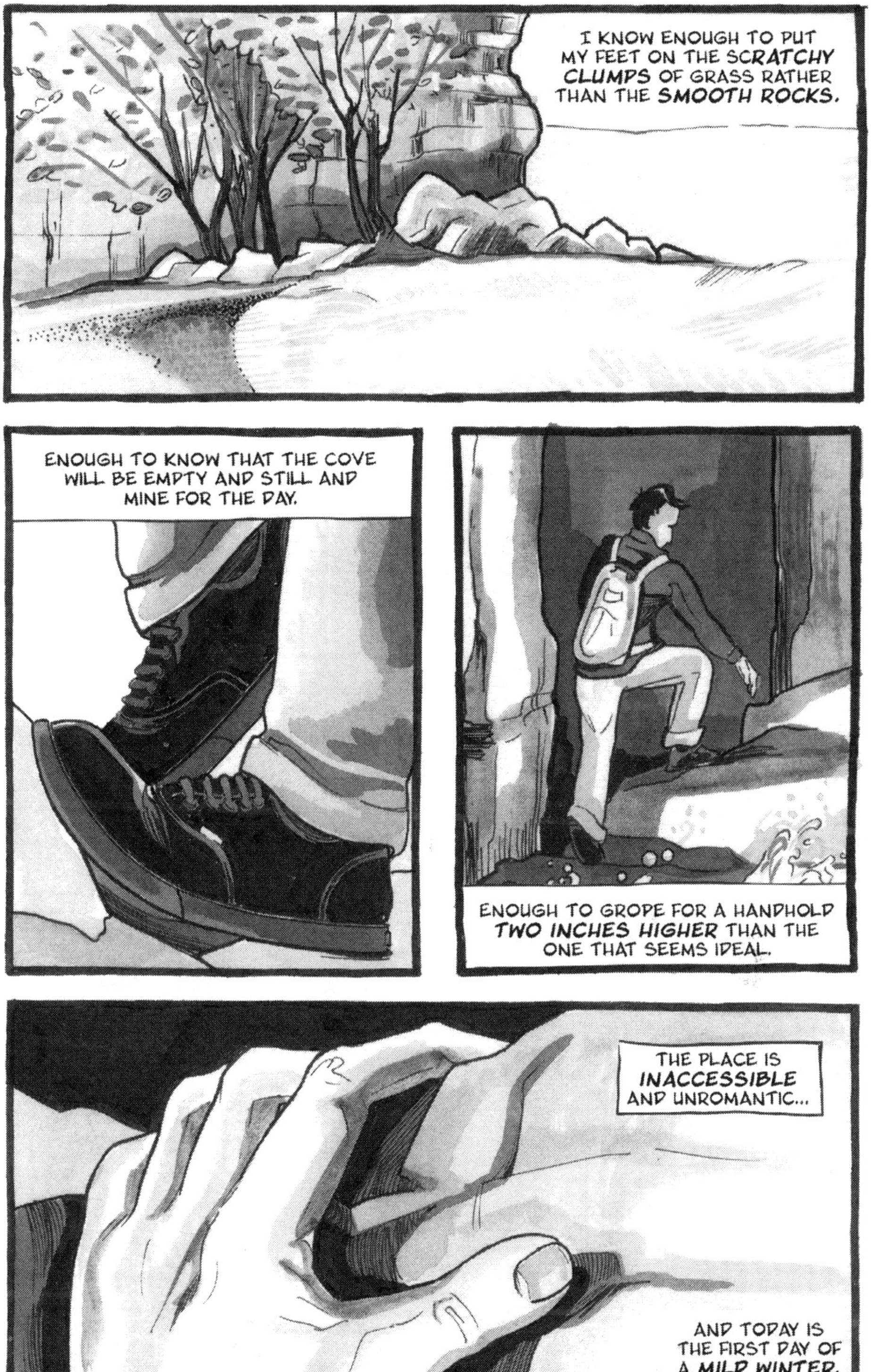
I KNOW ENOUGH TO PUT MY FEET ON THE SCRATCHY CLUMPS OF GRASS RATHER THAN THE SMOOTH ROCKS.
ENOUGH TO KNOW THAT THE COVE WILL BE EMPTY AND STILL AND MINE FOR THE DAY.
ENOUGH TO GROPE FOR A HANDHOLD TWO INCHES HIGHER THAN THE ONE THAT SEEMS IDEAL.
THE PLACE IS INACCESSIBLE AND UNROMANTIC...
AND TODAY IS THE FIRST DAY OF A MILD WINTER.

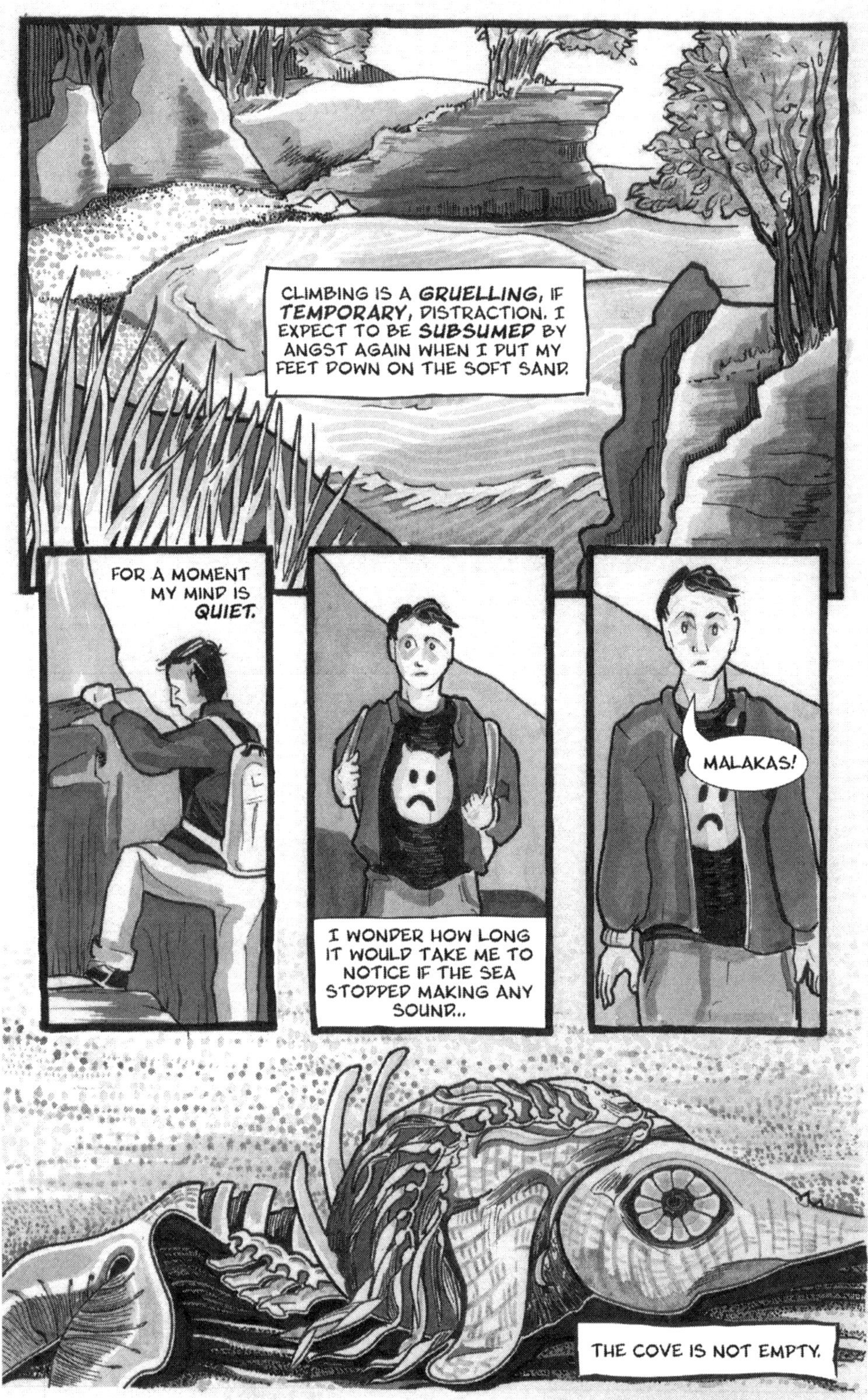
CLIMBING IS A GRUELLING, IF TEMPORARY, DISTRACTION. I EXPECT TO BE SUBSUMED BY ANGST AGAIN WHEN I PUT MY FEET DOWN ON THE SOFT SAND.
FOR A MOMENT MY MIND IS QUIET.
I WONDER HOW LONG IT WOULD TAKE ME TO NOTICE IF THE SEA STOPPED MAKING ANY SOUND...
MALAKAS!
THE COVE IS NOT EMPTY.

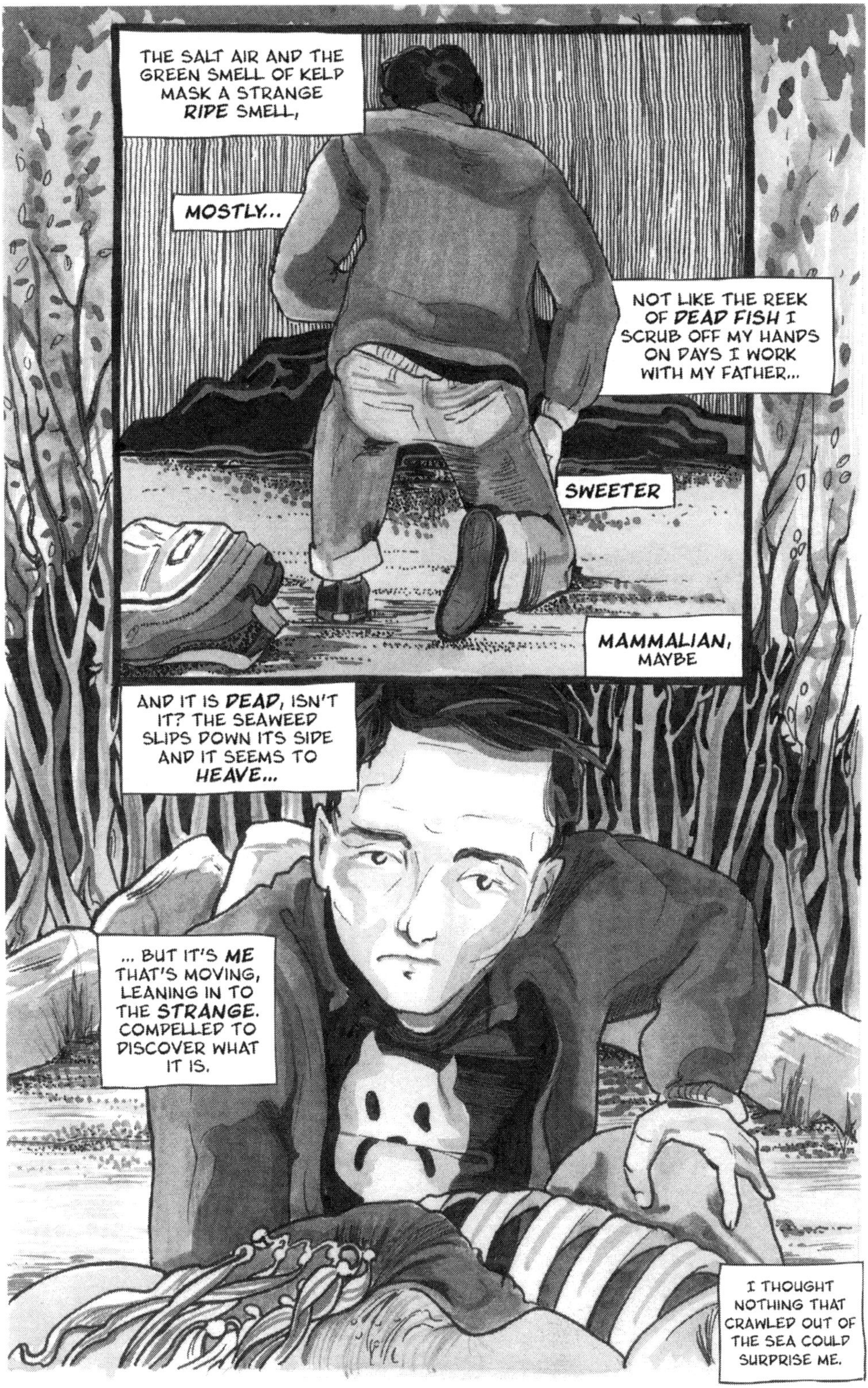
THE SALT AIR AND THE GREEN SMELL OF KELP MASK A STRANGE RIPE SMELL,
MOSTLY...
NOT LIKE THE REEK OF DEAD FISH I SCRUB OFF MY HANDS ON DAYS I WORK WITH MY FATHER...
SWEETER
MAMMALIAN, MAYBE
AND IT IS DEAD, ISN'T IT? THE SEAWEED SLIPS DOWN ITS SIDE AND IT SEEMS TO HEAVE...
... BUT IT'S ME THAT'S MOVING, LEANING IN TO THE STRANGE. COMPELLED TO DISCOVER WHAT IT IS.
I THOUGHT NOTHING THAT CRAWLED OUT OF THE SEA COULD SURPRISE ME.

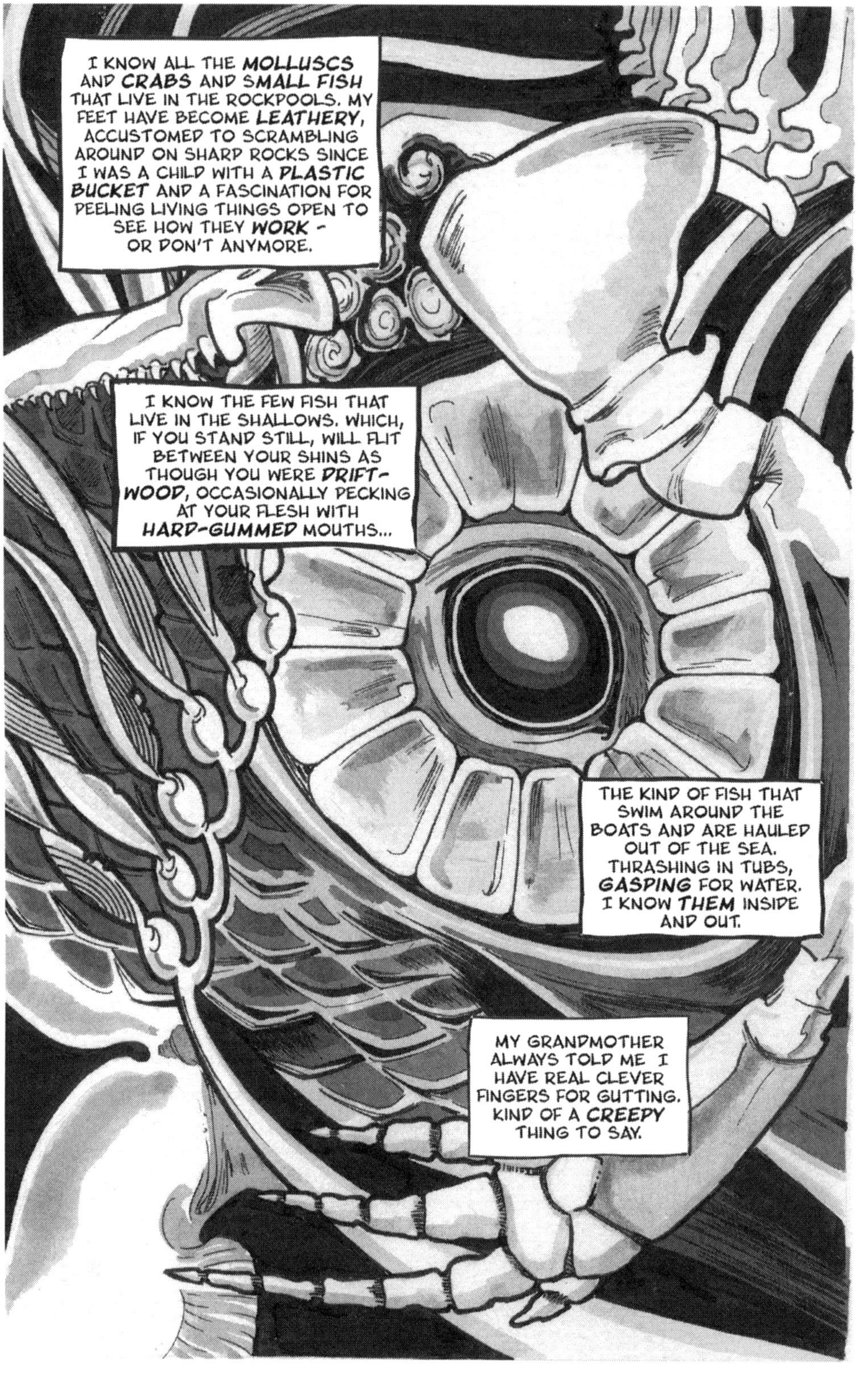
I KNOW ALL THE MOLLUSCS AND CRABS AND SMALL FISH THAT LIVE IN THE ROCKPOOLS. MY FEET HAVE BECOME LEATHERY, ACCUSTOMED TO SCRAMBLING AROUND ON SHARP ROCKS SINCE I WAS A CHILD WITH A PLASTIC BUCKET AND A FASCINATION FOR PEELING LIVING THINGS OPEN TO SEE HOW THEY WORK - OR DON'T ANYMORE.
I KNOW THE FEW FISH THAT LIVE IN THE SHALLOWS. WHICH, IF YOU STAND STILL, WILL FLIT BETWEEN YOUR SHINS AS THOUGH YOU WERE DRIFT-WOOD, OCCASIONALLY PECKING AT YOUR FLESH WITH HARD-GUMMED MOUTHS...
THE KIND OF FISH THAT SWIM AROUND THE BOATS AND ARE HAULED OUT OF THE SEA. THRASHING IN TUBS, GASPING FOR WATER. I KNOW THEM INSIDE AND OUT.
MY GRANDMOTHER ALWAYS TOLD ME I HAVE REAL CLEVER FINGERS FOR GUTTING. KIND OF A CREEPY THING TO SAY.

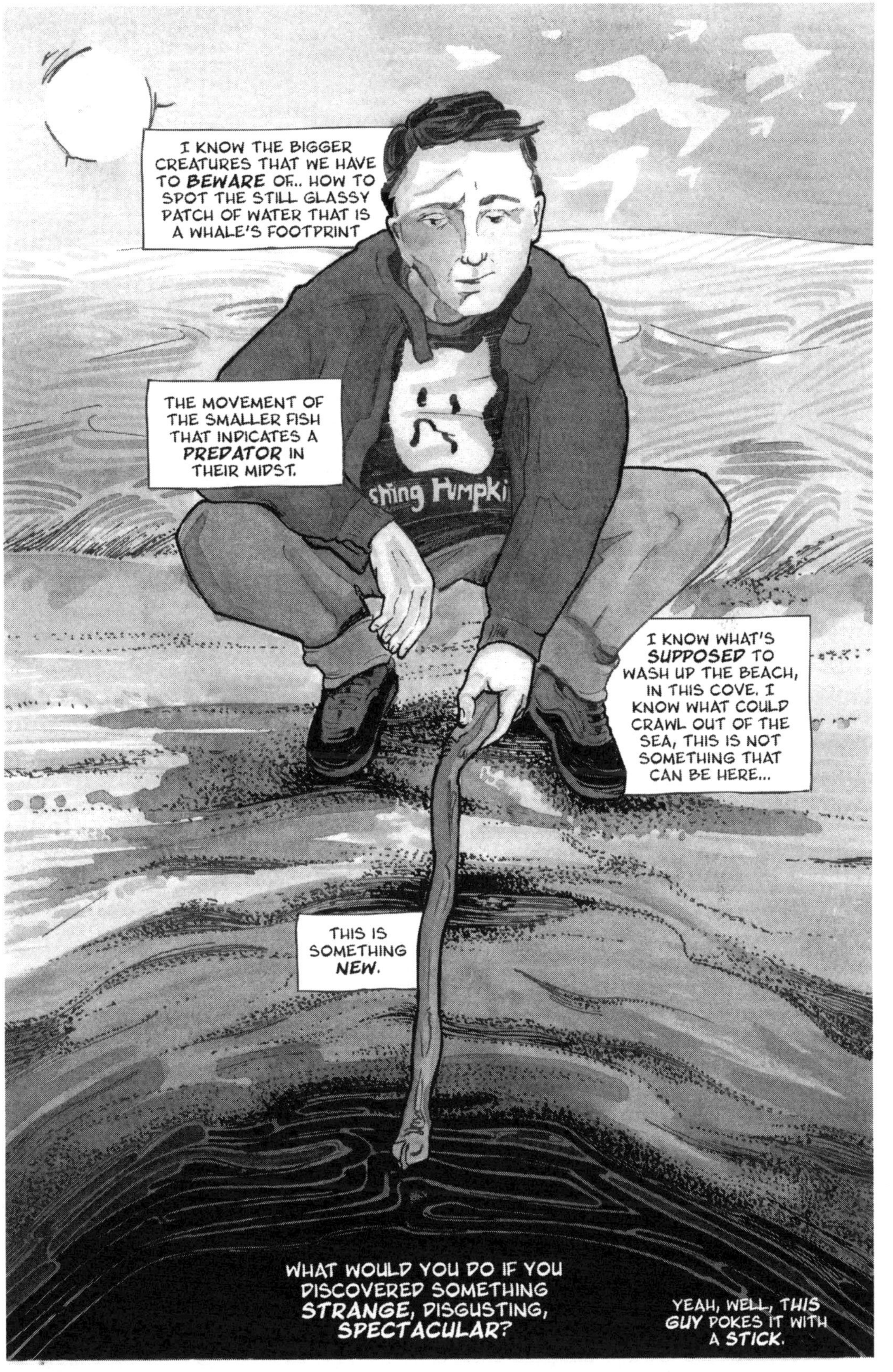
I KNOW THE BIGGER CREATURES THAT WE HAVE TO BEWARE OF.. HOW TO SPOT THE STILL GLASSY PATCH OF WATER THAT IS A WHALE'S FOOTPRINT
THE MOVEMENT OF THE SMALLER FISH THAT INDICATES A PREDATOR IN THEIR MIDST.
I KNOW WHAT'S SUPPOSED TO WASH UP THE BEACH, IN THIS COVE. I KNOW WHAT COULD CRAWL OUT OF THE SEA, THIS IS NOT SOMETHING THAT CAN BE HERE...
THIS IS SOMETHING NEW.
WHAT WOULD YOU DO IF YOU DISCOVERED SOMETHING STRANGE, DISGUSTING, SPECTACULAR?
YEAH, WELL, THIS GUY POKES IT WITH A STICK.

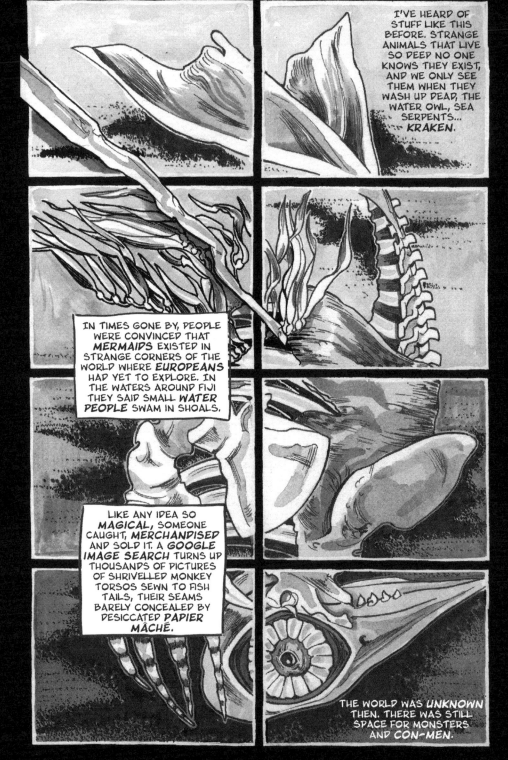

I'VE HEARD OF STUFF LIKE THIS BEFORE. STRANGE ANIMALS THAT LIVE SO DEEP NO ONE KNOWS THEY EXIST, AND WE ONLY SEE THEM WHEN THEY WASH UP DEAD; THE WATER OWL, SEA SERPENTS... *KRAKEN.*

IN TIMES GONE BY, PEOPLE WERE CONVINCED THAT *MERMAIDS* EXISTED IN STRANGE CORNERS OF THE WORLD WHERE *EUROPEANS* HAD YET TO EXPLORE. IN THE WATERS AROUND FIJI THEY SAID SMALL *WATER PEOPLE* SWAM IN SHOALS.

LIKE ANY IDEA SO *MAGICAL*, SOMEONE CAUGHT, *MERCHANDISED* AND SOLD IT. A *GOOGLE IMAGE SEARCH* TURNS UP THOUSANDS OF PICTURES OF SHRIVELLED MONKEY TORSOS SEWN TO FISH TAILS, THEIR SEAMS BARELY CONCEALED BY DESICCATED *PAPIER MÂCHÉ.*

THE WORLD WAS *UNKNOWN* THEN. THERE WAS STILL SPACE FOR MONSTERS AND *CON-MEN.*

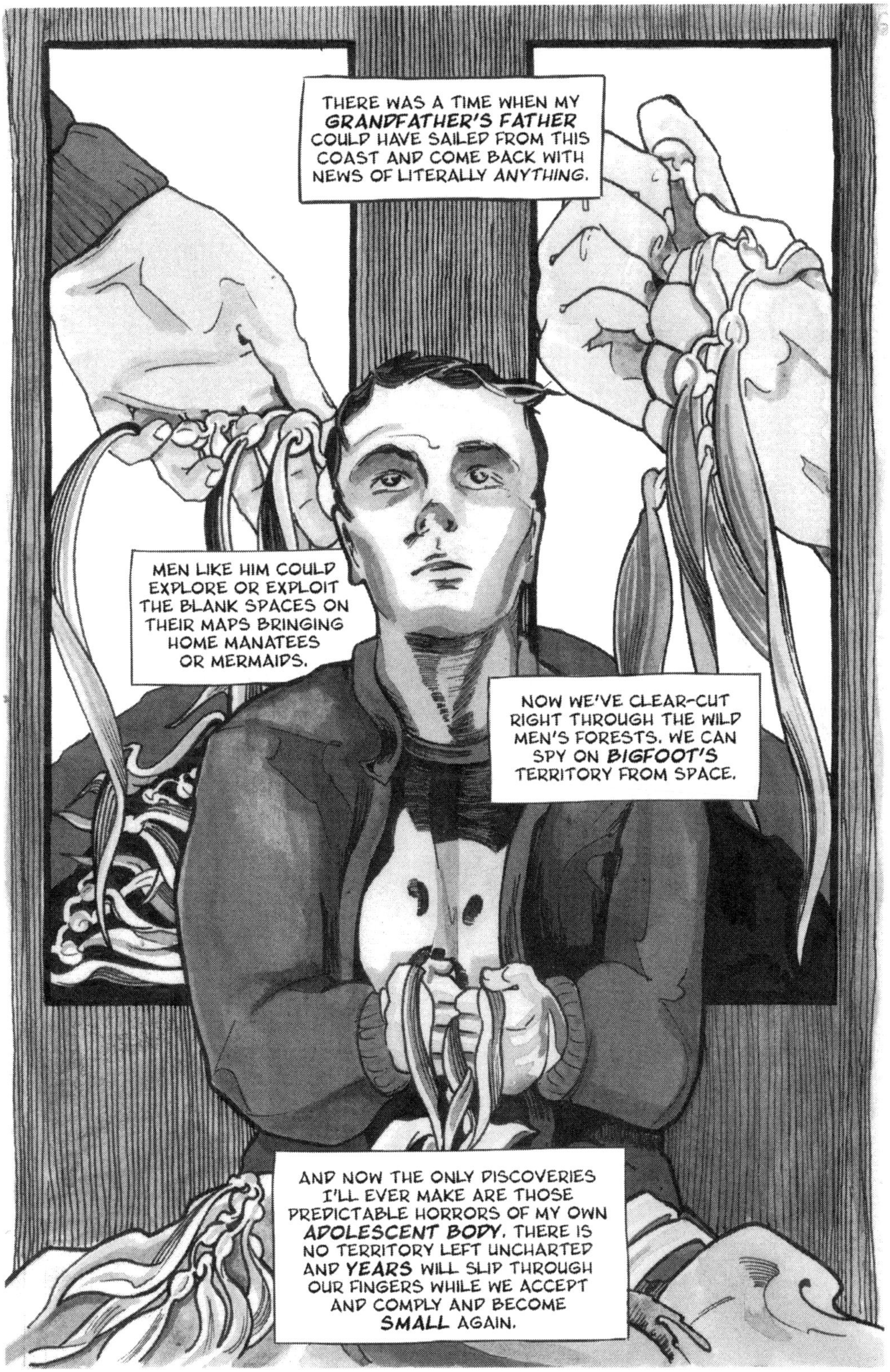
THERE WAS A TIME WHEN MY GRANDFATHER'S FATHER COULD HAVE SAILED FROM THIS COAST AND COME BACK WITH NEWS OF LITERALLY ANYTHING.
MEN LIKE HIM COULD EXPLORE OR EXPLOIT THE BLANK SPACES ON THEIR MAPS BRINGING HOME MANATEES OR MERMAIDS.
NOW WE'VE CLEAR-CUT RIGHT THROUGH THE WILD MEN'S FORESTS. WE CAN SPY ON BIGFOOT'S TERRITORY FROM SPACE.
AND NOW THE ONLY DISCOVERIES I'LL EVER MAKE ARE THOSE PREDICTABLE HORRORS OF MY OWN ADOLESCENT BODY. THERE IS NO TERRITORY LEFT UNCHARTED AND YEARS WILL SLIP THROUGH OUR FINGERS WHILE WE ACCEPT AND COMPLY AND BECOME SMALL AGAIN.

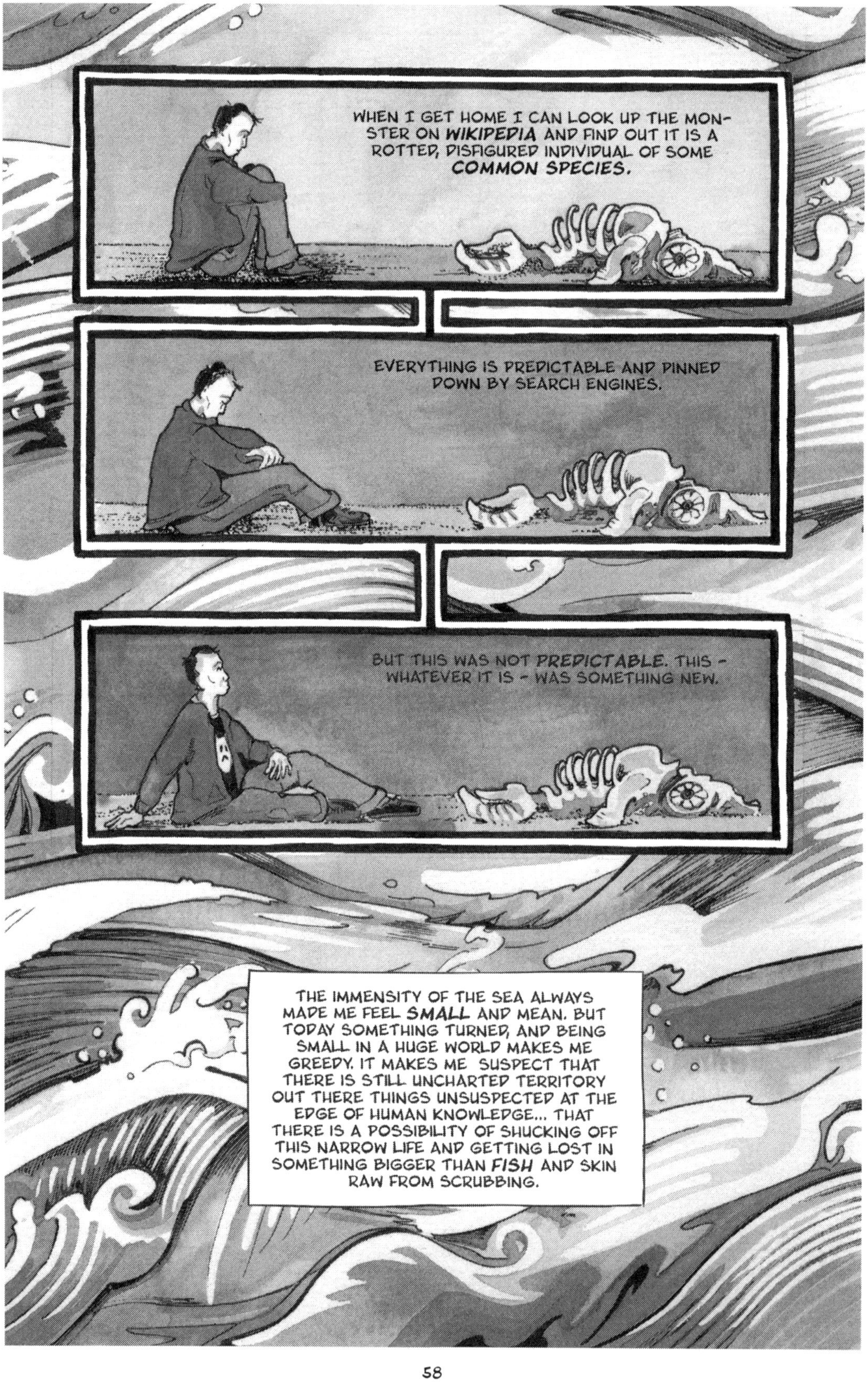
WHEN I GET HOME I CAN LOOK UP THE MONSTER ON WIKIPEDIA AND FIND OUT IT IS A ROTTED, DISFIGURED INDIVIDUAL OF SOME COMMON SPECIES.
EVERYTHING IS PREDICTABLE AND PINNED DOWN BY SEARCH ENGINES.
BUT THIS WAS NOT PREDICTABLE. THIS - WHATEVER IT IS - WAS SOMETHING NEW.
THE IMMENSITY OF THE SEA ALWAYS MADE ME FEEL SMALL AND MEAN. BUT TODAY SOMETHING TURNED, AND BEING SMALL IN A HUGE WORLD MAKES ME GREEDY. IT MAKES ME SUSPECT THAT THERE IS STILL UNCHARTED TERRITORY OUT THERE THINGS UNSUSPECTED AT THE EDGE OF HUMAN KNOWLEDGE... THAT THERE IS A POSSIBILITY OF SHUCKING OFF THIS NARROW LIFE AND GETTING LOST IN SOMETHING BIGGER THAN FISH AND SKIN RAW FROM SCRUBBING.

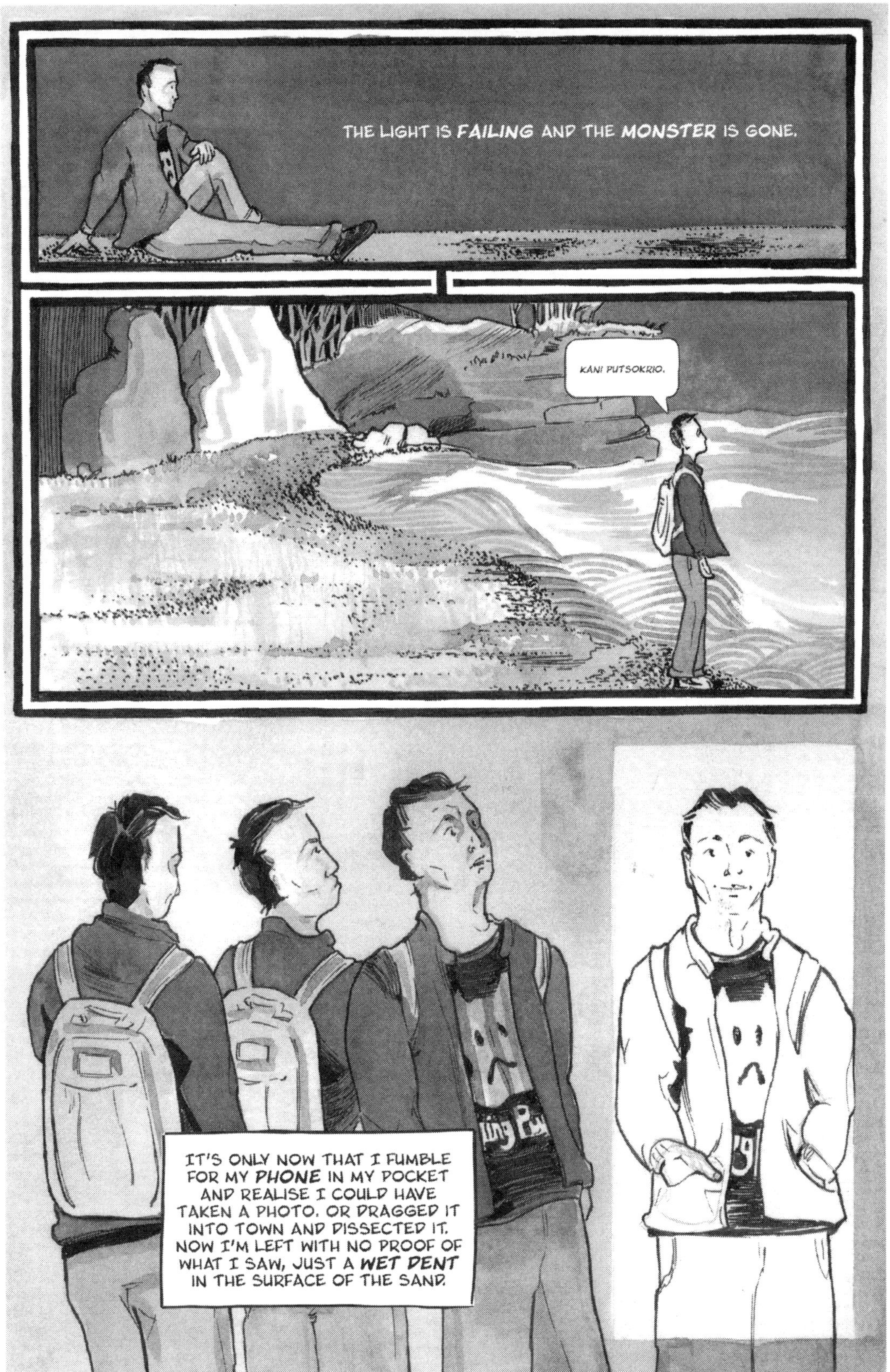
THE LIGHT IS FAILING AND THE MONSTER IS GONE.
KANI PUTSOKRIO.
IT'S ONLY NOW THAT I FUMBLE FOR MY PHONE IN MY POCKET AND REALISE I COULD HAVE TAKEN A PHOTO. OR DRAGGED IT INTO TOWN AND DISSECTED IT. NOW I'M LEFT WITH NO PROOF OF WHAT I SAW, JUST A WET DENT IN THE SURFACE OF THE SAND.

In a museum in the seaside town where I live, there is an imperfectly preserved specimen of a mermaid on display. Well, actually it's a mer*man*. The museum attendant corrected me when I mis-gendered the beast, pointing out that he only had one pair of nipples, unlike the females of his species.

This merman is one of the many Fiji mermaids produced in the early nineteenth century by sideshow curators. They are usually the torso of a monkey somehow attached to the tail of a fish displayed in inadequate light to obscure the artifice. The public would pay to see exhibits like this and marvel at the strange creatures that lived on the other side of the world. People were convinced by Fiji mermaids because there were so many strange tales coming from strange places at that time; was a mermaid anymore unlikely than a platypus or a giraffe?

Of course now we would never be so gullible. We understand evolution and the biological impossibility of a fish/primate hybrid. We have mapped out and classified almost all of the extant fauna on Earth. Even Bigfoot can't hide from Google Earth. It's tempting to think we know everything, or at least enough not to be fooled.

But a known universe would be a boring universe with no scope for discovery, awe or wonder. Thankfully, despite appearances, humanities ignorance is still epic. The stuff we don't know about the universe is the arena in which science operates and it is a gloriously vast field. From a NASA article on dark energy:

> *It turns out that roughly 68% of the Universe is dark energy. Dark matter makes up about 27%. The rest - everything on Earth, everything ever observed with all of our instruments, all normal matter - adds up to less than 5% of the Universe.*

Our maps don't have blank spaces — our maps are almost totally blank. We've charted less than five percent of the landscape. And now, while still high, the barriers of entry to exploring the universe are significantly lower than they ever have been. Thanks to technological innovation anyone with an internet connection can map the stars.

Just like in the nineteenth century, we have genuine explorers presenting us with amazing discoveries and there are frauds who exploit the gaps in our knowledge to sell tickets to their sideshows. The invocation of quantum mechanics, or at least the liberal use of quantum vocabulary, by new age gurus will (hopefully) seem as absurd to the scientifically literate population of the future as my merman does to us now.

When you find something strange on the beach, you have the choice whether to haul it back to civilisation and expose it to the rigorous testing and inquiry of science or to take a few blurry photographs and confabulate a story that you want to believe, or want to sell. Either choice is made in acknowledgement of the unknown but only the former gives proper respect to our collective ignorance. Because while con-men disguise or negate the unknown by providing false answers, true explorers must always work with a truly marvellous complex reality, that never fully satisfies us.

One of the reasons I moved to a coastal town a few years ago was because of an intense feeling that the sea provokes in me. When I explain it, some people nod in recognition and some crease their brow in concern. Freud popularised the term 'Oceanic Feeling' to describe the limitlessness feeling of connection that manifests in religion which he himself never felt. I'm not sure if I've had *the* Oceanic Feeling, but I get *an* Oceanic Feeling. When I'm standing on the shore and I look out over its expanse I feel small, but not as small as I actually am, and I'm tempted to go chasing mermaids.

More information, discussion and links at
doubtcomic.com/an-oceanic-feeling

MAYFLY

OUTSKIRTS OF JAIPUR, INDIA

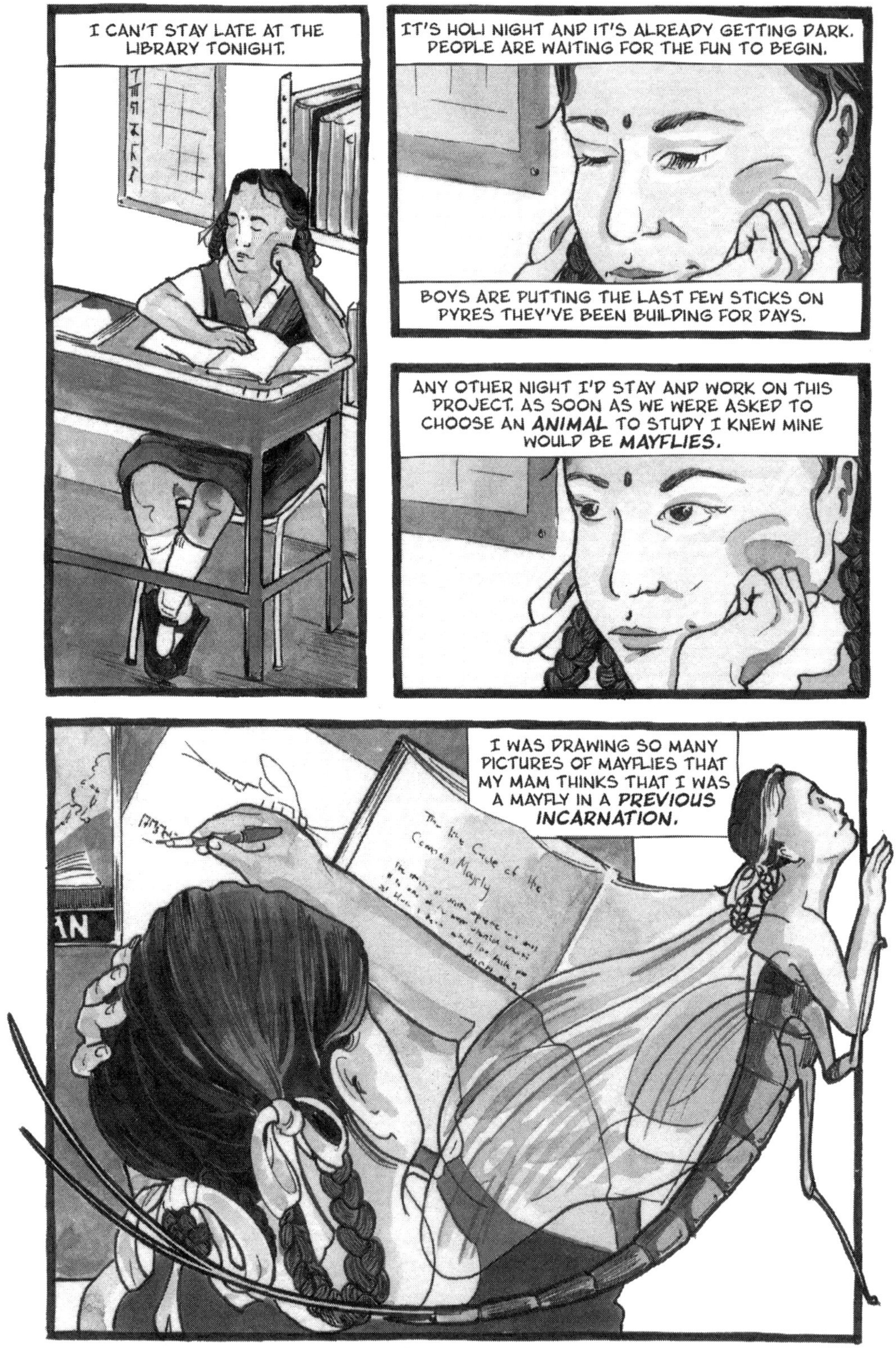
I CAN'T STAY LATE AT THE LIBRARY TONIGHT.
IT'S HOLI NIGHT AND IT'S ALREADY GETTING DARK. PEOPLE ARE WAITING FOR THE FUN TO BEGIN.
BOYS ARE PUTTING THE LAST FEW STICKS ON PYRES THEY'VE BEEN BUILDING FOR DAYS.
ANY OTHER NIGHT I'D STAY AND WORK ON THIS PROJECT. AS SOON AS WE WERE ASKED TO CHOOSE AN ANIMAL TO STUDY I KNEW MINE WOULD BE MAYFLIES.
I WAS DRAWING SO MANY PICTURES OF MAYFLIES THAT MY MAM THINKS THAT I WAS A MAYFLY IN A PREVIOUS INCARNATION.
The Life Cycle of the Common Mayfly

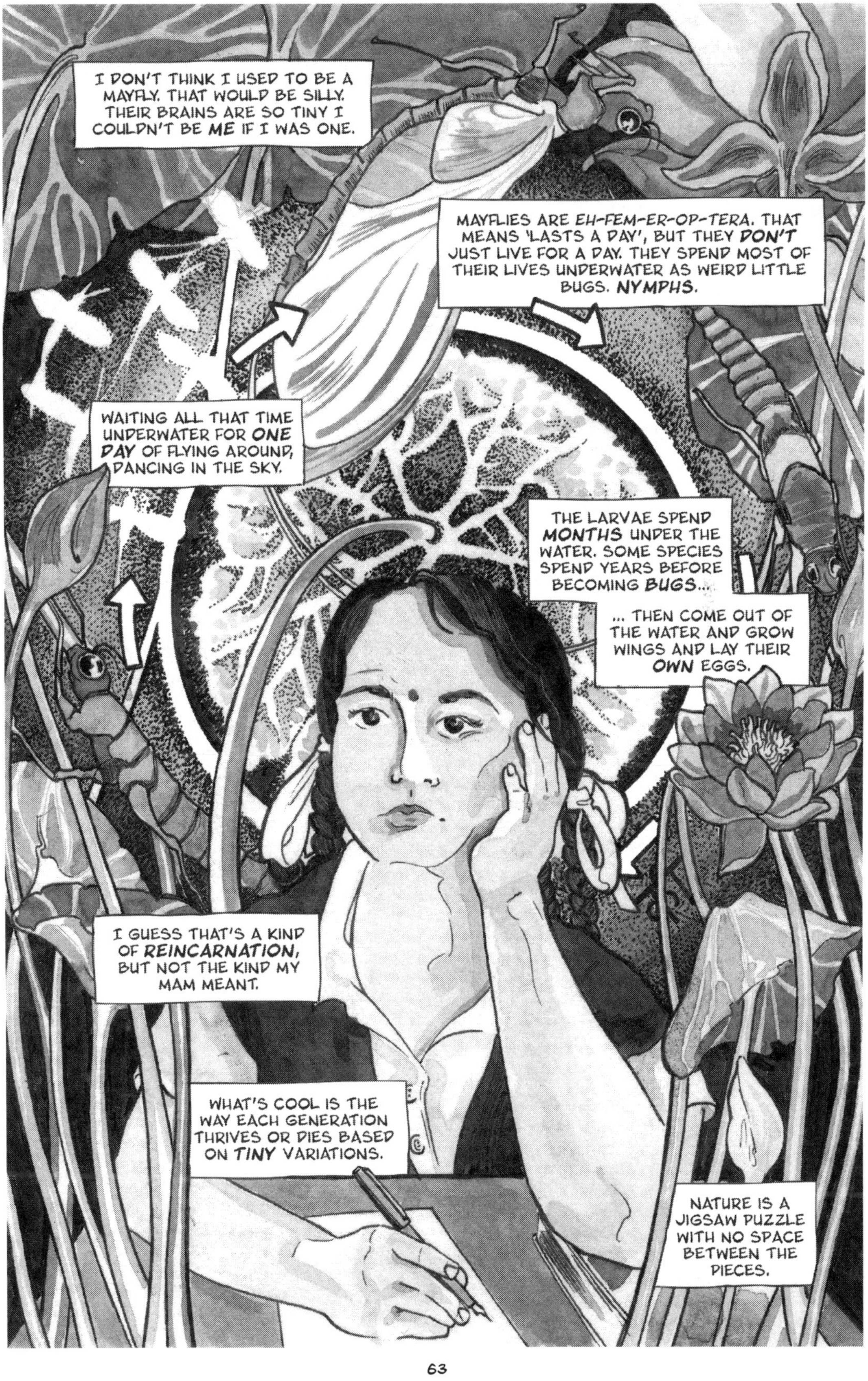
I DON'T THINK I USED TO BE A MAYFLY. THAT WOULD BE SILLY. THEIR BRAINS ARE SO TINY I COULDN'T BE ME IF I WAS ONE.
MAYFLIES ARE EH-FEM-ER-OP-TERA. THAT MEANS 'LASTS A DAY', BUT THEY DON'T JUST LIVE FOR A DAY. THEY SPEND MOST OF THEIR LIVES UNDERWATER AS WEIRD LITTLE BUGS. NYMPHS.
WAITING ALL THAT TIME UNDERWATER FOR ONE DAY OF FLYING AROUND, DANCING IN THE SKY.
THE LARVAE SPEND MONTHS UNDER THE WATER. SOME SPECIES SPEND YEARS BEFORE BECOMING BUGS...
... THEN COME OUT OF THE WATER AND GROW WINGS AND LAY THEIR OWN EGGS.
I GUESS THAT'S A KIND OF REINCARNATION, BUT NOT THE KIND MY MAM MEANT.
WHAT'S COOL IS THE WAY EACH GENERATION THRIVES OR DIES BASED ON TINY VARIATIONS.
NATURE IS A JIGSAW PUZZLE WITH NO SPACE BETWEEN THE PIECES.

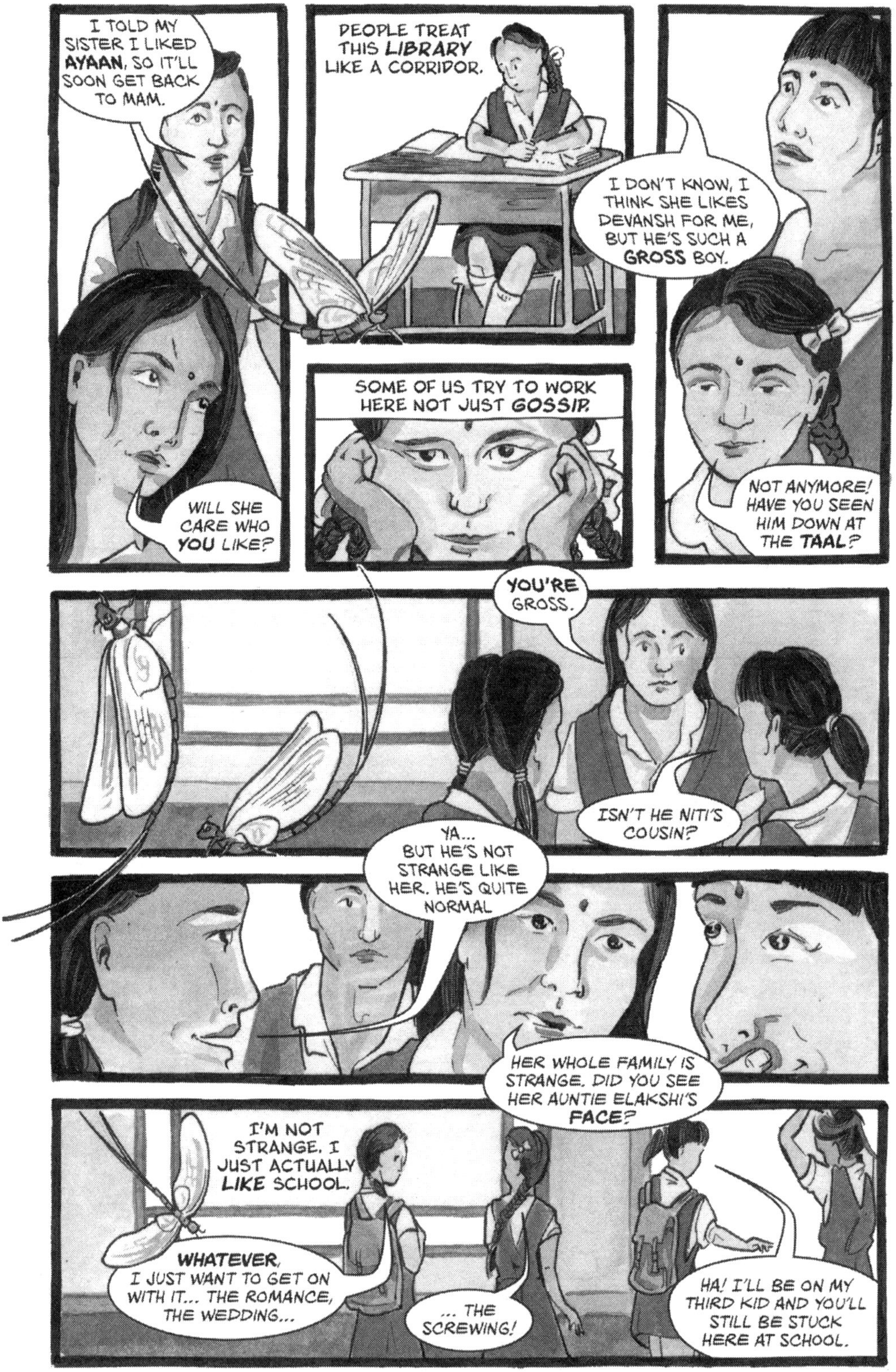
I TOLD MY SISTER I LIKED **AYAAN**, SO IT'LL SOON GET BACK TO MAM.
WILL SHE CARE WHO **YOU** LIKE?
PEOPLE TREAT THIS **LIBRARY** LIKE A CORRIDOR.
SOME OF US TRY TO WORK HERE NOT JUST **GOSSIP**.
I DON'T KNOW, I THINK SHE LIKES DEVANSH FOR ME, BUT HE'S SUCH A **GROSS** BOY.
NOT ANYMORE! HAVE YOU SEEN HIM DOWN AT THE **TAAL**?
YOU'RE GROSS.
ISN'T HE NITI'S COUSIN?
YA... BUT HE'S NOT STRANGE LIKE HER. HE'S QUITE NORMAL
HER WHOLE FAMILY IS STRANGE. DID YOU SEE HER AUNTIE ELAKSHI'S **FACE**?
I'M NOT STRANGE. I JUST ACTUALLY **LIKE** SCHOOL.
WHATEVER, I JUST WANT TO GET ON WITH IT... THE ROMANCE, THE WEDDING...
... THE SCREWING!
HA! I'LL BE ON MY THIRD KID AND YOU'LL STILL BE STUCK HERE AT SCHOOL.

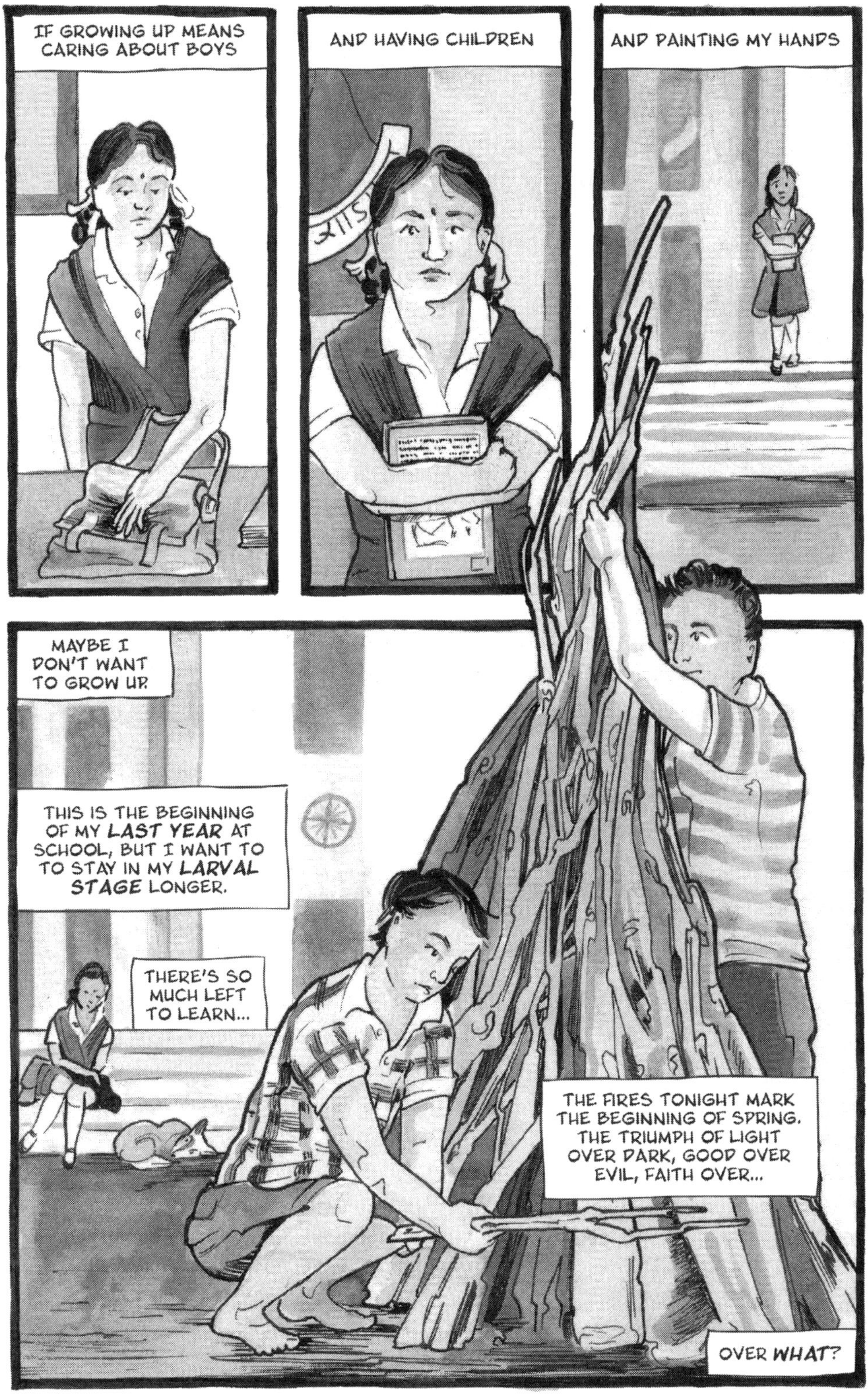
IF GROWING UP MEANS CARING ABOUT BOYS
AND HAVING CHILDREN
AND PAINTING MY HANDS
MAYBE I DON'T WANT TO GROW UP.
THIS IS THE BEGINNING OF MY **LAST YEAR** AT SCHOOL, BUT I WANT TO TO STAY IN MY **LARVAL STAGE** LONGER.
THERE'S SO MUCH LEFT TO LEARN...
THE FIRES TONIGHT MARK THE BEGINNING OF SPRING. THE TRIUMPH OF LIGHT OVER DARK, GOOD OVER EVIL, FAITH OVER...
OVER **WHAT**?

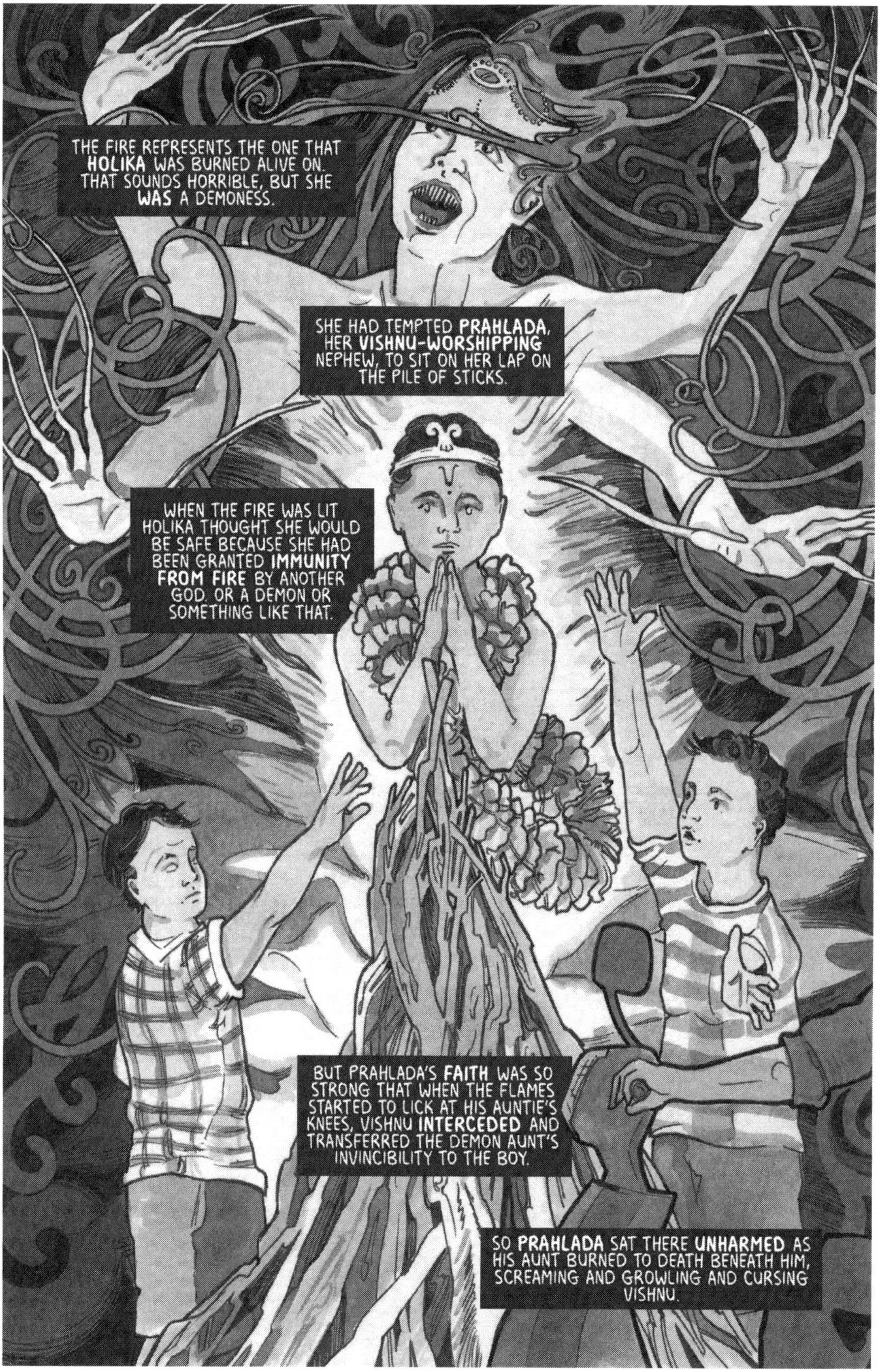
THE FIRE REPRESENTS THE ONE THAT HOLIKA WAS BURNED ALIVE ON. THAT SOUNDS HORRIBLE, BUT SHE WAS A DEMONESS.
SHE HAD TEMPTED PRAHLADA, HER VISHNU-WORSHIPPING NEPHEW, TO SIT ON HER LAP ON THE PILE OF STICKS.
WHEN THE FIRE WAS LIT HOLIKA THOUGHT SHE WOULD BE SAFE BECAUSE SHE HAD BEEN GRANTED IMMUNITY FROM FIRE BY ANOTHER GOD. OR A DEMON OR SOMETHING LIKE THAT.
BUT PRAHLADA'S FAITH WAS SO STRONG THAT WHEN THE FLAMES STARTED TO LICK AT HIS AUNTIE'S KNEES, VISHNU INTERCEDED AND TRANSFERRED THE DEMON AUNT'S INVINCIBILITY TO THE BOY.
SO PRAHLADA SAT THERE UNHARMED AS HIS AUNT BURNED TO DEATH BENEATH HIM, SCREAMING AND GROWLING AND CURSING VISHNU.

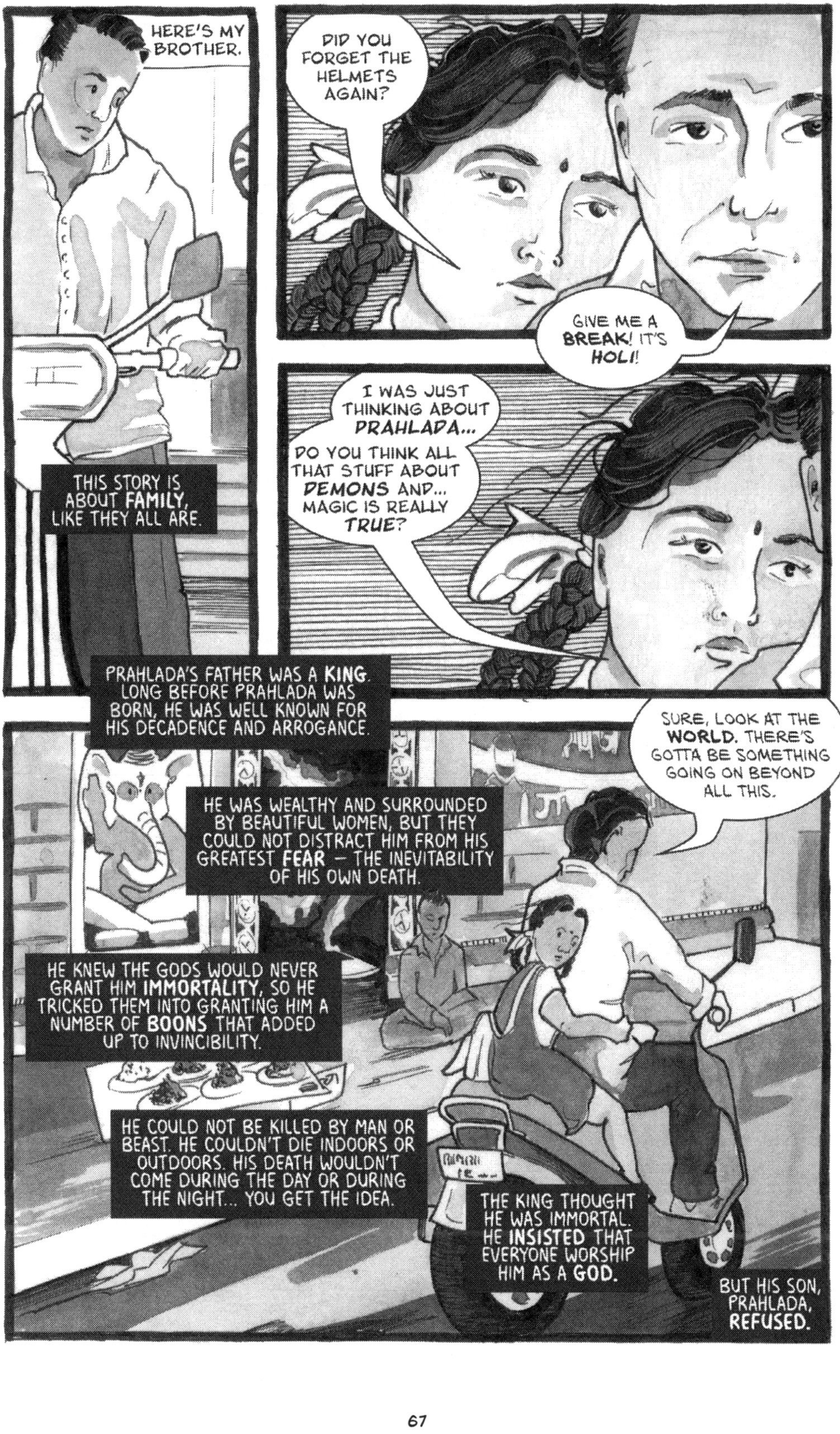
HERE'S MY BROTHER.
THIS STORY IS ABOUT FAMILY, LIKE THEY ALL ARE.
DID YOU FORGET THE HELMETS AGAIN?
GIVE ME A BREAK! IT'S HOLI!
I WAS JUST THINKING ABOUT PRAHLADA...
DO YOU THINK ALL THAT STUFF ABOUT DEMONS AND... MAGIC IS REALLY TRUE?
PRAHLADA'S FATHER WAS A KING. LONG BEFORE PRAHLADA WAS BORN, HE WAS WELL KNOWN FOR HIS DECADENCE AND ARROGANCE.
SURE, LOOK AT THE WORLD. THERE'S GOTTA BE SOMETHING GOING ON BEYOND ALL THIS.
HE WAS WEALTHY AND SURROUNDED BY BEAUTIFUL WOMEN, BUT THEY COULD NOT DISTRACT HIM FROM HIS GREATEST FEAR — THE INEVITABILITY OF HIS OWN DEATH.
HE KNEW THE GODS WOULD NEVER GRANT HIM IMMORTALITY, SO HE TRICKED THEM INTO GRANTING HIM A NUMBER OF BOONS THAT ADDED UP TO INVINCIBILITY.
HE COULD NOT BE KILLED BY MAN OR BEAST. HE COULDN'T DIE INDOORS OR OUTDOORS. HIS DEATH WOULDN'T COME DURING THE DAY OR DURING THE NIGHT... YOU GET THE IDEA.
THE KING THOUGHT HE WAS IMMORTAL. HE INSISTED THAT EVERYONE WORSHIP HIM AS A GOD.
BUT HIS SON, PRAHLADA, REFUSED.

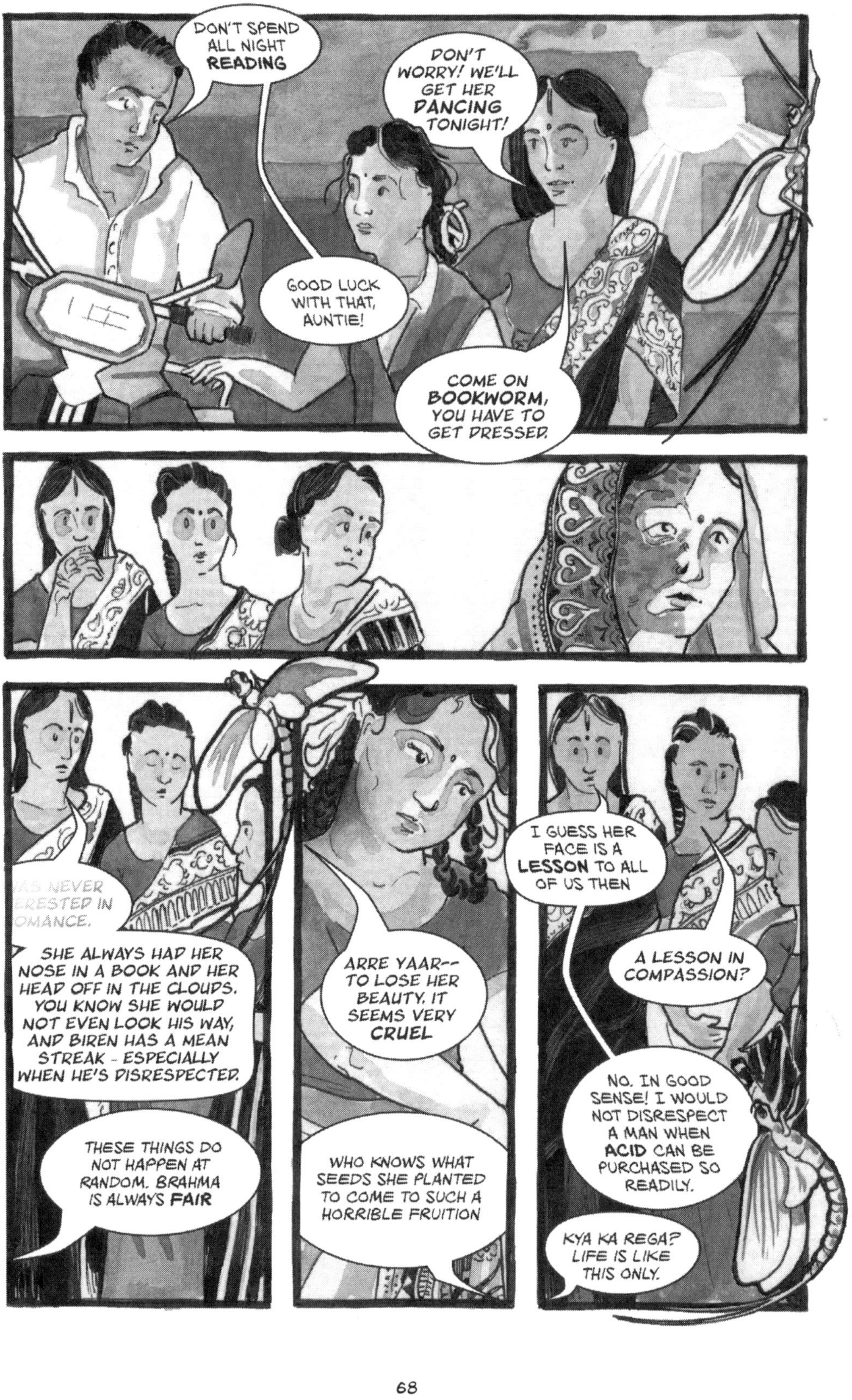
DON'T SPEND ALL NIGHT READING
DON'T WORRY! WE'LL GET HER DANCING TONIGHT!
GOOD LUCK WITH THAT, AUNTIE!
COME ON BOOKWORM, YOU HAVE TO GET DRESSED.
AS NEVER ERESTED IN OMANCE.
SHE ALWAYS HAD HER NOSE IN A BOOK AND HER HEAD OFF IN THE CLOUDS. YOU KNOW SHE WOULD NOT EVEN LOOK HIS WAY, AND BIREN HAS A MEAN STREAK - ESPECIALLY WHEN HE'S DISRESPECTED.
THESE THINGS DO NOT HAPPEN AT RANDOM. BRAHMA IS ALWAYS FAIR
ARRE YAAR-- TO LOSE HER BEAUTY. IT SEEMS VERY CRUEL
WHO KNOWS WHAT SEEDS SHE PLANTED TO COME TO SUCH A HORRIBLE FRUITION
I GUESS HER FACE IS A LESSON TO ALL OF US THEN
A LESSON IN COMPASSION?
NO. IN GOOD SENSE! I WOULD NOT DISRESPECT A MAN WHEN ACID CAN BE PURCHASED SO READILY.
KYA KA REGA? LIFE IS LIKE THIS ONLY.

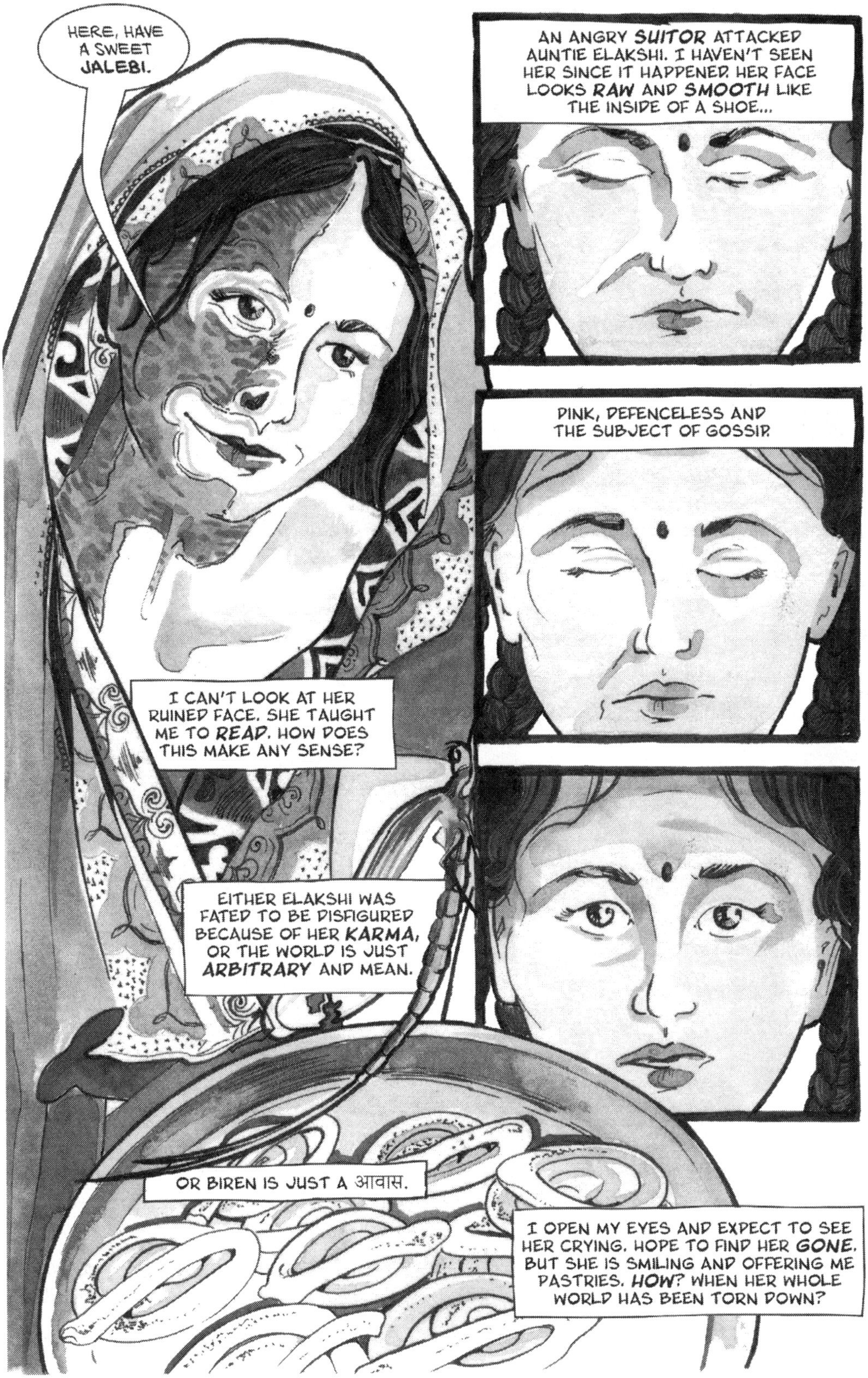
HERE, HAVE A SWEET JALEBI.
AN ANGRY SUITOR ATTACKED AUNTIE ELAKSHI. I HAVEN'T SEEN HER SINCE IT HAPPENED. HER FACE LOOKS RAW AND SMOOTH LIKE THE INSIDE OF A SHOE...
PINK, DEFENCELESS AND THE SUBJECT OF GOSSIP.
I CAN'T LOOK AT HER RUINED FACE. SHE TAUGHT ME TO READ. HOW DOES THIS MAKE ANY SENSE?
EITHER ELAKSHI WAS FATED TO BE DISFIGURED BECAUSE OF HER KARMA, OR THE WORLD IS JUST ARBITRARY AND MEAN.
OR BIREN IS JUST A आवास.
I OPEN MY EYES AND EXPECT TO SEE HER CRYING. HOPE TO FIND HER GONE. BUT SHE IS SMILING AND OFFERING ME PASTRIES. HOW? WHEN HER WHOLE WORLD HAS BEEN TORN DOWN?

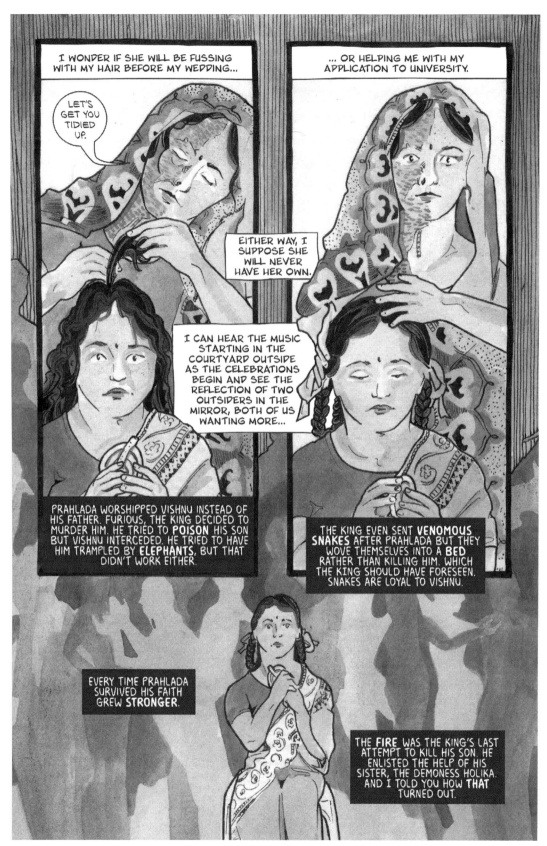

I WONDER IF SHE WILL BE FUSSING WITH MY HAIR BEFORE MY WEDDING...

... OR HELPING ME WITH MY APPLICATION TO UNIVERSITY.

LET'S GET YOU TIDIED UP.

EITHER WAY, I SUPPOSE SHE WILL NEVER HAVE HER OWN.

I CAN HEAR THE MUSIC STARTING IN THE COURTYARD OUTSIDE AS THE CELEBRATIONS BEGIN AND SEE THE REFLECTION OF TWO OUTSIDERS IN THE MIRROR, BOTH OF US WANTING MORE...

PRAHLADA WORSHIPPED VISHNU INSTEAD OF HIS FATHER. FURIOUS, THE KING DECIDED TO MURDER HIM. HE TRIED TO **POISON** HIS SON BUT VISHNU INTERCEDED. HE TRIED TO HAVE HIM TRAMPLED BY **ELEPHANTS**, BUT THAT DIDN'T WORK EITHER.

THE KING EVEN SENT **VENOMOUS SNAKES** AFTER PRAHLADA BUT THEY WOVE THEMSELVES INTO A **BED** RATHER THAN KILLING HIM, WHICH THE KING SHOULD HAVE FORESEEN. SNAKES ARE LOYAL TO VISHNU.

EVERY TIME PRAHLADA SURVIVED HIS FAITH GREW **STRONGER**.

THE **FIRE** WAS THE KING'S LAST ATTEMPT TO KILL HIS SON. HE ENLISTED THE HELP OF HIS SISTER, THE DEMONESS HOLIKA. AND I TOLD YOU HOW **THAT** TURNED OUT.

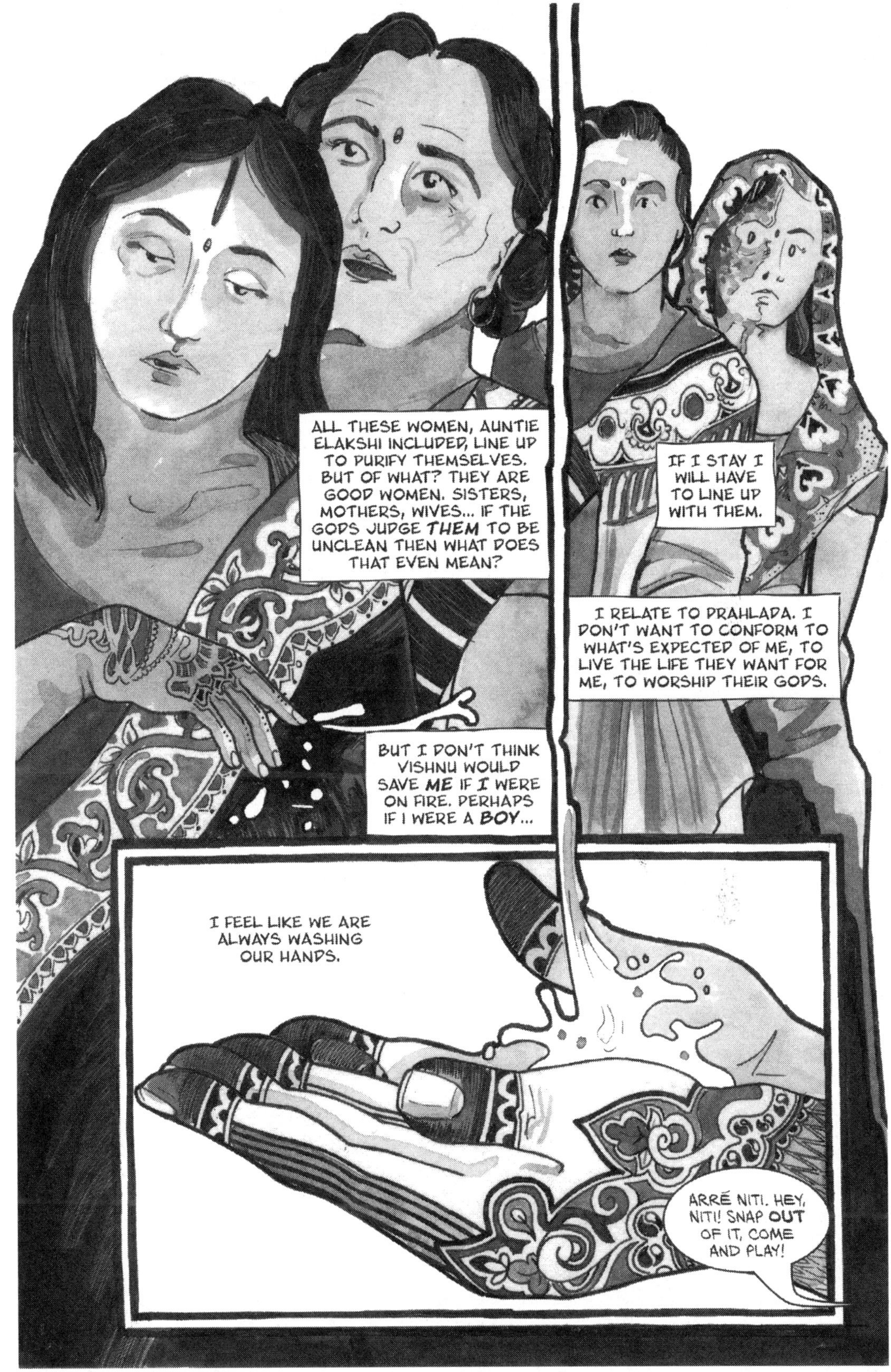
ALL THESE WOMEN, AUNTIE ELAKSHI INCLUDED, LINE UP TO PURIFY THEMSELVES. BUT OF WHAT? THEY ARE GOOD WOMEN. SISTERS, MOTHERS, WIVES... IF THE GODS JUDGE *THEM* TO BE UNCLEAN THEN WHAT DOES THAT EVEN MEAN?
IF I STAY I WILL HAVE TO LINE UP WITH THEM.
I RELATE TO PRAHLADA. I DON'T WANT TO CONFORM TO WHAT'S EXPECTED OF ME, TO LIVE THE LIFE THEY WANT FOR ME, TO WORSHIP THEIR GODS.
BUT I DON'T THINK VISHNU WOULD SAVE **ME** IF *I* WERE ON FIRE. PERHAPS IF I WERE A **BOY**...
I FEEL LIKE WE ARE ALWAYS WASHING OUR HANDS.
ARRÉ NITI. HEY, NITI! SNAP **OUT** OF IT, COME AND PLAY!

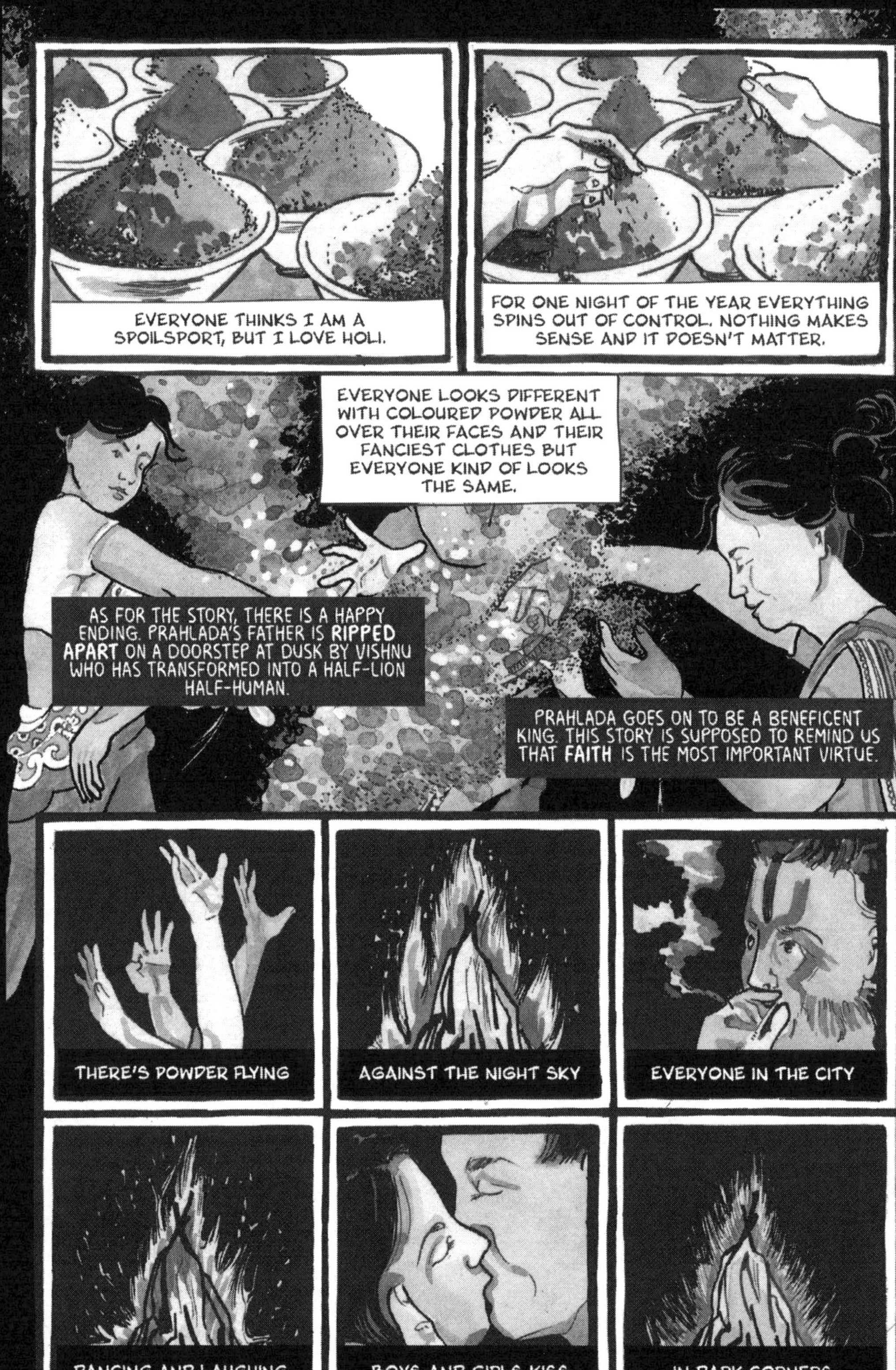
EVERYONE THINKS I AM A SPOILSPORT, BUT I LOVE HOLI.
FOR ONE NIGHT OF THE YEAR EVERYTHING SPINS OUT OF CONTROL. NOTHING MAKES SENSE AND IT DOESN'T MATTER.
EVERYONE LOOKS DIFFERENT WITH COLOURED POWDER ALL OVER THEIR FACES AND THEIR FANCIEST CLOTHES BUT EVERYONE KIND OF LOOKS THE SAME.
AS FOR THE STORY, THERE IS A HAPPY ENDING. PRAHLADA'S FATHER IS RIPPED APART ON A DOORSTEP AT DUSK BY VISHNU WHO HAS TRANSFORMED INTO A HALF-LION HALF-HUMAN.
PRAHLADA GOES ON TO BE A BENEFICENT KING. THIS STORY IS SUPPOSED TO REMIND US THAT FAITH IS THE MOST IMPORTANT VIRTUE.
THERE'S POWDER FLYING
AGAINST THE NIGHT SKY
EVERYONE IN THE CITY
DANCING AND LAUGHING
BOYS AND GIRLS KISS
IN DARK CORNERS

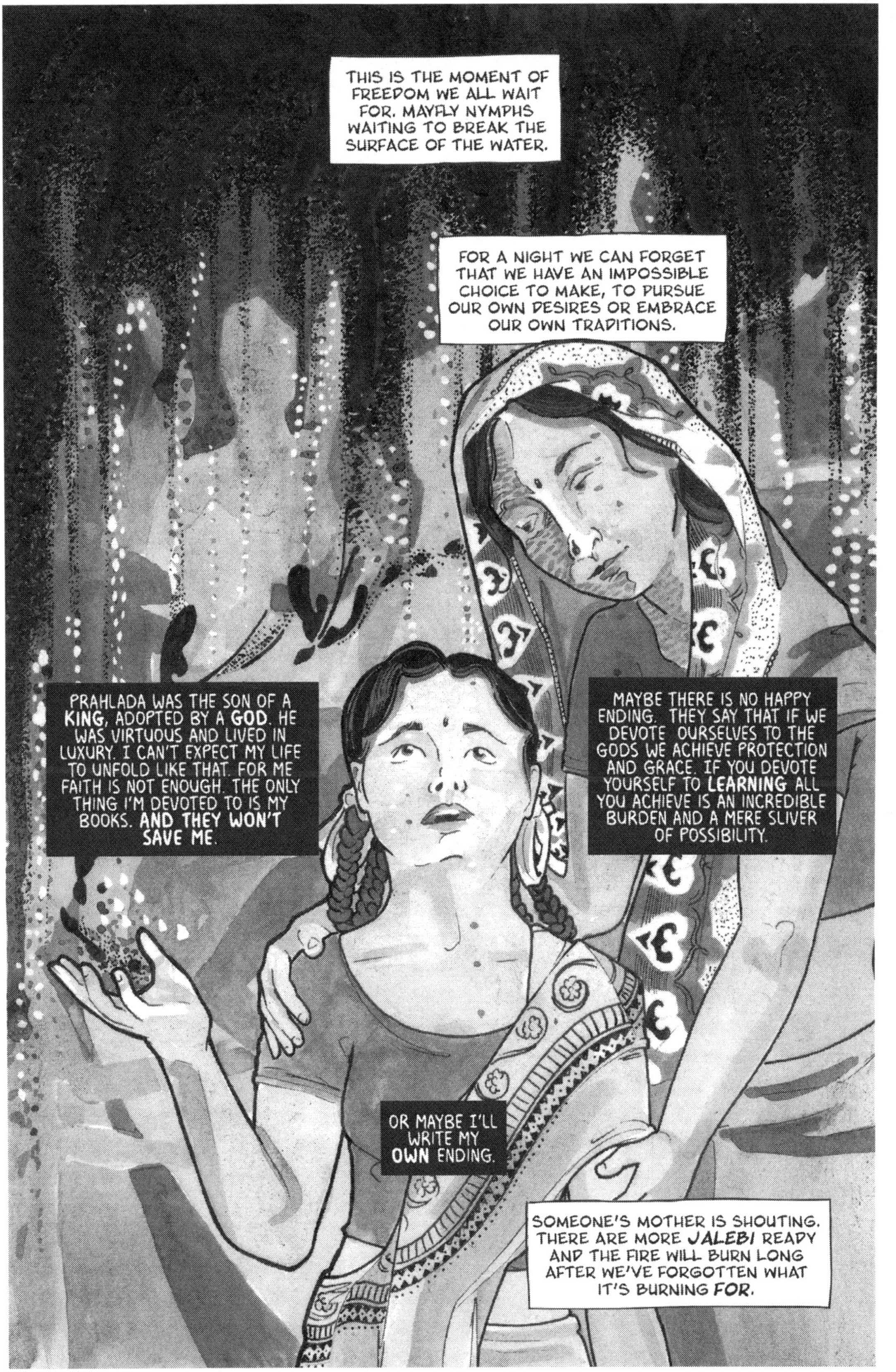
THIS IS THE MOMENT OF FREEDOM WE ALL WAIT FOR. MAYFLY NYMPHS WAITING TO BREAK THE SURFACE OF THE WATER.
FOR A NIGHT WE CAN FORGET THAT WE HAVE AN IMPOSSIBLE CHOICE TO MAKE, TO PURSUE OUR OWN DESIRES OR EMBRACE OUR OWN TRADITIONS.
PRAHLADA WAS THE SON OF A **KING**, ADOPTED BY A **GOD**. HE WAS VIRTUOUS AND LIVED IN LUXURY. I CAN'T EXPECT MY LIFE TO UNFOLD LIKE THAT. FOR ME FAITH IS NOT ENOUGH. THE ONLY THING I'M DEVOTED TO IS MY BOOKS. **AND THEY WON'T SAVE ME**.
MAYBE THERE IS NO HAPPY ENDING. THEY SAY THAT IF WE DEVOTE OURSELVES TO THE GODS WE ACHIEVE PROTECTION AND GRACE. IF YOU DEVOTE YOURSELF TO **LEARNING** ALL YOU ACHIEVE IS AN INCREDIBLE BURDEN AND A MERE SLIVER OF POSSIBILITY.
OR MAYBE I'LL WRITE MY **OWN** ENDING.
SOMEONE'S MOTHER IS SHOUTING. THERE ARE MORE ***JALEBI*** READY AND THE FIRE WILL BURN LONG AFTER WE'VE FORGOTTEN WHAT IT'S BURNING ***FOR***.

Once, in Nepal, on a bus to a Kali temple outside Kathmandu, I sat beside devotees clutching uncastrated male goats, chickens and marigold wreaths to offer in tribute to the goddess. Hindu legends often tell the story of a mortal who proves their extreme devotion to a deity and is rewarded by the gods' intervention in their life: smiting enemies, elevating them to positions of power or granting them supernatural powers. No one on the bus to Dakshinkali thought they would be granted super powers after their visit to the temple - most probably they hoped for not much more than a fun day out with their family - but the tradition of making offerings to the gods remains a powerful symbolic action.

Many Hindus believe honouring the gods confers protection and assistance, and they're right. By joining with your community for festivals, sacrifices and picnics on the lawns surrounding temples, you establish human connections that will support and nurture you throughout your life. The importance of tight-knit communities is even more obvious when travelling through rural areas that lack resources and technology. When food is short and the weather harsh, we humans rely on each other. Many anthropologists argue that it is our social nature that makes us such a successful species.

Because social ties are so important to us, we spend a lot of time cementing them with generous and gregarious behaviour, but we are also heavily invested in policing the boundaries of our social circles. People who do not take part in their culture's festivals, who refuse to conform to their social norms, who express disbelief in their Gods, are dangerous. They represent a threat to the cohesion of the community and it is our instinct to compel them to conform or expel them.

The charity Acid Survivors Foundation India works to support the victims of acid attacks across India – one of the countries where acid attacks are most common. An acid attack is a particularly horrific assault usually perpetrated on women. The assailant throws corrosive acid at the woman's face which causes extreme pain and disfigurement. Unlike many other types of violent assault, the victim cannot hide the fact that she has been attacked, and will often struggle to reintegrate into her community once her wounds have healed.

ASFI suggest that the disfigurement is not a side effect of these attacks but part of the purpose. The attacks are often motivated by the frustrated romantic intentions of the assailant. He does not just want to cause suffering to his victim, he wants to 'teach her a lesson' and by extension make an example of her to other women in the community who would consider defying him. The burnt face of an acid attack victim serves the same purpose as the scarlet letter sewn to a woman's chest: a manifestation of her stigma and a warning to other women who may be tempted to defy a patriarchal culture.

When charities seek to improve educational opportunities for girls, they are encouraging young women to defy their culture and the young women in rural villages in India are well aware of the potential costs of defying their social norms. It is not enough to provide the buildings and resources needed to educate, they seek to challenge and reform the social context that Indian girls grow up in, to remove the expectations of early marriage and to demonstrate the advantages of a well-educated female population.

Until there is a significant cultural shift these girls must make a stark choice: to pursue their education and risk ostracisation, or to conform to cultural expectations and never explore the limits of their intellectual capacities. No matter how devoted a young woman may be to her education the pantheon of men who wrote her textbooks are not going to step out from between the pages and rescue her.

More information, discussion and links at *doubtcomic.com/mayfly*

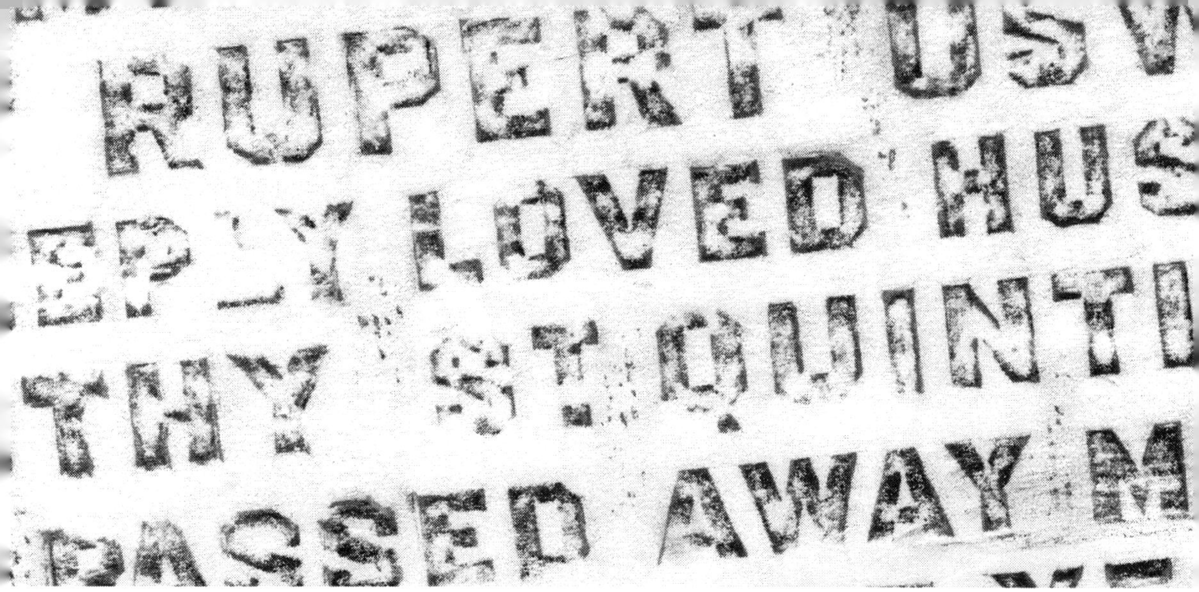
RUPERT US
LOVED HUS
QUINT
PASSED AWAY

AS ABOVE, SO BELOW

The New Forest, Southern England

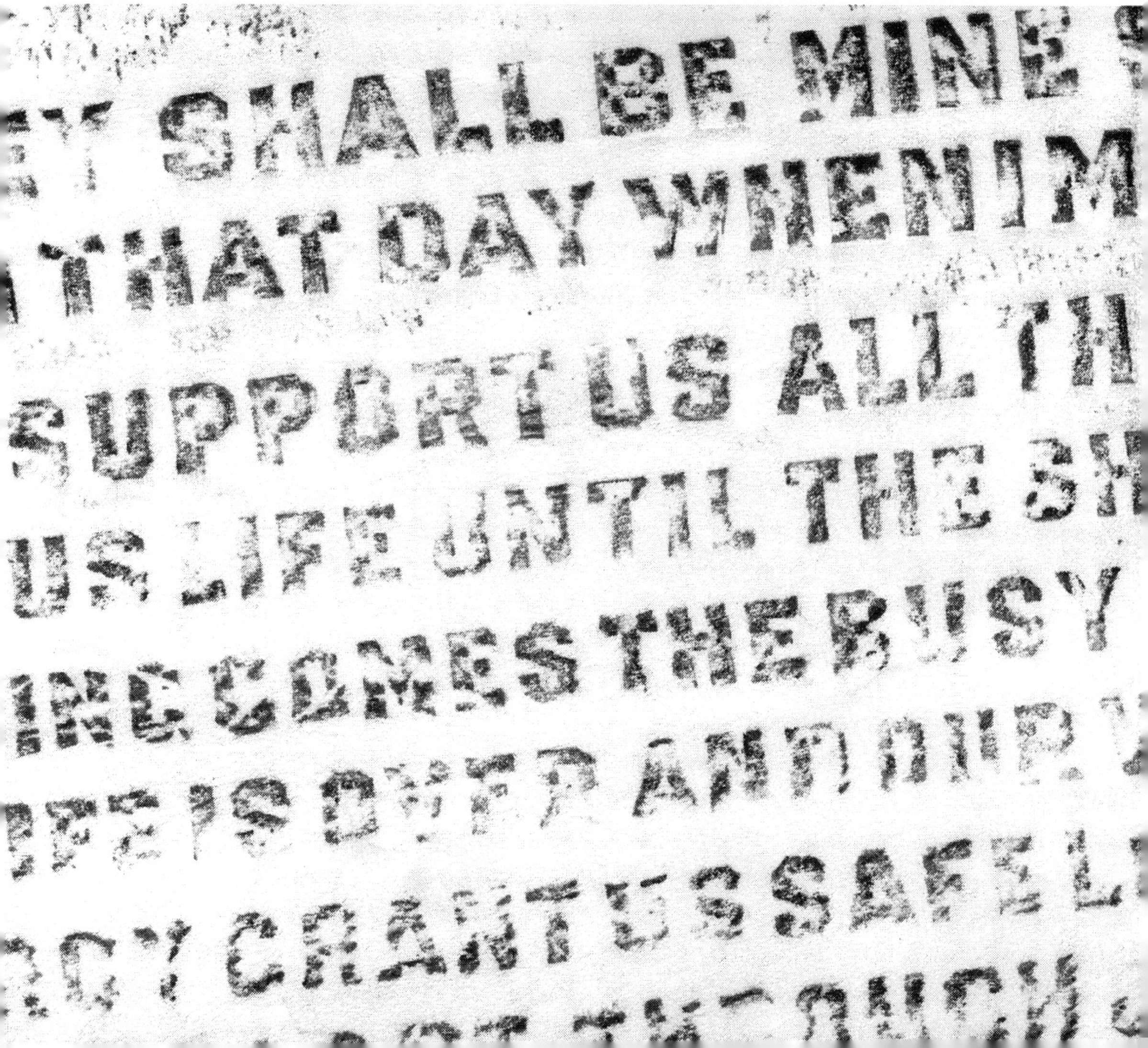
SHALL BE MINE
THAT DAY WHEN I M
SUPPORT US ALL TH
LIFE UNTIL THE SH
COMES THE BUSY
AND OUR
GRANT US SAFE L

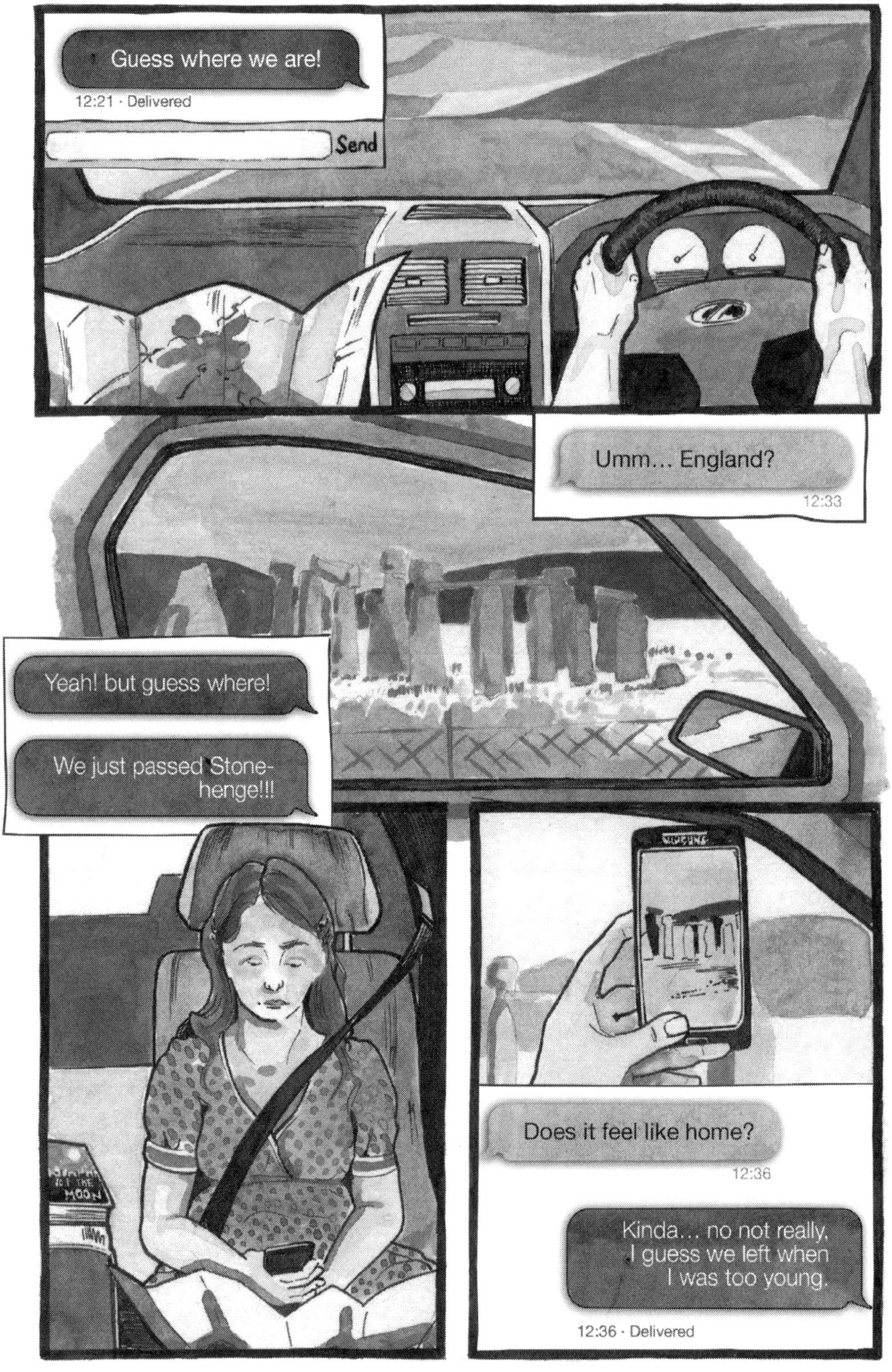
Guess where we are!
12:21 · Delivered
Send
Umm… England?
12:33
Yeah! but guess where!
We just passed Stone-henge!!!
Does it feel like home?
12:36
Kinda… no not really, I guess we left when I was too young.
12:36 · Delivered

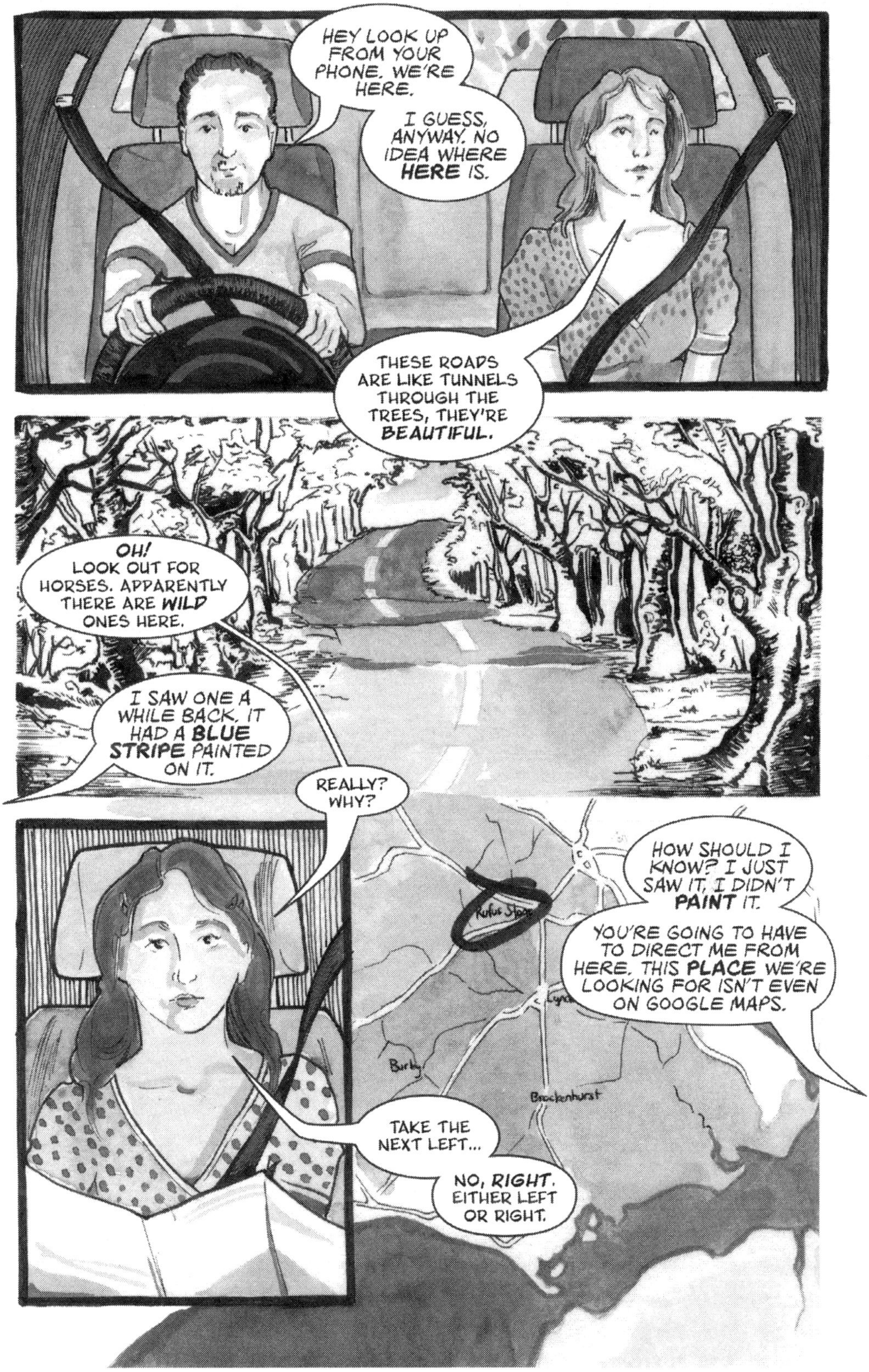
HEY LOOK UP FROM YOUR PHONE. WE'RE HERE.
I GUESS, ANYWAY. NO IDEA WHERE HERE IS.
THESE ROADS ARE LIKE TUNNELS THROUGH THE TREES, THEY'RE BEAUTIFUL.
OH! LOOK OUT FOR HORSES. APPARENTLY THERE ARE WILD ONES HERE.
I SAW ONE A WHILE BACK. IT HAD A BLUE STRIPE PAINTED ON IT.
REALLY? WHY?
HOW SHOULD I KNOW? I JUST SAW IT, I DIDN'T PAINT IT.
YOU'RE GOING TO HAVE TO DIRECT ME FROM HERE. THIS PLACE WE'RE LOOKING FOR ISN'T EVEN ON GOOGLE MAPS.
Brockenhurst
TAKE THE NEXT LEFT...
NO, RIGHT. EITHER LEFT OR RIGHT.

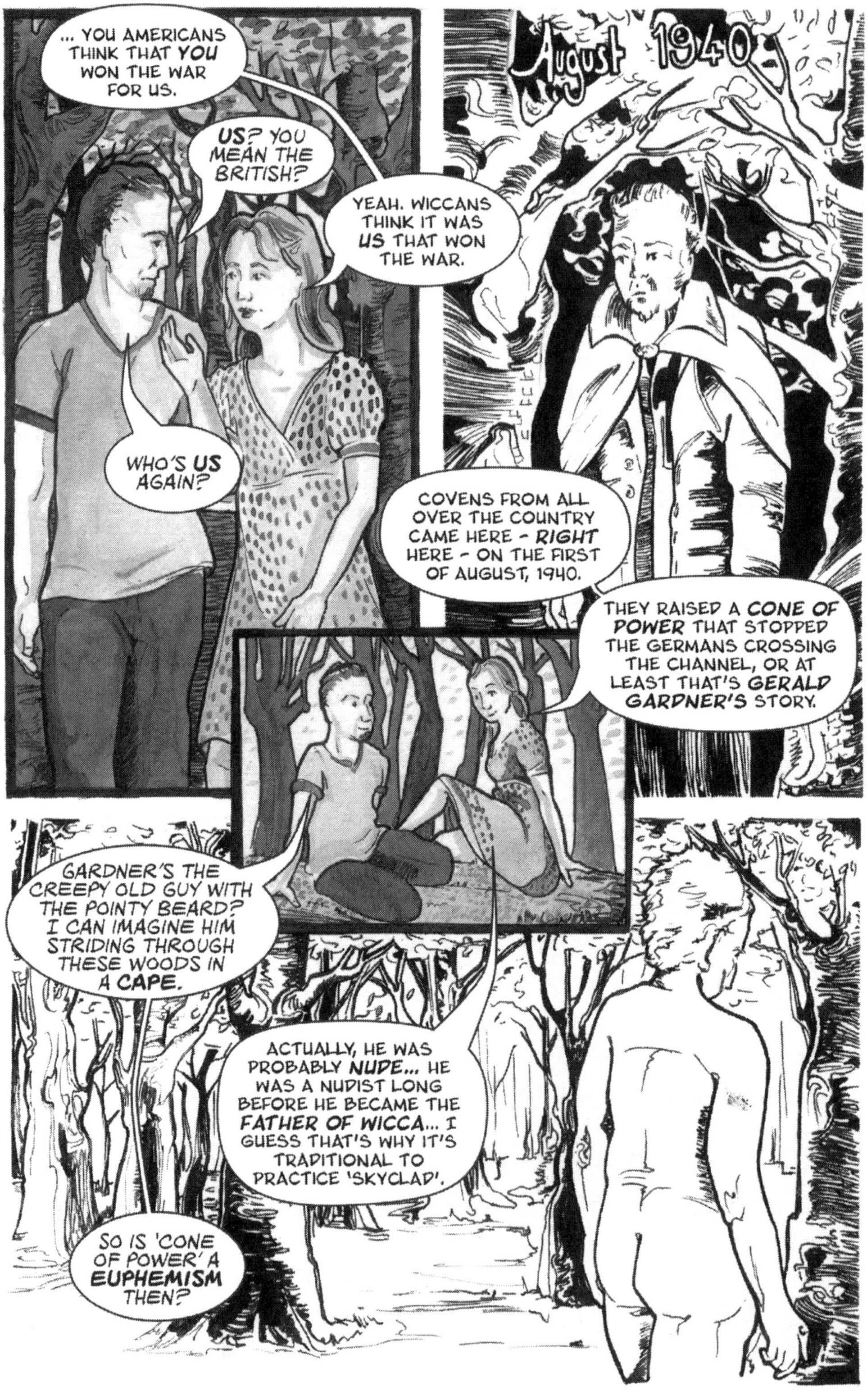

August 1940
... YOU AMERICANS THINK THAT YOU WON THE WAR FOR US.
US? YOU MEAN THE BRITISH?
YEAH. WICCANS THINK IT WAS US THAT WON THE WAR.
WHO'S US AGAIN?
COVENS FROM ALL OVER THE COUNTRY CAME HERE - RIGHT HERE - ON THE FIRST OF AUGUST, 1940.
THEY RAISED A CONE OF POWER THAT STOPPED THE GERMANS CROSSING THE CHANNEL, OR AT LEAST THAT'S GERALD GARDNER'S STORY.
GARDNER'S THE CREEPY OLD GUY WITH THE POINTY BEARD? I CAN IMAGINE HIM STRIDING THROUGH THESE WOODS IN A CAPE.
ACTUALLY, HE WAS PROBABLY NUDE... HE WAS A NUDIST LONG BEFORE HE BECAME THE FATHER OF WICCA... I GUESS THAT'S WHY IT'S TRADITIONAL TO PRACTICE 'SKYCLAD'.
SO IS 'CONE OF POWER' A EUPHEMISM THEN?

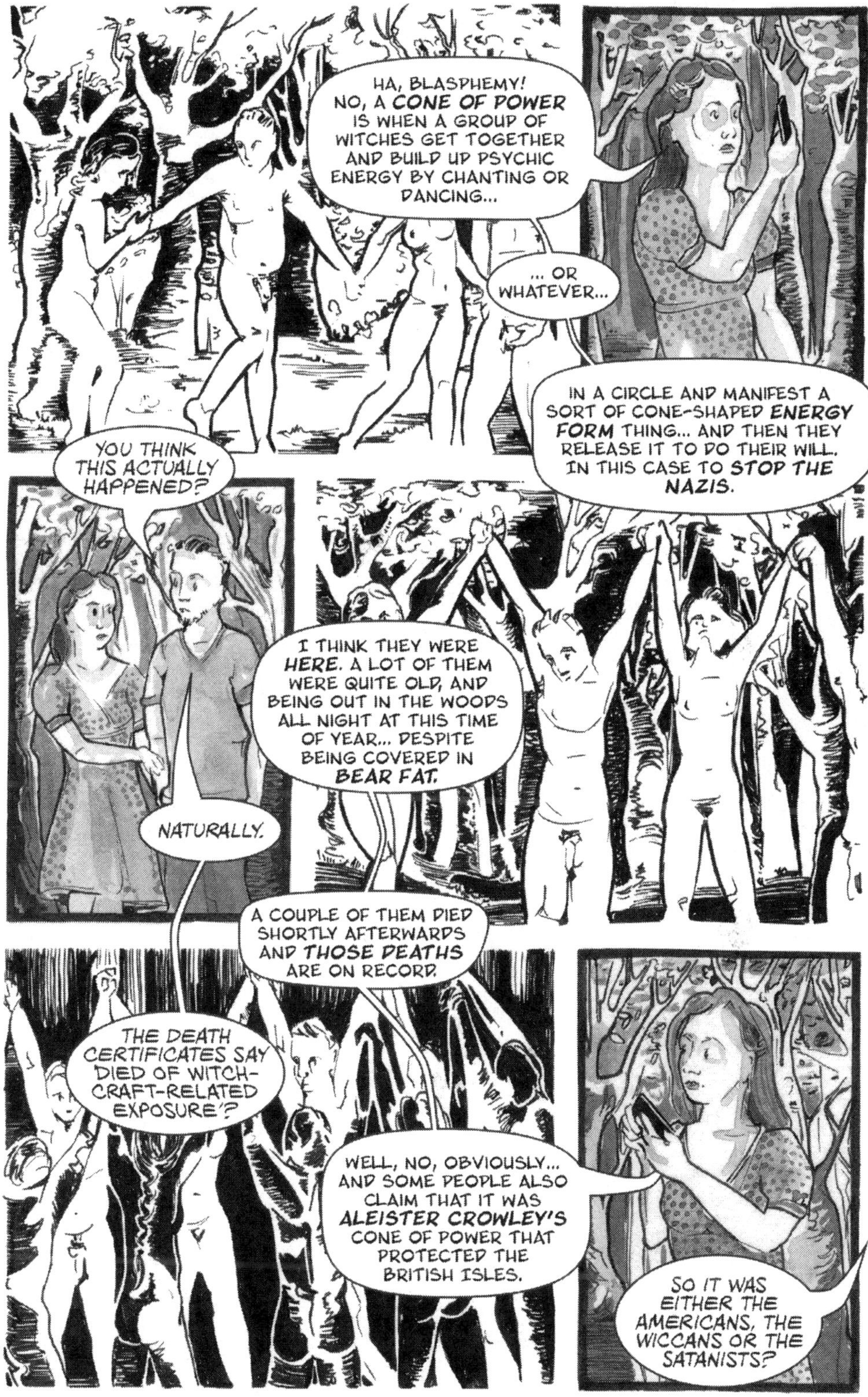
HA, BLASPHEMY! NO, A CONE OF POWER IS WHEN A GROUP OF WITCHES GET TOGETHER AND BUILD UP PSYCHIC ENERGY BY CHANTING OR DANCING...
... OR WHATEVER...
IN A CIRCLE AND MANIFEST A SORT OF CONE-SHAPED ENERGY FORM THING... AND THEN THEY RELEASE IT TO DO THEIR WILL. IN THIS CASE TO STOP THE NAZIS.
YOU THINK THIS ACTUALLY HAPPENED?
I THINK THEY WERE HERE. A LOT OF THEM WERE QUITE OLD, AND BEING OUT IN THE WOODS ALL NIGHT AT THIS TIME OF YEAR... DESPITE BEING COVERED IN BEAR FAT.
NATURALLY.
A COUPLE OF THEM DIED SHORTLY AFTERWARDS AND THOSE DEATHS ARE ON RECORD.
THE DEATH CERTIFICATES SAY 'DIED OF WITCH-CRAFT-RELATED EXPOSURE'?
WELL, NO, OBVIOUSLY... AND SOME PEOPLE ALSO CLAIM THAT IT WAS ALEISTER CROWLEY'S CONE OF POWER THAT PROTECTED THE BRITISH ISLES.
SO IT WAS EITHER THE AMERICANS, THE WICCANS OR THE SATANISTS?

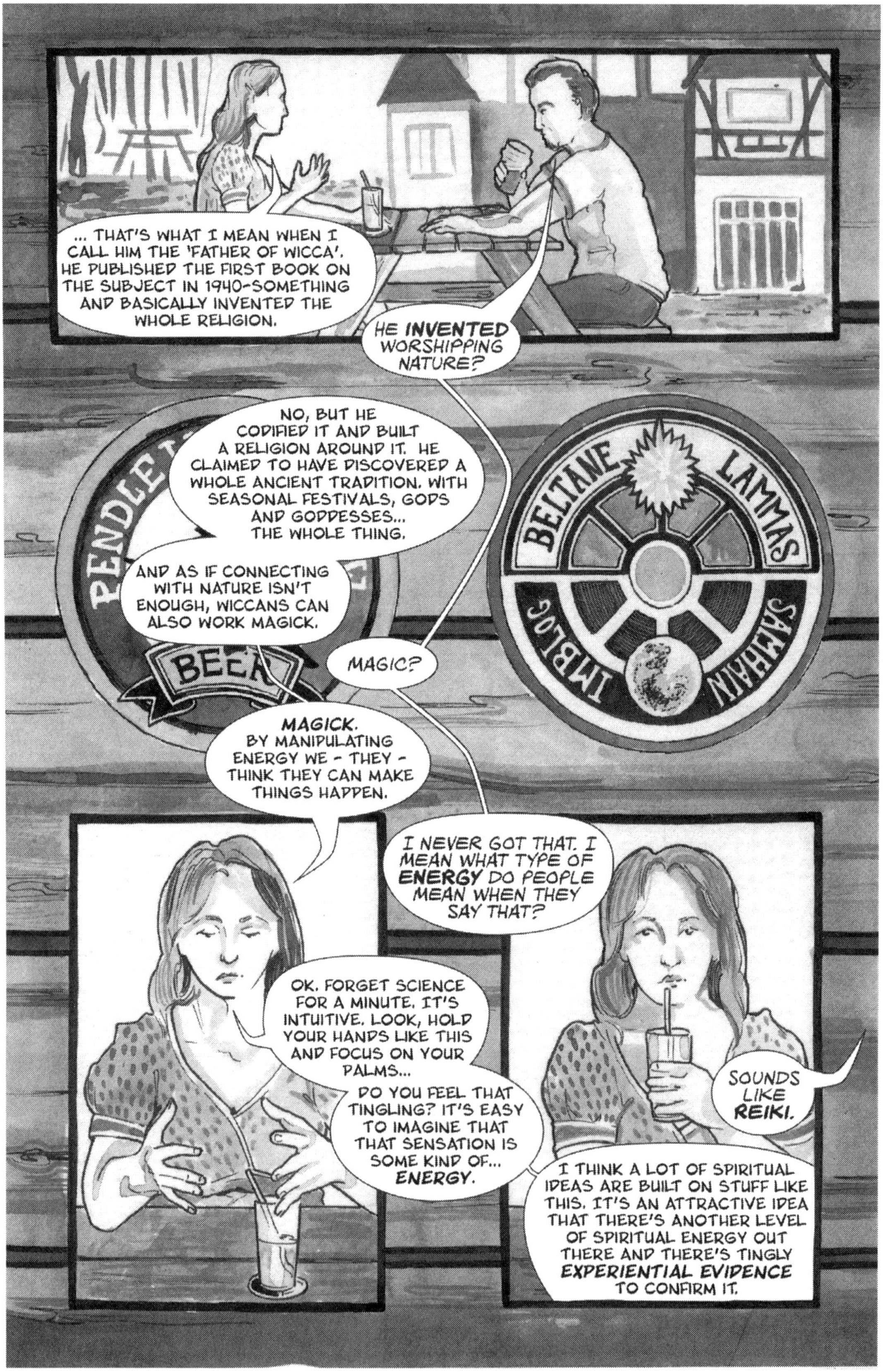

... THAT'S WHAT I MEAN WHEN I CALL HIM THE 'FATHER OF WICCA'. HE PUBLISHED THE FIRST BOOK ON THE SUBJECT IN 1940-SOMETHING AND BASICALLY INVENTED THE WHOLE RELIGION.
HE **INVENTED** WORSHIPPING NATURE?
NO, BUT HE CODIFIED IT AND BUILT A RELIGION AROUND IT. HE CLAIMED TO HAVE DISCOVERED A WHOLE ANCIENT TRADITION. WITH SEASONAL FESTIVALS, GODS AND GODDESSES... THE WHOLE THING.
AND AS IF CONNECTING WITH NATURE ISN'T ENOUGH, WICCANS CAN ALSO WORK MAGICK.
PENDLE
BEER
BELTANE
LAMMAS
SAMHAIN
MAGIC?
MAGICK. BY MANIPULATING ENERGY WE - THEY - THINK THEY CAN MAKE THINGS HAPPEN.
I NEVER GOT THAT. I MEAN WHAT TYPE OF **ENERGY** DO PEOPLE MEAN WHEN THEY SAY THAT?
OK. FORGET SCIENCE FOR A MINUTE. IT'S INTUITIVE. LOOK, HOLD YOUR HANDS LIKE THIS AND FOCUS ON YOUR PALMS...
DO YOU FEEL THAT TINGLING? IT'S EASY TO IMAGINE THAT THAT SENSATION IS SOME KIND OF... **ENERGY**.
SOUNDS LIKE **REIKI**.
I THINK A LOT OF SPIRITUAL IDEAS ARE BUILT ON STUFF LIKE THIS. IT'S AN ATTRACTIVE IDEA THAT THERE'S ANOTHER LEVEL OF SPIRITUAL ENERGY OUT THERE AND THERE'S TINGLY **EXPERIENTIAL EVIDENCE** TO CONFIRM IT.

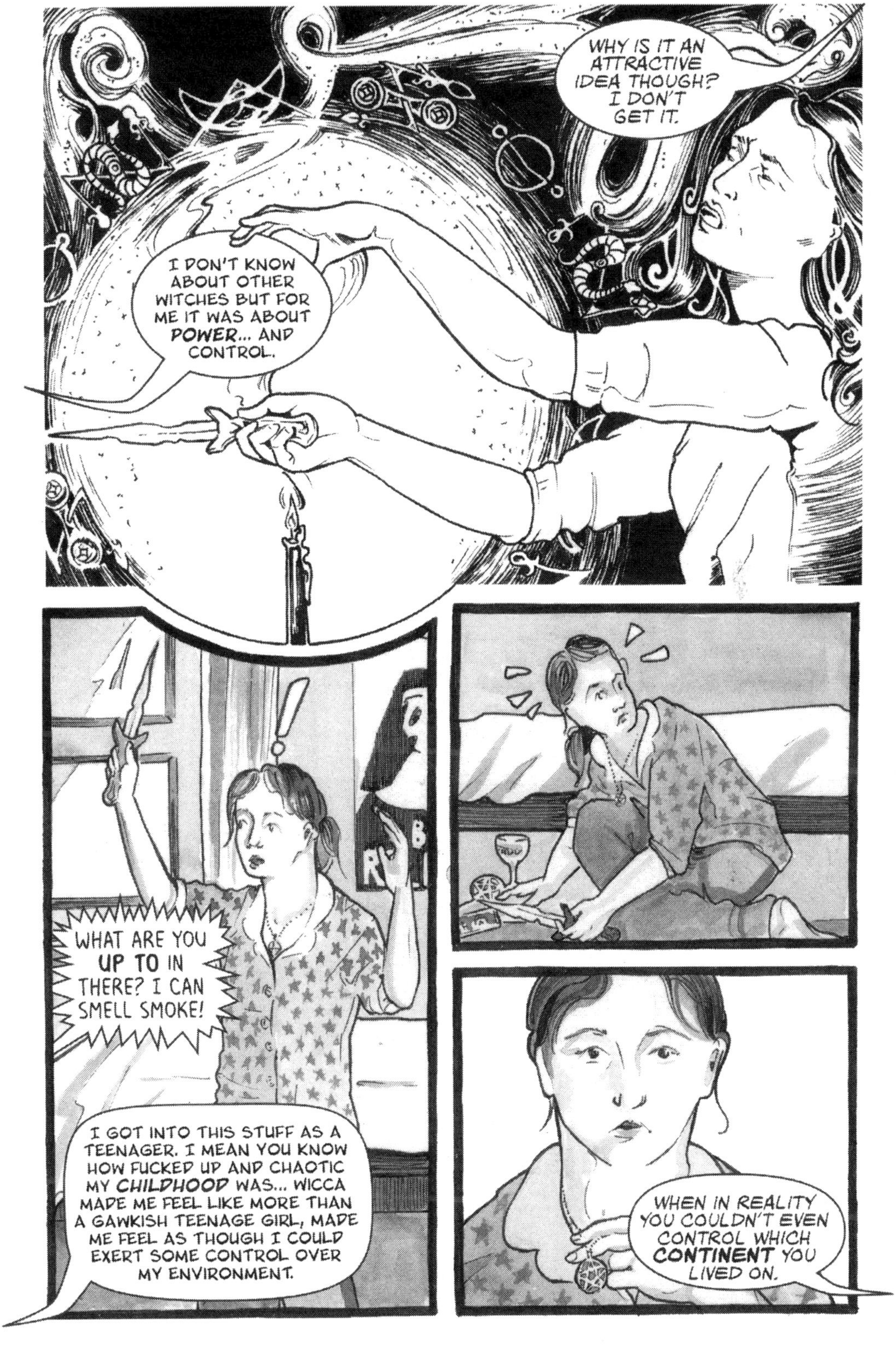
WHY IS IT AN ATTRACTIVE IDEA THOUGH? I DON'T GET IT.
I DON'T KNOW ABOUT OTHER WITCHES BUT FOR ME IT WAS ABOUT **POWER**... AND CONTROL.
WHAT ARE YOU **UP TO** IN THERE? I CAN SMELL SMOKE!
I GOT INTO THIS STUFF AS A TEENAGER. I MEAN YOU KNOW HOW FUCKED UP AND CHAOTIC MY **CHILDHOOD** WAS... WICCA MADE ME FEEL LIKE MORE THAN A GAWKISH TEENAGE GIRL, MADE ME FEEL AS THOUGH I COULD EXERT SOME CONTROL OVER MY ENVIRONMENT.
WHEN IN REALITY YOU COULDN'T EVEN CONTROL WHICH **CONTINENT** YOU LIVED ON.

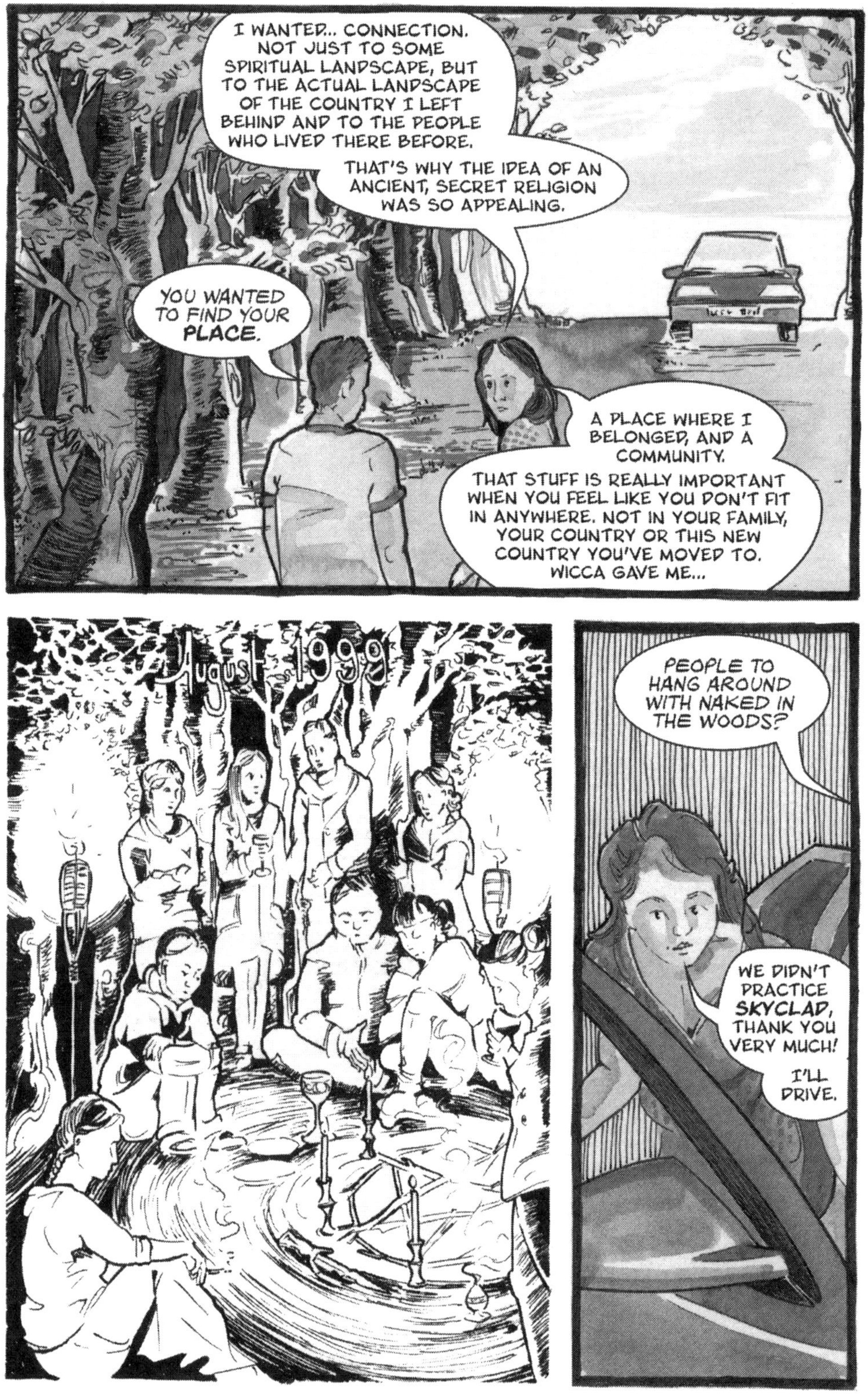
I WANTED... CONNECTION. NOT JUST TO SOME SPIRITUAL LANDSCAPE, BUT TO THE ACTUAL LANDSCAPE OF THE COUNTRY I LEFT BEHIND AND TO THE PEOPLE WHO LIVED THERE BEFORE.
THAT'S WHY THE IDEA OF AN ANCIENT, SECRET RELIGION WAS SO APPEALING.
YOU WANTED TO FIND YOUR **PLACE**.
A PLACE WHERE I BELONGED, AND A COMMUNITY.
THAT STUFF IS REALLY IMPORTANT WHEN YOU FEEL LIKE YOU DON'T FIT IN ANYWHERE. NOT IN YOUR FAMILY, YOUR COUNTRY OR THIS NEW COUNTRY YOU'VE MOVED TO. WICCA GAVE ME...
August 1999
PEOPLE TO HANG AROUND WITH NAKED IN THE WOODS?
WE DIDN'T PRACTICE **SKYCLAD**, THANK YOU VERY MUCH!
I'LL DRIVE.

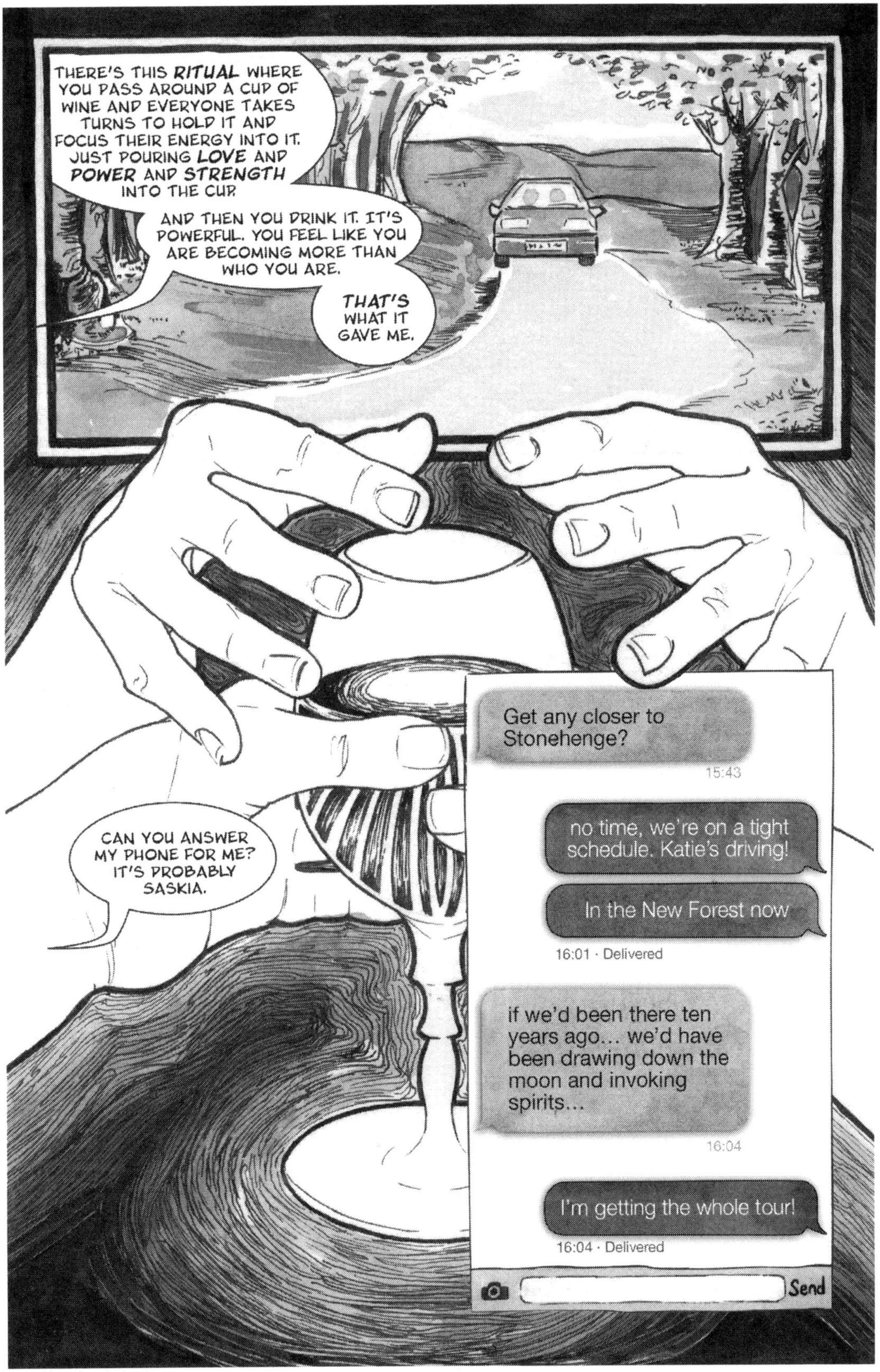
THERE'S THIS RITUAL WHERE YOU PASS AROUND A CUP OF WINE AND EVERYONE TAKES TURNS TO HOLD IT AND FOCUS THEIR ENERGY INTO IT. JUST POURING LOVE AND POWER AND STRENGTH INTO THE CUP.
AND THEN YOU DRINK IT. IT'S POWERFUL. YOU FEEL LIKE YOU ARE BECOMING MORE THAN WHO YOU ARE.
THAT'S WHAT IT GAVE ME.
CAN YOU ANSWER MY PHONE FOR ME? IT'S PROBABLY SASKIA.
Get any closer to Stonehenge?
15:43
no time, we're on a tight schedule. Katie's driving!
In the New Forest now
16:01 · Delivered
if we'd been there ten years ago… we'd have been drawing down the moon and invoking spirits…
16:04
I'm getting the whole tour!
16:04 · Delivered
Send

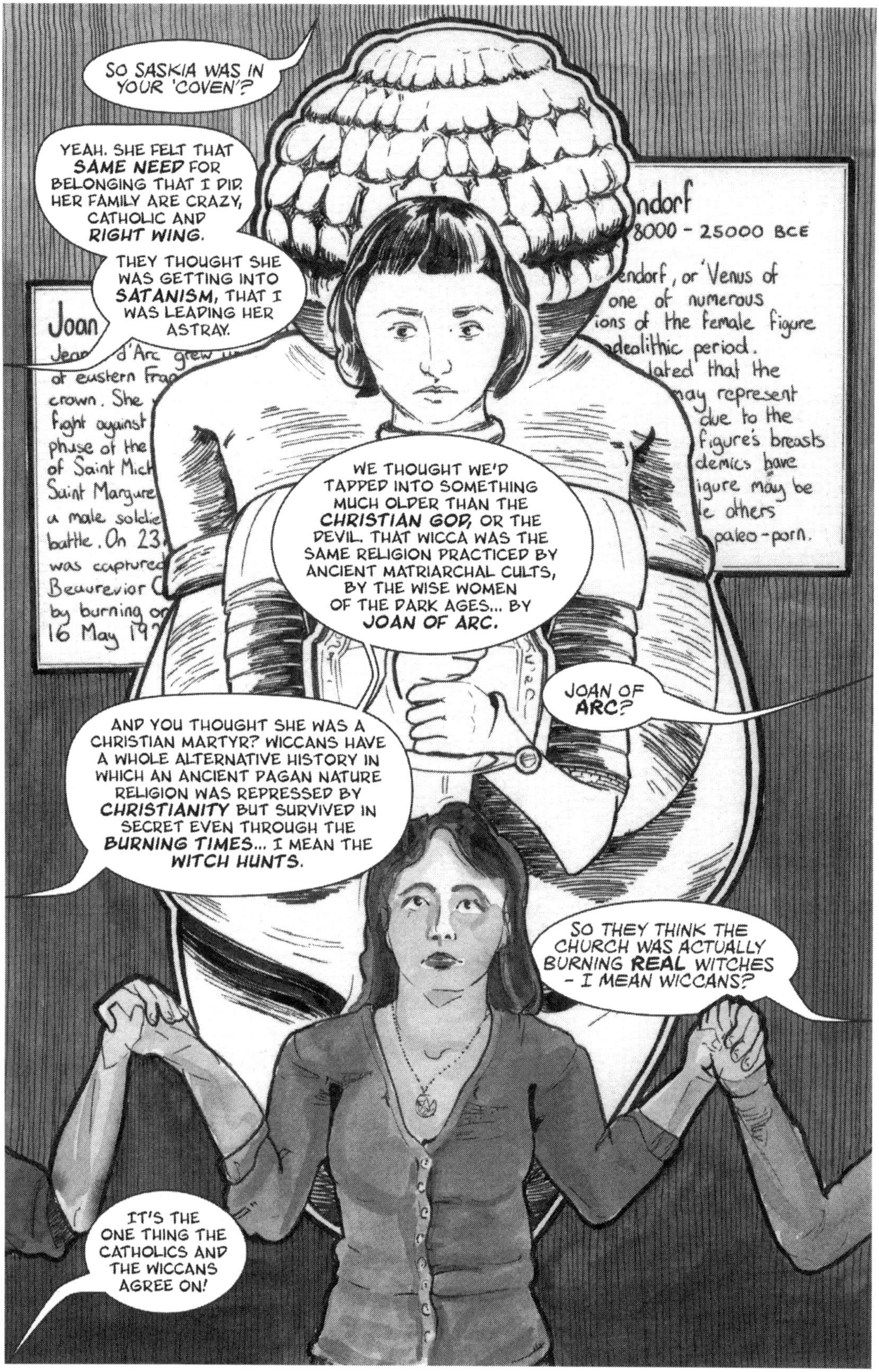
SO SASKIA WAS IN YOUR 'COVEN'?
YEAH. SHE FELT THAT SAME NEED FOR BELONGING THAT I DID. HER FAMILY ARE CRAZY, CATHOLIC AND RIGHT WING.
THEY THOUGHT SHE WAS GETTING INTO SATANISM, THAT I WAS LEADING HER ASTRAY.
WE THOUGHT WE'D TAPPED INTO SOMETHING MUCH OLDER THAN THE CHRISTIAN GOD, OR THE DEVIL. THAT WICCA WAS THE SAME RELIGION PRACTICED BY ANCIENT MATRIARCHAL CULTS, BY THE WISE WOMEN OF THE DARK AGES... BY JOAN OF ARC.
JOAN OF ARC?
AND YOU THOUGHT SHE WAS A CHRISTIAN MARTYR? WICCANS HAVE A WHOLE ALTERNATIVE HISTORY IN WHICH AN ANCIENT PAGAN NATURE RELIGION WAS REPRESSED BY CHRISTIANITY BUT SURVIVED IN SECRET EVEN THROUGH THE BURNING TIMES... I MEAN THE WITCH HUNTS.
SO THEY THINK THE CHURCH WAS ACTUALLY BURNING REAL WITCHES – I MEAN WICCANS?
IT'S THE ONE THING THE CATHOLICS AND THE WICCANS AGREE ON!

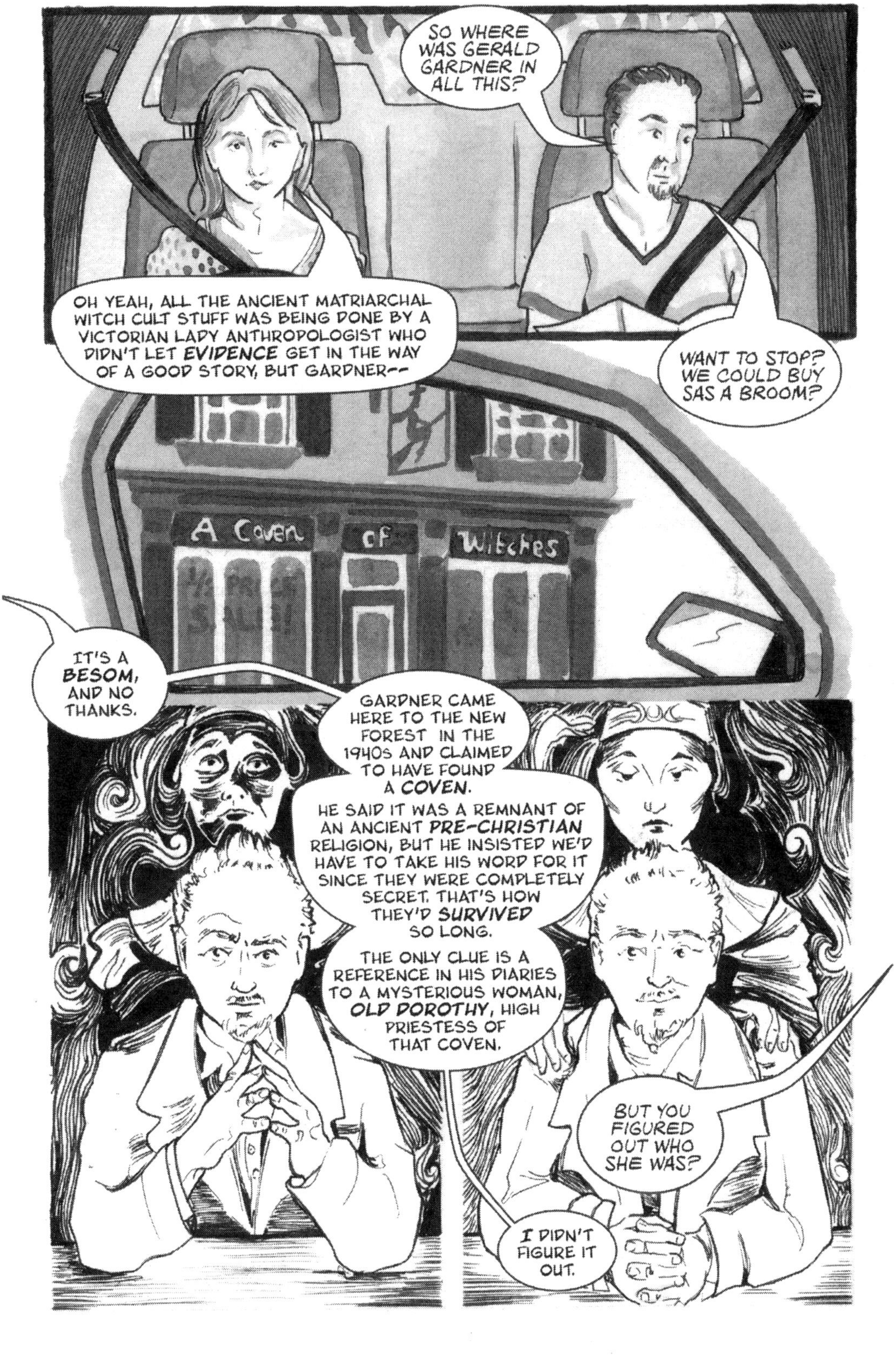
SO WHERE WAS GERALD GARDNER IN ALL THIS?
OH YEAH, ALL THE ANCIENT MATRIARCHAL WITCH CULT STUFF WAS BEING DONE BY A VICTORIAN LADY ANTHROPOLOGIST WHO DIDN'T LET EVIDENCE GET IN THE WAY OF A GOOD STORY, BUT GARDNER--
WANT TO STOP? WE COULD BUY SAS A BROOM?
A Coven of Witches
IT'S A BESOM, AND NO THANKS.
GARDNER CAME HERE TO THE NEW FOREST IN THE 1940S AND CLAIMED TO HAVE FOUND A COVEN.
HE SAID IT WAS A REMNANT OF AN ANCIENT PRE-CHRISTIAN RELIGION, BUT HE INSISTED WE'D HAVE TO TAKE HIS WORD FOR IT SINCE THEY WERE COMPLETELY SECRET. THAT'S HOW THEY'D SURVIVED SO LONG.
THE ONLY CLUE IS A REFERENCE IN HIS DIARIES TO A MYSTERIOUS WOMAN, OLD DOROTHY, HIGH PRIESTESS OF THAT COVEN.
BUT YOU FIGURED OUT WHO SHE WAS?
I DIDN'T FIGURE IT OUT.

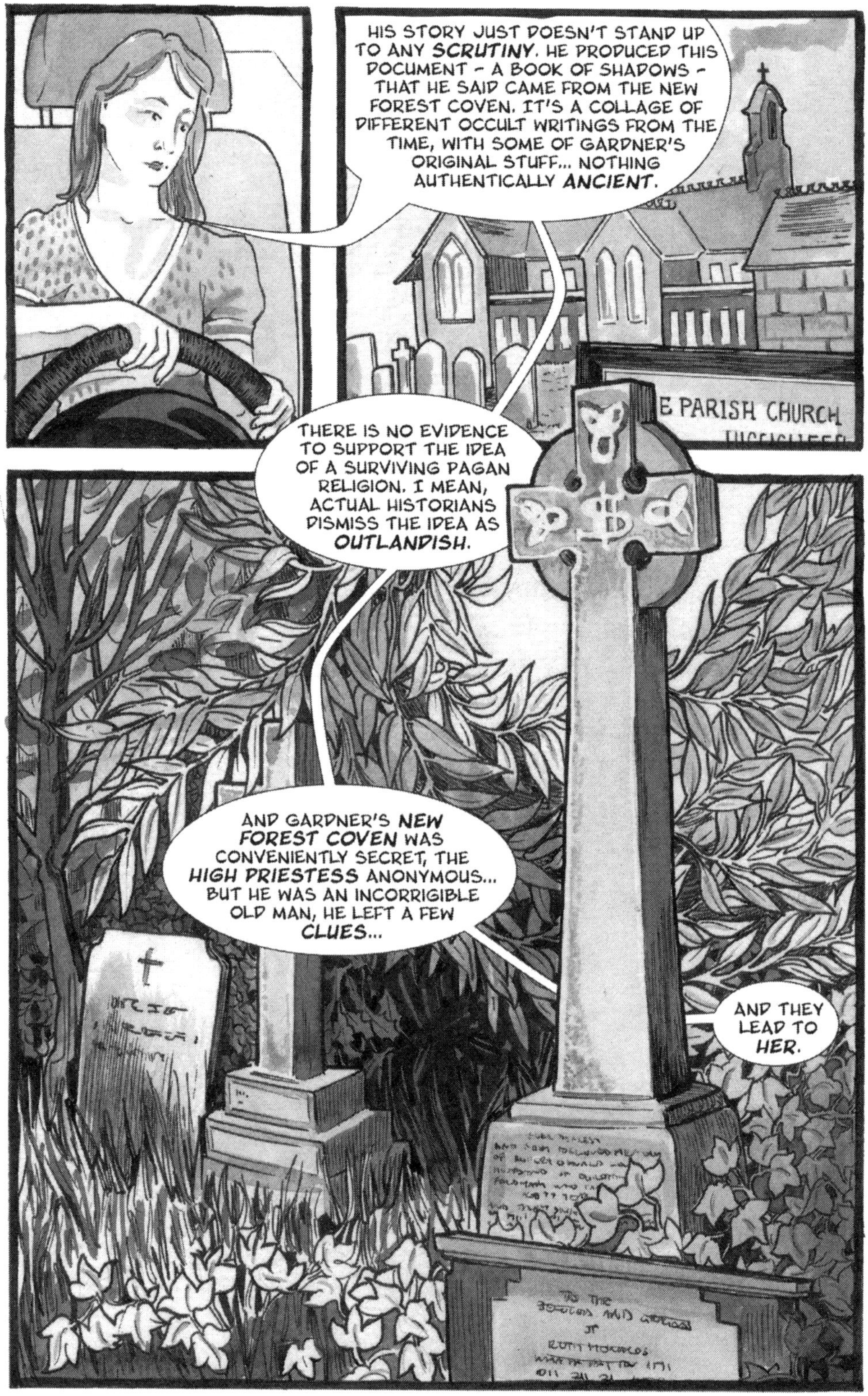
HIS STORY JUST DOESN'T STAND UP TO ANY SCRUTINY. HE PRODUCED THIS DOCUMENT - A BOOK OF SHADOWS - THAT HE SAID CAME FROM THE NEW FOREST COVEN. IT'S A COLLAGE OF DIFFERENT OCCULT WRITINGS FROM THE TIME, WITH SOME OF GARDNER'S ORIGINAL STUFF... NOTHING AUTHENTICALLY ANCIENT.
E PARISH CHURCH
THERE IS NO EVIDENCE TO SUPPORT THE IDEA OF A SURVIVING PAGAN RELIGION. I MEAN, ACTUAL HISTORIANS DISMISS THE IDEA AS OUTLANDISH.
AND GARDNER'S NEW FOREST COVEN WAS CONVENIENTLY SECRET, THE HIGH PRIESTESS ANONYMOUS... BUT HE WAS AN INCORRIGIBLE OLD MAN, HE LEFT A FEW CLUES...
AND THEY LEAD TO HER.

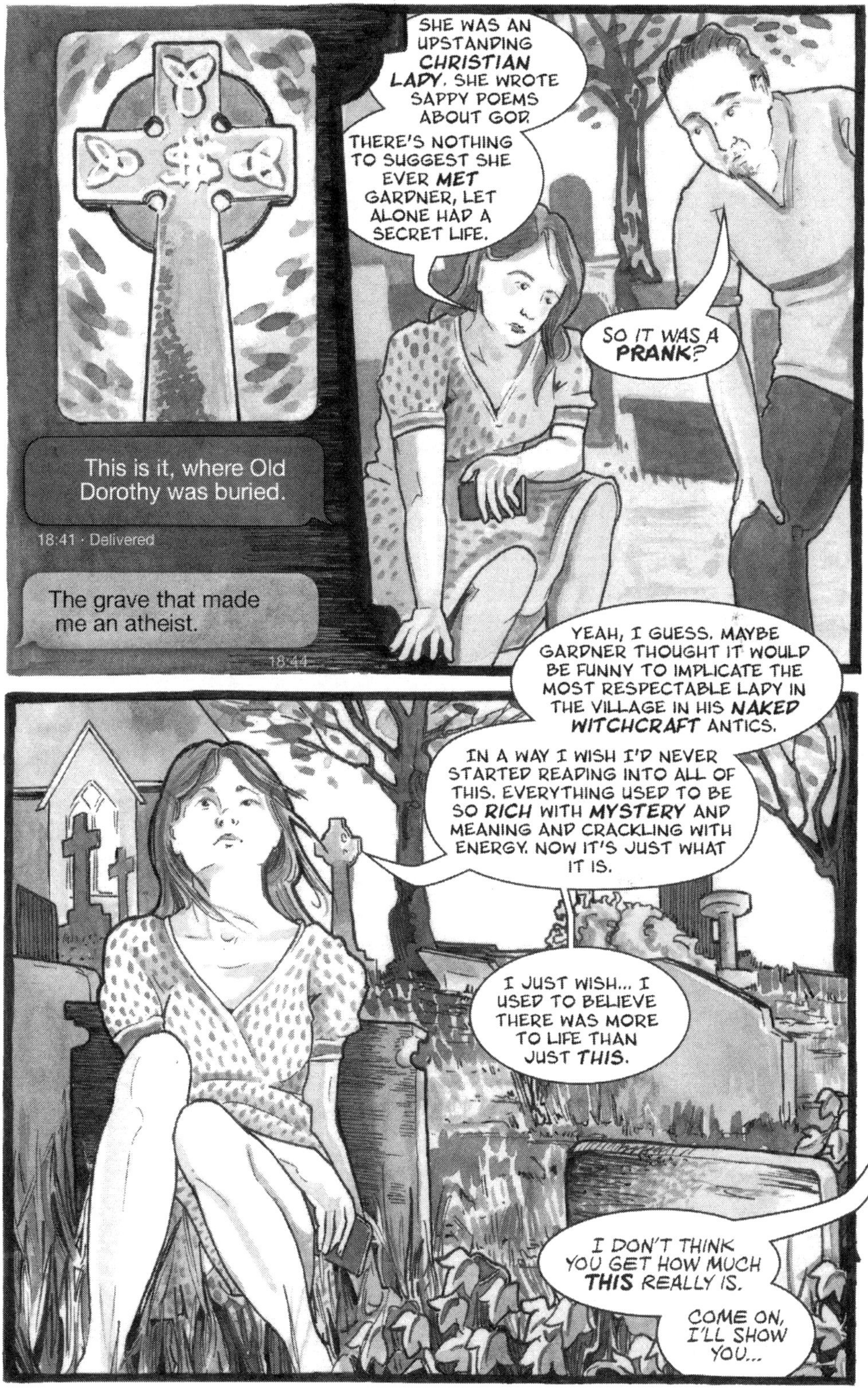

This is it, where Old Dorothy was buried.
18:41 · Delivered
The grave that made me an atheist.
18:44
SHE WAS AN UPSTANDING CHRISTIAN LADY. SHE WROTE SAPPY POEMS ABOUT GOD.
THERE'S NOTHING TO SUGGEST SHE EVER MET GARDNER, LET ALONE HAD A SECRET LIFE.
SO IT WAS A PRANK?
YEAH, I GUESS. MAYBE GARDNER THOUGHT IT WOULD BE FUNNY TO IMPLICATE THE MOST RESPECTABLE LADY IN THE VILLAGE IN HIS NAKED WITCHCRAFT ANTICS.
IN A WAY I WISH I'D NEVER STARTED READING INTO ALL OF THIS. EVERYTHING USED TO BE SO RICH WITH MYSTERY AND MEANING AND CRACKLING WITH ENERGY. NOW IT'S JUST WHAT IT IS.
I JUST WISH... I USED TO BELIEVE THERE WAS MORE TO LIFE THAN JUST THIS.
I DON'T THINK YOU GET HOW MUCH THIS REALLY IS.
COME ON, I'LL SHOW YOU...

LINEAGE IS VERY IMPORTANT IN MOST RELIGIONS. There is a sense of authenticity and truth that we feel any belief system earns when it reaches a certain age. Religions like Scientology and Mormonism are easier targets for criticism because their origins are so recent. The ideas that Joseph Smith and L. Ron Hubbard enshrined in their churches are no more ridiculous than the ones believed by Christians, Buddhists or Muslims, but they haven't had the benefit of centuries to obscure their origins or the character, a con-man and a pulp sci-fi author, of their originators.

In its infancy, Wicca, a neo-pagan reconstructionist religion, almost sidestepped this problem. Gerald Gardner was a retired British civil servant who spent most of his working life in Asia and his free time in the study of folklore and the occult. In 1945 the 1736 Witchcraft Act, which made it illegal to claim that any human being had magical powers or was guilty of practising witchcraft, was repealed and Gardner launched into promoting Wicca - not as a new religion, but as an ancient tradition that he had discovered.

Gardner claimed to have been initiated into a coven of witches who had been secretly practising the pre-Roman religion of Britain for centuries. Based on the text he copied from this coven, Gardner started his own coven and went public with the old ways, writing several books and becoming a popular media anti-hero.

The book which Gardner transcribed from the original ancient tome which he called simply 'Ye Bok', looks suspiciously like a collage of occult practices drawn from Freemasonry, the Golden Dawn and the writings of the famous occultist Aleister Crowley. Instead of being accepted and celebrated for his 'discovery', historians and the academic community dismissed Gardner's account of a surviving pagan religion. Partly because Gardner's Wicca bore very little similarity to what little is known of pre-Roman British traditions, and so much similarity to twentieth century occultism.

But Gardner's claims flourished in the public imagination. The industrial revolution had changed Britain dramatically and many city dwellers were fascinated by the allure of countryside folklore and the mysterious anti-science of the occult. The secrecy of the New Forest Coven enhanced public fascination rather than raising suspicion, and before long Wicca was out of Gardner's hands. Other people stepped forward as members of secret covens or ancient lineages and promoted their own traditions, rituals and spellcraft as authentic, or at least as authentic as Gardner's, Wicca.

When I first heard of Wicca as a teenager, I was told Gardner's myth: that the witchcraft practiced today was a continuation of an ancient religion. And I believed the Egyptologist, and enthusiastic amateur folklorist, Margaret Murray's unsupported and widely discredited, theory: that the 'witches' who were persecuted in the witch hunts of medieval Europe were Wiccans (as were many other historical figures including Joan of Arc). If the first text I'd read about Wicca had introduced it as a neo-pagan reconstructionist religion, founded by an eccentric old civil servant in the 1940s, I suspect it might have lost some of its initial appeal. But it didn't, so I became a witch.

I lost my belief in the supernatural long before I abandoned my traditions and identity as a Wiccan. When I thought critically about my religion, I was forced to accept that Wicca's ideas about a supernatural energy that pervades the universe and can be controlled and directed using spellcraft, lacked any evidence to support them. But the traditions and rituals were still by turns comforting and exhilarating in large part because I believed in their ancientness.

It took researching the legitimacy of Garner's claimed source, High Priestess of the New Forest Coven, and visiting the graveyard in which she buried her husband under a clearly Christian cross, for me to fully admit to myself that I had been one of many victims of Gardner's 'goatish' sense of humour.

More information, discussion and links at
doubtcomic.com/as-above-so-below

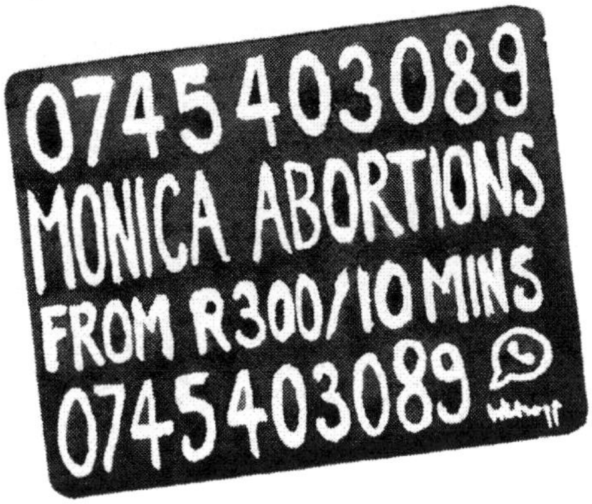
0745403089
MONICA ABORTIONS
FROM R300/10 MINS
0745403089

SNAKE OIL SHAMAN

KHAYELITSHA TOWNSHIP, SOUTH AFRICA

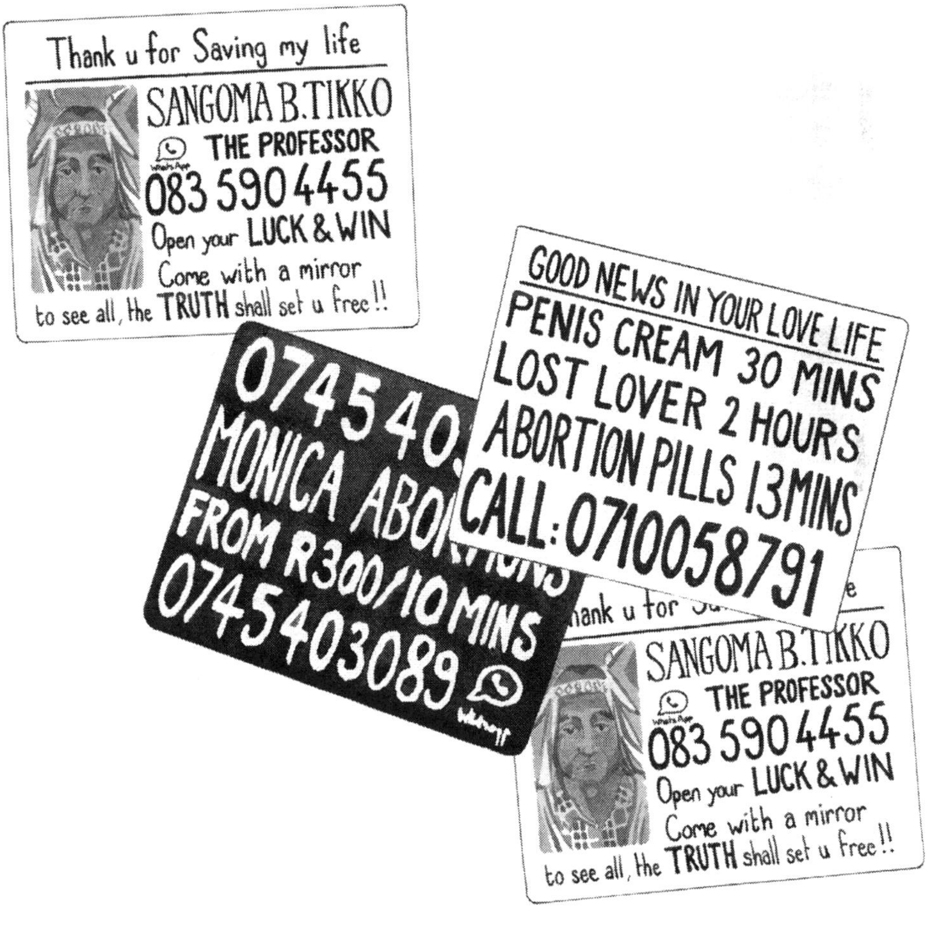
Thank u for Saving my life
SANGOMA B.TIKKO
THE PROFESSOR
083 590 4455
Open your LUCK & WIN
Come with a mirror
to see all, the TRUTH shall set u free!!
GOOD NEWS IN YOUR LOVE LIFE
PENIS CREAM 30 MINS
LOST LOVER 2 HOURS
ABORTION PILLS 13MINS
CALL: 0710058791
0745 40
MONICA ABO
FROM R300/10 MINS
0745403089
hank u for
SANGOMA B.TIKKO
THE PROFESSOR
083 590 4455
Open your LUCK & WIN
Come with a mirror
to see all, the TRUTH shall set u free!!

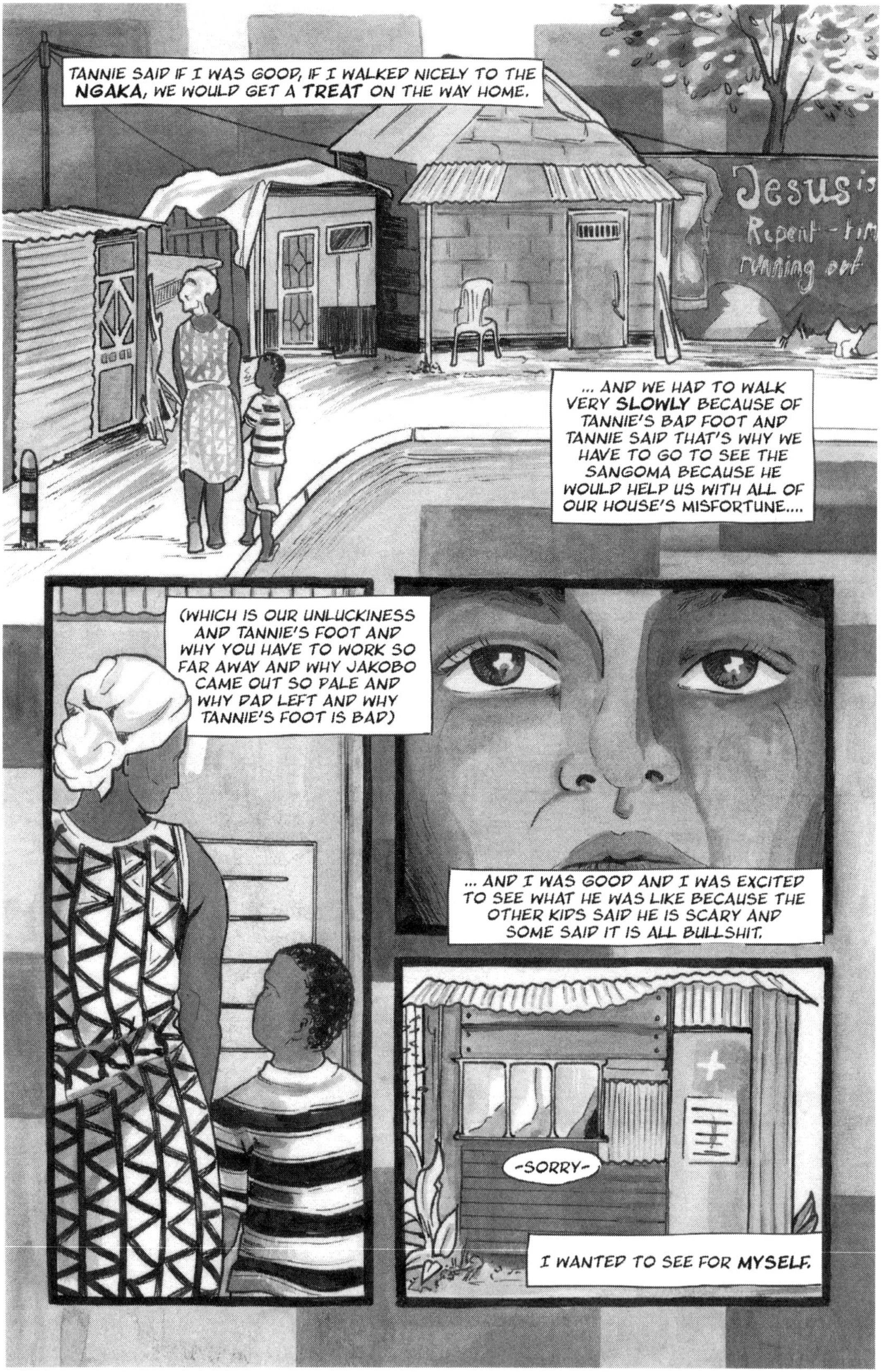
TANNIE SAID IF I WAS GOOD, IF I WALKED NICELY TO THE NGAKA, WE WOULD GET A TREAT ON THE WAY HOME.
Jesus is
Repent - time running out
... AND WE HAD TO WALK VERY SLOWLY BECAUSE OF TANNIE'S BAD FOOT AND TANNIE SAID THAT'S WHY WE HAVE TO GO TO SEE THE SANGOMA BECAUSE HE WOULD HELP US WITH ALL OF OUR HOUSE'S MISFORTUNE....
(WHICH IS OUR UNLUCKINESS AND TANNIE'S FOOT AND WHY YOU HAVE TO WORK SO FAR AWAY AND WHY JAKOBO CAME OUT SO PALE AND WHY DAD LEFT AND WHY TANNIE'S FOOT IS BAD)
... AND I WAS GOOD AND I WAS EXCITED TO SEE WHAT HE WAS LIKE BECAUSE THE OTHER KIDS SAID HE IS SCARY AND SOME SAID IT IS ALL BULLSHIT.
-SORRY-
I WANTED TO SEE FOR MYSELF.

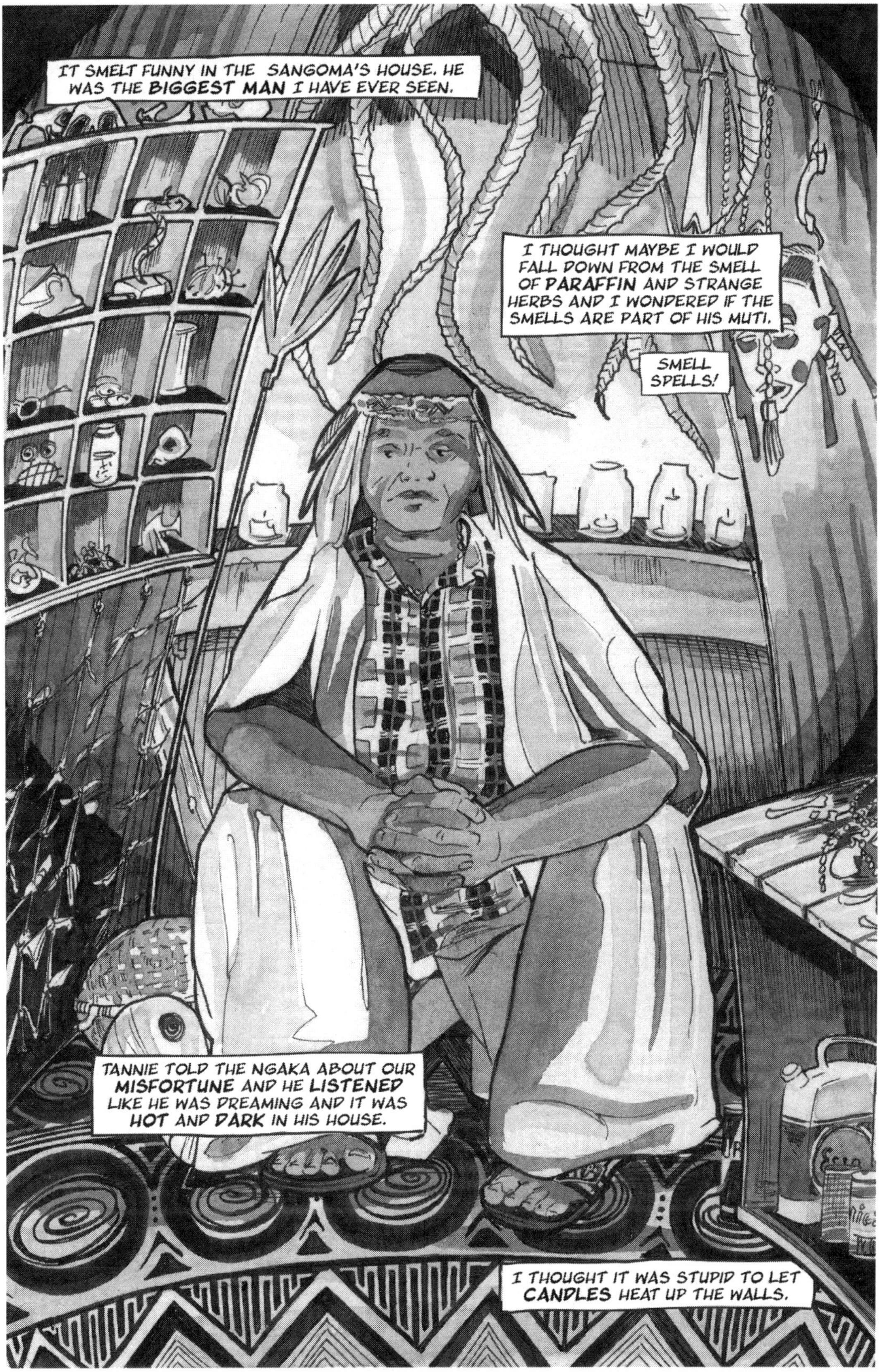
IT SMELT FUNNY IN THE SANGOMA'S HOUSE. HE WAS THE BIGGEST MAN I HAVE EVER SEEN.
I THOUGHT MAYBE I WOULD FALL DOWN FROM THE SMELL OF PARAFFIN AND STRANGE HERBS AND I WONDERED IF THE SMELLS ARE PART OF HIS MUTI.
SMELL SPELLS!
TANNIE TOLD THE NGAKA ABOUT OUR MISFORTUNE AND HE LISTENED LIKE HE WAS DREAMING AND IT WAS HOT AND DARK IN HIS HOUSE.
I THOUGHT IT WAS STUPID TO LET CANDLES HEAT UP THE WALLS.

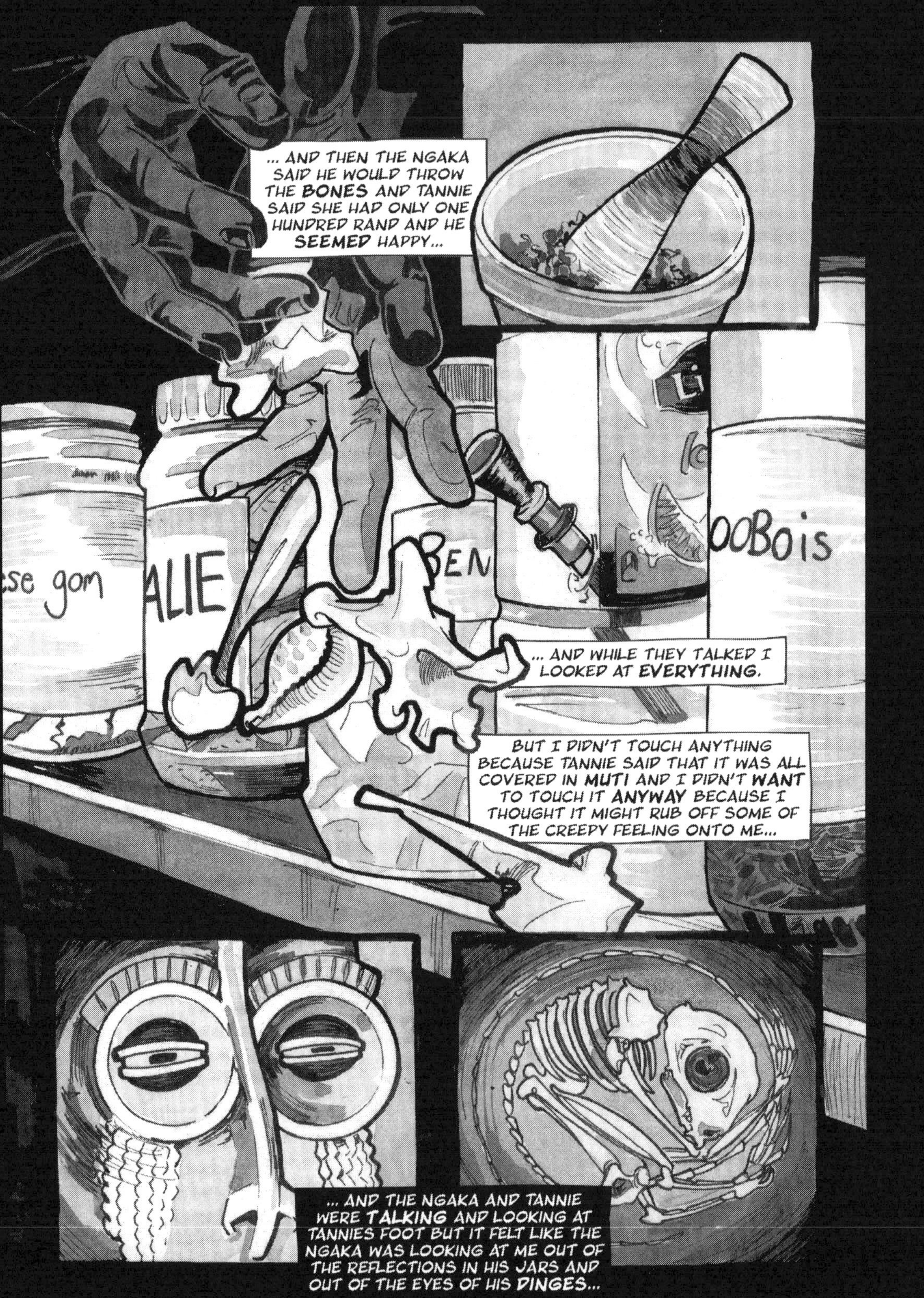
... AND THEN THE NGAKA SAID HE WOULD THROW THE BONES AND TANNIE SAID SHE HAD ONLY ONE HUNDRED RAND AND HE SEEMED HAPPY...
se gom
ALIE
BEN
OOBois
... AND WHILE THEY TALKED I LOOKED AT EVERYTHING.
BUT I DIDN'T TOUCH ANYTHING BECAUSE TANNIE SAID THAT IT WAS ALL COVERED IN MUTI AND I DIDN'T WANT TO TOUCH IT ANYWAY BECAUSE I THOUGHT IT MIGHT RUB OFF SOME OF THE CREEPY FEELING ONTO ME...
... AND THE NGAKA AND TANNIE WERE TALKING AND LOOKING AT TANNIES FOOT BUT IT FELT LIKE THE NGAKA WAS LOOKING AT ME OUT OF THE REFLECTIONS IN HIS JARS AND OUT OF THE EYES OF HIS DINGES...

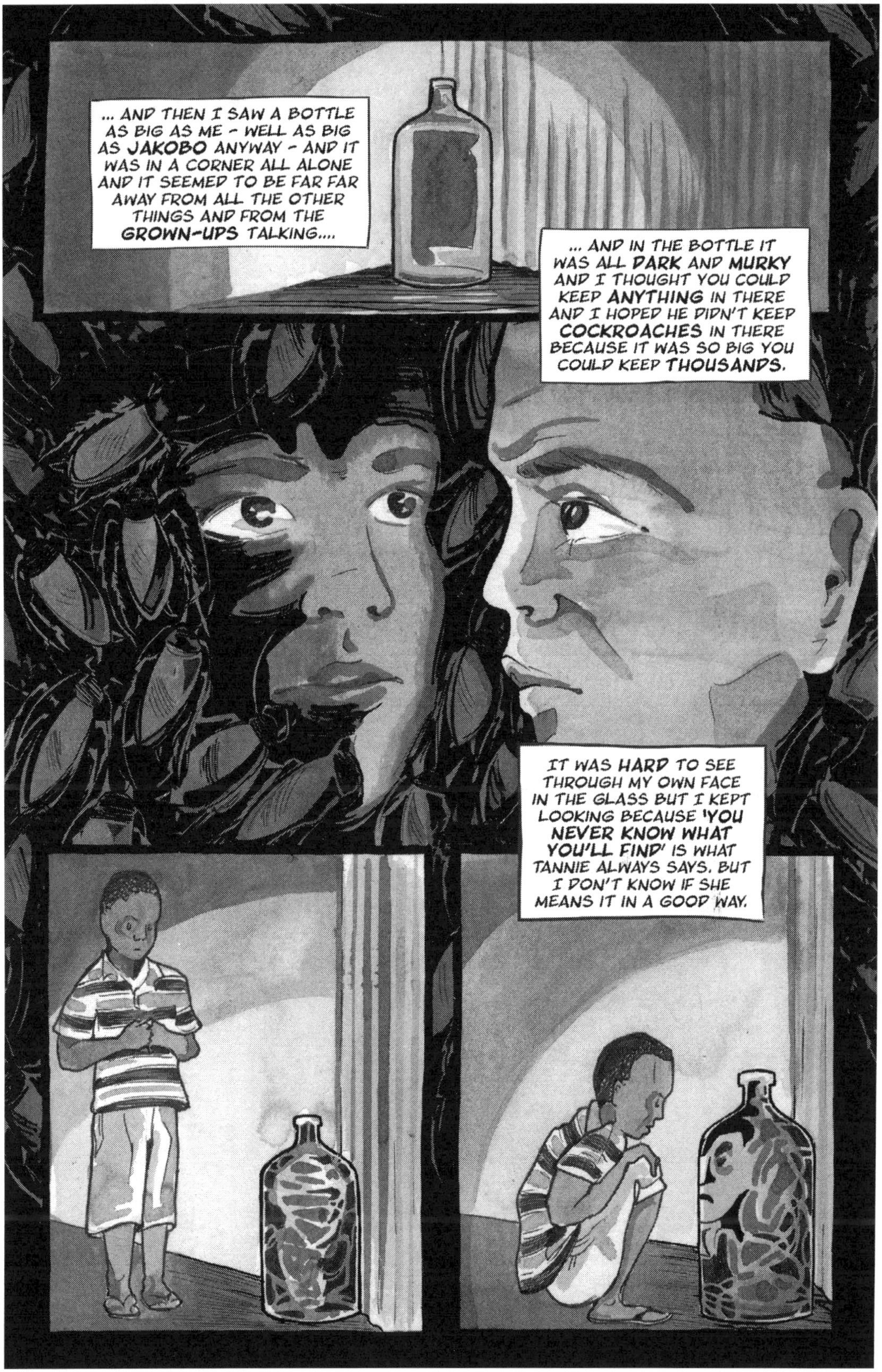
... AND THEN I SAW A BOTTLE AS BIG AS ME - WELL AS BIG AS JAKOBO ANYWAY - AND IT WAS IN A CORNER ALL ALONE AND IT SEEMED TO BE FAR FAR AWAY FROM ALL THE OTHER THINGS AND FROM THE GROWN-UPS TALKING....
... AND IN THE BOTTLE IT WAS ALL DARK AND MURKY AND I THOUGHT YOU COULD KEEP ANYTHING IN THERE AND I HOPED HE DIDN'T KEEP COCKROACHES IN THERE BECAUSE IT WAS SO BIG YOU COULD KEEP THOUSANDS.
IT WAS HARD TO SEE THROUGH MY OWN FACE IN THE GLASS BUT I KEPT LOOKING BECAUSE 'YOU NEVER KNOW WHAT YOU'LL FIND' IS WHAT TANNIE ALWAYS SAYS. BUT I DON'T KNOW IF SHE MEANS IT IN A GOOD WAY.

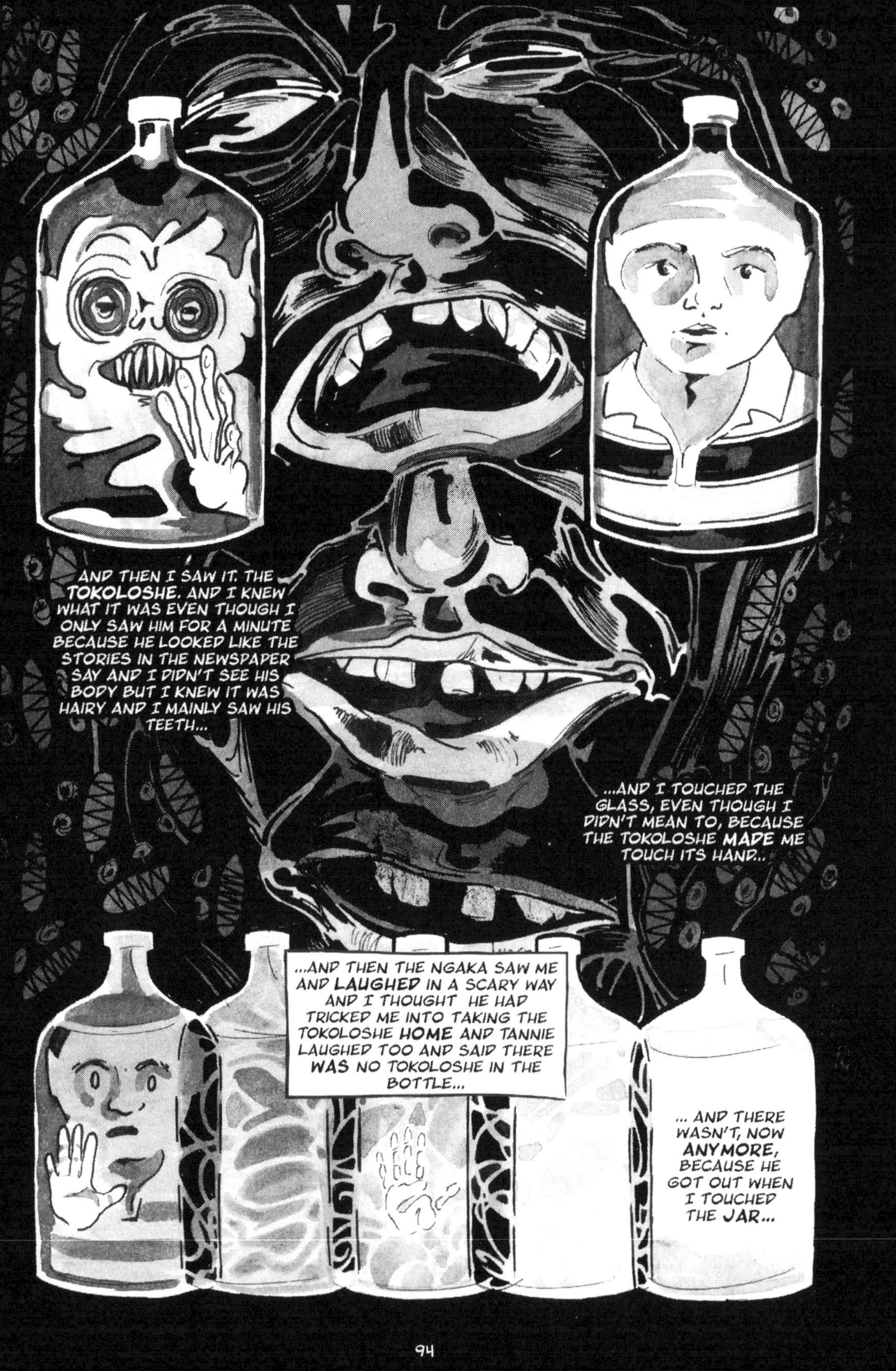
AND THEN I SAW IT. THE TOKOLOSHE. AND I KNEW WHAT IT WAS EVEN THOUGH I ONLY SAW HIM FOR A MINUTE BECAUSE HE LOOKED LIKE THE STORIES IN THE NEWSPAPER SAY AND I DIDN'T SEE HIS BODY BUT I KNEW IT WAS HAIRY AND I MAINLY SAW HIS TEETH...
...AND I TOUCHED THE GLASS, EVEN THOUGH I DIDN'T MEAN TO, BECAUSE THE TOKOLOSHE MADE ME TOUCH ITS HAND...
...AND THEN THE NGAKA SAW ME AND LAUGHED IN A SCARY WAY AND I THOUGHT HE HAD TRICKED ME INTO TAKING THE TOKOLOSHE HOME AND TANNIE LAUGHED TOO AND SAID THERE WAS NO TOKOLOSHE IN THE BOTTLE...
... AND THERE WASN'T, NOW ANYMORE, BECAUSE HE GOT OUT WHEN I TOUCHED THE JAR...

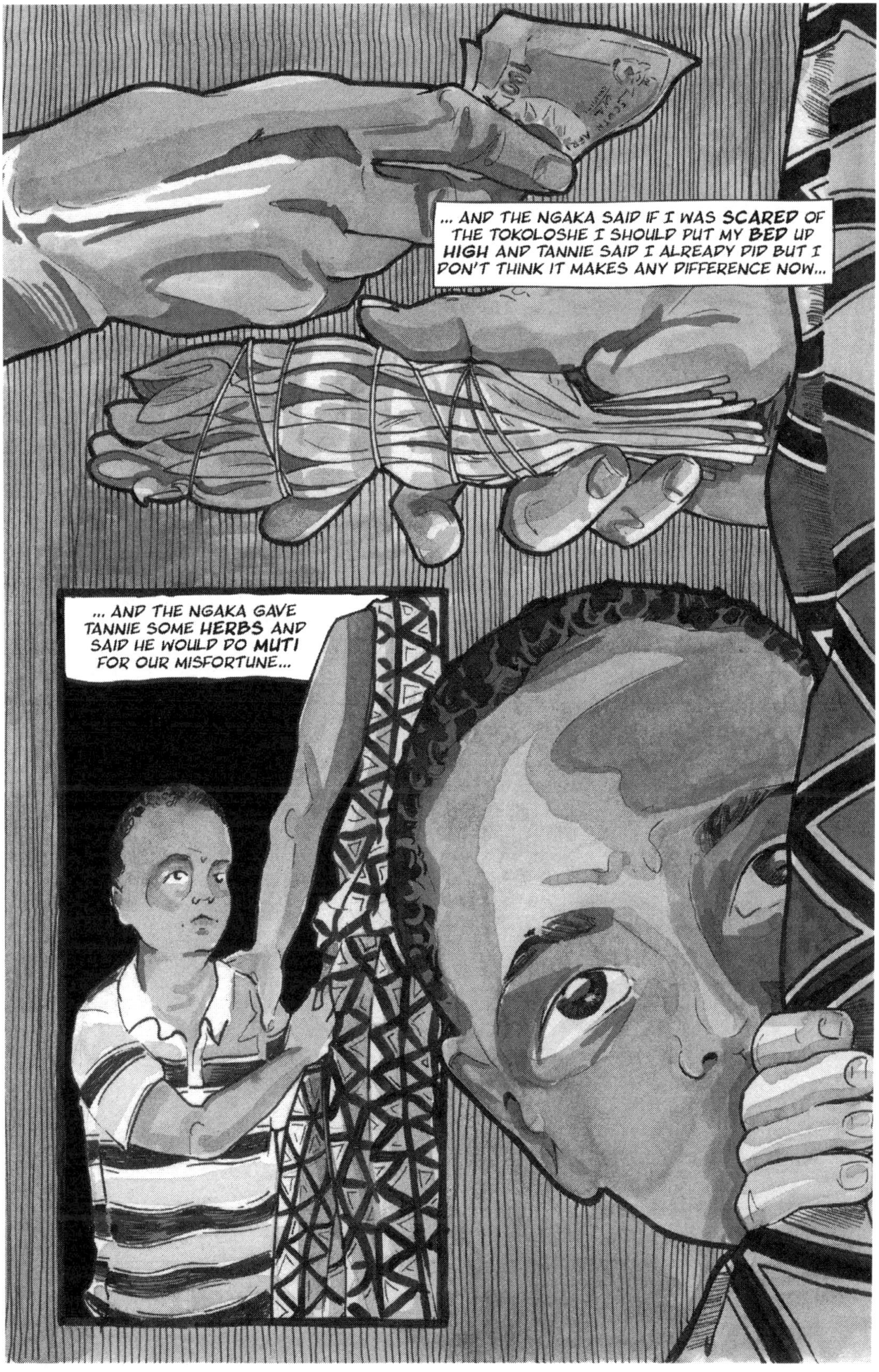
... AND THE NGAKA SAID IF I WAS SCARED OF THE TOKOLOSHE I SHOULD PUT MY BED UP HIGH AND TANNIE SAID I ALREADY DID BUT I DON'T THINK IT MAKES ANY DIFFERENCE NOW...
... AND THE NGAKA GAVE TANNIE SOME HERBS AND SAID HE WOULD DO MUTI FOR OUR MISFORTUNE...

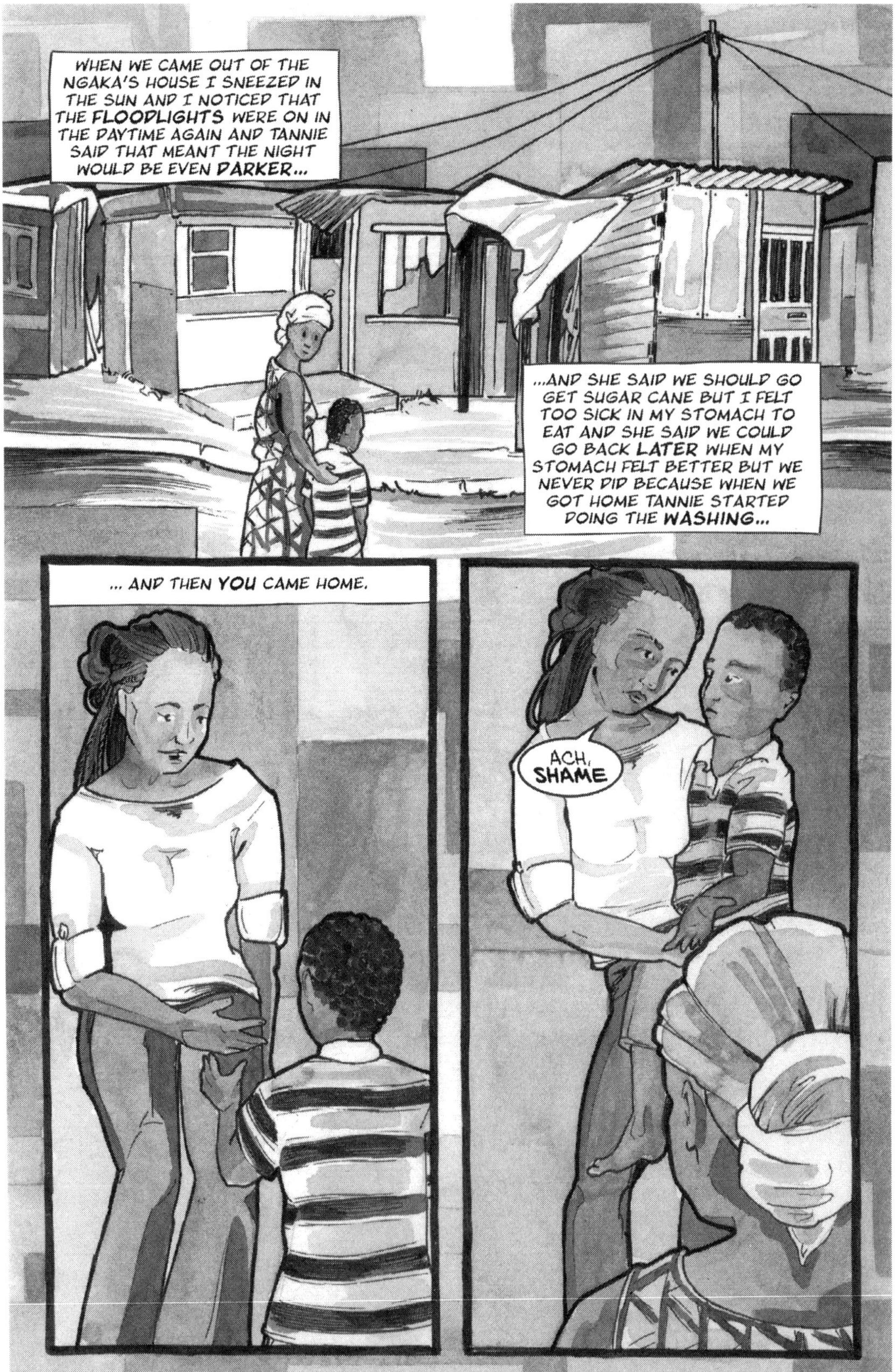
WHEN WE CAME OUT OF THE NGAKA'S HOUSE I SNEEZED IN THE SUN AND I NOTICED THAT THE FLOODLIGHTS WERE ON IN THE DAYTIME AGAIN AND TANNIE SAID THAT MEANT THE NIGHT WOULD BE EVEN DARKER...
...AND SHE SAID WE SHOULD GO GET SUGAR CANE BUT I FELT TOO SICK IN MY STOMACH TO EAT AND SHE SAID WE COULD GO BACK LATER WHEN MY STOMACH FELT BETTER BUT WE NEVER DID BECAUSE WHEN WE GOT HOME TANNIE STARTED DOING THE WASHING...
... AND THEN YOU CAME HOME.
ACH, SHAME

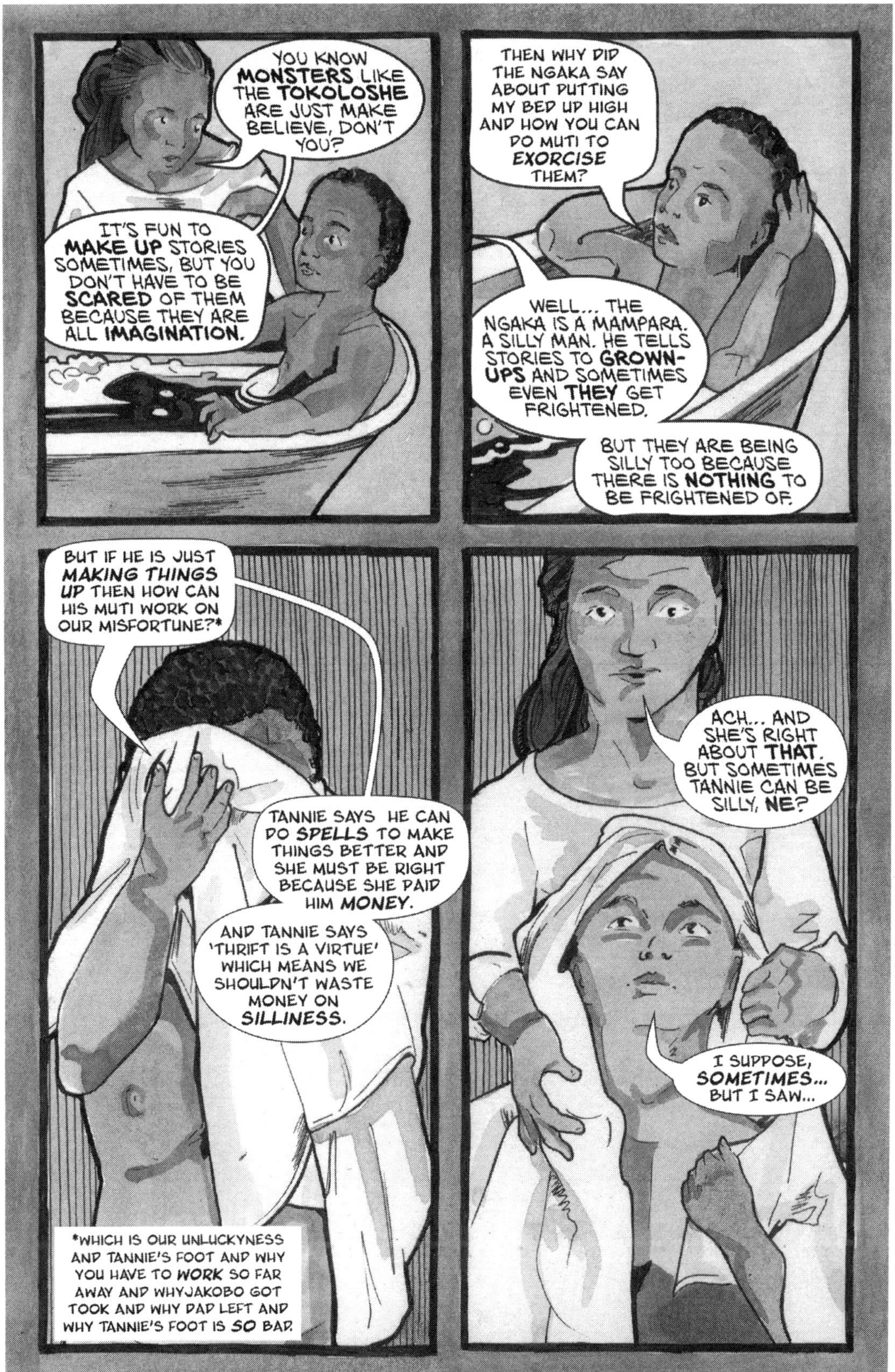
YOU KNOW MONSTERS LIKE THE TOKOLOSHE ARE JUST MAKE BELIEVE, DON'T YOU?
IT'S FUN TO MAKE UP STORIES SOMETIMES, BUT YOU DON'T HAVE TO BE SCARED OF THEM BECAUSE THEY ARE ALL IMAGINATION.
THEN WHY DID THE NGAKA SAY ABOUT PUTTING MY BED UP HIGH AND HOW YOU CAN DO MUTI TO EXORCISE THEM?
WELL... THE NGAKA IS A MAMPARA. A SILLY MAN. HE TELLS STORIES TO GROWN-UPS AND SOMETIMES EVEN THEY GET FRIGHTENED.
BUT THEY ARE BEING SILLY TOO BECAUSE THERE IS NOTHING TO BE FRIGHTENED OF.
BUT IF HE IS JUST MAKING THINGS UP THEN HOW CAN HIS MUTI WORK ON OUR MISFORTUNE?*
TANNIE SAYS HE CAN DO SPELLS TO MAKE THINGS BETTER AND SHE MUST BE RIGHT BECAUSE SHE PAID HIM MONEY.
AND TANNIE SAYS 'THRIFT IS A VIRTUE' WHICH MEANS WE SHOULDN'T WASTE MONEY ON SILLINESS.
*WHICH IS OUR UNLUCKYNESS AND TANNIE'S FOOT AND WHY YOU HAVE TO WORK SO FAR AWAY AND WHYJAKOBO GOT TOOK AND WHY DAD LEFT AND WHY TANNIE'S FOOT IS SO BAD.
ACH... AND SHE'S RIGHT ABOUT THAT. BUT SOMETIMES TANNIE CAN BE SILLY, NE?
I SUPPOSE, SOMETIMES... BUT I SAW...

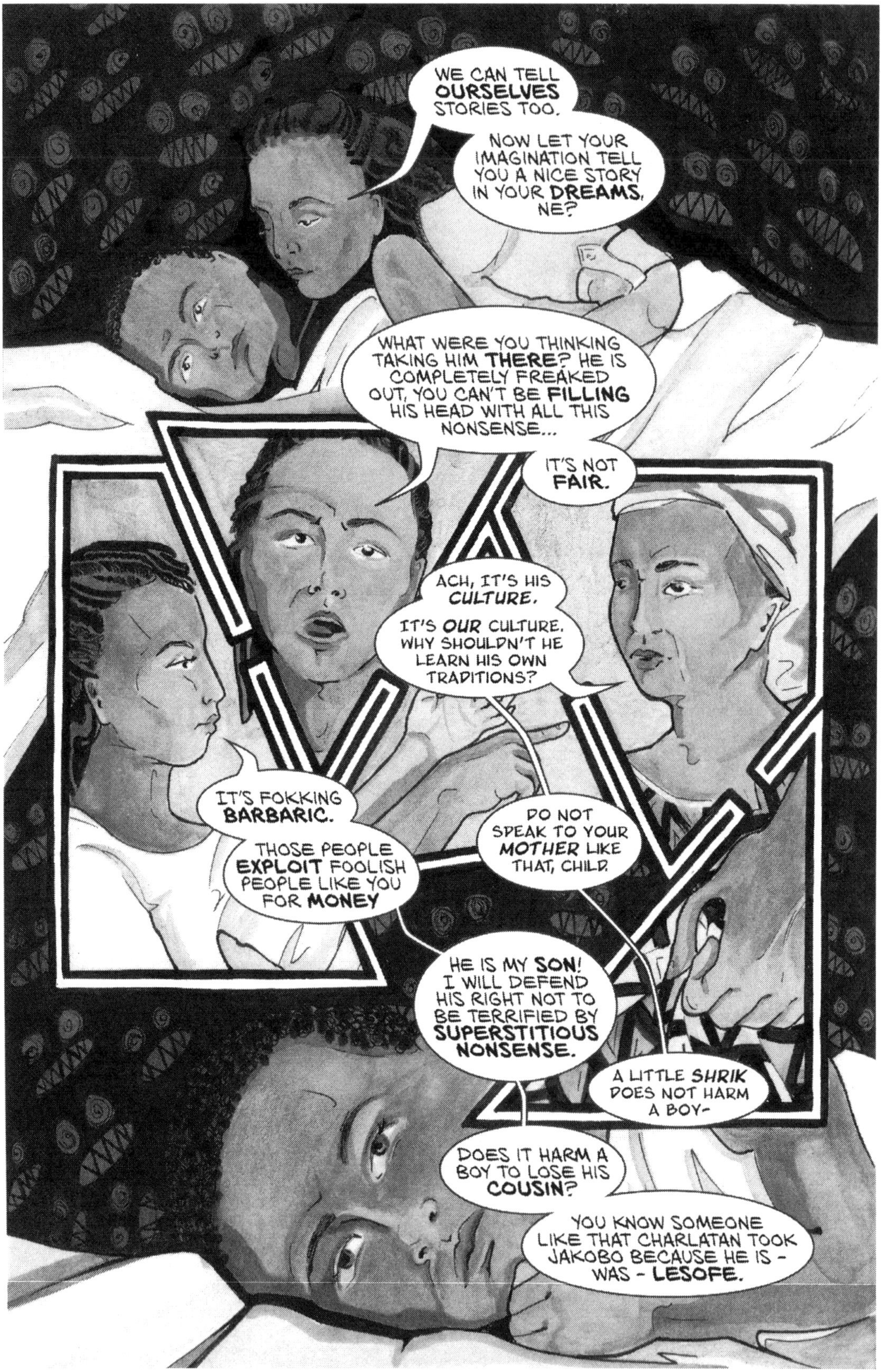
WE CAN TELL OURSELVES STORIES TOO.
NOW LET YOUR IMAGINATION TELL YOU A NICE STORY IN YOUR DREAMS, NE?
WHAT WERE YOU THINKING TAKING HIM THERE? HE IS COMPLETELY FREAKED OUT, YOU CAN'T BE FILLING HIS HEAD WITH ALL THIS NONSENSE...
IT'S NOT FAIR.
ACH, IT'S HIS CULTURE.
IT'S OUR CULTURE. WHY SHOULDN'T HE LEARN HIS OWN TRADITIONS?
IT'S FOKKING BARBARIC.
THOSE PEOPLE EXPLOIT FOOLISH PEOPLE LIKE YOU FOR MONEY
DO NOT SPEAK TO YOUR MOTHER LIKE THAT, CHILD.
HE IS MY SON! I WILL DEFEND HIS RIGHT NOT TO BE TERRIFIED BY SUPERSTITIOUS NONSENSE.
A LITTLE SHRIK DOES NOT HARM A BOY-
DOES IT HARM A BOY TO LOSE HIS COUSIN?
YOU KNOW SOMEONE LIKE THAT CHARLATAN TOOK JAKOBO BECAUSE HE IS - WAS - LESOFE.

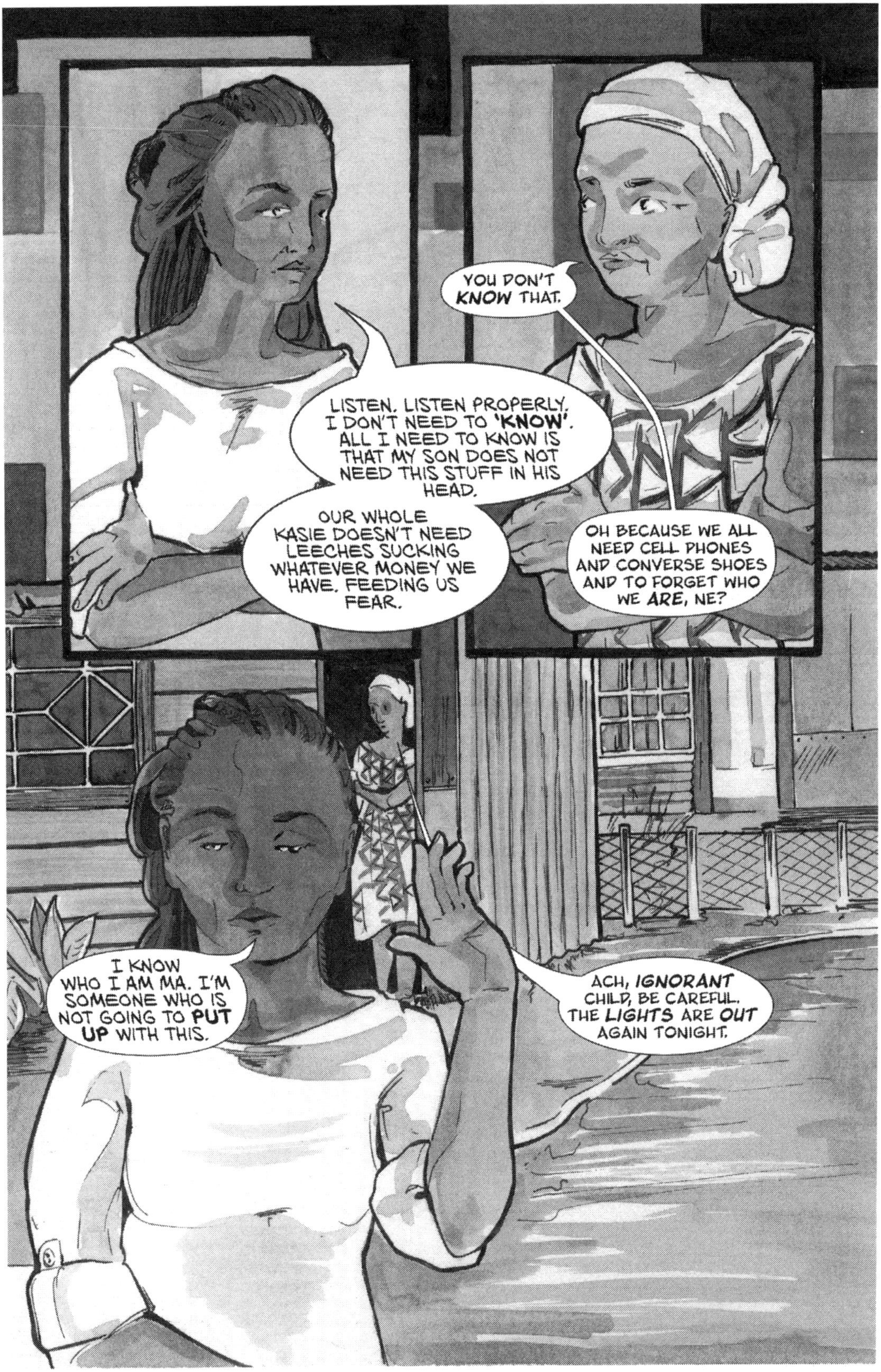
YOU DON'T KNOW THAT.
LISTEN. LISTEN PROPERLY. I DON'T NEED TO 'KNOW'. ALL I NEED TO KNOW IS THAT MY SON DOES NOT NEED THIS STUFF IN HIS HEAD.
OUR WHOLE KASIE DOESN'T NEED LEECHES SUCKING WHATEVER MONEY WE HAVE. FEEDING US FEAR.
OH BECAUSE WE ALL NEED CELL PHONES AND CONVERSE SHOES AND TO FORGET WHO WE ARE, NE?
I KNOW WHO I AM MA. I'M SOMEONE WHO IS NOT GOING TO PUT UP WITH THIS.
ACH, IGNORANT CHILD, BE CAREFUL. THE LIGHTS ARE OUT AGAIN TONIGHT.

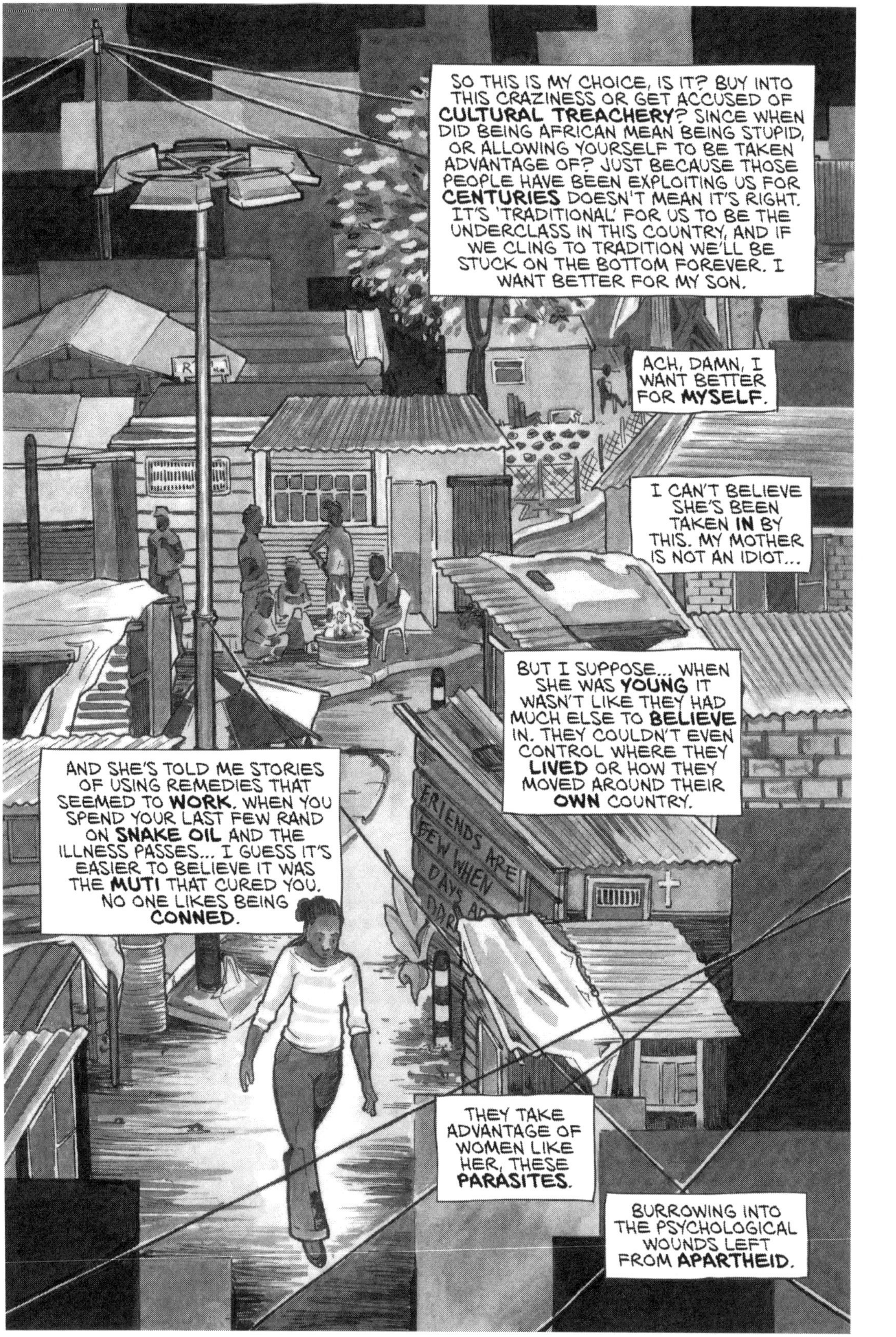
SO THIS IS MY CHOICE, IS IT? BUY INTO THIS CRAZINESS OR GET ACCUSED OF **CULTURAL TREACHERY**? SINCE WHEN DID BEING AFRICAN MEAN BEING STUPID, OR ALLOWING YOURSELF TO BE TAKEN ADVANTAGE OF? JUST BECAUSE THOSE PEOPLE HAVE BEEN EXPLOITING US FOR **CENTURIES** DOESN'T MEAN IT'S RIGHT. IT'S 'TRADITIONAL' FOR US TO BE THE UNDERCLASS IN THIS COUNTRY, AND IF WE CLING TO TRADITION WE'LL BE STUCK ON THE BOTTOM FOREVER. I WANT BETTER FOR MY SON.
ACH, DAMN, I WANT BETTER FOR **MYSELF**.
I CAN'T BELIEVE SHE'S BEEN TAKEN **IN** BY THIS. MY MOTHER IS NOT AN IDIOT...
BUT I SUPPOSE... WHEN SHE WAS **YOUNG** IT WASN'T LIKE THEY HAD MUCH ELSE TO **BELIEVE** IN. THEY COULDN'T EVEN CONTROL WHERE THEY **LIVED** OR HOW THEY MOVED AROUND THEIR **OWN** COUNTRY.
AND SHE'S TOLD ME STORIES OF USING REMEDIES THAT SEEMED TO **WORK**. WHEN YOU SPEND YOUR LAST FEW RAND ON **SNAKE OIL** AND THE ILLNESS PASSES... I GUESS IT'S EASIER TO BELIEVE IT WAS THE **MUTI** THAT CURED YOU. NO ONE LIKES BEING **CONNED**.
FRIENDS ARE
FEW WHEN
THEY TAKE ADVANTAGE OF WOMEN LIKE HER, THESE **PARASITES**.
BURROWING INTO THE PSYCHOLOGICAL WOUNDS LEFT FROM **APARTHEID**.

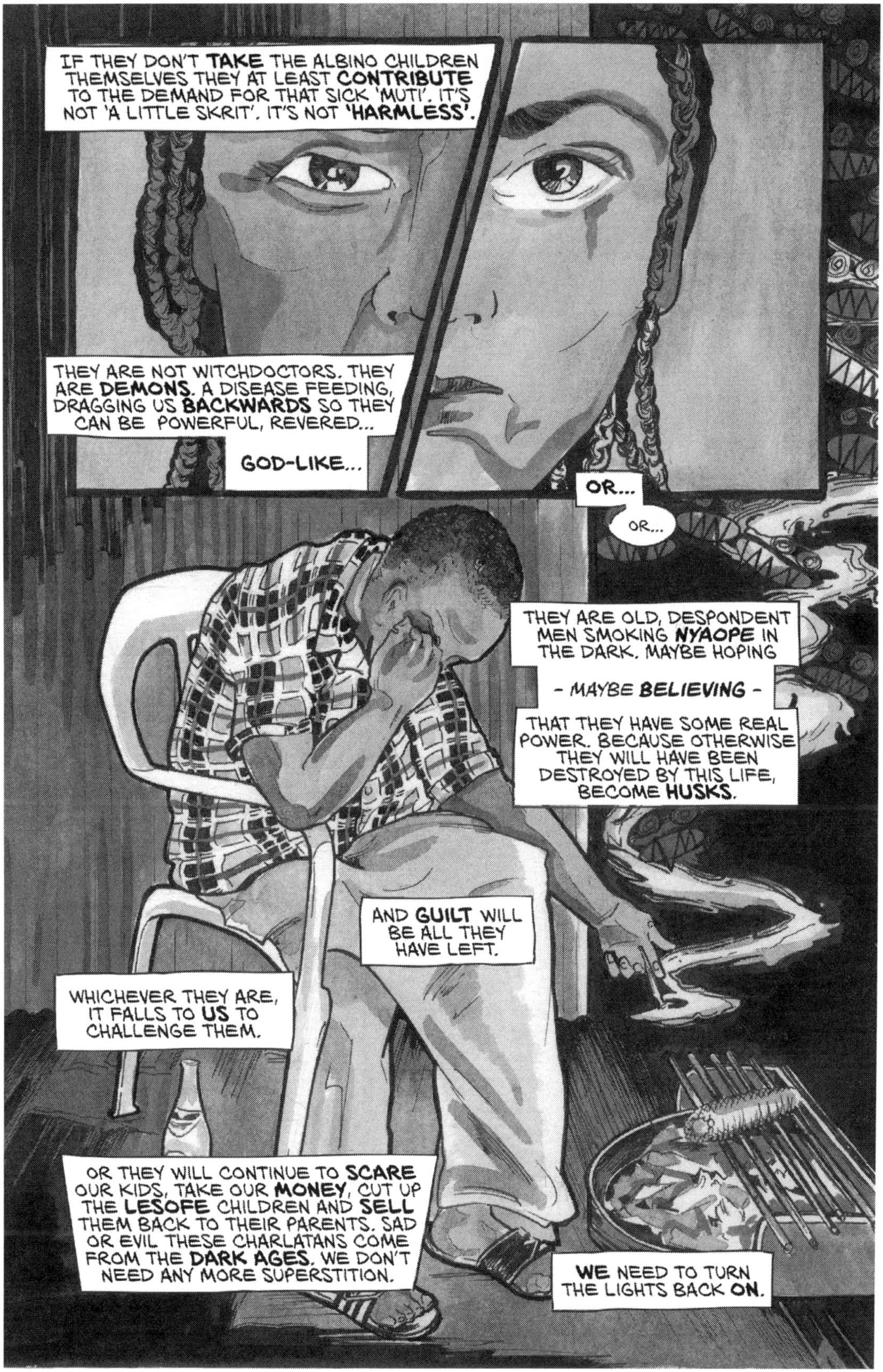
IF THEY DON'T TAKE THE ALBINO CHILDREN THEMSELVES THEY AT LEAST CONTRIBUTE TO THE DEMAND FOR THAT SICK 'MUTI'. IT'S NOT 'A LITTLE SKRIT'. IT'S NOT 'HARMLESS'.
THEY ARE NOT WITCHDOCTORS. THEY ARE DEMONS. A DISEASE FEEDING, DRAGGING US BACKWARDS SO THEY CAN BE POWERFUL, REVERED...
GOD-LIKE...
OR...
OR...
THEY ARE OLD, DESPONDENT MEN SMOKING NYAOPE IN THE DARK. MAYBE HOPING
- MAYBE BELIEVING -
THAT THEY HAVE SOME REAL POWER. BECAUSE OTHERWISE THEY WILL HAVE BEEN DESTROYED BY THIS LIFE, BECOME HUSKS.
AND GUILT WILL BE ALL THEY HAVE LEFT.
WHICHEVER THEY ARE, IT FALLS TO US TO CHALLENGE THEM.
OR THEY WILL CONTINUE TO SCARE OUR KIDS, TAKE OUR MONEY, CUT UP THE LESOFE CHILDREN AND SELL THEM BACK TO THEIR PARENTS. SAD OR EVIL THESE CHARLATANS COME FROM THE DARK AGES. WE DON'T NEED ANY MORE SUPERSTITION.
WE NEED TO TURN THE LIGHTS BACK ON.

Plastered on the walls of the second class train carriages of Cape Town's public rail system are white stickers advertising services in bold fonts. Each has the phone number of a doctor or a witch doctor to call. You can get a good luck charm, a herbal potion, or even an abortion 'WITHIN 10MIN/R300'. The stickers are symptomatic of an underlying condition.

Former president of South Africa Thabo Mbeki denied the connection between HIV and AIDS. Mbeki suggested that AIDS was a western invention: either a propaganda campaign to sell expensive western medicine, or a man-made disease designed to exterminate Africans. Mbeki's government promoted the idea that HIV could be cured with a healthy diet and that AIDS could be cured by ingesting an untested herbal remedy. Mbeki believed that antiretroviral drugs, the only successful treatment for HIV, do more harm than good so he prevented aid agencies from dispensing them. It is partly thanks to his legacy that, today, impoverished South Africans buy and sell magic and medicine interchangeably.

In his *Manifesto for a Skeptical Africa*, Nigerian human rights advocate Leo Igwe, explains that in Africa 'science, critical thinking and tech savvy' are seen as Western values. By taking a rational approach, he says, one betrays one's culture. This was made evident in South Africa when Mbeki's health minister dismissed The Durban Declaration (a statement signed by over 5,000 physicians and scientists, affirming that HIV is the cause of AIDS) as an 'elitist document'.

African hostility to Western intervention is not unjustified. In South Africa people have recent memories of an oppressive white establishment denying them rights. Across the continent, there are living memories of European and American doctors conducting unethical medical trials, exploiting Africa's poorest people's poverty, scientific illiteracy and desperation.

One of the most horrific consequences of Africa's rejection of critical thinking is the persecution of people with albinism. In parts of northern Africa, people with albinism are murdered in witch hunts perpetuated by Christian ministers. In southern Africa they live in fear of being killed or dismembered, cut up and sold as charms that promise luck, money or fertility. The persistent myth that underlies these crimes is that people with albinism are not really people. In the words of the Albinism Society of South Africa: '[it is believed that] when people with albinism die, they simply vanish.'

Reasonable suspicion of Western ideas has metastasized into either rejection or confusion about science and critical thinking. Leo Igwe is one of many African rationalists calling for an African Enlightenment to protect his continent from deadly diseases, superstitious killings and exploitation. For that to happen, people like him have to speak the truth, and people outside Africa must support them. In the words of Nozizwe Madlala-Routledge, the former deputy health minister of South Africa, who sacrificed her career under Mbeki by contradicting his AIDS denialism:

> *It is important that I say the truth, because that is what sustains me. This is not 'my' truth. But it is* the *truth. The values that taught us it is possible to fight an enemy like apartheid, which appeared impossible to defeat. It is that truth.*

Our ancestors used the truth to scare away bogeymen like the tokoloshe from under their children's beds. To create a better future for children in Africa we need to be unapologetic advocates for this same truth. Not *our* truth, but *the* truth.

More information, discussion and links at
doubtcomic.com/snake-oil-shaman

CHAKRAS DON'T SPIN

Yoga Studio, Coogee, Sydney, Australia

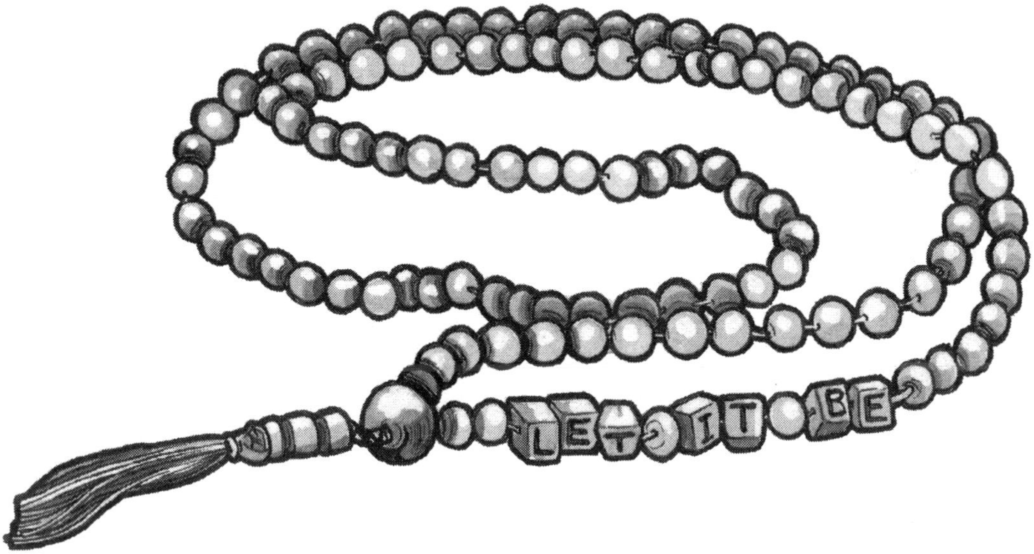

LET IT BE

YEAH, THAT'S WHAT HE SAID. I JUST HEARD SO MANY STORIES ABOUT PEOPLE BEING *MIRACULOUSLY* 'FIXED' AFTER THEIR FIRST ADJUSTMENT THAT I WAS *DISAPPOINTED*, YOU KNOW?

...MORE SESSIONS BEFORE IT STARTS *WORKING.*

I JUST FEEL SORT OF *CLEANER.* I DIDN'T FEEL *BAD* BEFORE, BUT LOOKING BACK I WAS TIRED A LOT AND JUST GENERALLY *'DOWN'.*

ARE YOU STILL TAKING THAT HOMEOPATHIC *TINCTURE?*

...NOT SURPRISED, ...ST THINK OF ALL ...E *CHEMICALS* AND ...NESS KNOWS WHAT ...HAT YOU *USED* TO BE EATING.

OH THE *BYRONIA.* YES, MAYBE IT'S HELPING A BIT, BUT I STILL HAVE THE *PAIN* AND IT'S REALLY BAD TOWARDS THE END OF THE DAY.

MAYBE IT'S NON-PHYSICAL...? ... MEAN IT MIGHT B... AN *EMOTIONAL* PAIN JUST SORT ... LOCKED INTO YOU... BACK?

WELL, I'M SURE I'M STILL EATING *SOME* GMOS. YOU NEVER KNOW WHAT'S IN *RESTAURANT* FOOD OR WHATEVER...

...BUT AT LEAST ...VERYTHING YOU ...AKE YOURSELF IS *NATURAL.*

EVERY YOGA CLASS I'VE EVER BEEN TO HAS THIS SAME VIBE. ATTRACTIVE MIDDLE-AGED WOMEN PERHAPS OVERLY CONCERNED ABOUT THEIR SPIRITUAL AND PHYSICAL HEALTH. OPEN-MINDED ENOUGH TO TRY *ALTERNATIVE* IDEAS.

IT'S A CULTURE THAT FEELS FAMILIAR AND *COMFORTABLE.* TOTALLY NON-JUDGEMENTAL.

WE SETTLE DOWN. CONVERSATIONS HUSH AND WE LIE JUST BREATHING TOGETHER.

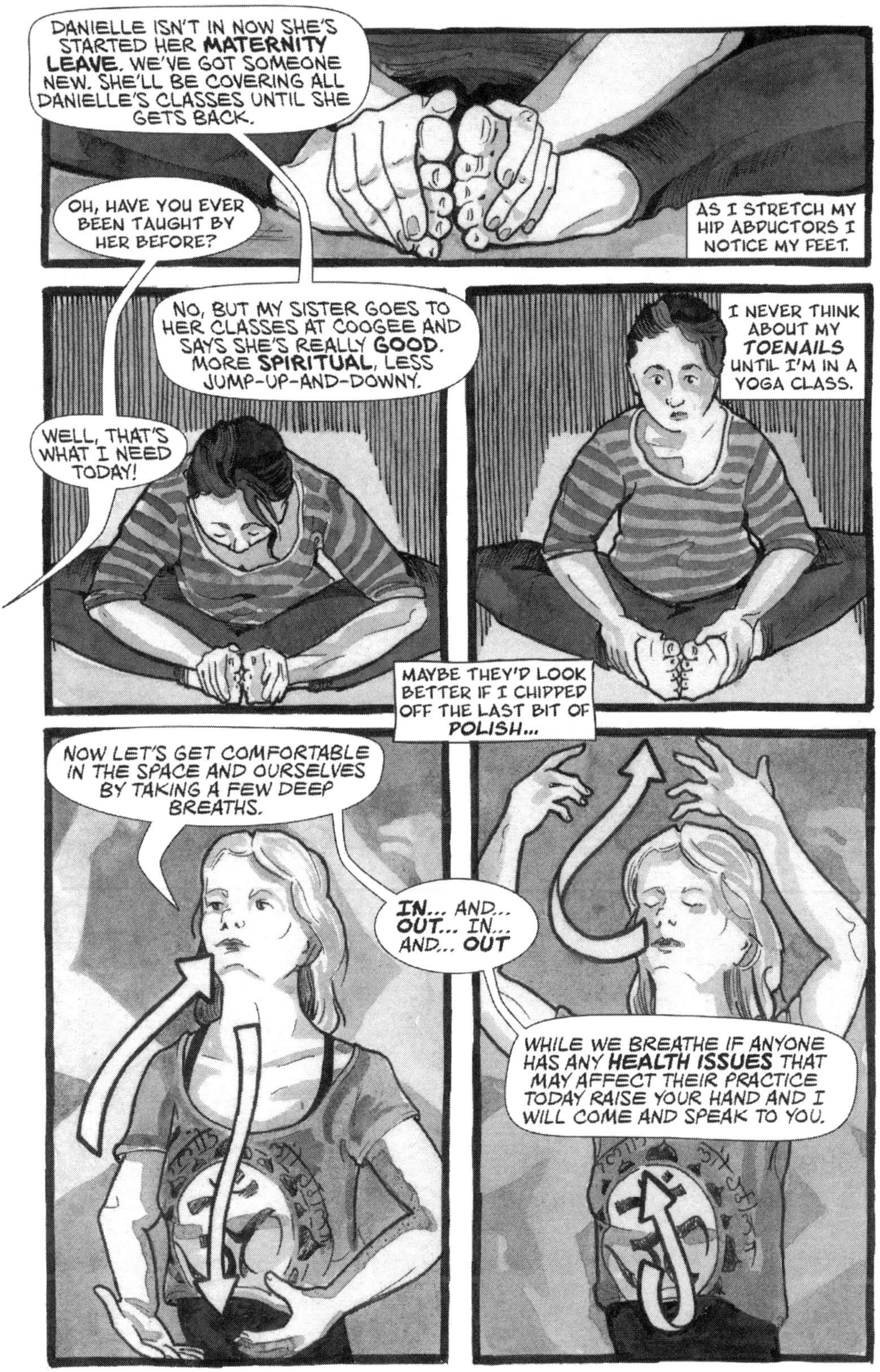
DANIELLE ISN'T IN NOW SHE'S STARTED HER **MATERNITY LEAVE**. WE'VE GOT SOMEONE NEW. SHE'LL BE COVERING ALL DANIELLE'S CLASSES UNTIL SHE GETS BACK.
OH, HAVE YOU EVER BEEN TAUGHT BY HER BEFORE?
AS I STRETCH MY HIP ABDUCTORS I NOTICE MY FEET.
NO, BUT MY SISTER GOES TO HER CLASSES AT COOGEE AND SAYS SHE'S REALLY **GOOD**. MORE **SPIRITUAL**, LESS JUMP-UP-AND-DOWNY.
WELL, THAT'S WHAT I NEED TODAY!
I NEVER THINK ABOUT MY ***TOENAILS*** UNTIL I'M IN A YOGA CLASS.
MAYBE THEY'D LOOK BETTER IF I CHIPPED OFF THE LAST BIT OF ***POLISH...***
NOW LET'S GET COMFORTABLE IN THE SPACE AND OURSELVES BY TAKING A FEW DEEP BREATHS.
IN... AND... ***OUT...*** IN... AND... ***OUT***
WHILE WE BREATHE IF ANYONE HAS ANY ***HEALTH ISSUES*** THAT MAY AFFECT THEIR PRACTICE TODAY RAISE YOUR HAND AND I WILL COME AND SPEAK TO YOU.

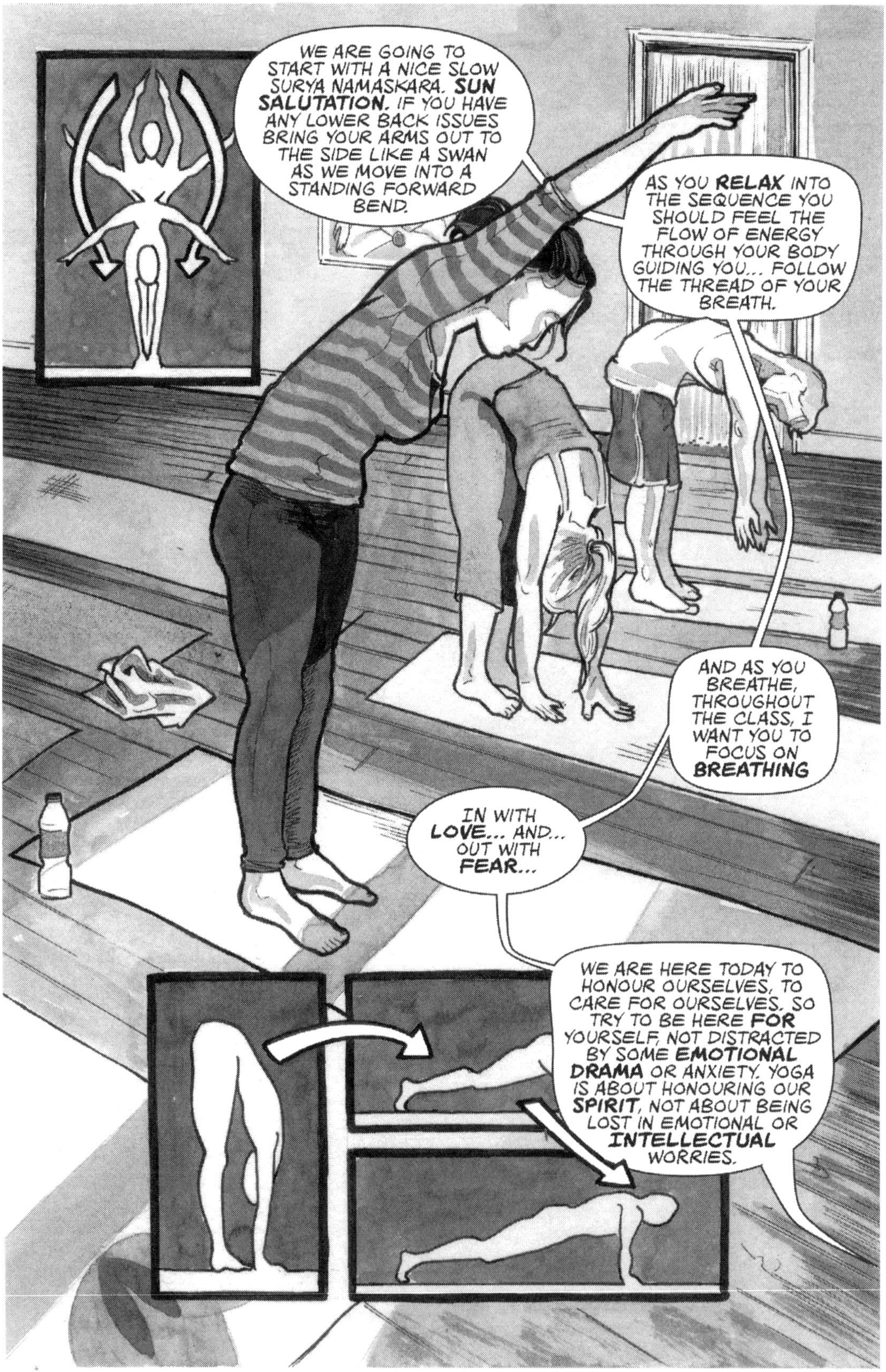
WE ARE GOING TO START WITH A NICE SLOW SURYA NAMASKARA. **SUN SALUTATION.** IF YOU HAVE ANY LOWER BACK ISSUES BRING YOUR ARMS OUT TO THE SIDE LIKE A SWAN AS WE MOVE INTO A STANDING FORWARD BEND.
AS YOU **RELAX** INTO THE SEQUENCE YOU SHOULD FEEL THE FLOW OF ENERGY THROUGH YOUR BODY GUIDING YOU... FOLLOW THE THREAD OF YOUR BREATH.
AND AS YOU BREATHE, THROUGHOUT THE CLASS, I WANT YOU TO FOCUS ON **BREATHING**
IN WITH **LOVE...** AND... OUT WITH **FEAR...**
WE ARE HERE TODAY TO HONOUR OURSELVES, TO CARE FOR OURSELVES. SO TRY TO BE HERE **FOR** YOURSELF, NOT DISTRACTED BY SOME **EMOTIONAL DRAMA** OR ANXIETY. YOGA IS ABOUT HONOURING OUR **SPIRIT**, NOT ABOUT BEING LOST IN EMOTIONAL OR **INTELLECTUAL** WORRIES.

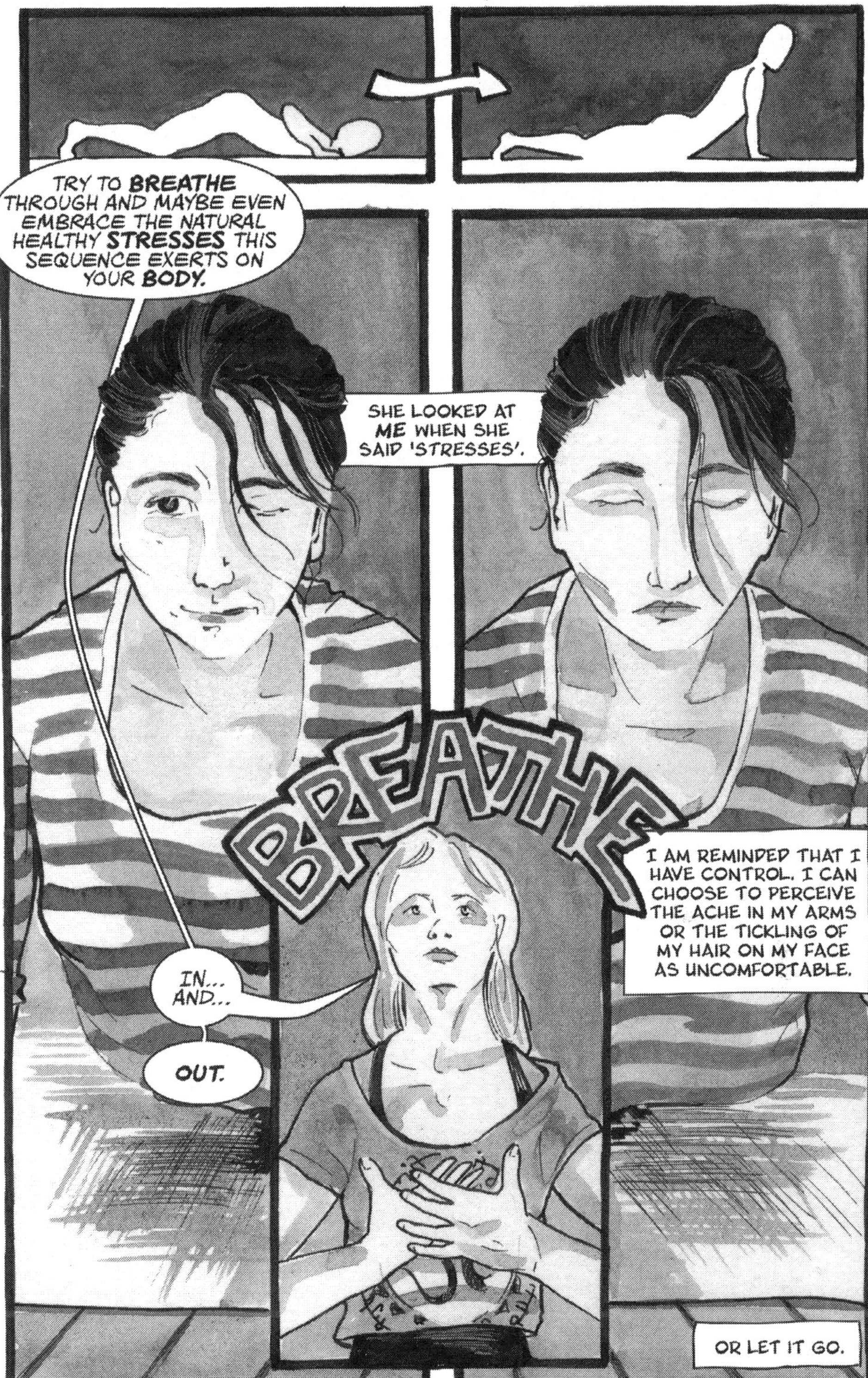
TRY TO BREATHE THROUGH AND MAYBE EVEN EMBRACE THE NATURAL HEALTHY STRESSES THIS SEQUENCE EXERTS ON YOUR BODY.
SHE LOOKED AT ME WHEN SHE SAID 'STRESSES'.
BREATHE
IN... AND...
OUT.
I AM REMINDED THAT I HAVE CONTROL. I CAN CHOOSE TO PERCEIVE THE ACHE IN MY ARMS OR THE TICKLING OF MY HAIR ON MY FACE AS UNCOMFORTABLE.
OR LET IT GO.

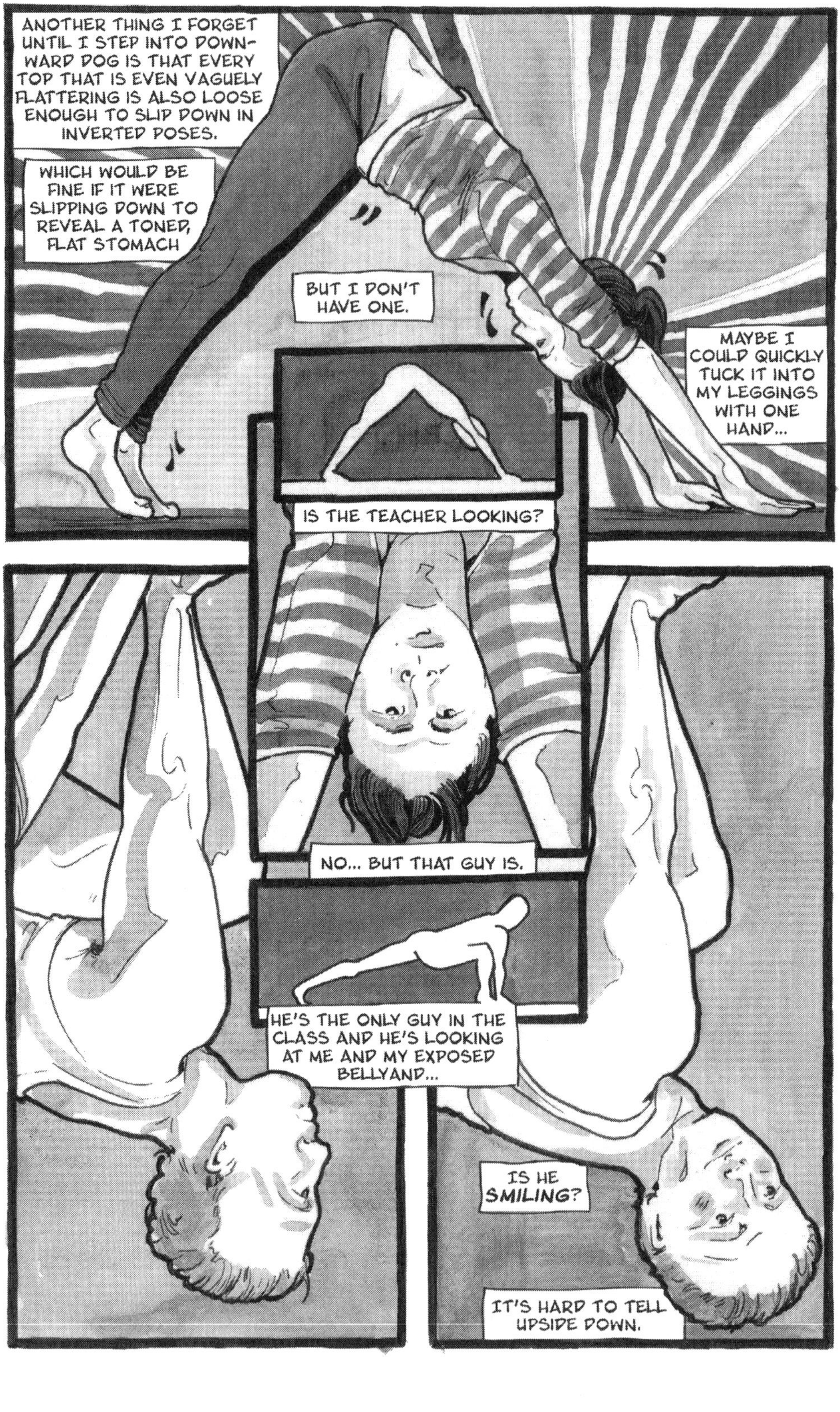
ANOTHER THING I FORGET UNTIL I STEP INTO DOWNWARD DOG IS THAT EVERY TOP THAT IS EVEN VAGUELY FLATTERING IS ALSO LOOSE ENOUGH TO SLIP DOWN IN INVERTED POSES.
WHICH WOULD BE FINE IF IT WERE SLIPPING DOWN TO REVEAL A TONED, FLAT STOMACH
BUT I DON'T HAVE ONE.
MAYBE I COULD QUICKLY TUCK IT INTO MY LEGGINGS WITH ONE HAND...
IS THE TEACHER LOOKING?
NO... BUT THAT GUY IS.
HE'S THE ONLY GUY IN THE CLASS AND HE'S LOOKING AT ME AND MY EXPOSED BELLYAND...
IS HE SMILING?
IT'S HARD TO TELL UPSIDE DOWN.

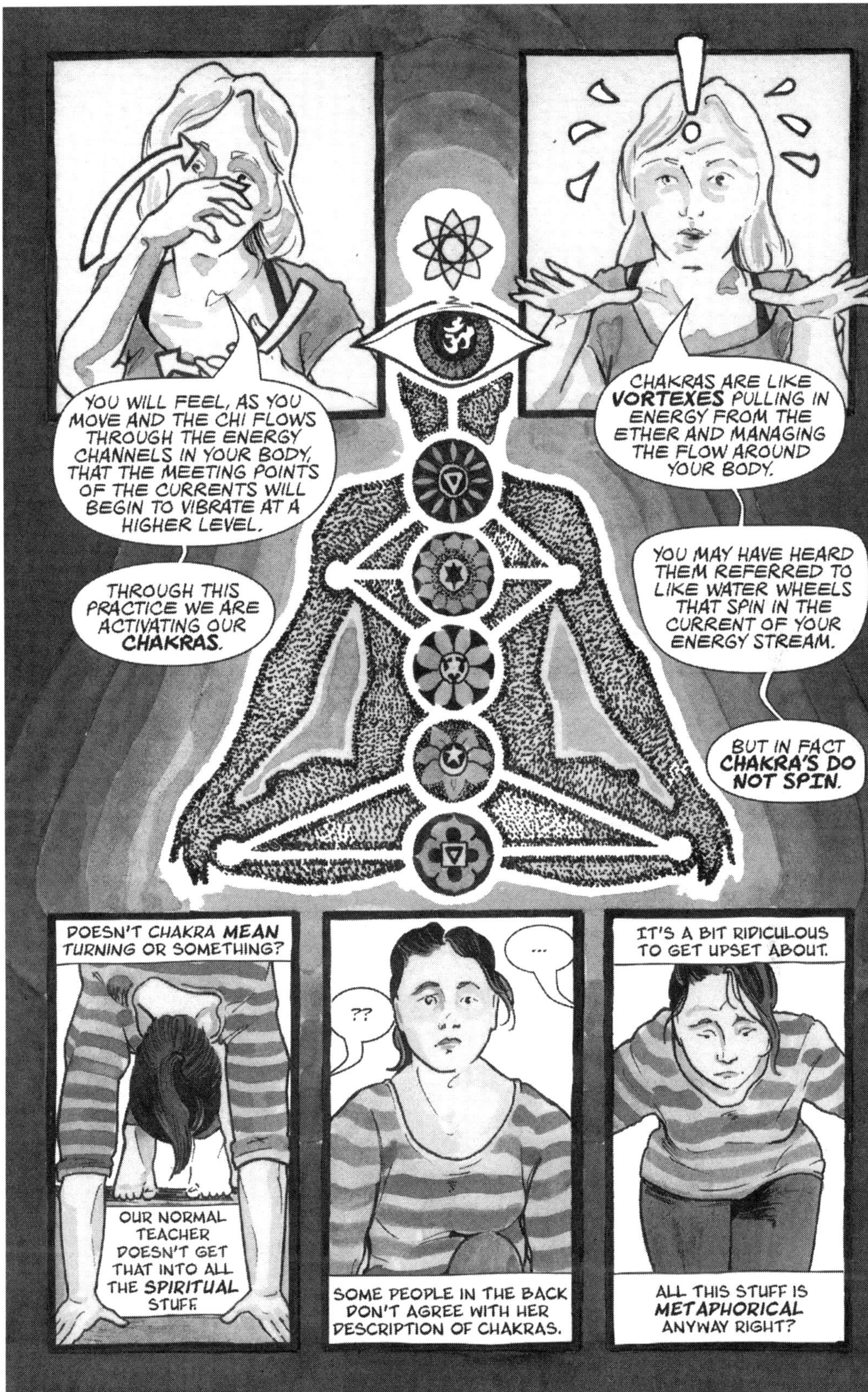

YOU WILL FEEL, AS YOU MOVE AND THE CHI FLOWS THROUGH THE ENERGY CHANNELS IN YOUR BODY, THAT THE MEETING POINTS OF THE CURRENTS WILL BEGIN TO VIBRATE AT A HIGHER LEVEL.
THROUGH THIS PRACTICE WE ARE ACTIVATING OUR CHAKRAS.
CHAKRAS ARE LIKE VORTEXES PULLING IN ENERGY FROM THE ETHER AND MANAGING THE FLOW AROUND YOUR BODY.
YOU MAY HAVE HEARD THEM REFERRED TO LIKE WATER WHEELS THAT SPIN IN THE CURRENT OF YOUR ENERGY STREAM.
BUT IN FACT CHAKRA'S DO NOT SPIN.
DOESN'T CHAKRA MEAN TURNING OR SOMETHING?
OUR NORMAL TEACHER DOESN'T GET THAT INTO ALL THE SPIRITUAL STUFF.
??
...
SOME PEOPLE IN THE BACK DON'T AGREE WITH HER DESCRIPTION OF CHAKRAS.
IT'S A BIT RIDICULOUS TO GET UPSET ABOUT.
ALL THIS STUFF IS METAPHORICAL ANYWAY RIGHT?

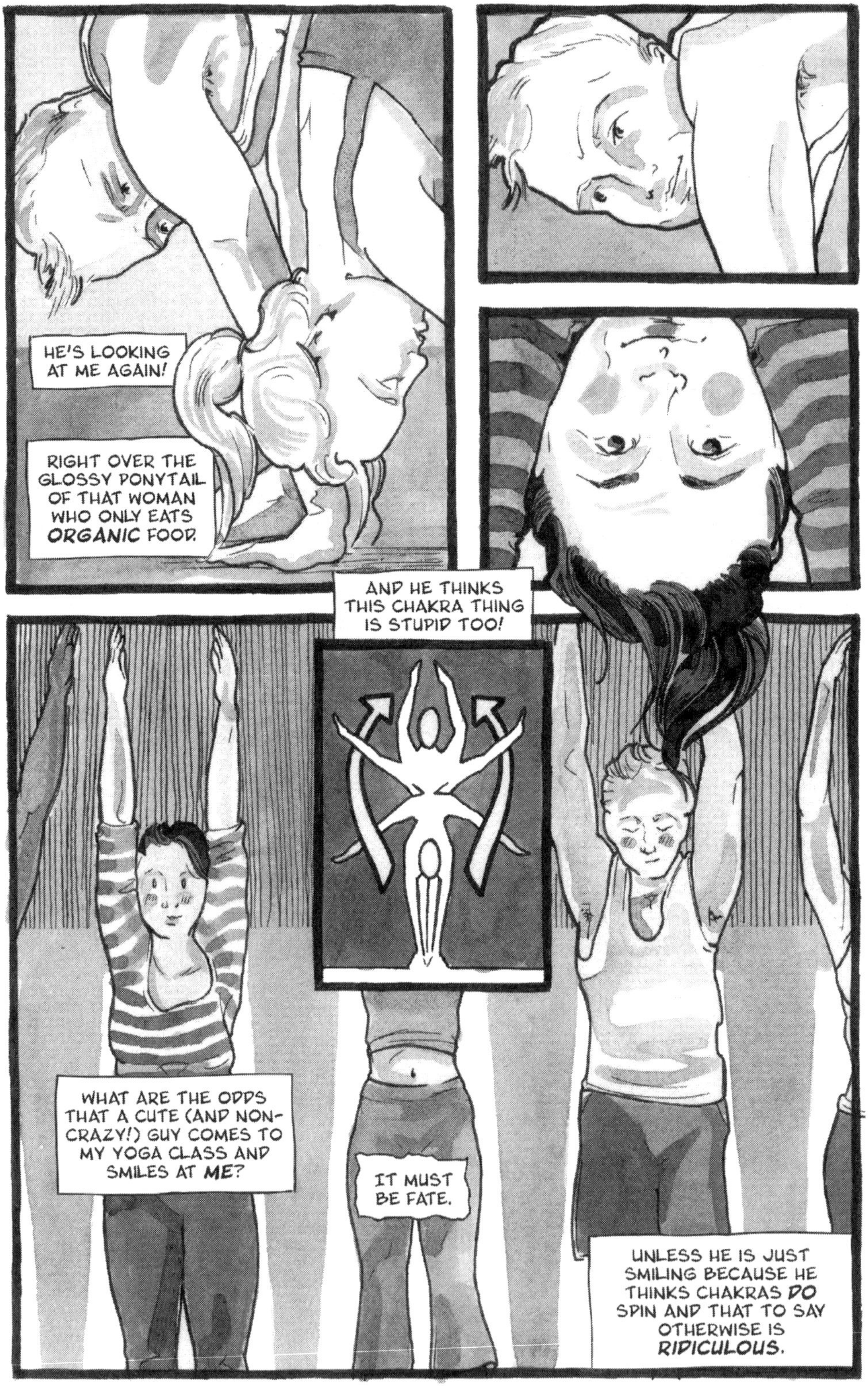
HE'S LOOKING AT ME AGAIN!
RIGHT OVER THE GLOSSY PONYTAIL OF THAT WOMAN WHO ONLY EATS ORGANIC FOOD.
AND HE THINKS THIS CHAKRA THING IS STUPID TOO!
WHAT ARE THE ODDS THAT A CUTE (AND NON-CRAZY!) GUY COMES TO MY YOGA CLASS AND SMILES AT ME?
IT MUST BE FATE.
UNLESS HE IS JUST SMILING BECAUSE HE THINKS CHAKRAS DO SPIN AND THAT TO SAY OTHERWISE IS RIDICULOUS.

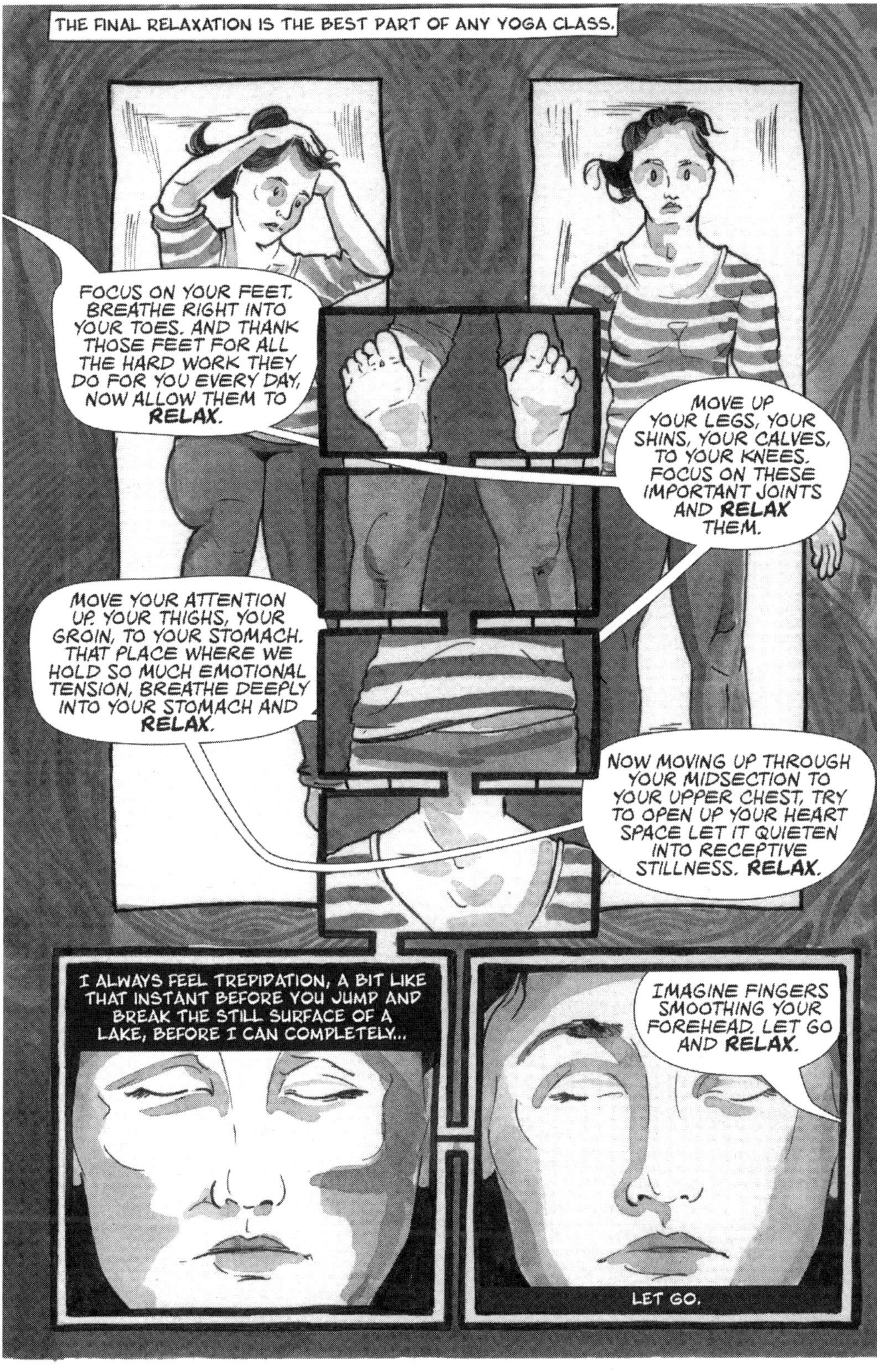
THE FINAL RELAXATION IS THE BEST PART OF ANY YOGA CLASS.
FOCUS ON YOUR FEET. BREATHE RIGHT INTO YOUR TOES. AND THANK THOSE FEET FOR ALL THE HARD WORK THEY DO FOR YOU EVERY DAY, NOW ALLOW THEM TO **RELAX**.
MOVE UP YOUR LEGS, YOUR SHINS, YOUR CALVES, TO YOUR KNEES. FOCUS ON THESE IMPORTANT JOINTS AND **RELAX** THEM.
MOVE YOUR ATTENTION UP. YOUR THIGHS, YOUR GROIN, TO YOUR STOMACH. THAT PLACE WHERE WE HOLD SO MUCH EMOTIONAL TENSION, BREATHE DEEPLY INTO YOUR STOMACH AND **RELAX**.
NOW MOVING UP THROUGH YOUR MIDSECTION TO YOUR UPPER CHEST, TRY TO OPEN UP YOUR HEART SPACE LET IT QUIETEN INTO RECEPTIVE STILLNESS. **RELAX**.
I ALWAYS FEEL TREPIDATION, A BIT LIKE THAT INSTANT BEFORE YOU JUMP AND BREAK THE STILL SURFACE OF A LAKE, BEFORE I CAN COMPLETELY...
IMAGINE FINGERS SMOOTHING YOUR FOREHEAD. LET GO AND **RELAX**.
LET GO.

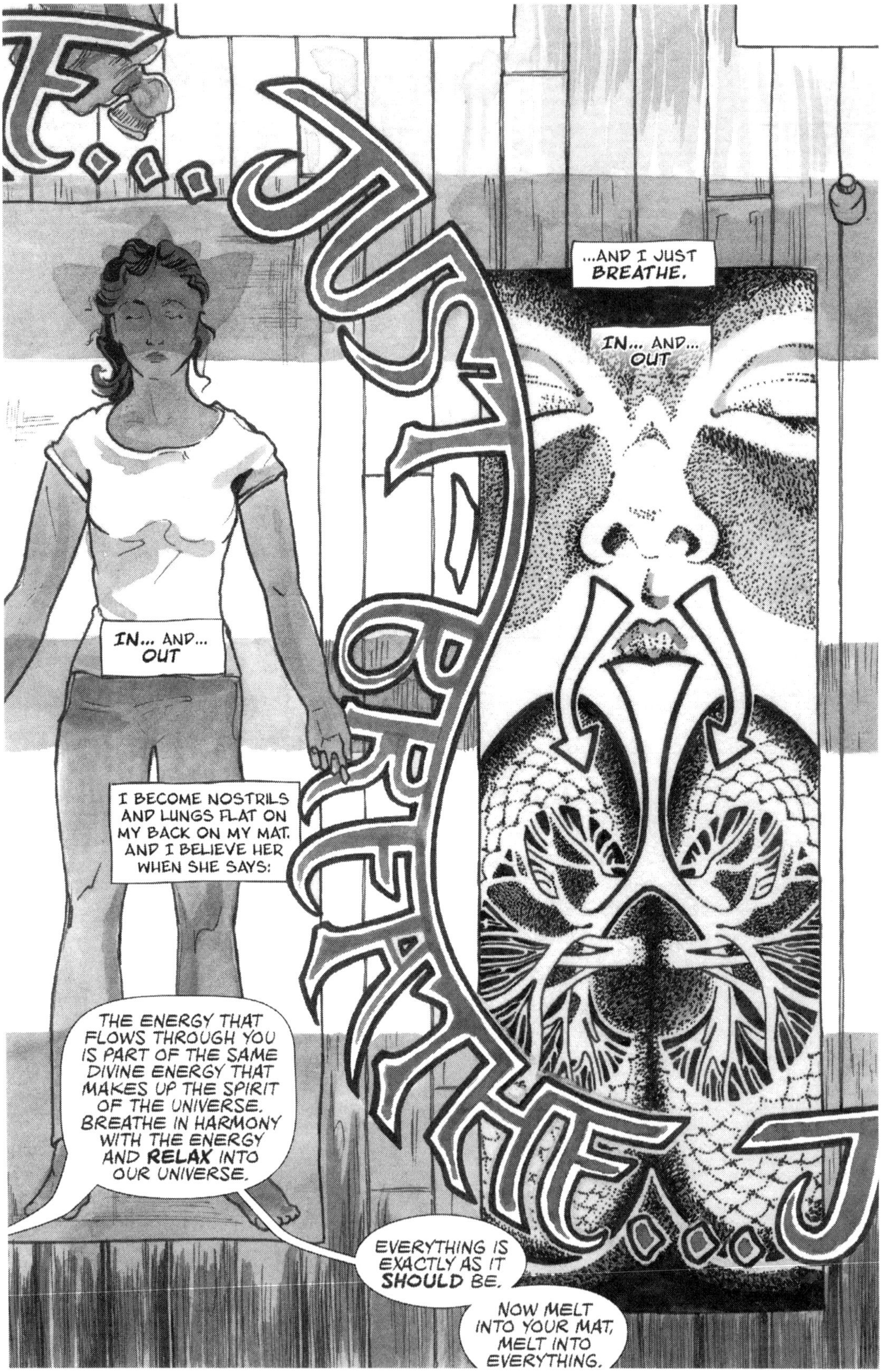

...JUST BREATHE...
...AND I JUST BREATHE.
IN... AND... OUT
IN... AND... OUT
I BECOME NOSTRILS AND LUNGS FLAT ON MY BACK ON MY MAT. AND I BELIEVE HER WHEN SHE SAYS:
THE ENERGY THAT FLOWS THROUGH YOU IS PART OF THE SAME DIVINE ENERGY THAT MAKES UP THE SPIRIT OF THE UNIVERSE. BREATHE IN HARMONY WITH THE ENERGY AND RELAX INTO OUR UNIVERSE.
EVERYTHING IS EXACTLY AS IT SHOULD BE.
NOW MELT INTO YOUR MAT, MELT INTO EVERYTHING.

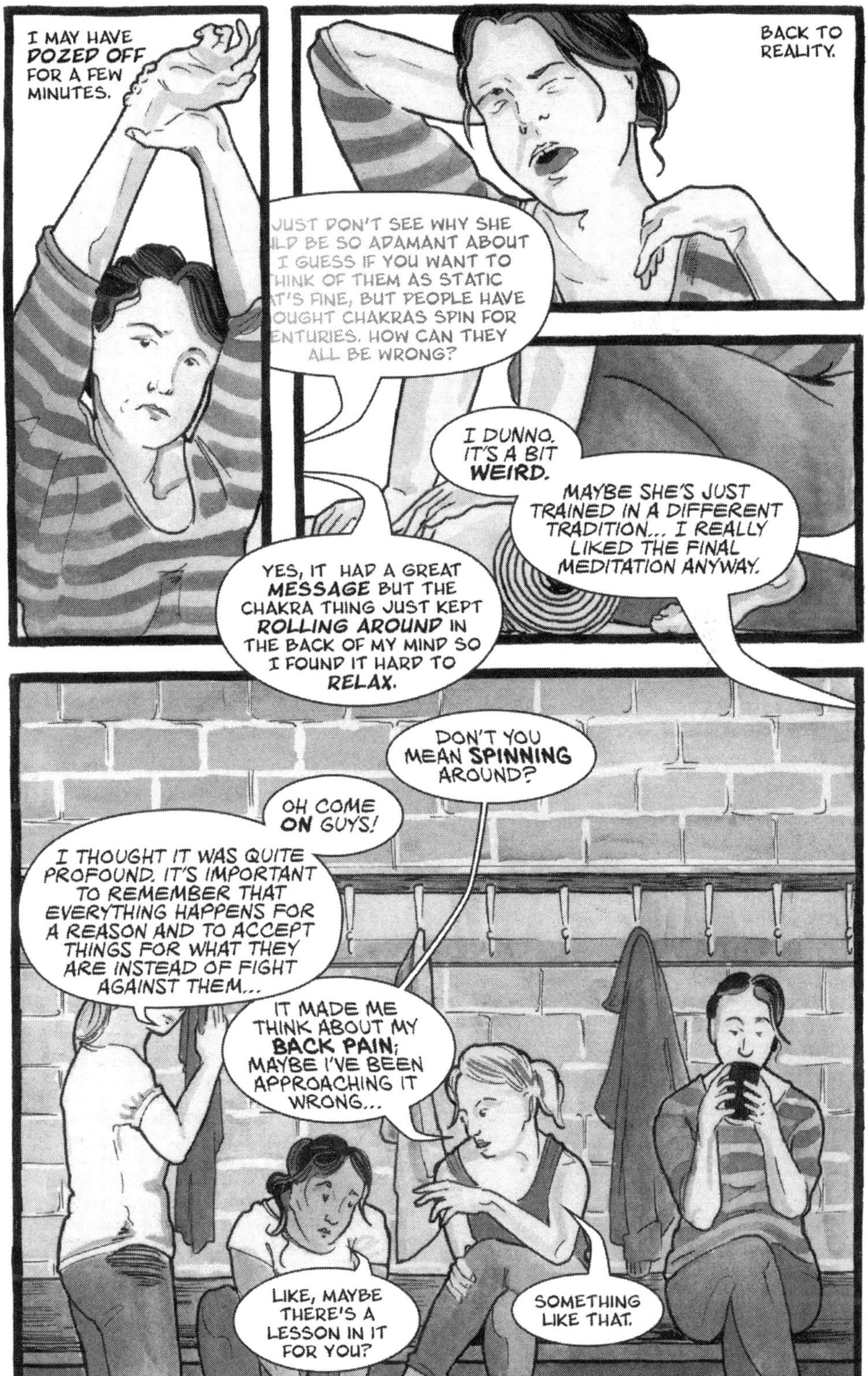
I MAY HAVE **DOZED OFF** FOR A FEW MINUTES.
BACK TO REALITY.
JUST DON'T SEE WHY SHE ULD BE SO ADAMANT ABOUT I GUESS IF YOU WANT TO THINK OF THEM AS STATIC AT'S FINE, BUT PEOPLE HAVE OUGHT CHAKRAS SPIN FOR ENTURIES. HOW CAN THEY ALL BE WRONG?
I DUNNO. IT'S A BIT **WEIRD.**
MAYBE SHE'S JUST TRAINED IN A DIFFERENT TRADITION... I REALLY LIKED THE FINAL MEDITATION ANYWAY.
YES, IT HAD A GREAT **MESSAGE** BUT THE CHAKRA THING JUST KEPT **ROLLING AROUND** IN THE BACK OF MY MIND SO I FOUND IT HARD TO **RELAX.**
DON'T YOU MEAN **SPINNING** AROUND?
OH COME **ON** GUYS!
I THOUGHT IT WAS QUITE PROFOUND. IT'S IMPORTANT TO REMEMBER THAT EVERYTHING HAPPENS FOR A REASON AND TO ACCEPT THINGS FOR WHAT THEY ARE INSTEAD OF FIGHT AGAINST THEM...
IT MADE ME THINK ABOUT MY **BACK PAIN**; MAYBE I'VE BEEN APPROACHING IT WRONG...
LIKE, MAYBE THERE'S A LESSON IN IT FOR YOU?
SOMETHING LIKE THAT.

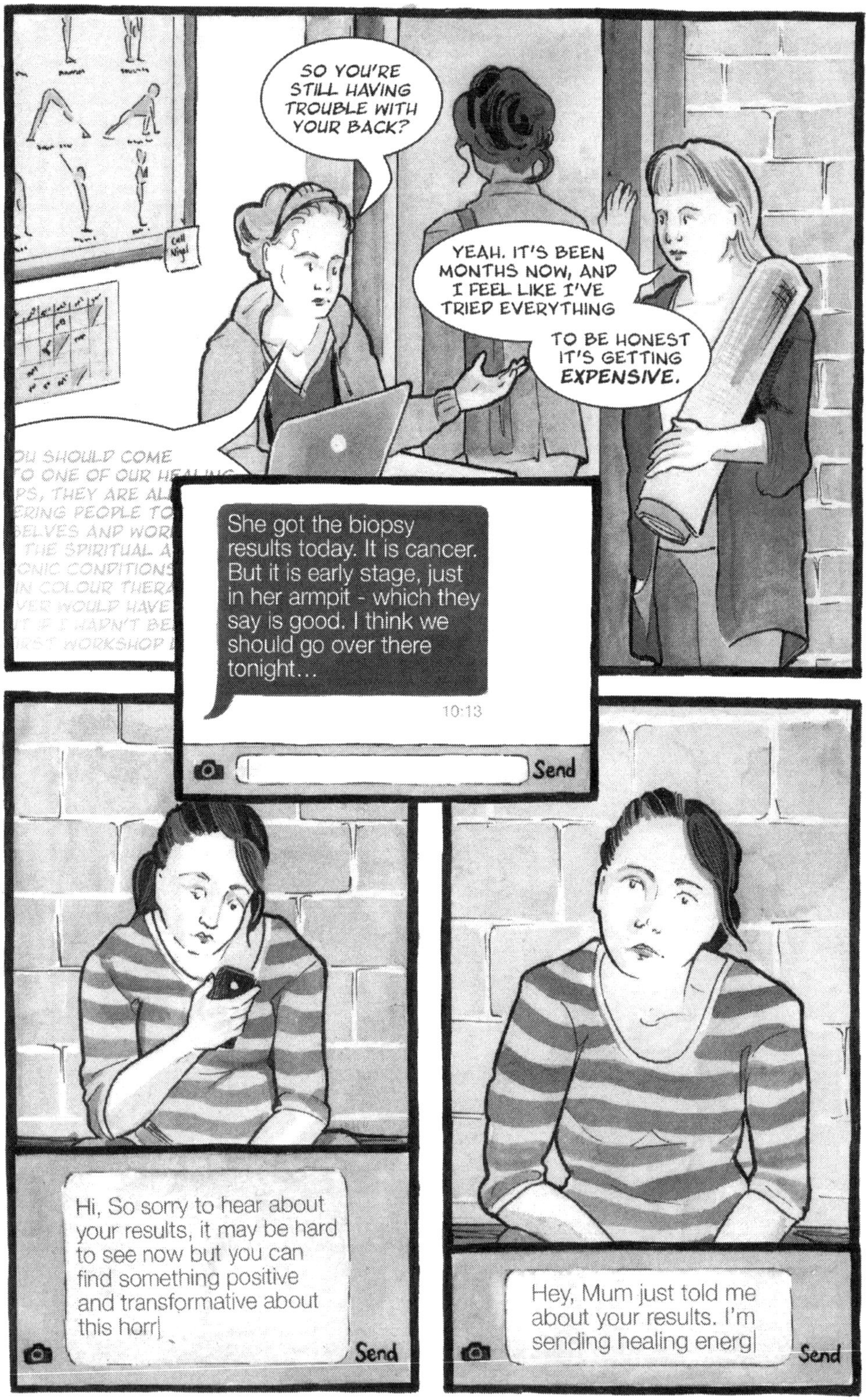
SO YOU'RE STILL HAVING TROUBLE WITH YOUR BACK?
YEAH. IT'S BEEN MONTHS NOW, AND I FEEL LIKE I'VE TRIED EVERYTHING
TO BE HONEST IT'S GETTING EXPENSIVE.
OU SHOULD COME
TO ONE OF OUR HE
PS, THEY ARE AL
ERING PEOPLE TO
SELVES AND WOR
THE SPIRITUAL A
ONIC CONDITIONS
N COLOUR THERA
VER WOULD HAVE
T IF I HADN'T BE
RST WORKSHOP
She got the biopsy results today. It is cancer. But it is early stage, just in her armpit - which they say is good. I think we should go over there tonight…
10:13
Send
Hi, So sorry to hear about your results, it may be hard to see now but you can find something positive and transformative about this horr|
Send
Hey, Mum just told me about your results. I'm sending healing energ|
Send

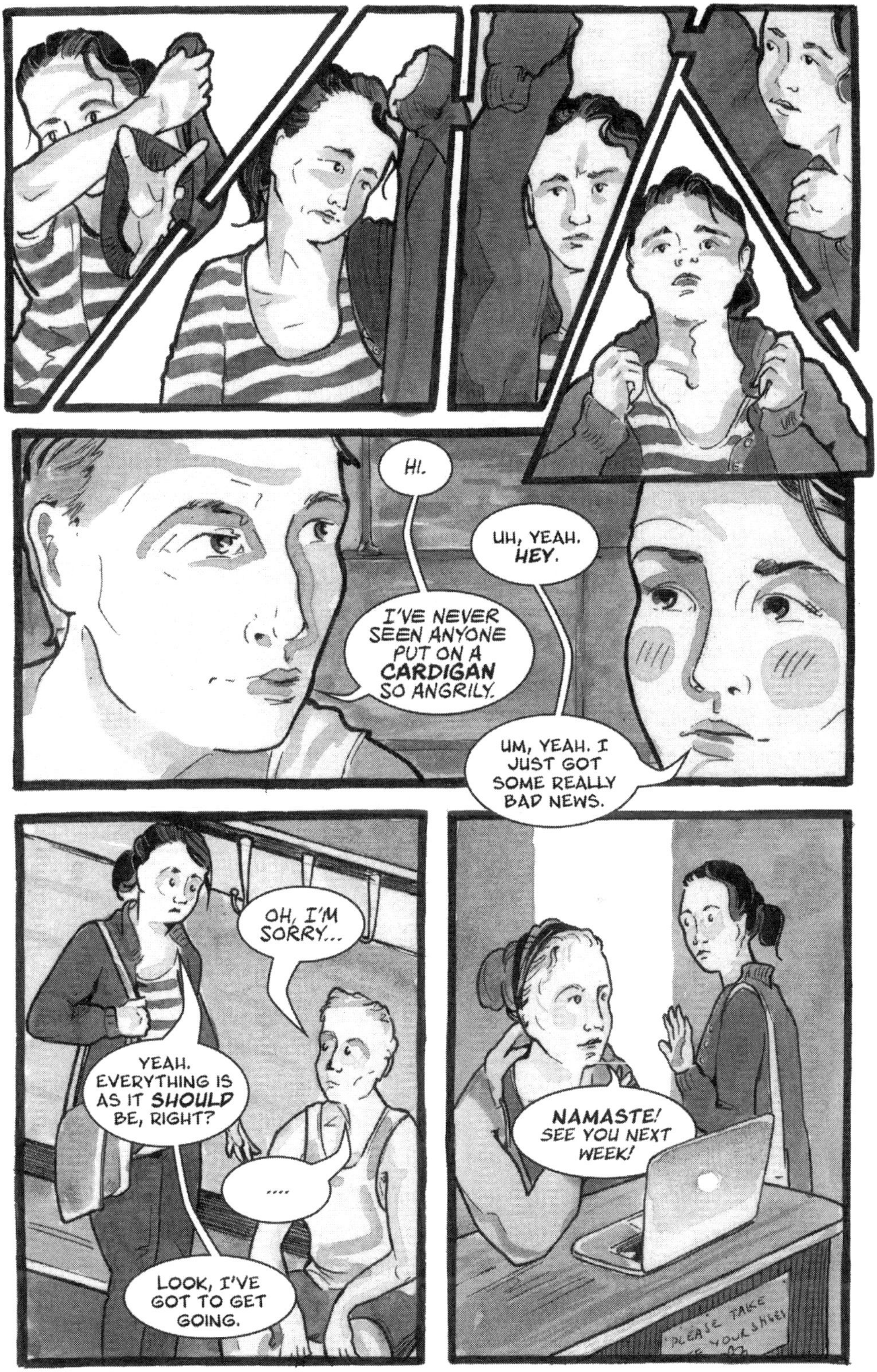
HI.
UH, YEAH. **HEY**.
I'VE NEVER SEEN ANYONE PUT ON A **CARDIGAN** SO ANGRILY.
UM, YEAH. I JUST GOT SOME REALLY BAD NEWS.
OH, I'M SORRY...
YEAH. EVERYTHING IS AS IT **SHOULD** BE, RIGHT?
....
LOOK, I'VE GOT TO GET GOING.
NAMASTE!
SEE YOU NEXT WEEK!
PLEASE TAKE

New Age ideas once seemed, well, new. Now they seem to have integrated into middle class Western culture. As someone who enjoys gentle exercise and a plant-based diet, I often find myself surrounded by aisles of alternative medicine and esoteric ideas in the yoga studio, vegan cafe or health food shop.

Complementary (or 'alternative') medicine is a long parade of remedies, interventions and practices. Some are ancient, some are modern, some have evidence suggestive of possible efficacy, many have evidence of non-efficacy or harm. The commonality that these types of 'medicines' share is that none originate in evidence gathered using the scientific method. As Tim Minchin opines in his jazz poem *Storm*:

> *By definition, I begin*
> *Alternative Medicine, I continue,*
> *Has either not been proved to work,*
> *Or been proved not to work.*
> *Do you know what they call*
> *Alternative medicine*
> *That's been proved to work?*
> *Medicine.*

The New Age ideas that populate these venues are as diverse as the forms of alternative medicine, but may be even harder to define. Perhaps the closest thing they have to a defining characteristic is that they all employ some foundational belief in a supernatural force or 'energy'.

One conception of the supernatural is the idea of some sort of divine balance, or purpose. The common phrase 'everything happens for a reason' is an expression of this principle. This is an example of the just-world hypothesis – a cognitive bias that leads people to think that there is a universal force which ensures a moral balance, sometimes characterised as karma, fate or destiny.

You can see why believing that 'everything is as it should be' would be comforting. No matter what discomfort you are currently undergoing, you can be sure it is either a just punishment from which you will learn or a necessary hardship to undergo before you are rewarded. It's particularly comforting if you are in a position of powerlessness, accepting the inevitable instead of fighting against it is not unwise.

Social psychologist Melvin Lerner, who coined the term 'just-world hypothesis', was curious about why people accept situations that cause suffering in themselves and others. In his studies he found that his subjects were quick to derogate those who were suffering, be they mentally ill, impoverished or losers in an experimental game. He theorised that we want to see the world as ordered and fair, and when we see something that seems to negate that vision, we are more likely to blame the victim of misfortune than accept the world may be random or cruel.

The people in the health food shops and yoga studios I frequent are predominantly middle class women in their early adulthood. They are the women who have the time for daytime yoga classes or making healthy food from scratch; often stay at home mothers or people with flexible work schedules. In previous generations, women in this demographic worked in charitable organisations, volunteered as Sunday School teachers, founded the feminist movement and won us the right to vote. It was their dissatisfaction with the status quo that motivated them to change the world.

If you think the world should be fair, and you see evidence that it is not you have two choices. One is to disregard the evidence and accept that whatever may appear to be wrong is part of some bigger plan. The second is to recognise the injustice and rally against it.

I resent the aspects of this culture that perpetuate irrationality and panglossianism because they stifle intelligent, compassionate people. Instead of changing the world, we are discouraged from critical thinking by those who want to sell us placebos. They take our money and our dissatisfaction in return for false hope and apathy.

More information, discussion and links at
doubtcomic.com/chrakras-dont-spin

BORN OF WATER
MEDIUM-SIZED TOWN, NORTH AMERICA

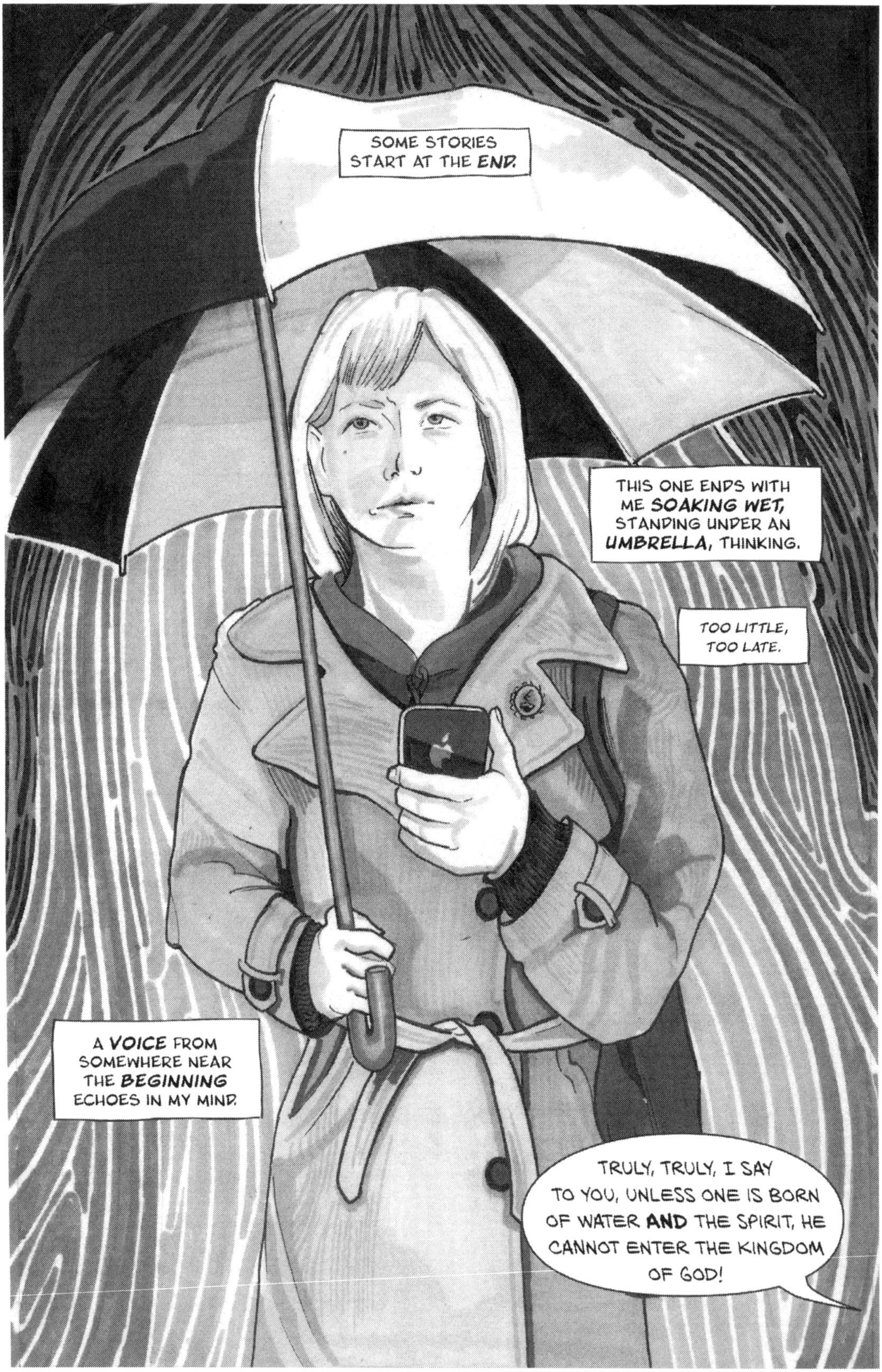
SOME STORIES START AT THE **END.**
THIS ONE ENDS WITH ME **SOAKING WET,** STANDING UNDER AN **UMBRELLA,** THINKING.
TOO LITTLE, TOO LATE.
A **VOICE** FROM SOMEWHERE NEAR THE **BEGINNING** ECHOES IN MY MIND.
TRULY, TRULY, I SAY TO YOU, UNLESS ONE IS BORN OF WATER **AND** THE SPIRIT, HE CANNOT ENTER THE KINGDOM OF GOD!

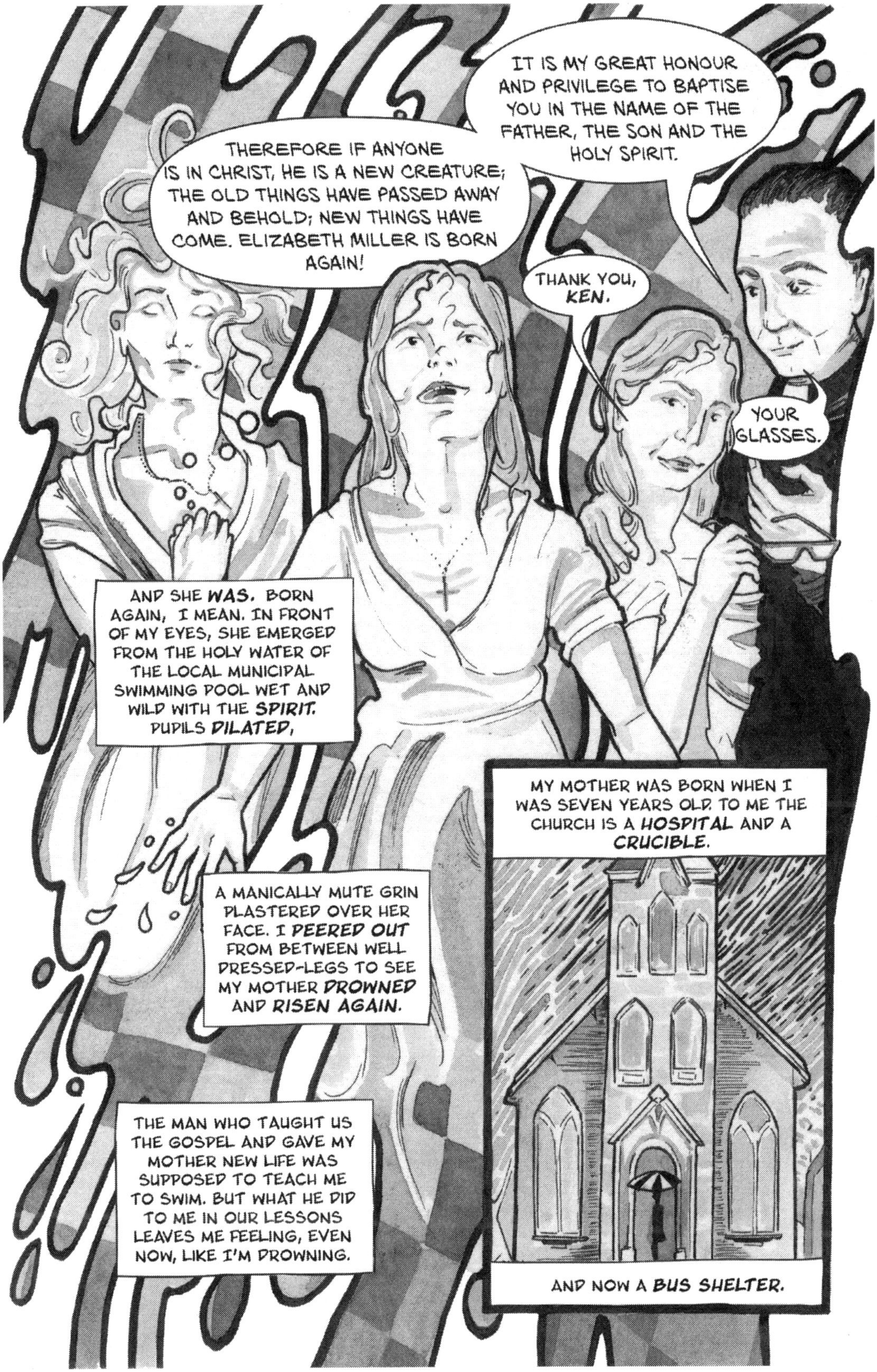
THEREFORE IF ANYONE IS IN CHRIST, HE IS A NEW CREATURE; THE OLD THINGS HAVE PASSED AWAY AND BEHOLD; NEW THINGS HAVE COME. ELIZABETH MILLER IS BORN AGAIN!
IT IS MY GREAT HONOUR AND PRIVILEGE TO BAPTISE YOU IN THE NAME OF THE FATHER, THE SON AND THE HOLY SPIRIT.
THANK YOU, KEN.
YOUR GLASSES.
AND SHE WAS. BORN AGAIN, I MEAN. IN FRONT OF MY EYES, SHE EMERGED FROM THE HOLY WATER OF THE LOCAL MUNICIPAL SWIMMING POOL WET AND WILD WITH THE SPIRIT. PUPILS DILATED,
A MANICALLY MUTE GRIN PLASTERED OVER HER FACE. I PEERED OUT FROM BETWEEN WELL DRESSED-LEGS TO SEE MY MOTHER DROWNED AND RISEN AGAIN.
THE MAN WHO TAUGHT US THE GOSPEL AND GAVE MY MOTHER NEW LIFE WAS SUPPOSED TO TEACH ME TO SWIM. BUT WHAT HE DID TO ME IN OUR LESSONS LEAVES ME FEELING, EVEN NOW, LIKE I'M DROWNING.
MY MOTHER WAS BORN WHEN I WAS SEVEN YEARS OLD. TO ME THE CHURCH IS A HOSPITAL AND A CRUCIBLE.
AND NOW A BUS SHELTER.

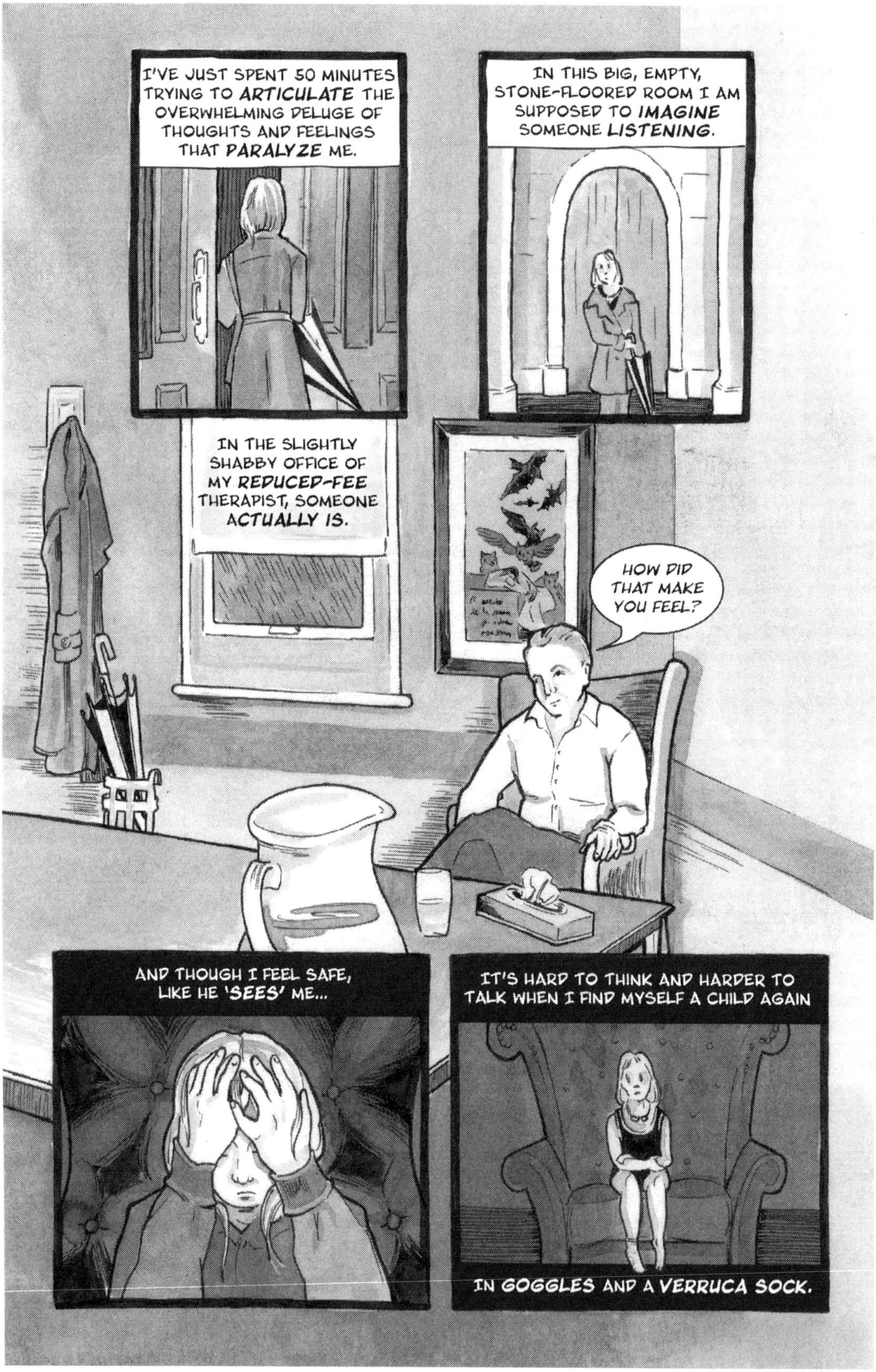
I'VE JUST SPENT 50 MINUTES TRYING TO ARTICULATE THE OVERWHELMING DELUGE OF THOUGHTS AND FEELINGS THAT PARALYZE ME.
IN THIS BIG, EMPTY, STONE-FLOORED ROOM I AM SUPPOSED TO IMAGINE SOMEONE LISTENING.
IN THE SLIGHTLY SHABBY OFFICE OF MY REDUCED-FEE THERAPIST, SOMEONE ACTUALLY IS.
HOW DID THAT MAKE YOU FEEL?
AND THOUGH I FEEL SAFE, LIKE HE 'SEES' ME...
IT'S HARD TO THINK AND HARDER TO TALK WHEN I FIND MYSELF A CHILD AGAIN
IN GOGGLES AND A VERRUCA SOCK.

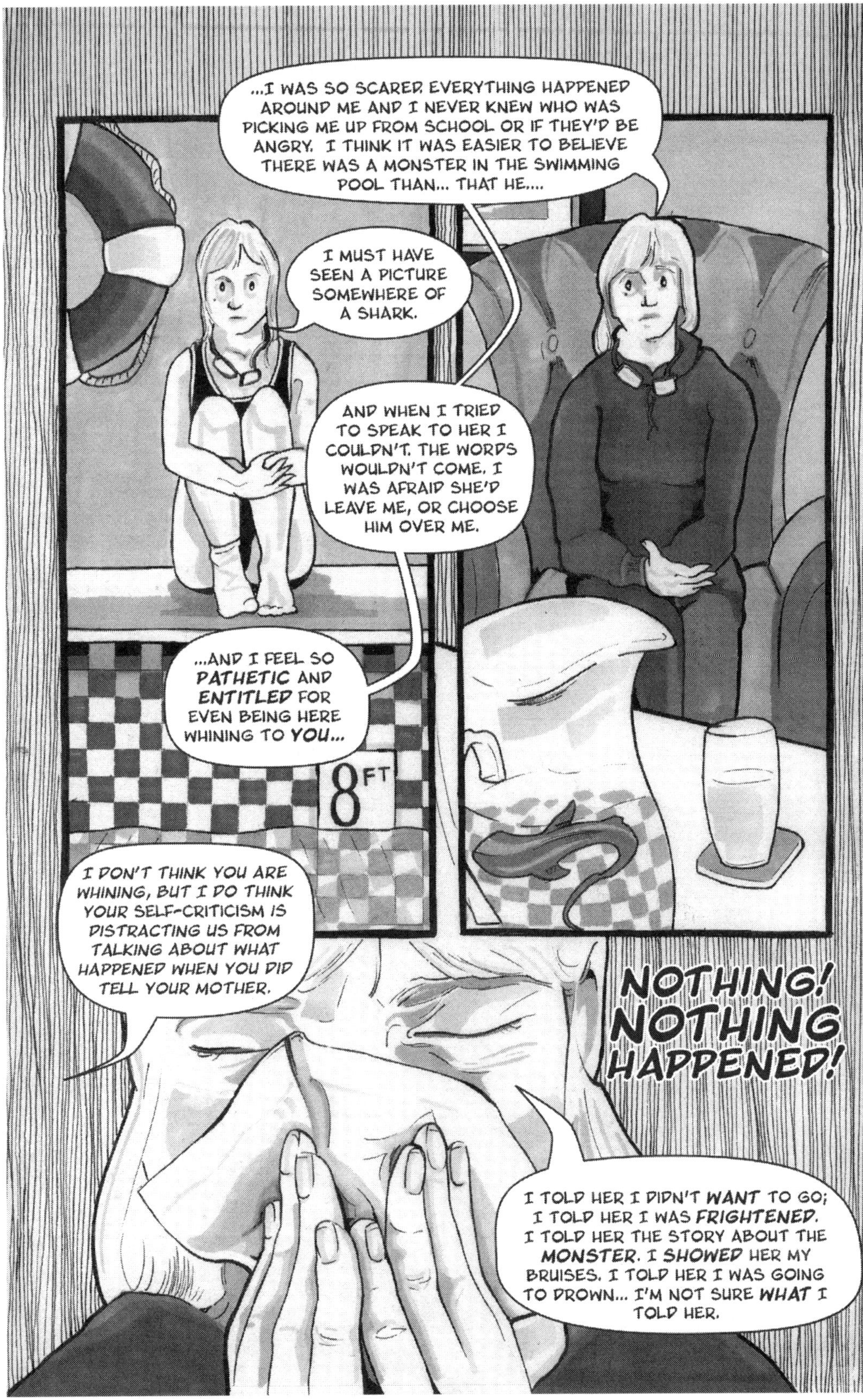
...I WAS SO SCARED. EVERYTHING HAPPENED AROUND ME AND I NEVER KNEW WHO WAS PICKING ME UP FROM SCHOOL OR IF THEY'D BE ANGRY. I THINK IT WAS EASIER TO BELIEVE THERE WAS A MONSTER IN THE SWIMMING POOL THAN... THAT HE....
I MUST HAVE SEEN A PICTURE SOMEWHERE OF A SHARK.
AND WHEN I TRIED TO SPEAK TO HER I COULDN'T. THE WORDS WOULDN'T COME. I WAS AFRAID SHE'D LEAVE ME, OR CHOOSE HIM OVER ME.
...AND I FEEL SO PATHETIC AND ENTITLED FOR EVEN BEING HERE WHINING TO YOU...
8FT
I DON'T THINK YOU ARE WHINING, BUT I DO THINK YOUR SELF-CRITICISM IS DISTRACTING US FROM TALKING ABOUT WHAT HAPPENED WHEN YOU DID TELL YOUR MOTHER.
NOTHING! NOTHING HAPPENED!
I TOLD HER I DIDN'T WANT TO GO; I TOLD HER I WAS FRIGHTENED. I TOLD HER THE STORY ABOUT THE MONSTER. I SHOWED HER MY BRUISES. I TOLD HER I WAS GOING TO DROWN... I'M NOT SURE WHAT I TOLD HER.

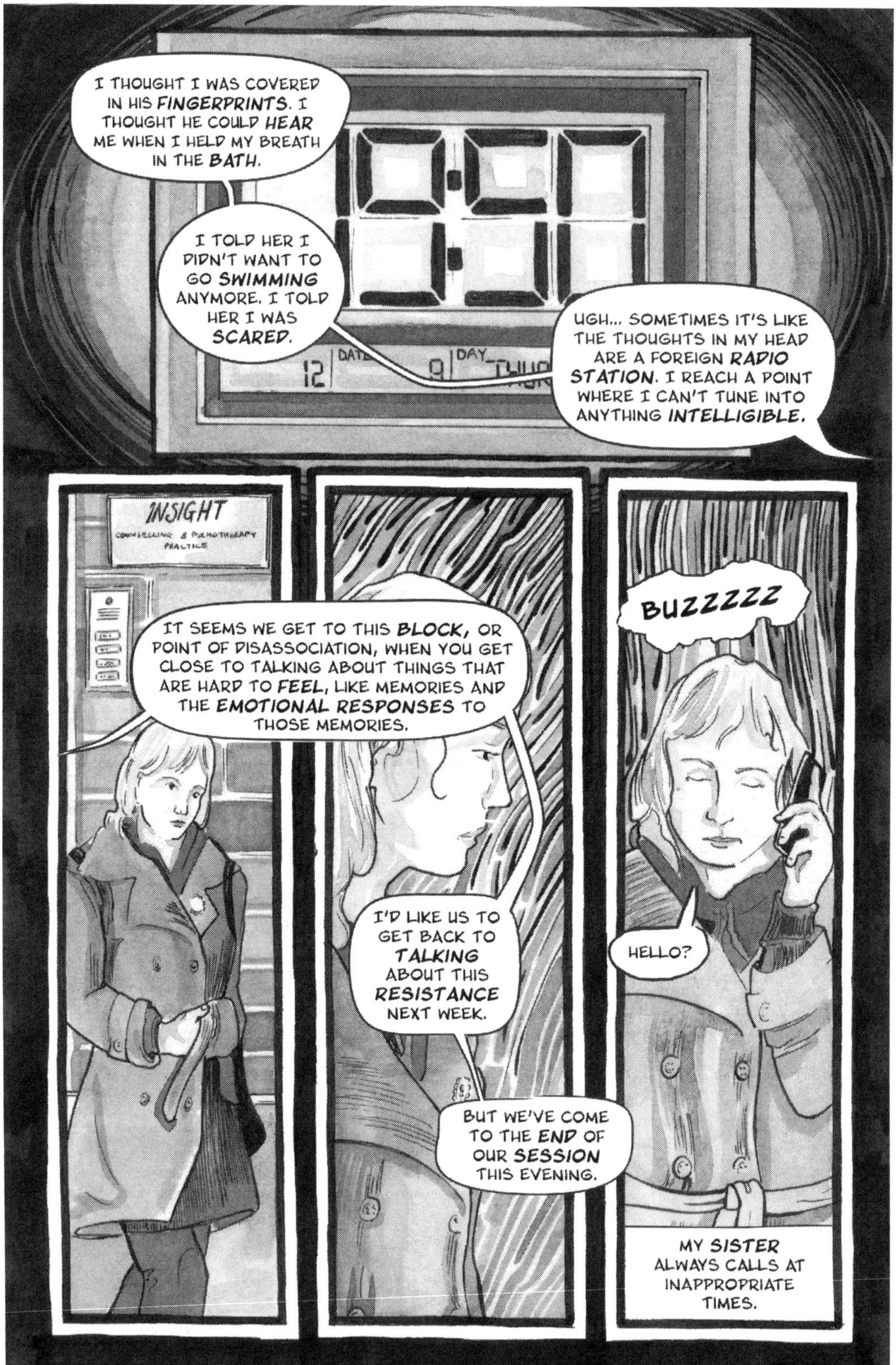
I THOUGHT I WAS COVERED IN HIS FINGERPRINTS. I THOUGHT HE COULD HEAR ME WHEN I HELD MY BREATH IN THE BATH.
I TOLD HER I DIDN'T WANT TO GO SWIMMING ANYMORE. I TOLD HER I WAS SCARED.
12 DATE 9 DAY THUR
UGH... SOMETIMES IT'S LIKE THE THOUGHTS IN MY HEAD ARE A FOREIGN RADIO STATION. I REACH A POINT WHERE I CAN'T TUNE INTO ANYTHING INTELLIGIBLE.
INSIGHT
IT SEEMS WE GET TO THIS BLOCK, OR POINT OF DISASSOCIATION, WHEN YOU GET CLOSE TO TALKING ABOUT THINGS THAT ARE HARD TO FEEL, LIKE MEMORIES AND THE EMOTIONAL RESPONSES TO THOSE MEMORIES.
I'D LIKE US TO GET BACK TO TALKING ABOUT THIS RESISTANCE NEXT WEEK.
BUT WE'VE COME TO THE END OF OUR SESSION THIS EVENING.
BUZZZZZ
HELLO?
MY SISTER ALWAYS CALLS AT INAPPROPRIATE TIMES.

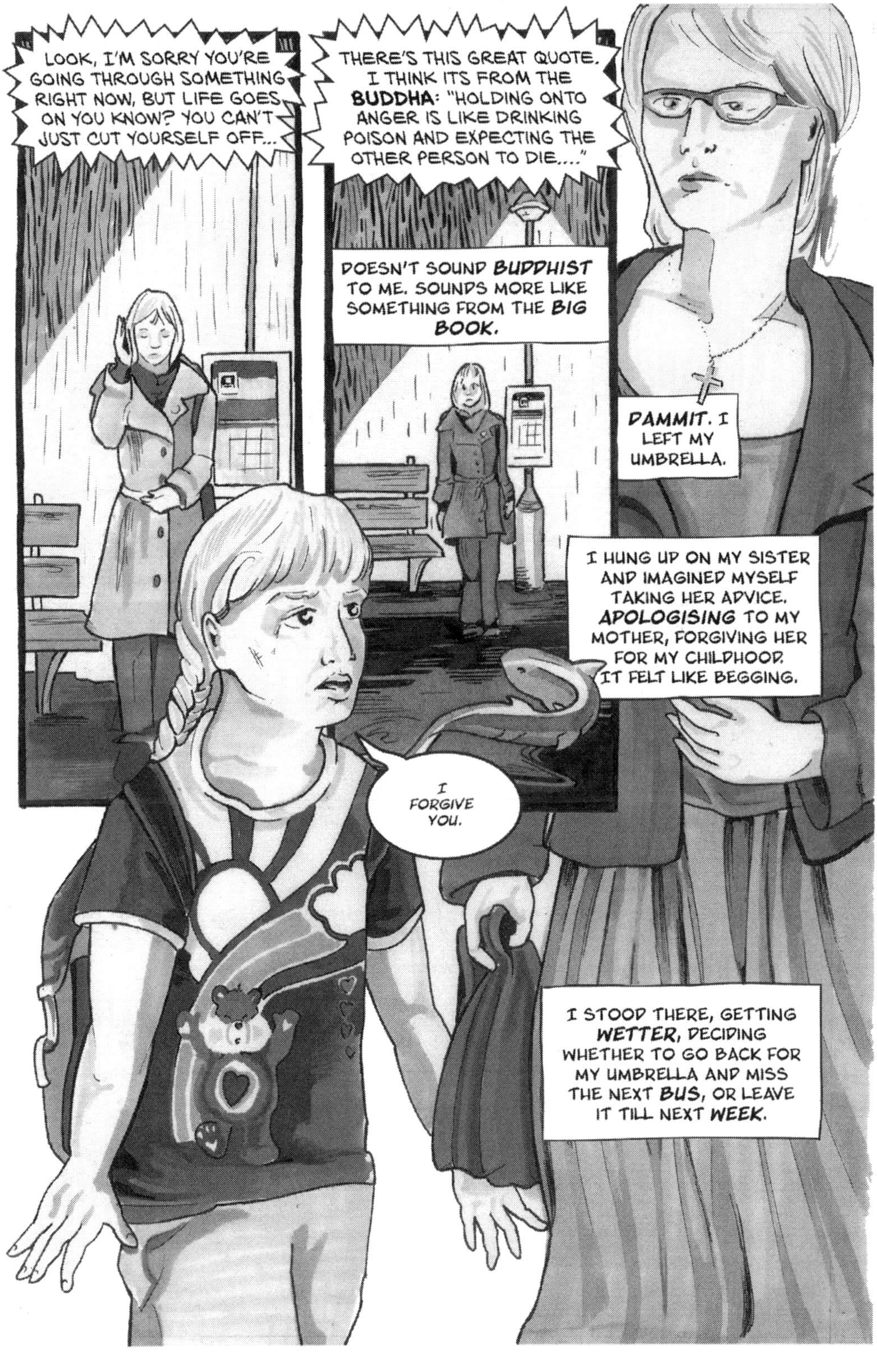
LOOK, I'M SORRY YOU'RE GOING THROUGH SOMETHING RIGHT NOW, BUT LIFE GOES ON YOU KNOW? YOU CAN'T JUST CUT YOURSELF OFF...
THERE'S THIS GREAT QUOTE. I THINK ITS FROM THE BUDDHA: "HOLDING ONTO ANGER IS LIKE DRINKING POISON AND EXPECTING THE OTHER PERSON TO DIE...."
DOESN'T SOUND BUDDHIST TO ME. SOUNDS MORE LIKE SOMETHING FROM THE BIG BOOK.
DAMMIT. I LEFT MY UMBRELLA.
I HUNG UP ON MY SISTER AND IMAGINED MYSELF TAKING HER ADVICE. APOLOGISING TO MY MOTHER, FORGIVING HER FOR MY CHILDHOOD. IT FELT LIKE BEGGING.
I FORGIVE YOU.
I STOOD THERE, GETTING WETTER, DECIDING WHETHER TO GO BACK FOR MY UMBRELLA AND MISS THE NEXT BUS, OR LEAVE IT TILL NEXT WEEK.

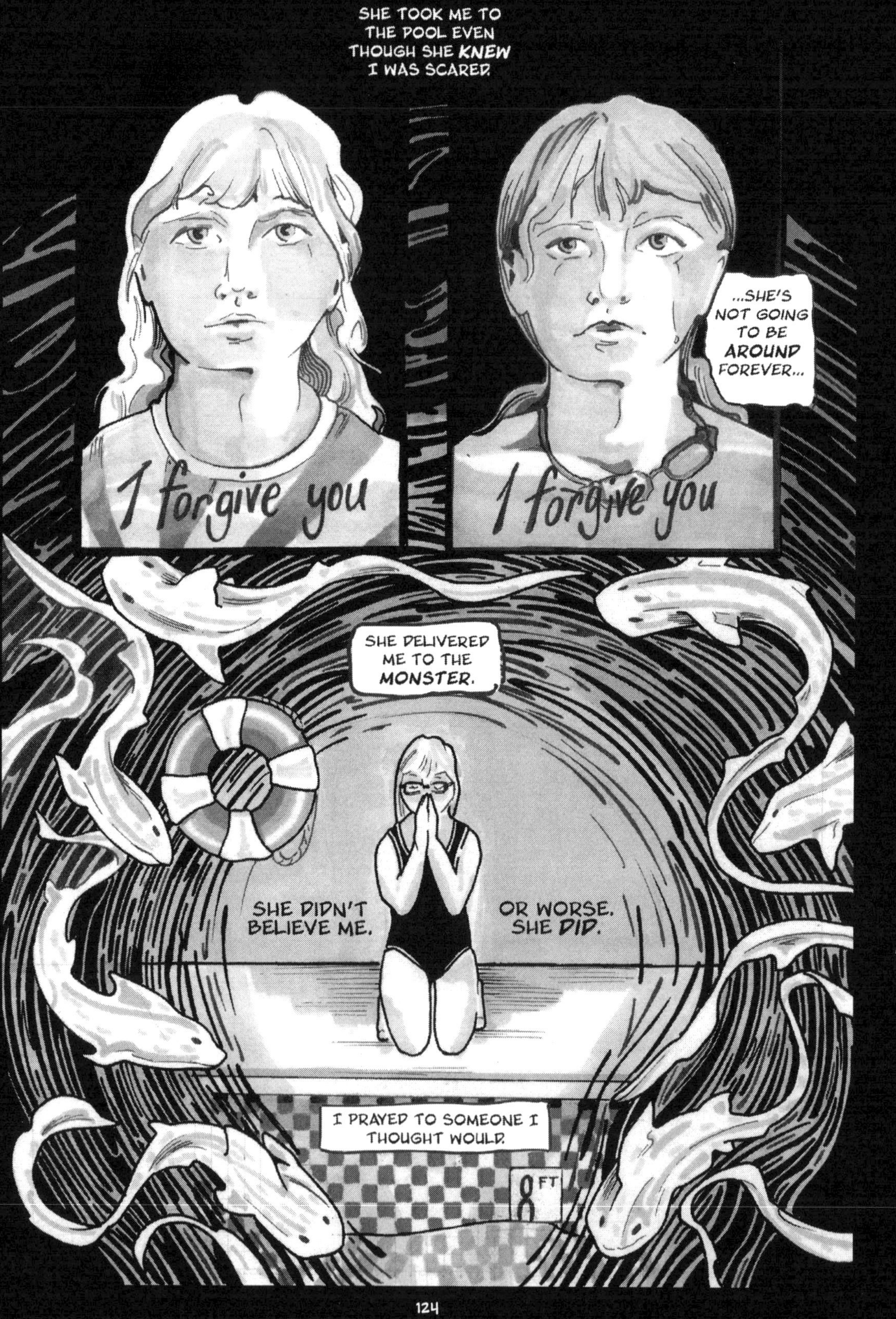
SHE TOOK ME TO THE POOL EVEN THOUGH SHE KNEW I WAS SCARED.
I forgive you
I forgive you
...SHE'S NOT GOING TO BE AROUND FOREVER...
SHE DELIVERED ME TO THE MONSTER.
SHE DIDN'T BELIEVE ME.
OR WORSE. SHE DID.
I PRAYED TO SOMEONE I THOUGHT WOULD.
8 FT

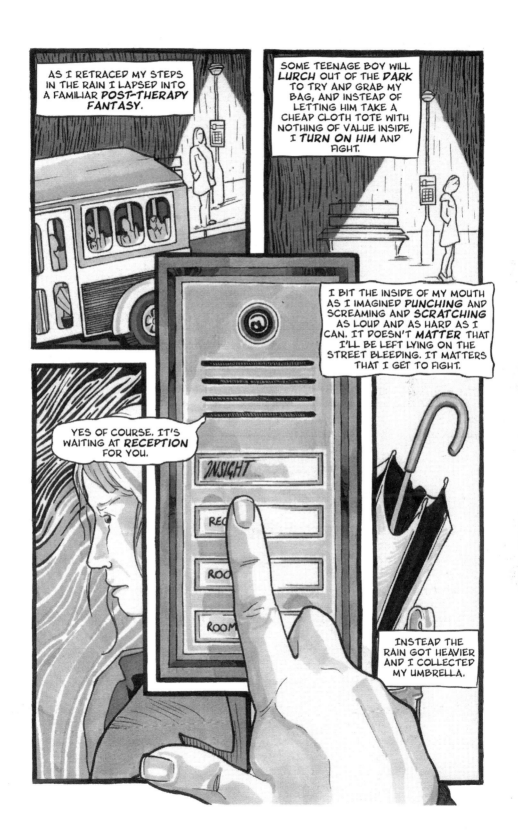

AS I RETRACED MY STEPS IN THE RAIN I LAPSED INTO A FAMILIAR *POST-THERAPY FANTASY.*

SOME TEENAGE BOY WILL *LURCH* OUT OF THE *DARK* TO TRY AND GRAB MY BAG, AND INSTEAD OF LETTING HIM TAKE A CHEAP CLOTH TOTE WITH NOTHING OF VALUE INSIDE, I *TURN ON HIM* AND FIGHT.

I BIT THE INSIDE OF MY MOUTH AS I IMAGINED *PUNCHING* AND SCREAMING AND *SCRATCHING* AS LOUD AND AS HARD AS I CAN. IT DOESN'T *MATTER* THAT I'LL BE LEFT LYING ON THE STREET BLEEDING. IT MATTERS THAT I GET TO FIGHT.

YES OF COURSE. IT'S WAITING AT *RECEPTION* FOR YOU.

INSTEAD THE RAIN GOT HEAVIER AND I COLLECTED MY UMBRELLA.

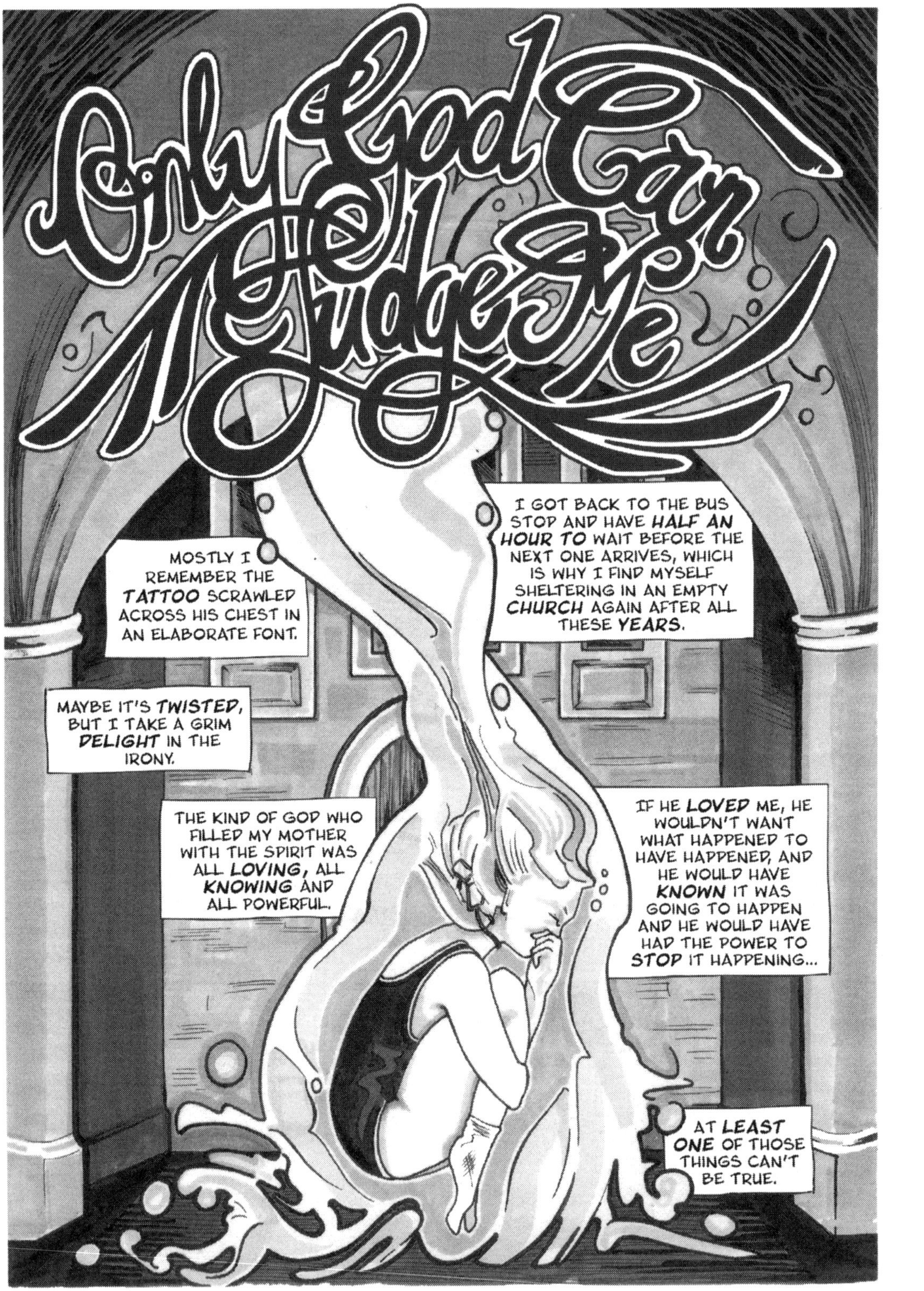
Only God Can Judge Me
MOSTLY I REMEMBER THE TATTOO SCRAWLED ACROSS HIS CHEST IN AN ELABORATE FONT.
I GOT BACK TO THE BUS STOP AND HAVE HALF AN HOUR TO WAIT BEFORE THE NEXT ONE ARRIVES, WHICH IS WHY I FIND MYSELF SHELTERING IN AN EMPTY CHURCH AGAIN AFTER ALL THESE YEARS.
MAYBE IT'S TWISTED, BUT I TAKE A GRIM DELIGHT IN THE IRONY.
THE KIND OF GOD WHO FILLED MY MOTHER WITH THE SPIRIT WAS ALL LOVING, ALL KNOWING AND ALL POWERFUL.
IF HE LOVED ME, HE WOULDN'T WANT WHAT HAPPENED TO HAVE HAPPENED, AND HE WOULD HAVE KNOWN IT WAS GOING TO HAPPEN AND HE WOULD HAVE HAD THE POWER TO STOP IT HAPPENING...
AT LEAST ONE OF THOSE THINGS CAN'T BE TRUE.

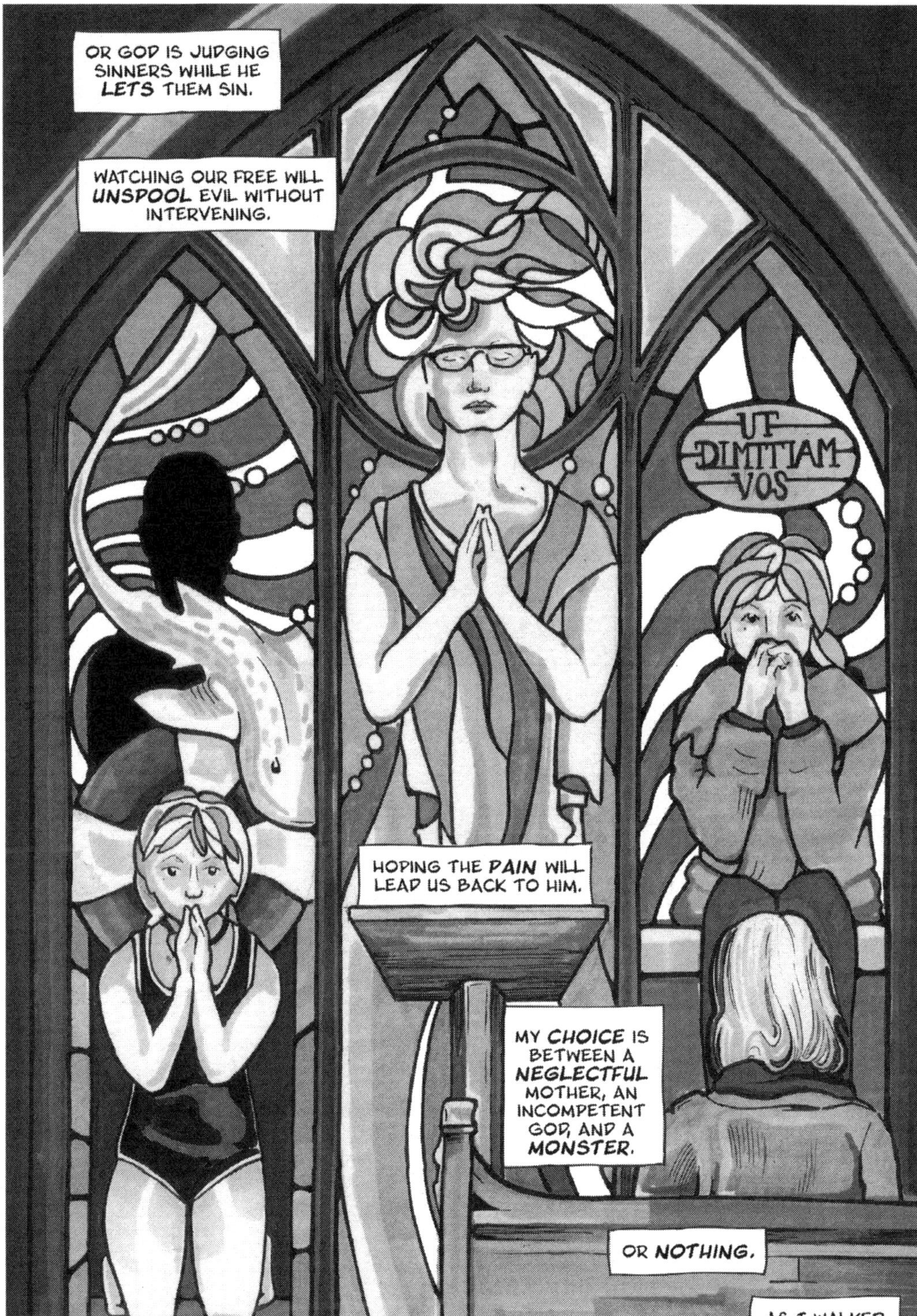
OR GOD IS JUDGING SINNERS WHILE HE LETS THEM SIN.
WATCHING OUR FREE WILL UNSPOOL EVIL WITHOUT INTERVENING.
UT DIMITTIAM VOS
HOPING THE PAIN WILL LEAD US BACK TO HIM.
MY CHOICE IS BETWEEN A NEGLECTFUL MOTHER, AN INCOMPETENT GOD, AND A MONSTER.
OR NOTHING.
AS I WALKED IN THIS PLACE DID FEEL...

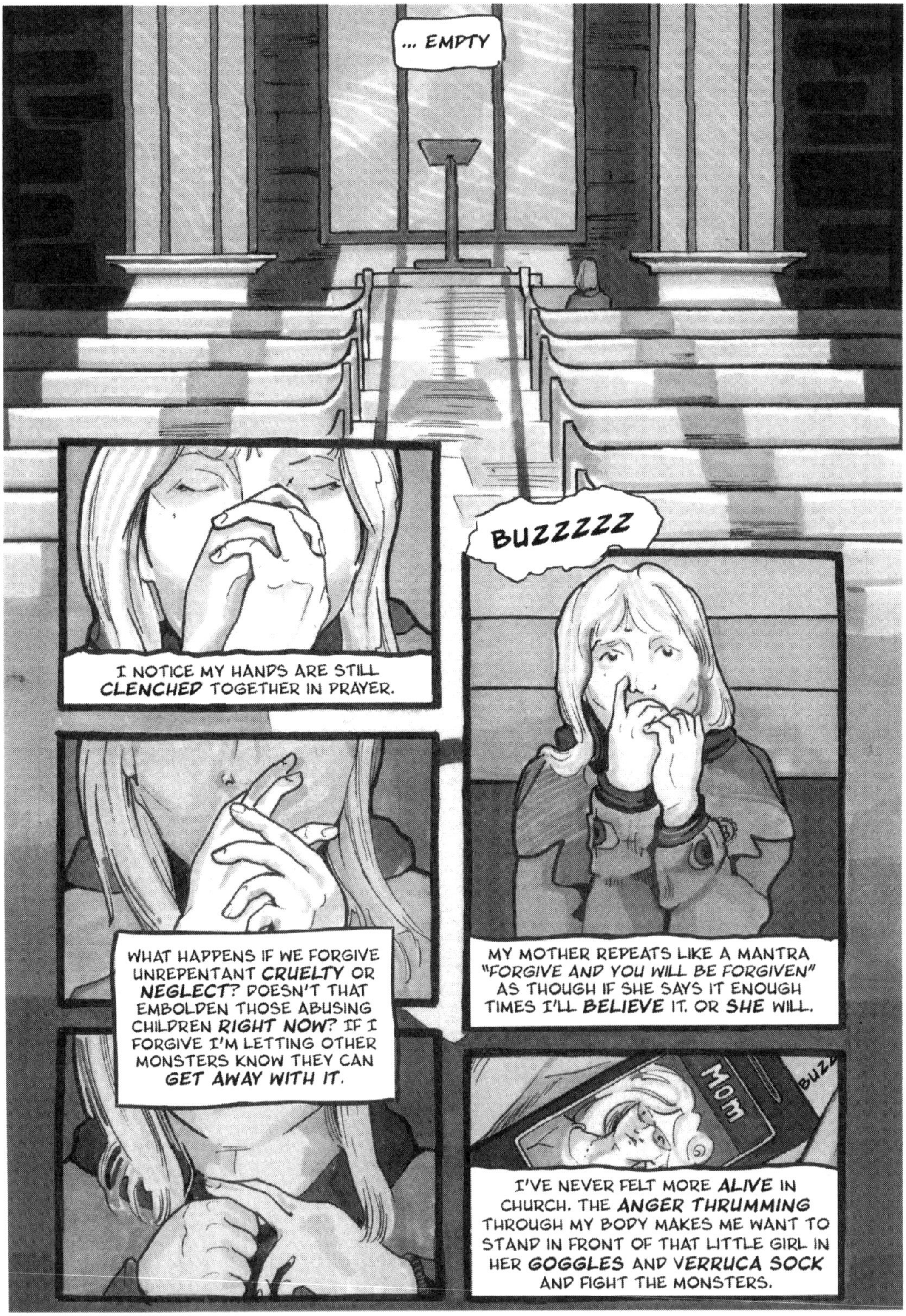
... EMPTY
I NOTICE MY HANDS ARE STILL CLENCHED TOGETHER IN PRAYER.
BUZZZZZ
MY MOTHER REPEATS LIKE A MANTRA "FORGIVE AND YOU WILL BE FORGIVEN" AS THOUGH IF SHE SAYS IT ENOUGH TIMES I'LL BELIEVE IT. OR SHE WILL.
WHAT HAPPENS IF WE FORGIVE UNREPENTANT CRUELTY OR NEGLECT? DOESN'T THAT EMBOLDEN THOSE ABUSING CHILDREN RIGHT NOW? IF I FORGIVE I'M LETTING OTHER MONSTERS KNOW THEY CAN GET AWAY WITH IT.
MOM
I'VE NEVER FELT MORE ALIVE IN CHURCH. THE ANGER THRUMMING THROUGH MY BODY MAKES ME WANT TO STAND IN FRONT OF THAT LITTLE GIRL IN HER GOGGLES AND VERRUCA SOCK AND FIGHT THE MONSTERS.

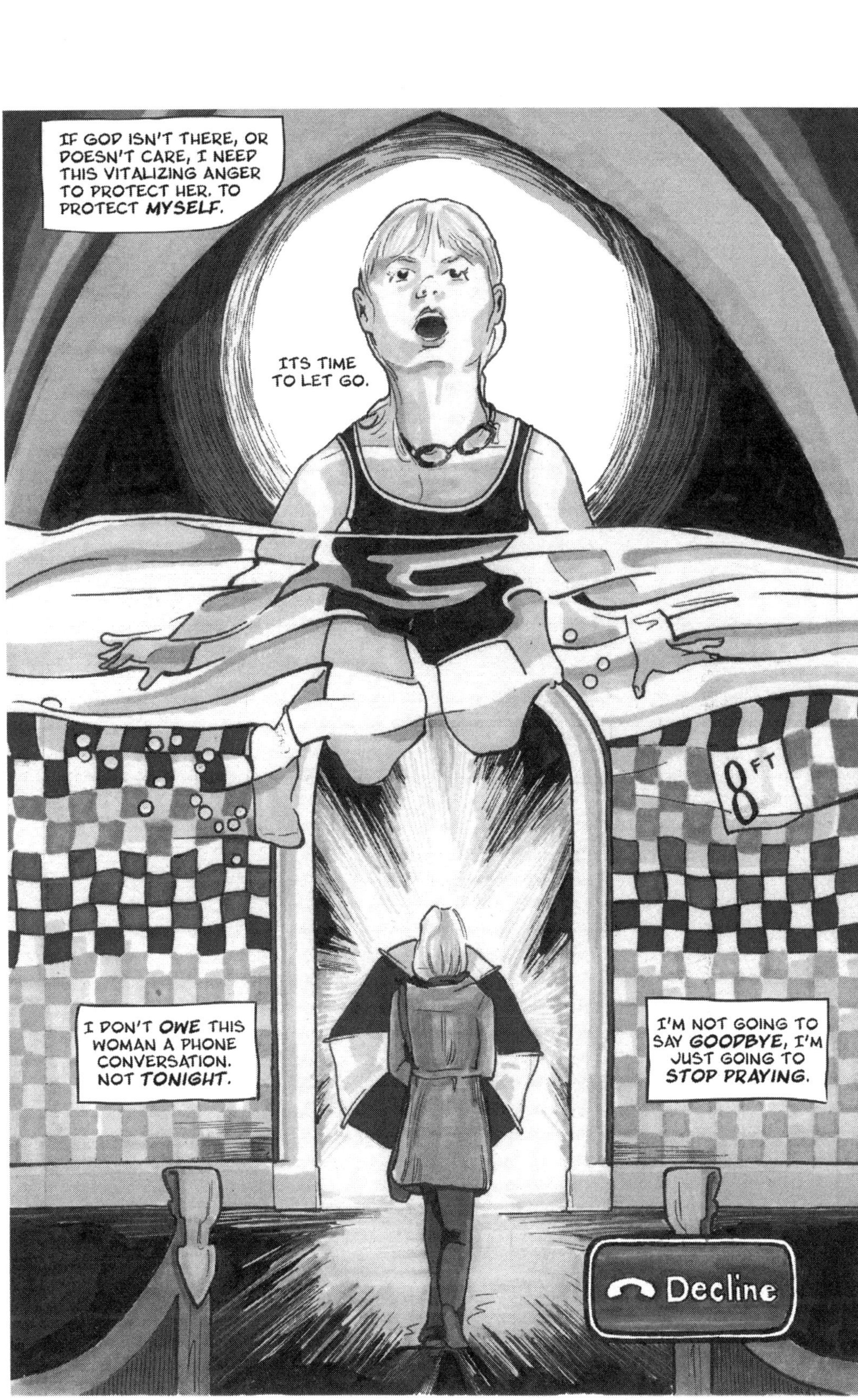
IF GOD ISN'T THERE, OR DOESN'T CARE, I NEED THIS VITALIZING ANGER TO PROTECT HER. TO PROTECT MYSELF.
ITS TIME TO LET GO.
8 FT
I DON'T OWE THIS WOMAN A PHONE CONVERSATION. NOT TONIGHT.
I'M NOT GOING TO SAY GOODBYE, I'M JUST GOING TO STOP PRAYING.
Decline

In almost every vampire novel I've ever read, and I read more than my fair share as a teenager, there is a scene in which a human agonises over the prospect of becoming a vampire. It's usually a lengthy consideration, but I can't remember a single case of a human turning that offer down.

The deal is immortality in exchange for the sacrifice of a mortal life, abandonment of human friends and family, and accepting the inconveniences of subsisting on human blood. Evangelical Christians aren't known for drinking blood (they specifically object to the doctrine of transubstantiation) or avoiding sunlight and holy objects (they quite like crucifixes) but there are some similarities between being 'born again' and accepting the 'dark gift'.

When a Christian is born again they believe they become immortal. They are no longer condemned to die when their mortal bodies wear out; they will live forever in heaven. They are 'saved' from a life without Jesus, from their sins, and from death itself.

From our mortal perspective the plight of humans and animals on our planet seems of paramount importance. The suffering and death of fifty billion children seems, to us, like an atrocity. In his article *Theodicy's Problem*, philosopher Gregory Paul estimates that the number of children who have died from non-human causes before they reached the age at which they could accept Christ as their personal saviour is at least fifty billion.

> *If a creator exists, then it has chosen to fashion a habitat that has maximised the level of suffering and death among young humans that are due to factors beyond the control of humans for most of history.*

Christians don't want to give up any of the three qualities they ascribe to God—omnipotence, omniscience and omnibenevolence—so they redefine the terms or diminish the problem. Yes; God can be kind *and* allow the torture of innocents. No; suffering a horrific death isn't a big deal in the great scheme of things. It may seem like a big deal to us but to an immortal being it is barely relevant.

We are the patina of stains that accumulate on a more-or-less blank slate. Clean that slate and you wipe yourself away. A true factory reset would be almost indistinguishable from suicide. When we say we're starting over we mean that we are resolving to do better. We're not pretending that we can wash our sins away.

The few evangelical Christians that I've met have been eager to tell me of their past lives and the vices they succumbed to. Maybe this is a strategy for connecting with apparent sinners like myself, or maybe they just enjoy recounting stories of wasted youth. Either way, the product they are selling is rebirth. You don't have to live with your past indiscretions. You can have a fresh start.

And like new vampires, new born again Christians are encouraged to distance themselves from friends and family. At least those friends and family who refuse to look for, or can't find, Jesus. Christ enjoins his followers to prioritise God over their families:

> *Everyone who has left [family] for my sake will receive a hundred times as much, and inherit eternal life.* (Matthew 19:29)

To fantasise about being reborn is to ignore the fact that without the events of our past, we would not be ourselves. It is to ignore the people who, if we truly started over, would be bereft at our leaving. The people who love us or rely on us don't want us to become new people, they want us to stay and figure it out with them.

People can forgive themselves. They can believe they've been granted divine absolution or be born again, but the only people really empowered to forgive are those who have been hurt. You can't squirm out from under your victim's judgement by claiming 'only God can judge me'.

It's much harder to look someone you've hurt in the eye and try to make amends than it is to turn away from humanity to the divine. Can you look at the fifty billion children who died before they could be saved and tell them that this is the best of all possible worlds? The only being I can think of that might be capable of such a feat would be an omniscient, omnipotent God.

More information, discussion and links at
doubtcomic.com/born-of-water

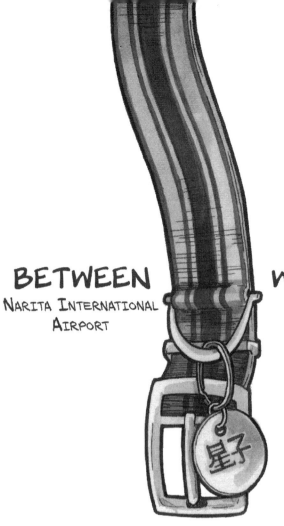

BETWEEN WORLDS

NARITA INTERNATIONAL
AIRPORT

TOKYO,
JAPAN

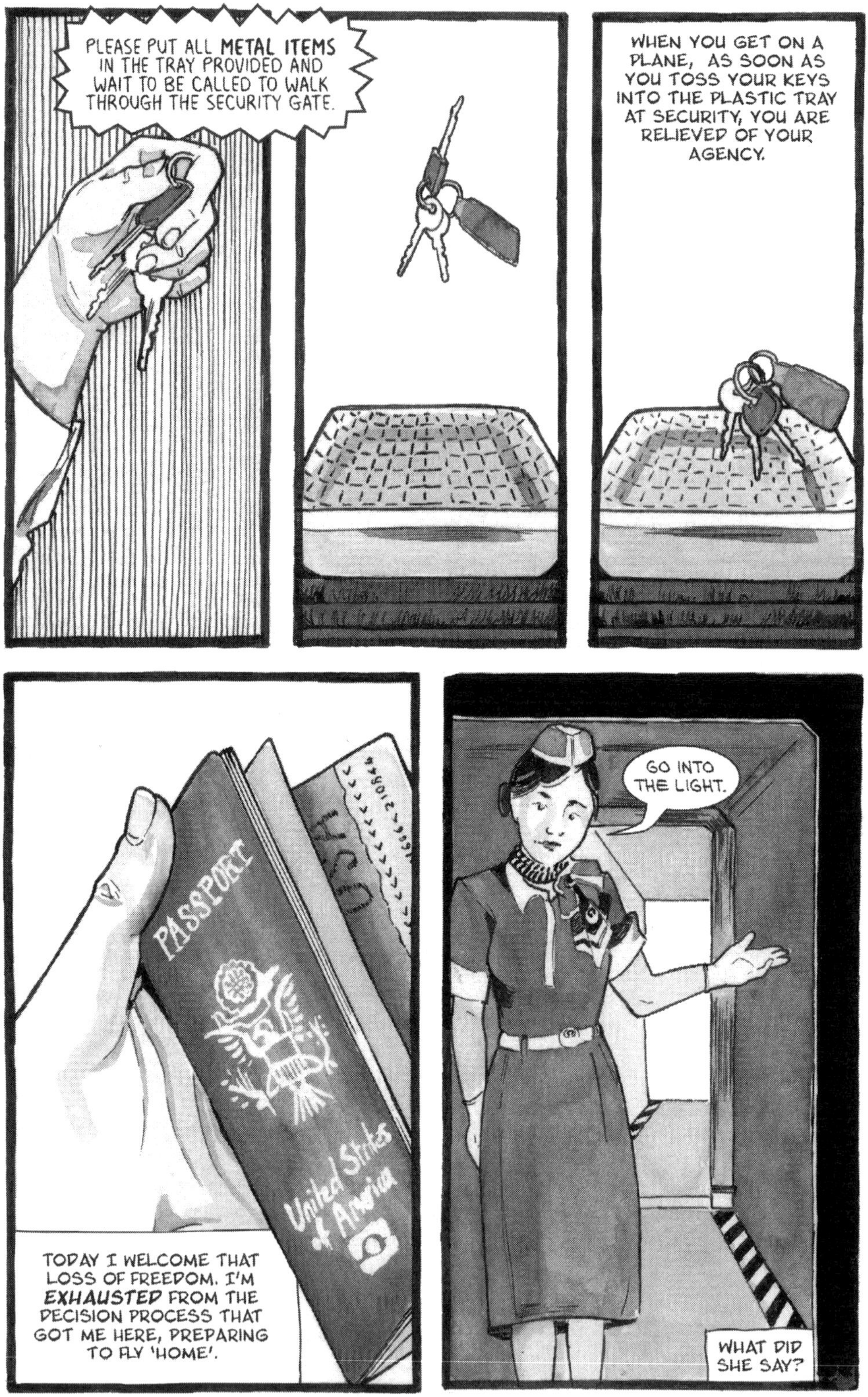
PLEASE PUT ALL METAL ITEMS IN THE TRAY PROVIDED AND WAIT TO BE CALLED TO WALK THROUGH THE SECURITY GATE.
WHEN YOU GET ON A PLANE, AS SOON AS YOU TOSS YOUR KEYS INTO THE PLASTIC TRAY AT SECURITY, YOU ARE RELIEVED OF YOUR AGENCY.
PASSPORT
United States of America
TODAY I WELCOME THAT LOSS OF FREEDOM. I'M EXHAUSTED FROM THE DECISION PROCESS THAT GOT ME HERE, PREPARING TO FLY 'HOME'.
GO INTO THE LIGHT.
WHAT DID SHE SAY?

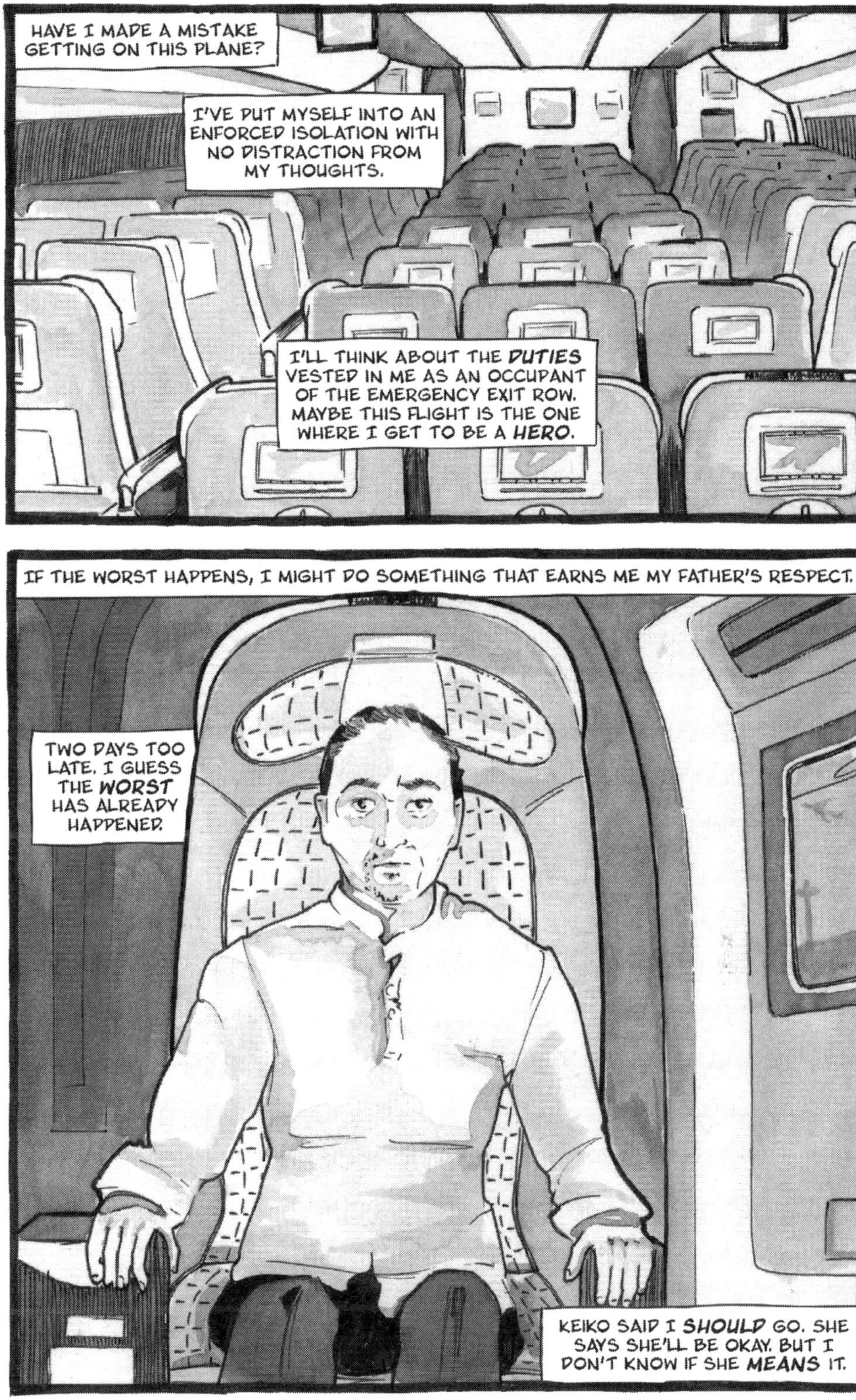
HAVE I MADE A MISTAKE GETTING ON THIS PLANE?
I'VE PUT MYSELF INTO AN ENFORCED ISOLATION WITH NO DISTRACTION FROM MY THOUGHTS.
I'LL THINK ABOUT THE DUTIES VESTED IN ME AS AN OCCUPANT OF THE EMERGENCY EXIT ROW. MAYBE THIS FLIGHT IS THE ONE WHERE I GET TO BE A HERO.
IF THE WORST HAPPENS, I MIGHT DO SOMETHING THAT EARNS ME MY FATHER'S RESPECT.
TWO DAYS TOO LATE. I GUESS THE WORST HAS ALREADY HAPPENED.
KEIKO SAID I SHOULD GO. SHE SAYS SHE'LL BE OKAY. BUT I DON'T KNOW IF SHE MEANS IT.

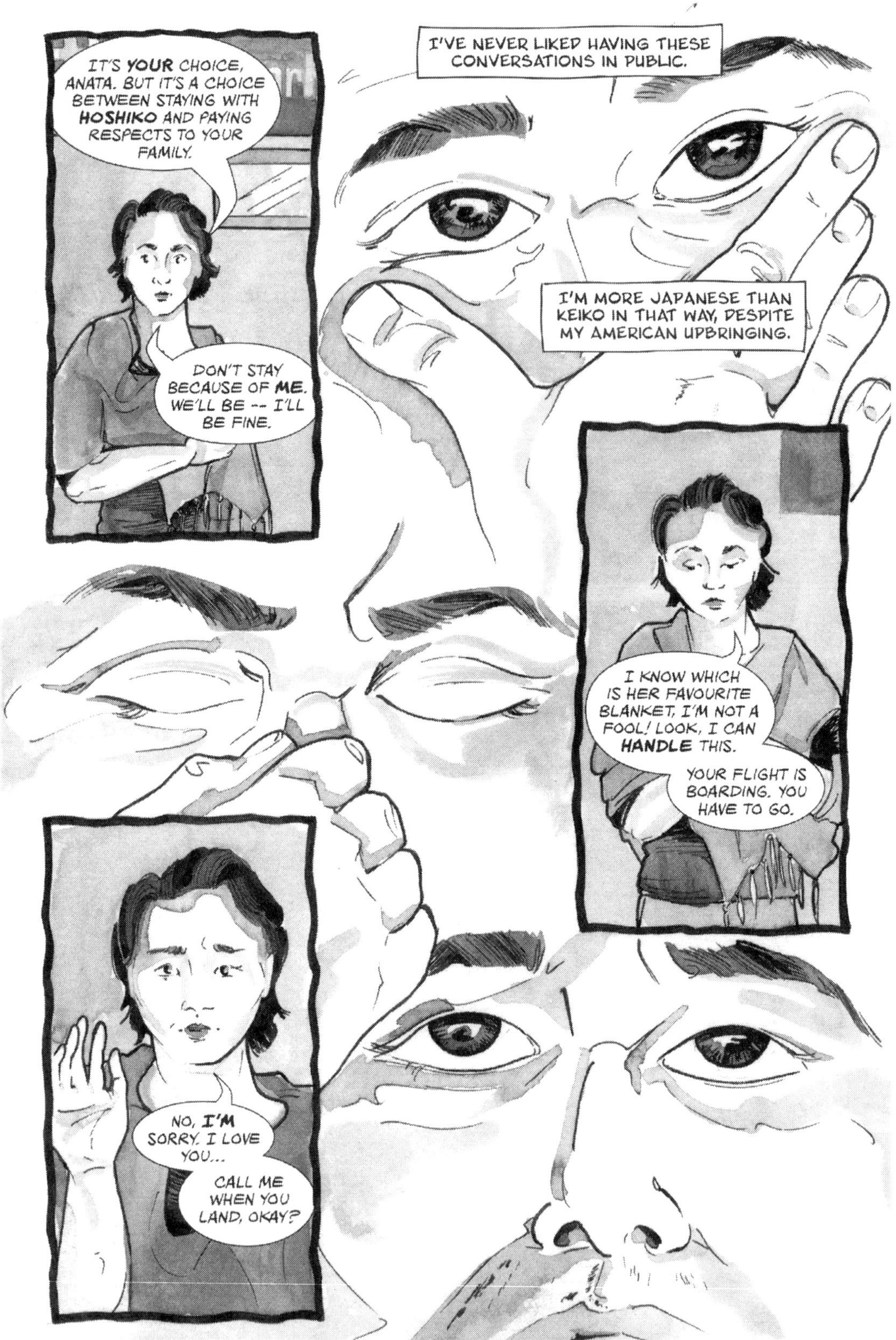
IT'S YOUR CHOICE, ANATA. BUT IT'S A CHOICE BETWEEN STAYING WITH HOSHIKO AND PAYING RESPECTS TO YOUR FAMILY.
I'VE NEVER LIKED HAVING THESE CONVERSATIONS IN PUBLIC.
DON'T STAY BECAUSE OF ME. WE'LL BE -- I'LL BE FINE.
I'M MORE JAPANESE THAN KEIKO IN THAT WAY, DESPITE MY AMERICAN UPBRINGING.
I KNOW WHICH IS HER FAVOURITE BLANKET, I'M NOT A FOOL! LOOK, I CAN HANDLE THIS.
YOUR FLIGHT IS BOARDING. YOU HAVE TO GO.
NO, I'M SORRY. I LOVE YOU...
CALL ME WHEN YOU LAND, OKAY?

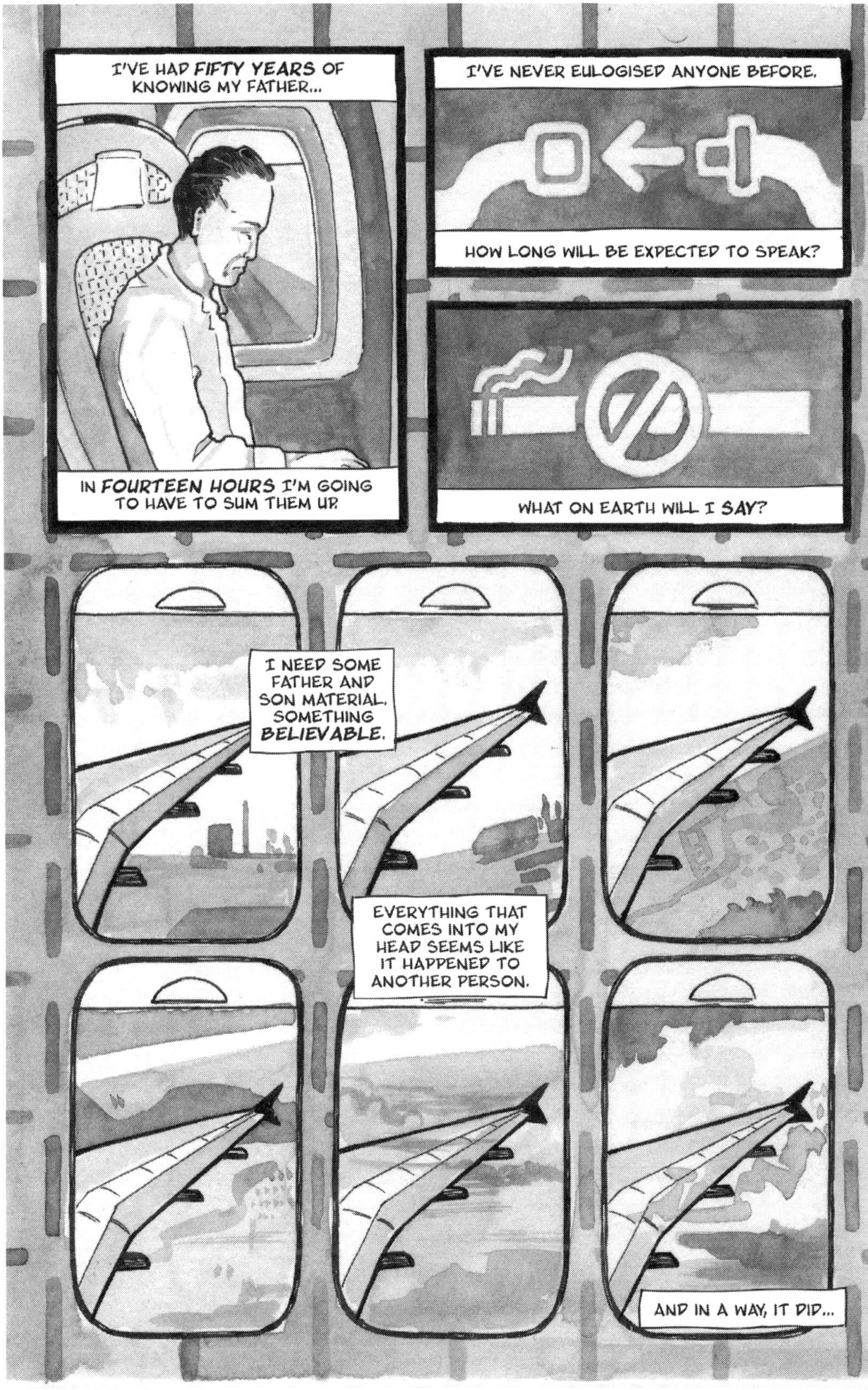
I'VE HAD FIFTY YEARS OF KNOWING MY FATHER...
IN FOURTEEN HOURS I'M GOING TO HAVE TO SUM THEM UP.
I'VE NEVER EULOGISED ANYONE BEFORE.
HOW LONG WILL BE EXPECTED TO SPEAK?
WHAT ON EARTH WILL I SAY?
I NEED SOME FATHER AND SON MATERIAL. SOMETHING BELIEVABLE.
EVERYTHING THAT COMES INTO MY HEAD SEEMS LIKE IT HAPPENED TO ANOTHER PERSON.
AND IN A WAY, IT DID...

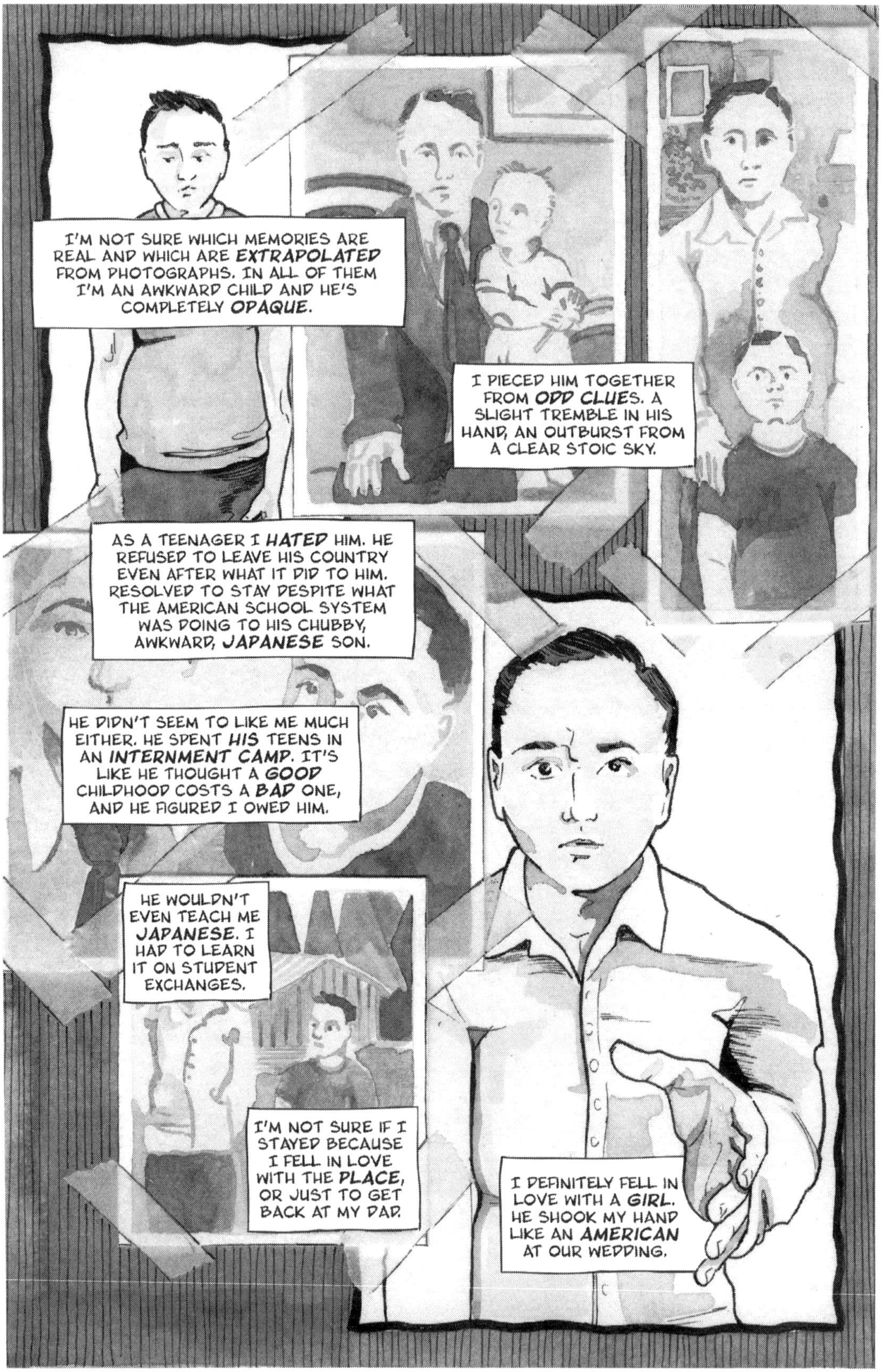
I'M NOT SURE WHICH MEMORIES ARE REAL AND WHICH ARE EXTRAPOLATED FROM PHOTOGRAPHS. IN ALL OF THEM I'M AN AWKWARD CHILD AND HE'S COMPLETELY OPAQUE.
I PIECED HIM TOGETHER FROM ODD CLUES. A SLIGHT TREMBLE IN HIS HAND, AN OUTBURST FROM A CLEAR STOIC SKY.
AS A TEENAGER I HATED HIM. HE REFUSED TO LEAVE HIS COUNTRY EVEN AFTER WHAT IT DID TO HIM. RESOLVED TO STAY DESPITE WHAT THE AMERICAN SCHOOL SYSTEM WAS DOING TO HIS CHUBBY, AWKWARD, JAPANESE SON.
HE DIDN'T SEEM TO LIKE ME MUCH EITHER. HE SPENT HIS TEENS IN AN INTERNMENT CAMP. IT'S LIKE HE THOUGHT A GOOD CHILDHOOD COSTS A BAD ONE, AND HE FIGURED I OWED HIM.
HE WOULDN'T EVEN TEACH ME JAPANESE. I HAD TO LEARN IT ON STUDENT EXCHANGES.
I'M NOT SURE IF I STAYED BECAUSE I FELL IN LOVE WITH THE PLACE, OR JUST TO GET BACK AT MY DAD.
I DEFINITELY FELL IN LOVE WITH A GIRL. HE SHOOK MY HAND LIKE AN AMERICAN AT OUR WEDDING.

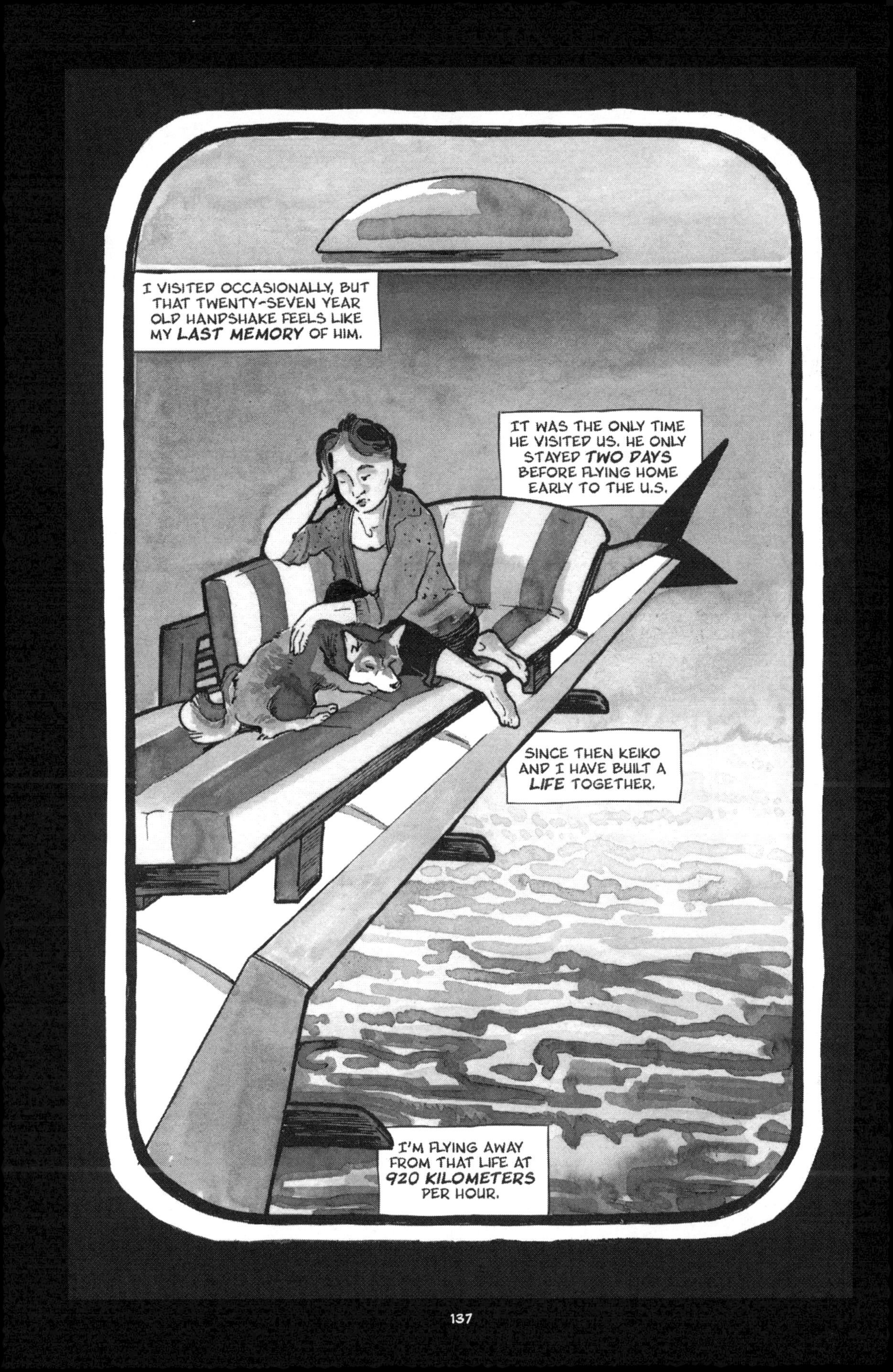
I VISITED OCCASIONALLY, BUT THAT TWENTY-SEVEN YEAR OLD HANDSHAKE FEELS LIKE MY **LAST MEMORY** OF HIM.
IT WAS THE ONLY TIME HE VISITED US. HE ONLY STAYED **TWO DAYS** BEFORE FLYING HOME EARLY TO THE U.S.
SINCE THEN KEIKO AND I HAVE BUILT A **LIFE** TOGETHER.
I'M FLYING AWAY FROM THAT LIFE AT **920 KILOMETERS** PER HOUR.

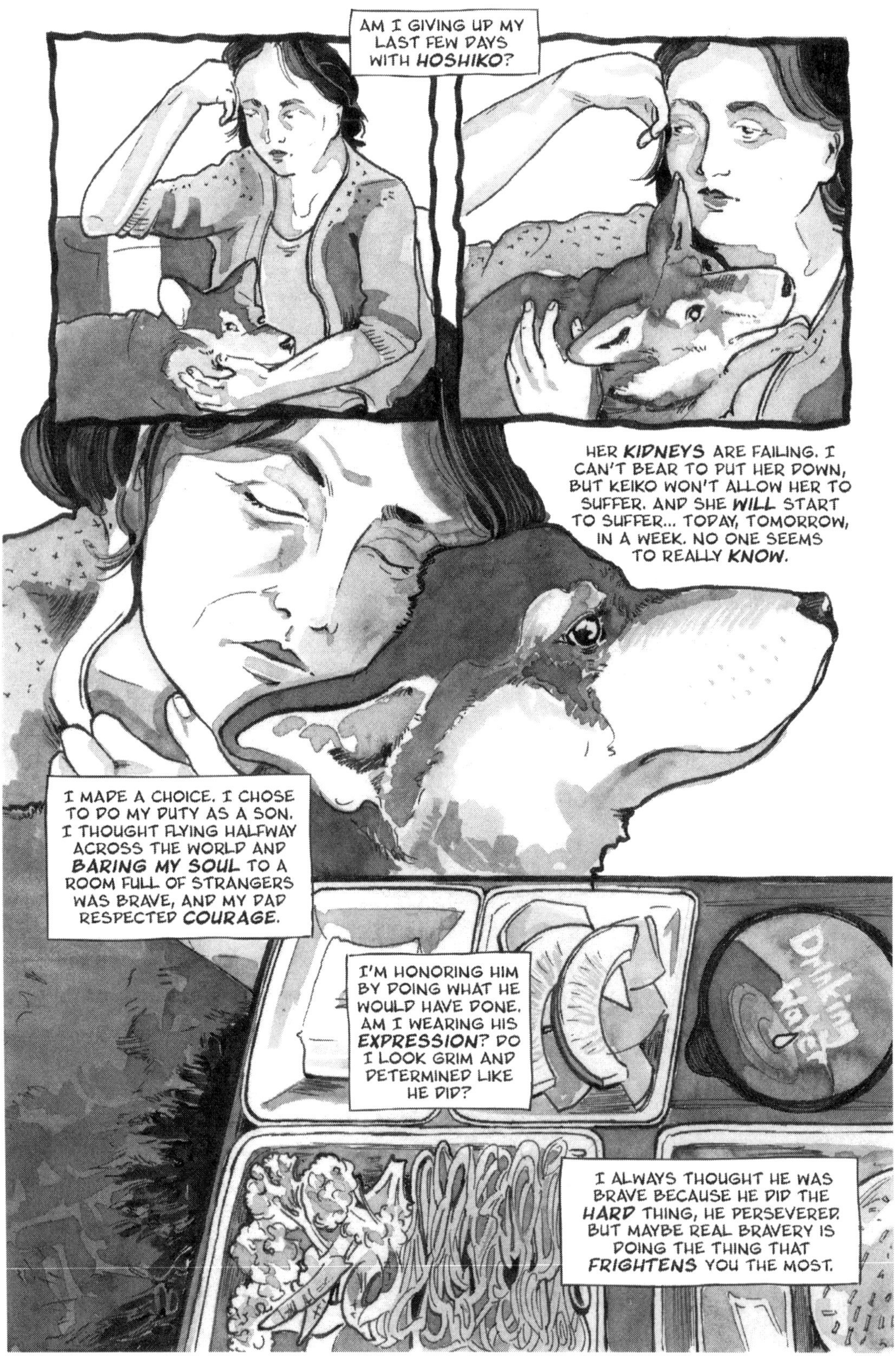
AM I GIVING UP MY LAST FEW DAYS WITH HOSHIKO?
HER KIDNEYS ARE FAILING. I CAN'T BEAR TO PUT HER DOWN, BUT KEIKO WON'T ALLOW HER TO SUFFER. AND SHE WILL START TO SUFFER... TODAY, TOMORROW, IN A WEEK. NO ONE SEEMS TO REALLY KNOW.
I MADE A CHOICE. I CHOSE TO DO MY DUTY AS A SON. I THOUGHT FLYING HALFWAY ACROSS THE WORLD AND BARING MY SOUL TO A ROOM FULL OF STRANGERS WAS BRAVE, AND MY DAD RESPECTED COURAGE.
I'M HONORING HIM BY DOING WHAT HE WOULD HAVE DONE. AM I WEARING HIS EXPRESSION? DO I LOOK GRIM AND DETERMINED LIKE HE DID?
I ALWAYS THOUGHT HE WAS BRAVE BECAUSE HE DID THE HARD THING, HE PERSEVERED. BUT MAYBE REAL BRAVERY IS DOING THE THING THAT FRIGHTENS YOU THE MOST.

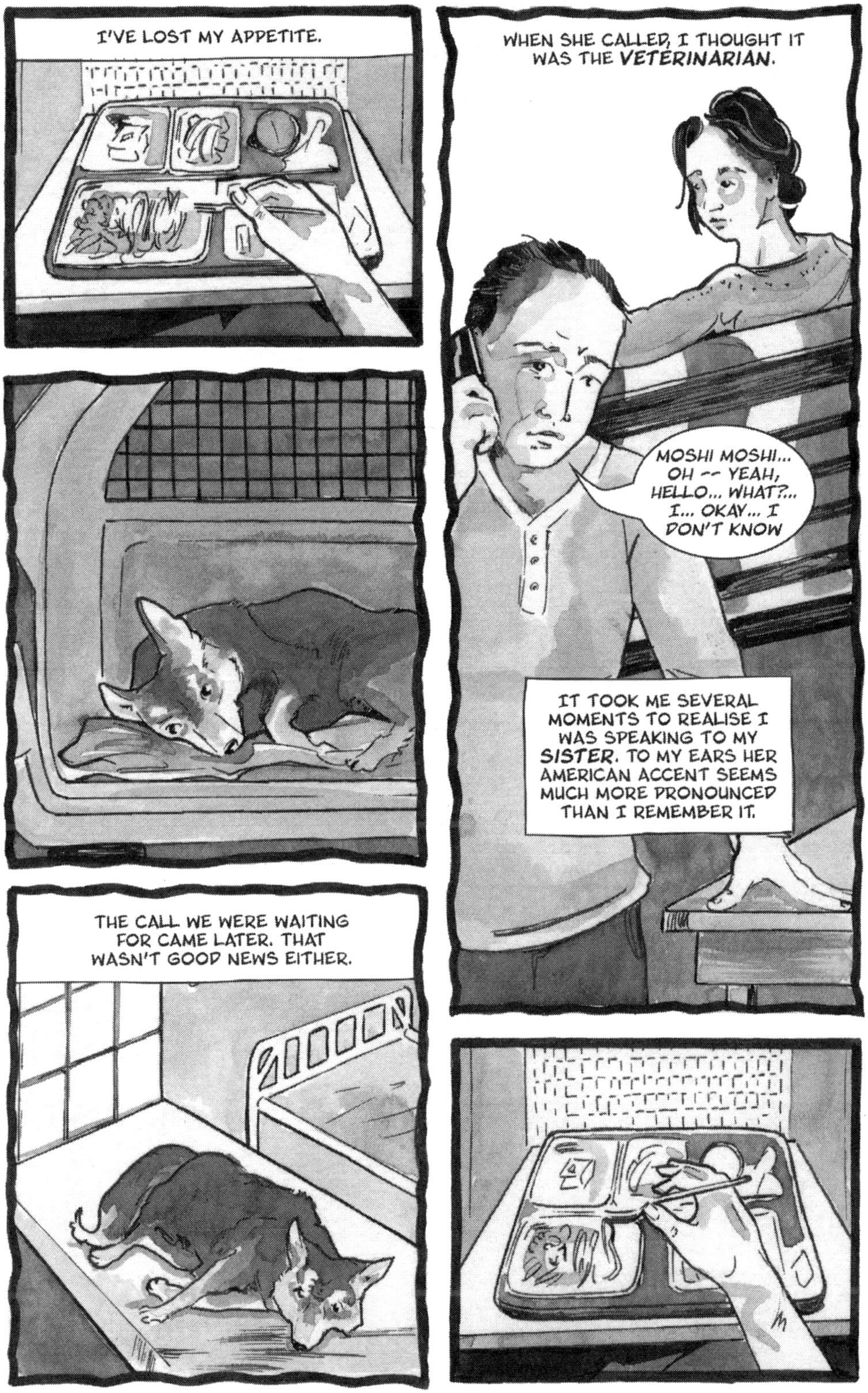
I'VE LOST MY APPETITE.
WHEN SHE CALLED, I THOUGHT IT WAS THE **VETERINARIAN**.
MOSHI MOSHI... OH -- YEAH, HELLO... WHAT?... I... OKAY... I DON'T KNOW
IT TOOK ME SEVERAL MOMENTS TO REALISE I WAS SPEAKING TO MY **SISTER**. TO MY EARS HER AMERICAN ACCENT SEEMS MUCH MORE PRONOUNCED THAN I REMEMBER IT.
THE CALL WE WERE WAITING FOR CAME LATER. THAT WASN'T GOOD NEWS EITHER.

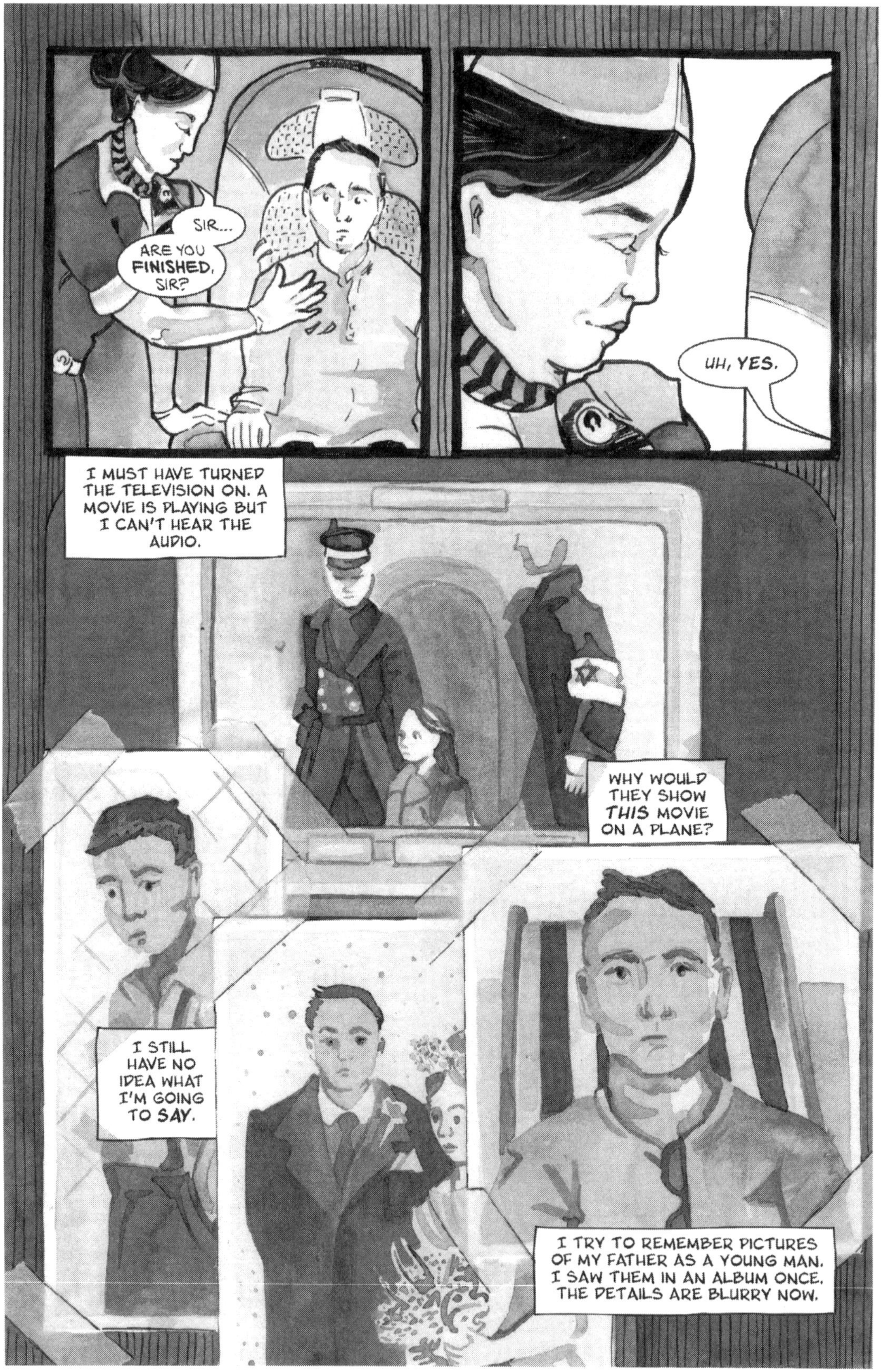
SIR...
ARE YOU FINISHED, SIR?
UH, YES.
I MUST HAVE TURNED THE TELEVISION ON. A MOVIE IS PLAYING BUT I CAN'T HEAR THE AUDIO.
WHY WOULD THEY SHOW THIS MOVIE ON A PLANE?
I STILL HAVE NO IDEA WHAT I'M GOING TO SAY.
I TRY TO REMEMBER PICTURES OF MY FATHER AS A YOUNG MAN. I SAW THEM IN AN ALBUM ONCE. THE DETAILS ARE BLURRY NOW.

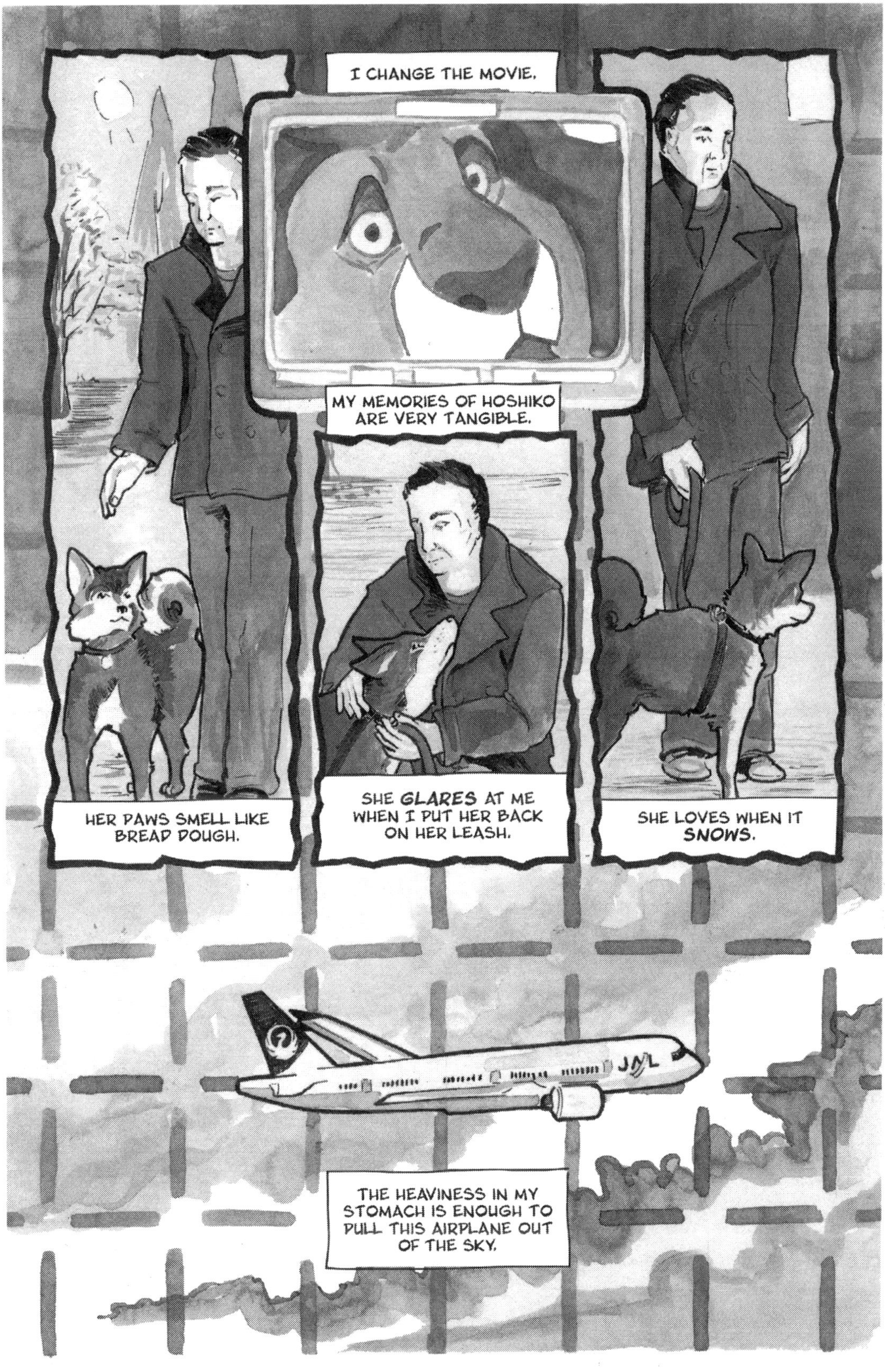
I CHANGE THE MOVIE.
MY MEMORIES OF HOSHIKO ARE VERY TANGIBLE.
HER PAWS SMELL LIKE BREAD DOUGH.
SHE GLARES AT ME WHEN I PUT HER BACK ON HER LEASH.
SHE LOVES WHEN IT SNOWS.
JAL
THE HEAVINESS IN MY STOMACH IS ENOUGH TO PULL THIS AIRPLANE OUT OF THE SKY.

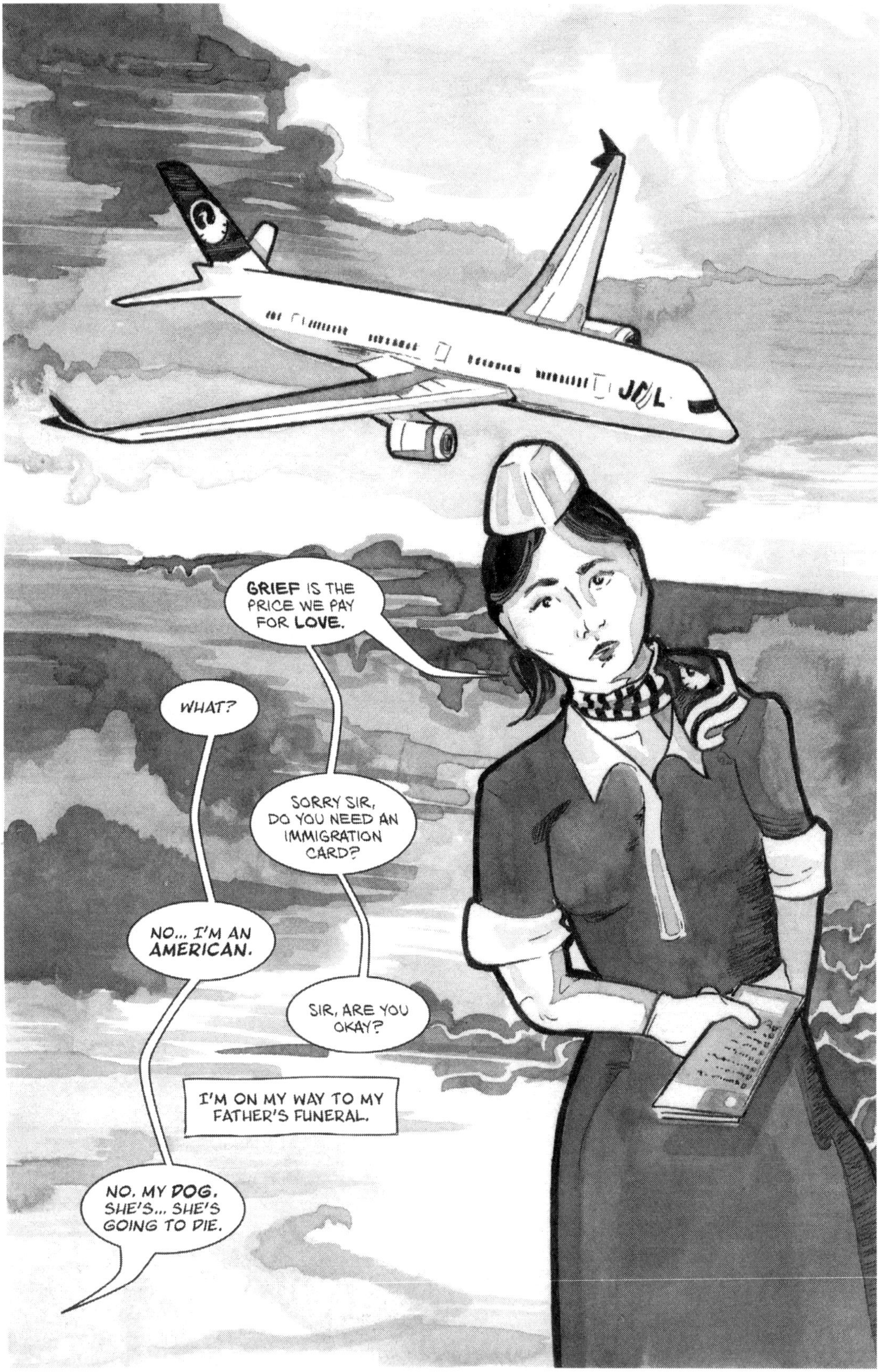
JAL
GRIEF IS THE PRICE WE PAY FOR LOVE.
WHAT?
SORRY SIR, DO YOU NEED AN IMMIGRATION CARD?
NO... I'M AN AMERICAN.
SIR, ARE YOU OKAY?
I'M ON MY WAY TO MY FATHER'S FUNERAL.
NO. MY DOG. SHE'S... SHE'S GOING TO DIE.

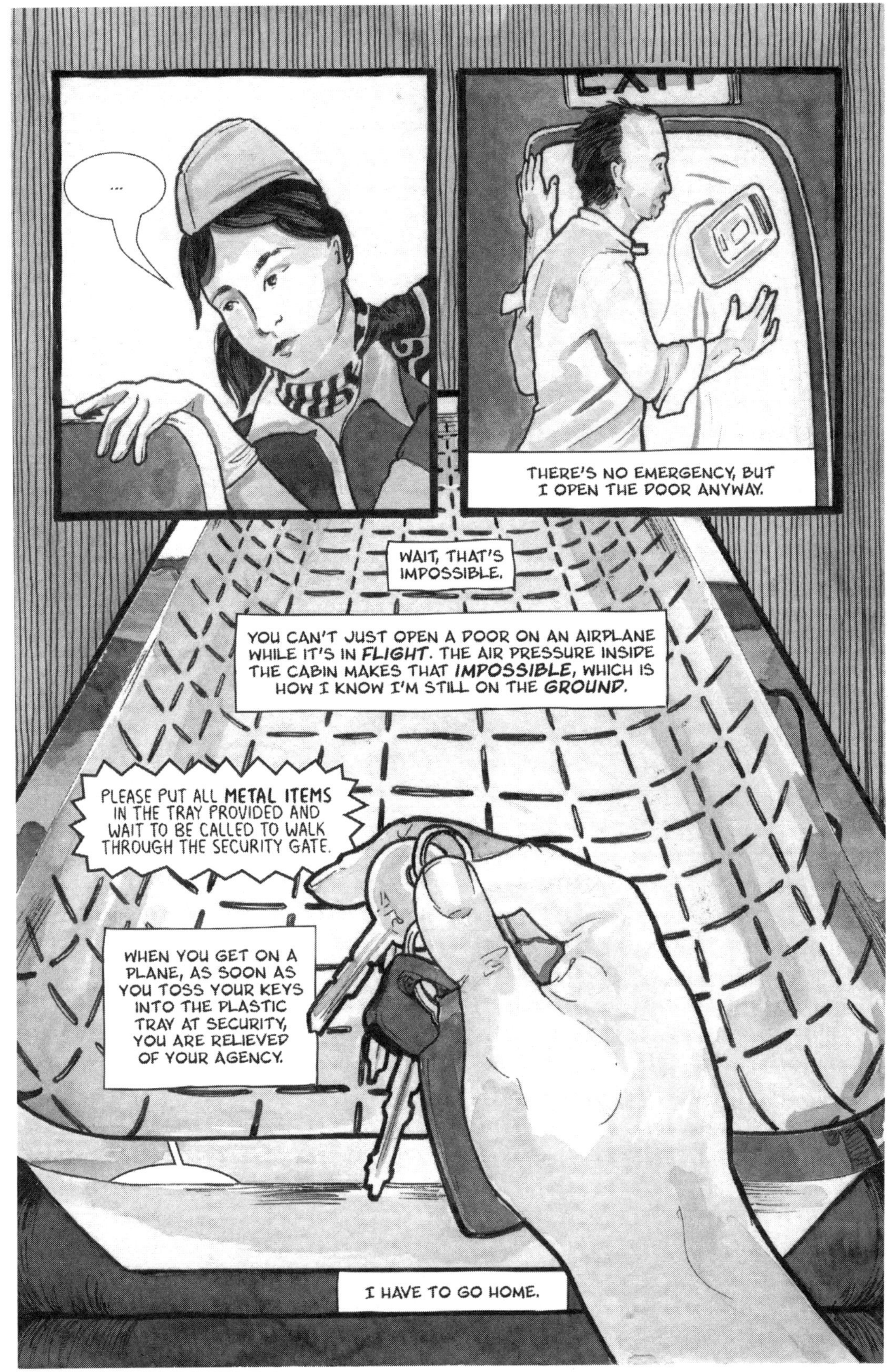
...
THERE'S NO EMERGENCY, BUT I OPEN THE DOOR ANYWAY.
WAIT, THAT'S IMPOSSIBLE.
YOU CAN'T JUST OPEN A DOOR ON AN AIRPLANE WHILE IT'S IN FLIGHT. THE AIR PRESSURE INSIDE THE CABIN MAKES THAT IMPOSSIBLE, WHICH IS HOW I KNOW I'M STILL ON THE GROUND.
PLEASE PUT ALL METAL ITEMS IN THE TRAY PROVIDED AND WAIT TO BE CALLED TO WALK THROUGH THE SECURITY GATE.
WHEN YOU GET ON A PLANE, AS SOON AS YOU TOSS YOUR KEYS INTO THE PLASTIC TRAY AT SECURITY, YOU ARE RELIEVED OF YOUR AGENCY.
I HAVE TO GO HOME.

I USED TO BE A REALLY ENTHUSIASTIC FLYER. In my early twenties I travelled extensively and took many ultra-long haul flights. I spent countless hours wandering around airports in a kind of jet lagged delirium, not entirely sure which country I was in.

On one such flight, from somewhere to somewhere else, I had a strange experience. I had got up in the middle of the night and walked through the dark cabin to the toilet. As I returned down the aisle to find my seat I had the sensation that I could get into any seat I chose; that I was disembodied and could slide into any of the sleeping bodies around me and carry on their life.

This uncanny experience led me to appreciate the literal and psychological distance that you get from your life when in the air. I'm not frightened of flying, so instead of thinking about how my loved ones would react in the unlikely event that my plane plunges unexpectedly back down to Earth, I think about who my loved ones are – and who I am.

We are all born into a relationship with parents and with a country. From our first moments most of us have a family name and a nationality that will define us - even if we change them both - for the rest of our lives. Our culture, traditions and religions encourage us to prioritise these unchosen relationships to ensure social harmony and solidarity.

During World War Two over 100,000 Japanese Americans found themselves cornered at the junction of two identities. In March of 1942, Japanese Americans living on the west coast were forcibly relocated to camps in the interior of the country. People who had been American citizens in February became people with 'enemy ancestry' in March, and their civil rights were summarily dismissed. *A Los Angeles Times* editorial read:

> *A viper is nonetheless a viper wherever the egg is hatched.... So, a Japanese American born of Japanese parents, nurtured upon Japanese traditions, living in a transplanted Japanese atmosphere... notwithstanding his nominal brand of accidental citizenship almost inevitably and with the rarest exceptions grows up to be a Japanese, and not an American.... Thus, while it might cause injustice to a few to treat them all as potential enemies, I cannot escape the conclusion... that such treatment... should be accorded to each and all of them while we are at war with their race.*

The writer is articulating a popular sentiment of the time which disgusts us now, but his underlying premises are still ubiquitous. The idea that birth into a race, culture, religion or nationality could ever be non-accidental is absurd. All circumstances of our births are unchosen and therefore accidental. That categories such as race, citizenship or nationality can be redefined demonstrates their subjective quality.

During Apartheid in South Africa the government measured people's faces and assigned them racial categories; in Nazi Germany, people of many different beliefs were gassed as Jews because of their lineage; and in America in the 1940s, people with more than one sixteenth Japanese heritage were incarcerated. Nothing about these people changed. The categories that defined them were reassigned without their consent.

The urge to label each other and ourselves seems inescapable. The very nature of language is a sophisticated labelling system that allows us to communicate complex or ephemeral ideas. But from the vantage point of 10,000 feet above ground, it seems strange that the arbitrary categories that we are born into are prioritised over those we choose. That we are encouraged to value most highly the relationships we fall into by an accident of birth rather than those we build ourselves based on mutual values, interests and respect.

It is only when our country or family reject us, or when we find ourselves inhabiting a duelling identity, that we begin to question our affiliations... or when we are on a plane.

More information, discussion and links at
doubtcomic.com/between-worlds

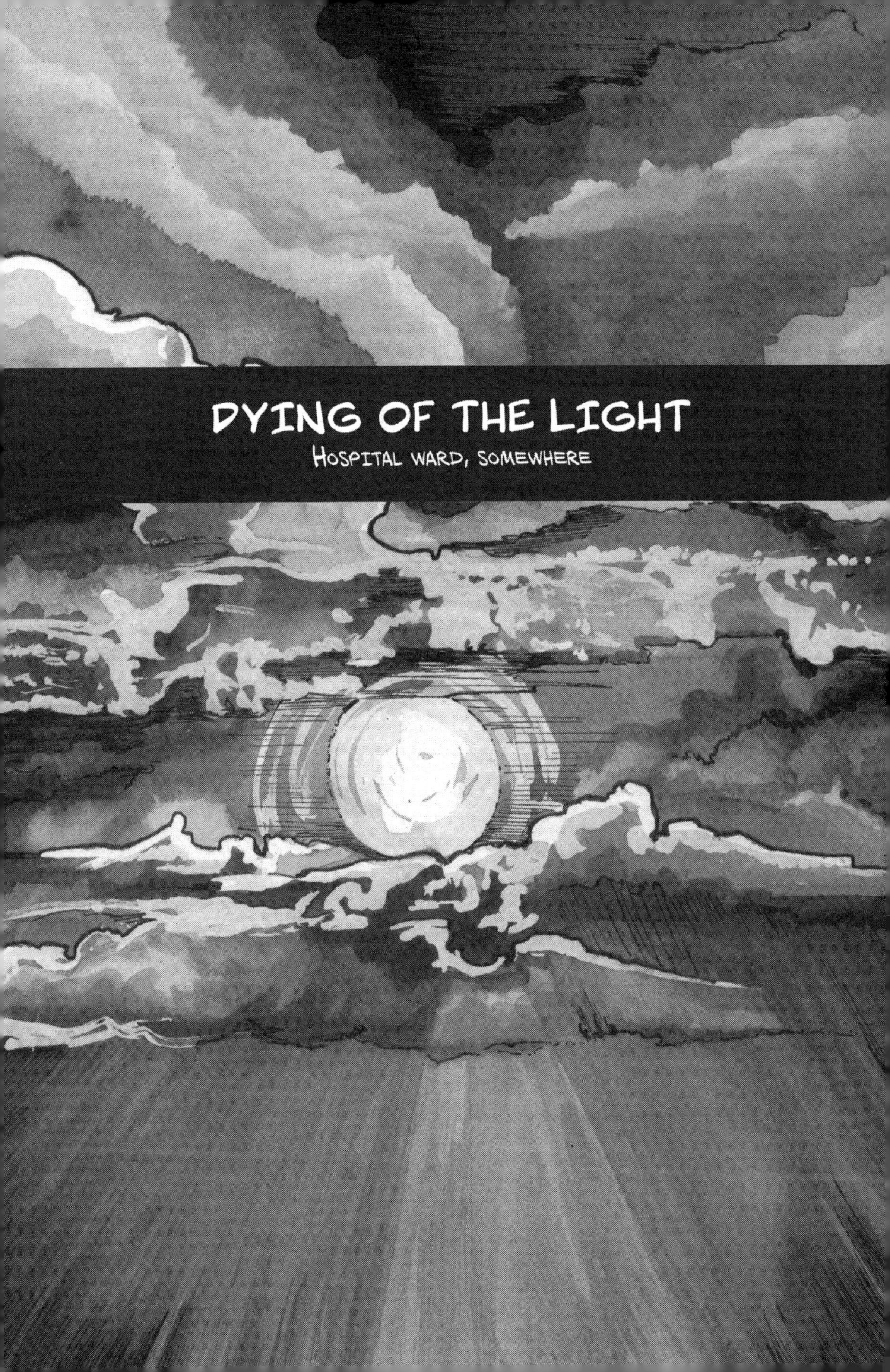
DYING OF THE LIGHT
Hospital ward, somewhere

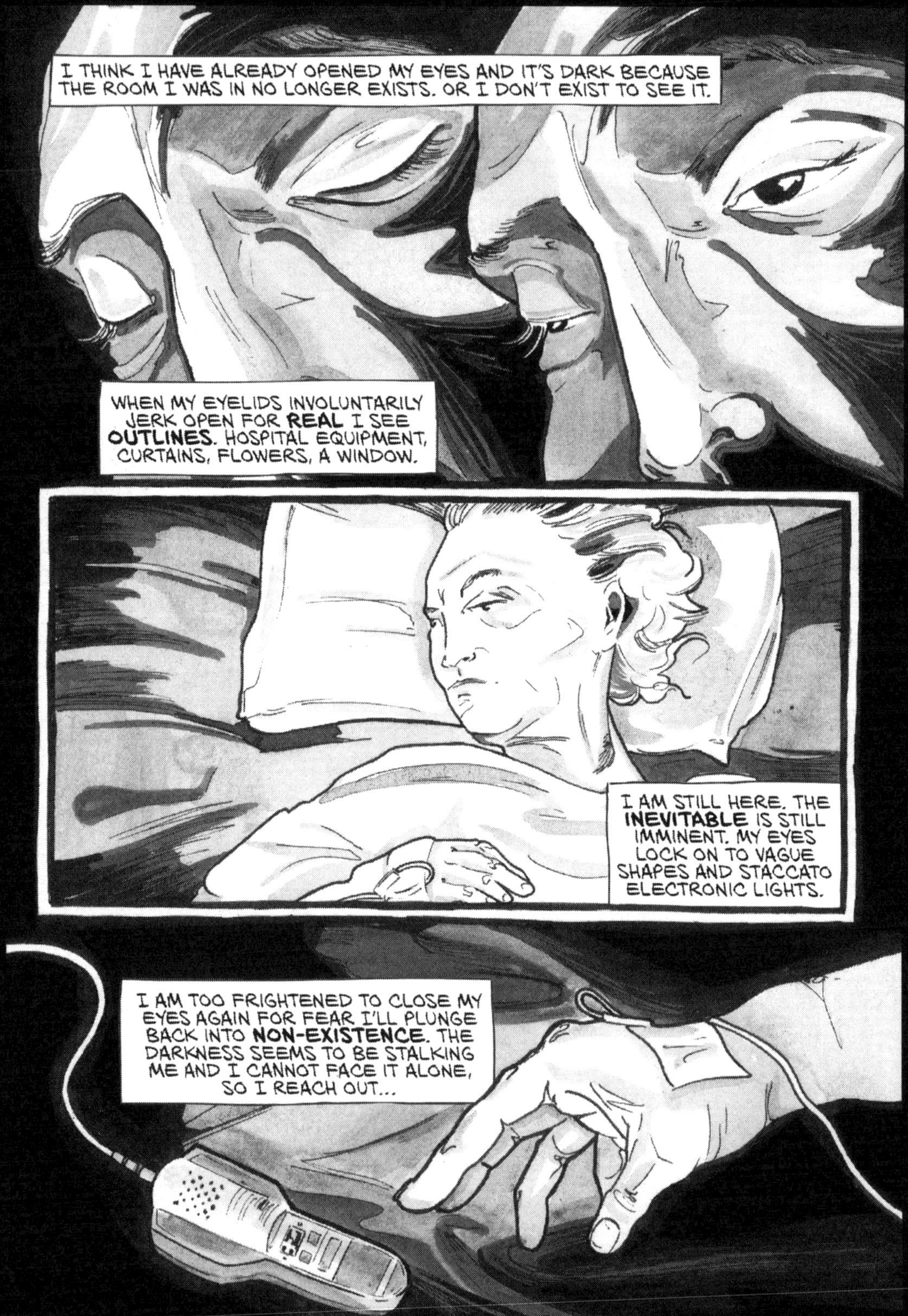
I THINK I HAVE ALREADY OPENED MY EYES AND IT'S DARK BECAUSE THE ROOM I WAS IN NO LONGER EXISTS. OR I DON'T EXIST TO SEE IT.
WHEN MY EYELIDS INVOLUNTARILY JERK OPEN FOR **REAL** I SEE **OUTLINES**. HOSPITAL EQUIPMENT, CURTAINS, FLOWERS, A WINDOW.
I AM STILL HERE. THE **INEVITABLE** IS STILL IMMINENT. MY EYES LOCK ON TO VAGUE SHAPES AND STACCATO ELECTRONIC LIGHTS.
I AM TOO FRIGHTENED TO CLOSE MY EYES AGAIN FOR FEAR I'LL PLUNGE BACK INTO **NON-EXISTENCE**. THE DARKNESS SEEMS TO BE STALKING ME AND I CANNOT FACE IT ALONE, SO I REACH OUT...

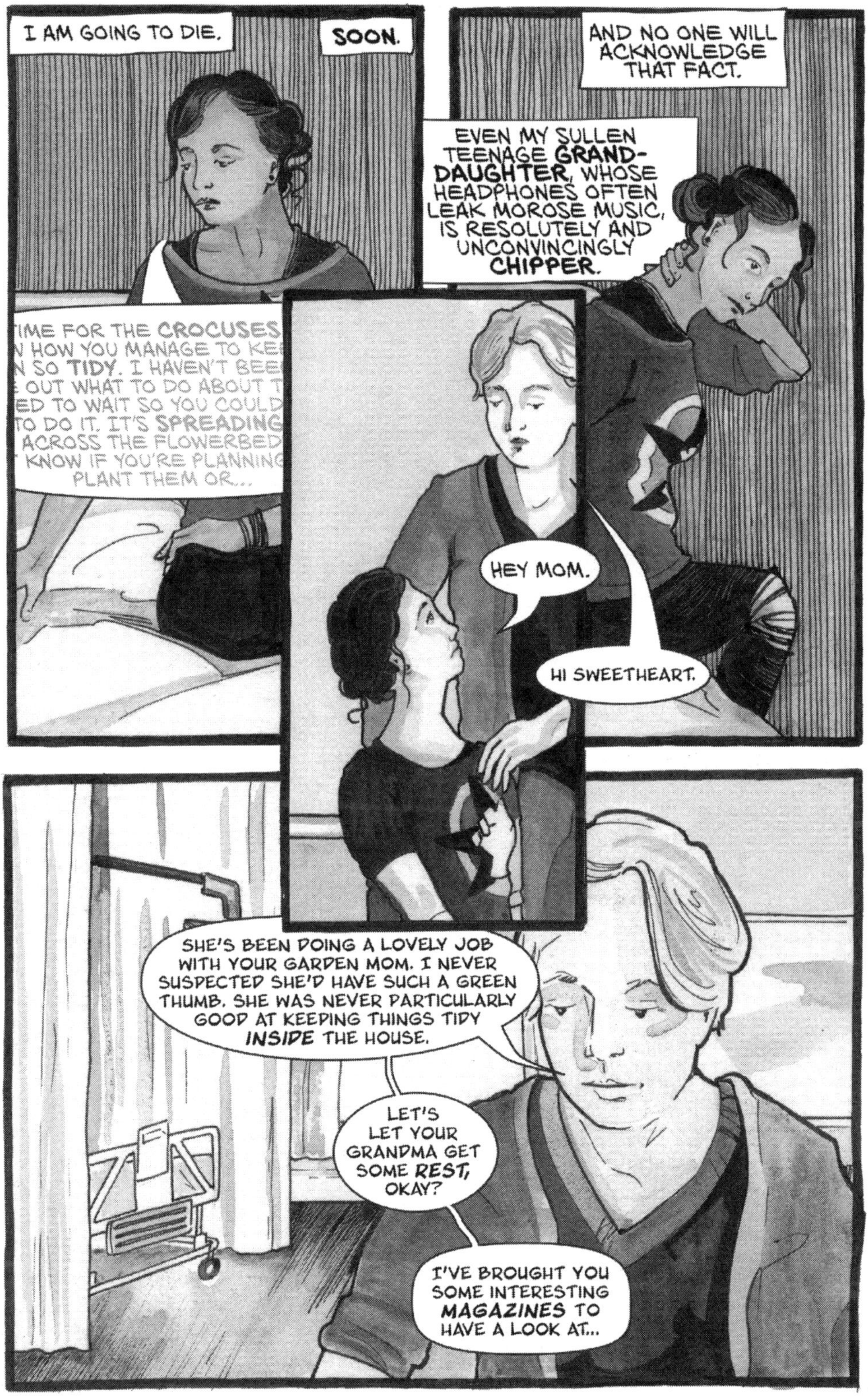
I AM GOING TO DIE.
SOON.
AND NO ONE WILL ACKNOWLEDGE THAT FACT.
EVEN MY SULLEN TEENAGE GRAND-DAUGHTER, WHOSE HEADPHONES OFTEN LEAK MOROSE MUSIC, IS RESOLUTELY AND UNCONVINCINGLY CHIPPER.
TIME FOR THE CROCUSES
N HOW YOU MANAGE TO KEE
N SO TIDY. I HAVEN'T BEE
OUT WHAT TO DO ABOUT T
ED TO WAIT SO YOU COULD
TO DO IT. IT'S SPREADING
ACROSS THE FLOWERBED
KNOW IF YOU'RE PLANNING
PLANT THEM OR...
HEY MOM.
HI SWEETHEART.
SHE'S BEEN DOING A LOVELY JOB WITH YOUR GARDEN MOM. I NEVER SUSPECTED SHE'D HAVE SUCH A GREEN THUMB. SHE WAS NEVER PARTICULARLY GOOD AT KEEPING THINGS TIDY INSIDE THE HOUSE.
LET'S LET YOUR GRANDMA GET SOME REST, OKAY?
I'VE BROUGHT YOU SOME INTERESTING MAGAZINES TO HAVE A LOOK AT...

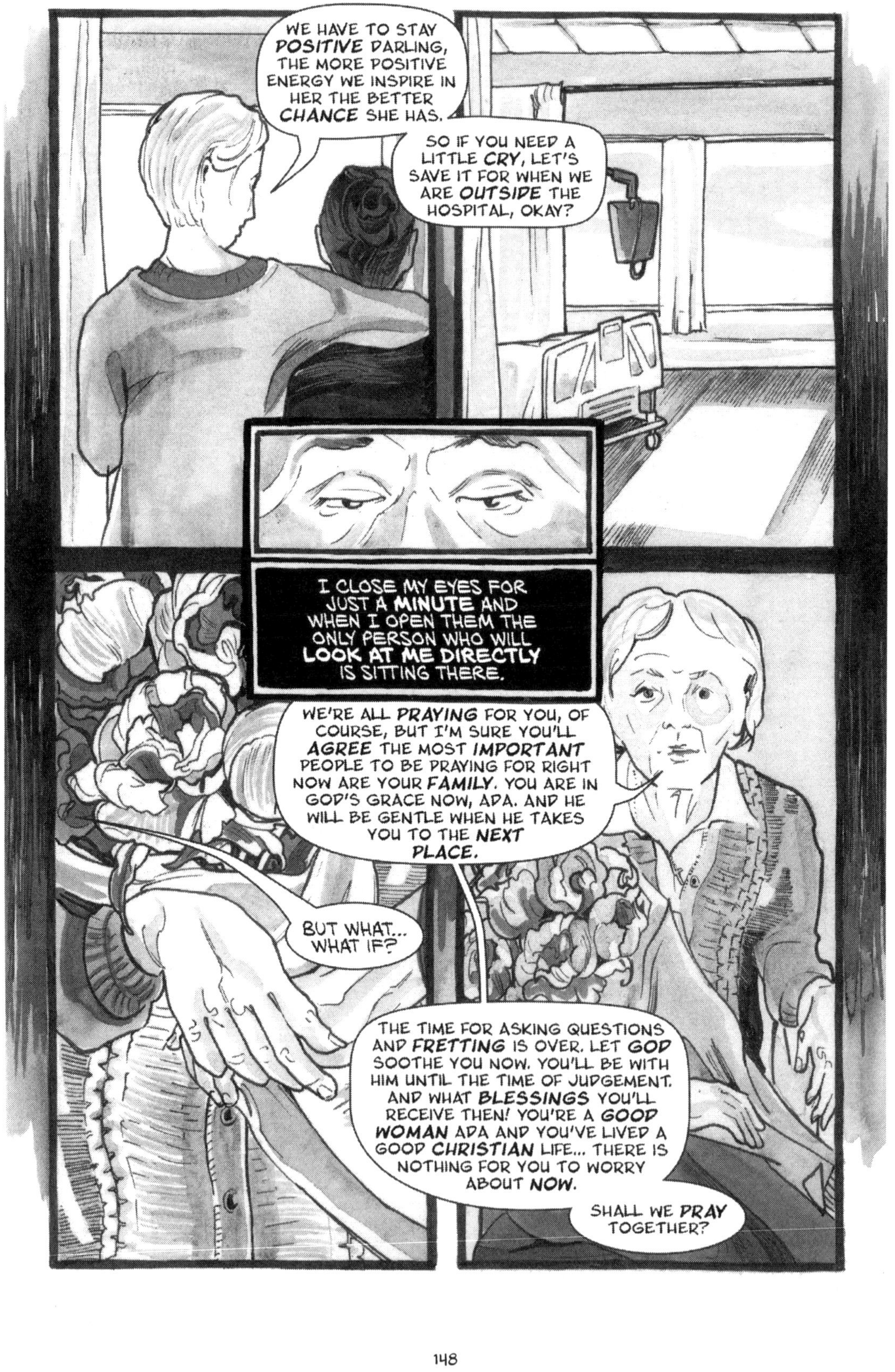
WE HAVE TO STAY POSITIVE DARLING, THE MORE POSITIVE ENERGY WE INSPIRE IN HER THE BETTER CHANCE SHE HAS.
SO IF YOU NEED A LITTLE CRY, LET'S SAVE IT FOR WHEN WE ARE OUTSIDE THE HOSPITAL, OKAY?
I CLOSE MY EYES FOR JUST A MINUTE AND WHEN I OPEN THEM THE ONLY PERSON WHO WILL LOOK AT ME DIRECTLY IS SITTING THERE.
WE'RE ALL PRAYING FOR YOU, OF COURSE, BUT I'M SURE YOU'LL AGREE THE MOST IMPORTANT PEOPLE TO BE PRAYING FOR RIGHT NOW ARE YOUR FAMILY. YOU ARE IN GOD'S GRACE NOW, ADA. AND HE WILL BE GENTLE WHEN HE TAKES YOU TO THE NEXT PLACE.
BUT WHAT... WHAT IF?
THE TIME FOR ASKING QUESTIONS AND FRETTING IS OVER. LET GOD SOOTHE YOU NOW. YOU'LL BE WITH HIM UNTIL THE TIME OF JUDGEMENT. AND WHAT BLESSINGS YOU'LL RECEIVE THEN! YOU'RE A GOOD WOMAN ADA AND YOU'VE LIVED A GOOD CHRISTIAN LIFE... THERE IS NOTHING FOR YOU TO WORRY ABOUT NOW.
SHALL WE PRAY TOGETHER?

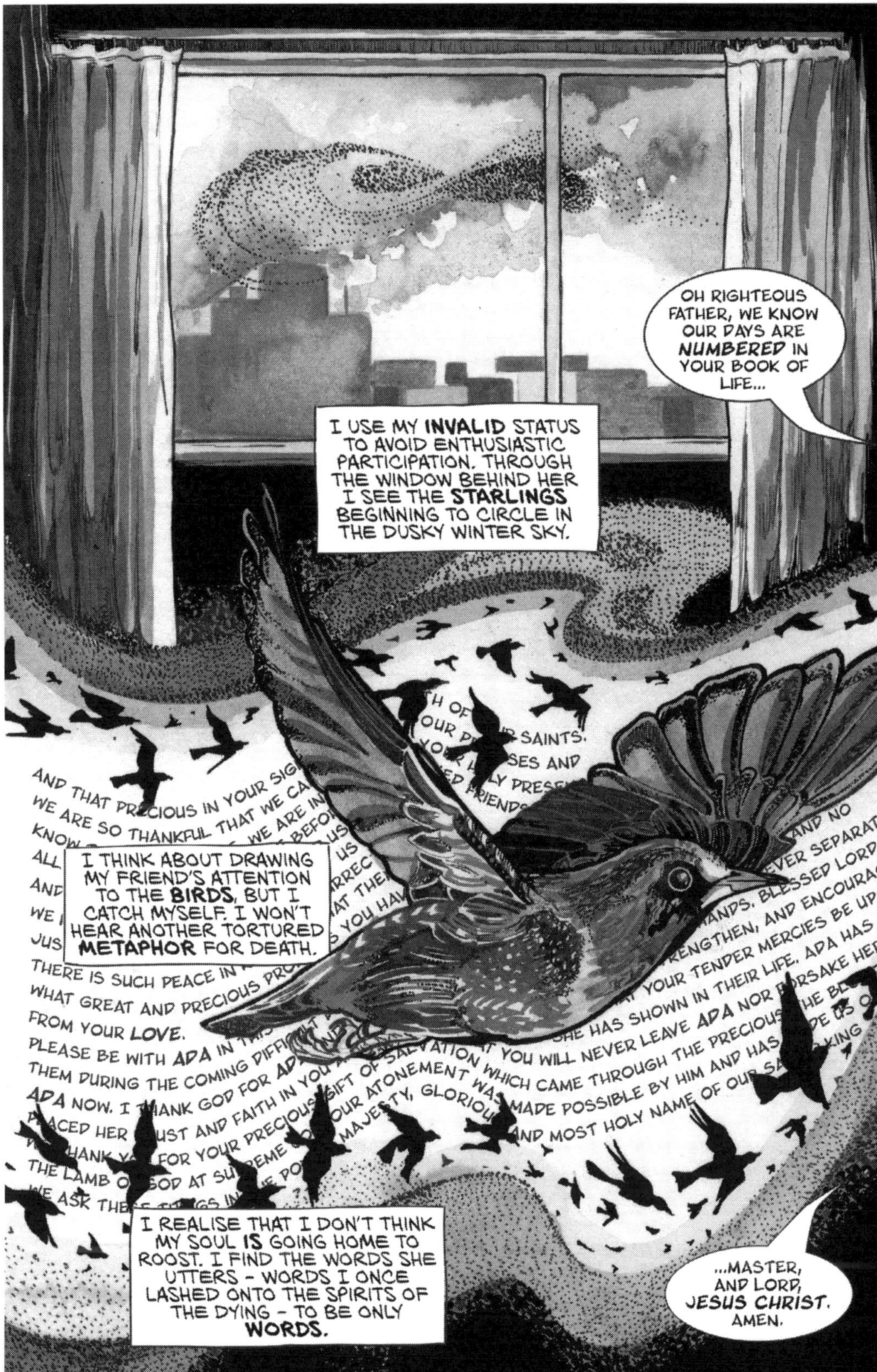
OH RIGHTEOUS FATHER, WE KNOW OUR DAYS ARE NUMBERED IN YOUR BOOK OF LIFE...
I USE MY INVALID STATUS TO AVOID ENTHUSIASTIC PARTICIPATION. THROUGH THE WINDOW BEHIND HER I SEE THE STARLINGS BEGINNING TO CIRCLE IN THE DUSKY WINTER SKY.
I THINK ABOUT DRAWING MY FRIEND'S ATTENTION TO THE BIRDS, BUT I CATCH MYSELF. I WON'T HEAR ANOTHER TORTURED METAPHOR FOR DEATH.
I REALISE THAT I DON'T THINK MY SOUL IS GOING HOME TO ROOST. I FIND THE WORDS SHE UTTERS - WORDS I ONCE LASHED ONTO THE SPIRITS OF THE DYING - TO BE ONLY WORDS.
...MASTER, AND LORD, JESUS CHRIST. AMEN.

NOW, STEPPING INTO THAT DARKNESS FOR MYSELF, I AM IN NEED OF MORE THAN **POETRY** TO DEFEND MYSELF AGAINST WHAT SEEMS LIKE THE MOST **PLAUSIBLE** POSSIBILITY:

THAT THERE WILL BE **NOTHING**.

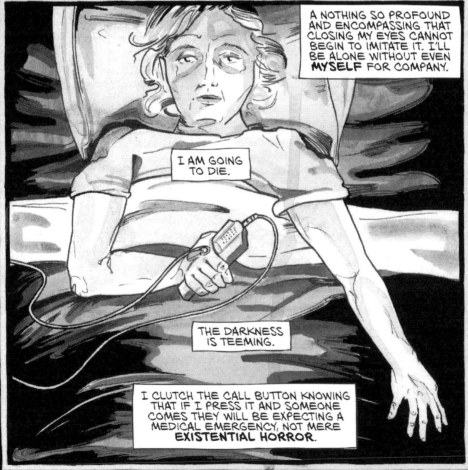

A NOTHING SO PROFOUND AND ENCOMPASSING THAT CLOSING MY EYES CANNOT BEGIN TO IMITATE IT. I'LL BE ALONE WITHOUT EVEN **MYSELF** FOR COMPANY.

I AM GOING TO DIE.

THE DARKNESS IS TEEMING.

I CLUTCH THE CALL BUTTON KNOWING THAT IF I PRESS IT AND SOMEONE COMES THEY WILL BE EXPECTING A MEDICAL EMERGENCY, NOT MERE **EXISTENTIAL HORROR**.

WHEN THE HORROR COMES FOR ME **TONIGHT** I WILL FACE IT WELL-MANICURED.

WORK ON SOMEONE WHO OBVIOU HAS TAKEN SUCH GOOD CARE OF T SKIN. YOUR *DAUGHTER* MENTIONE ARE A KEEN GARDENER BUT I CA HARDLY BELIEVE IT. WHENEVER I S BEAUTIFUL FLOWER BED I SHUDDER THINK OF THE *CALLOUSED* HANDS CREATED IT, DON'T YOU? IT USED T COMMON PRACTICE FOR WOMEN-E *YOUNG* WOMEN-TO USE A GOOD O NIGHT COLD CREAM BUT I DON'T PEOPLE DOING THAT NOWADAYS E THOSE WHO REALLY SHOULD, LIK GARD

HER PERFORMANCE IS EXCELLENT, **OSCAR WORTHY**. I WONDER IF SHE ONLY PAINTS THE NAILS OF THE **DYING** OR IF SHE DOES THIS AS A VOLUNTEER JOB. A DAY OFF FROM HOLDING THE HANDS OF THE LIVING.

MY DAUGHTER IS TALKING BEHIND THE CURTAIN.

THERE'S THIS **GAME** WE ALL PLAY IN HOSPITALS WHERE WE PRETEND THIN **COTTON** IS **CONCRETE**, IMPENETRABLE AND **SOUNDPROOF**.

... I KNOW, BUT YOUR GRANDMA HAS LIVED A LONG HAPPY LIFE, YOU HAVE TO COMFORT YOURSELF WITH *THAT THOUGHT*. THIS *TEMPORARY* SUFFERING WILL BE OVER WHEN SHE PASSES *ON* AND *THROUGH*. WE'LL MISS HER. WE SHOULD BE *CELEBRATING* HER NEW LIFE IN...

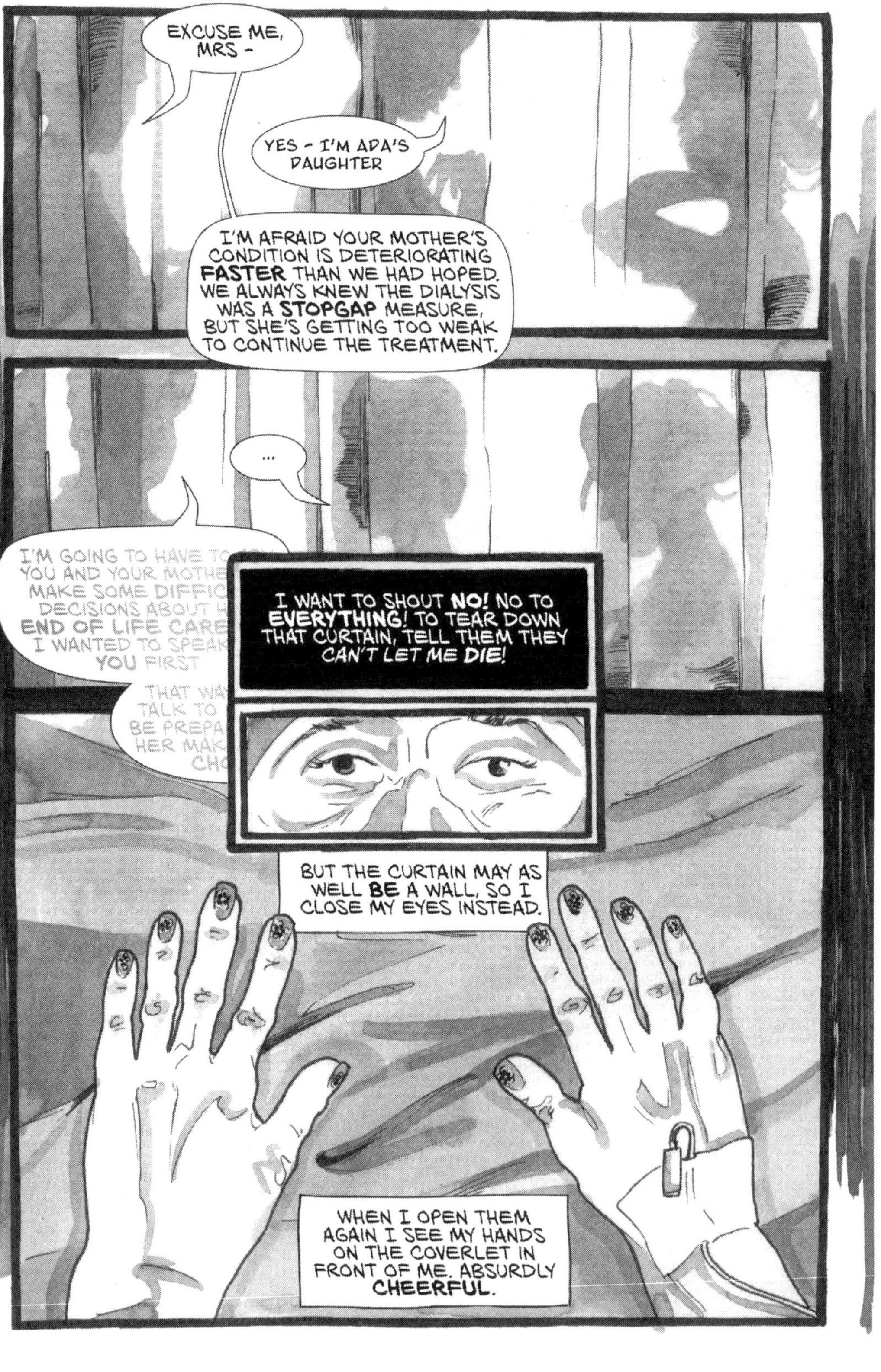
EXCUSE ME, MRS -
YES - I'M ADA'S DAUGHTER
I'M AFRAID YOUR MOTHER'S CONDITION IS DETERIORATING **FASTER** THAN WE HAD HOPED. WE ALWAYS KNEW THE DIALYSIS WAS A **STOPGAP** MEASURE, BUT SHE'S GETTING TOO WEAK TO CONTINUE THE TREATMENT.
...
I'M GOING TO HAVE TO YOU AND YOUR MAKE SOME DECISIONS ABOUT END OF LIFE I WANTED TO SPEAK YOU FIRST
TALK TO
I WANT TO SHOUT **NO!** NO TO **EVERYTHING!** TO TEAR DOWN THAT CURTAIN, TELL THEM THEY *CAN'T LET ME **DIE**!*
BUT THE CURTAIN MAY AS WELL **BE** A WALL, SO I CLOSE MY EYES INSTEAD.
WHEN I OPEN THEM AGAIN I SEE MY HANDS ON THE COVERLET IN FRONT OF ME. ABSURDLY **CHEERFUL**.

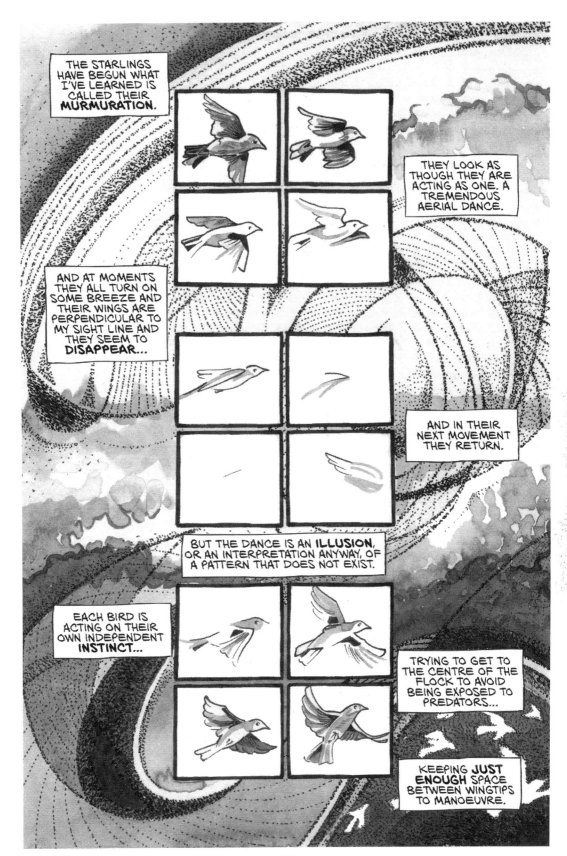

THE STARLINGS HAVE BEGUN WHAT I'VE LEARNED IS CALLED THEIR **MURMURATION.**

THEY LOOK AS THOUGH THEY ARE ACTING AS ONE. A TREMENDOUS AERIAL DANCE.

AND AT MOMENTS THEY ALL TURN ON SOME BREEZE AND THEIR WINGS ARE PERPENDICULAR TO MY SIGHT LINE AND THEY SEEM TO **DISAPPEAR...**

AND IN THEIR NEXT MOVEMENT THEY RETURN.

BUT THE DANCE IS AN **ILLUSION,** OR AN INTERPRETATION ANYWAY, OF A PATTERN THAT DOES NOT EXIST.

EACH BIRD IS ACTING ON THEIR OWN INDEPENDENT **INSTINCT...**

TRYING TO GET TO THE CENTRE OF THE FLOCK TO AVOID BEING EXPOSED TO PREDATORS...

KEEPING **JUST ENOUGH** SPACE BETWEEN WINGTIPS TO MANOEUVRE.

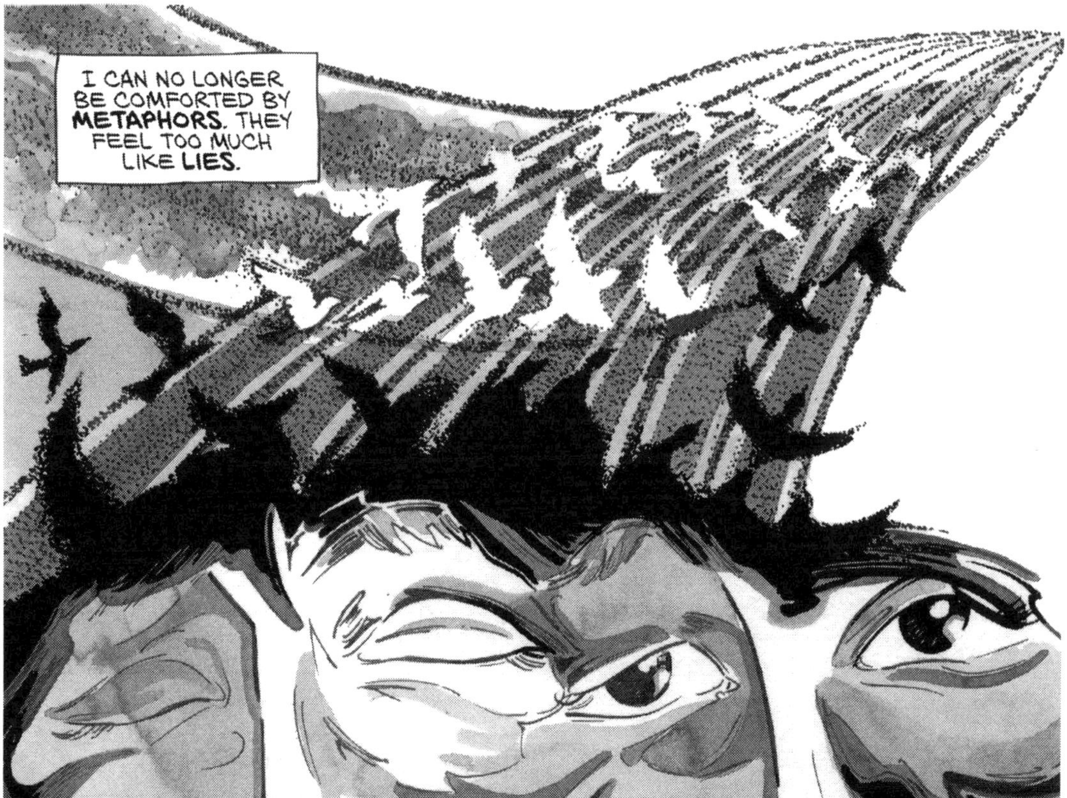
I CAN NO LONGER BE COMFORTED BY **METAPHORS**. THEY FEEL TOO MUCH LIKE **LIES**.
WHEN I OPEN MY EYES IT IS DARK AND I AM GOING TO DIE.

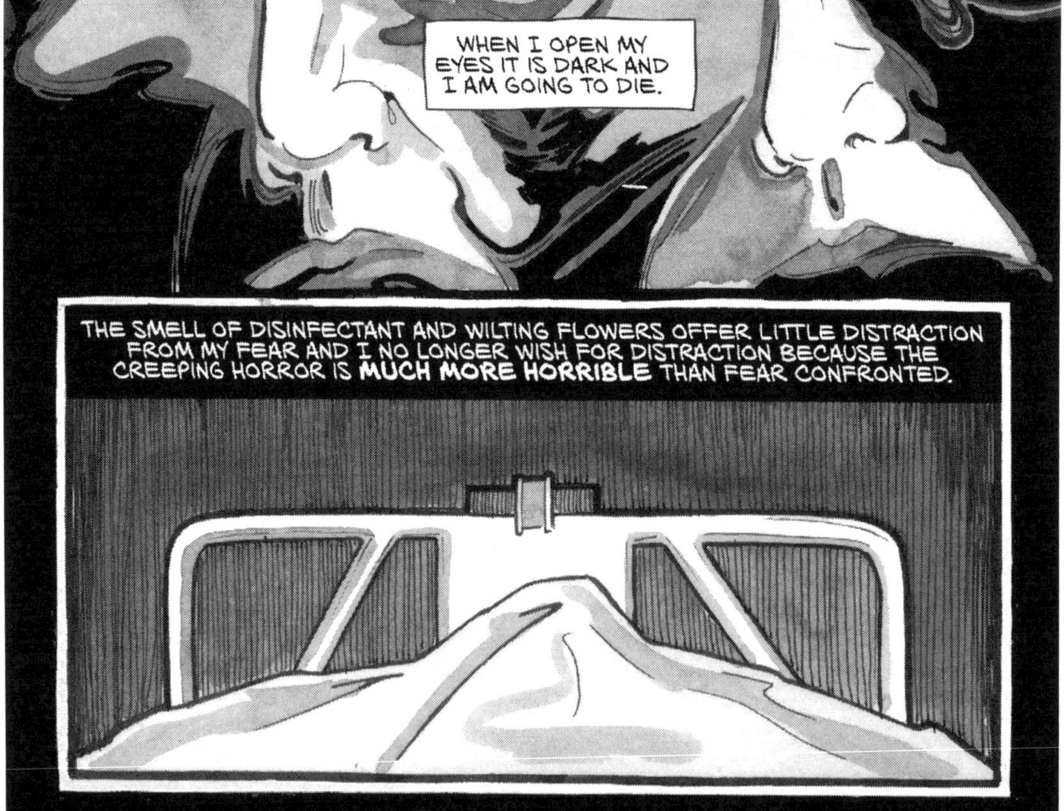
THE SMELL OF DISINFECTANT AND WILTING FLOWERS OFFER LITTLE DISTRACTION FROM MY FEAR AND I NO LONGER WISH FOR DISTRACTION BECAUSE THE CREEPING HORROR IS **MUCH MORE HORRIBLE** THAN FEAR CONFRONTED.

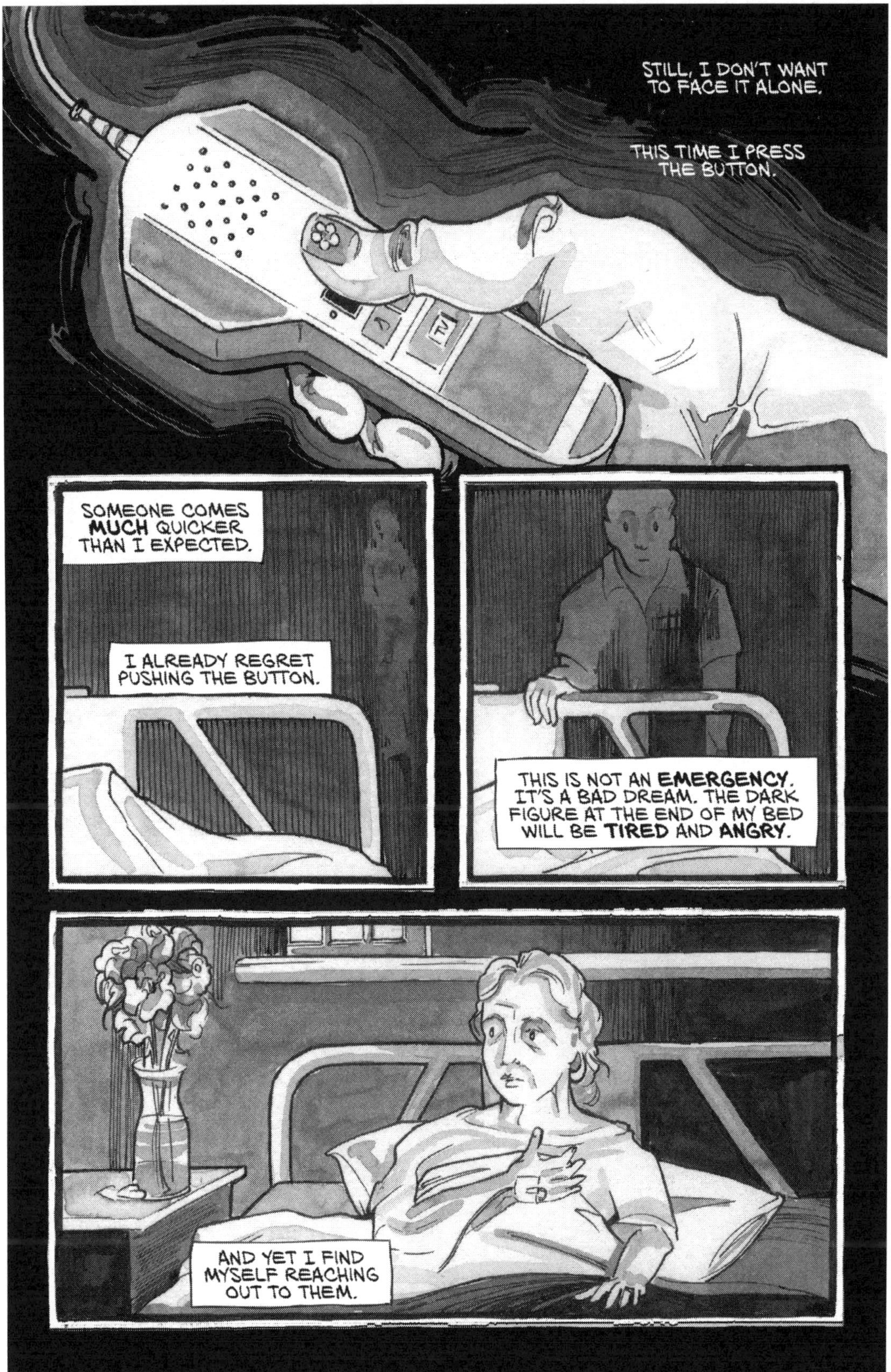
STILL, I DON'T WANT TO FACE IT ALONE.
THIS TIME I PRESS THE BUTTON.
SOMEONE COMES **MUCH** QUICKER THAN I EXPECTED.
I ALREADY REGRET PUSHING THE BUTTON.
THIS IS NOT AN **EMERGENCY**. IT'S A BAD DREAM. THE DARK FIGURE AT THE END OF MY BED WILL BE **TIRED** AND **ANGRY**.
AND YET I FIND MYSELF REACHING OUT TO THEM.

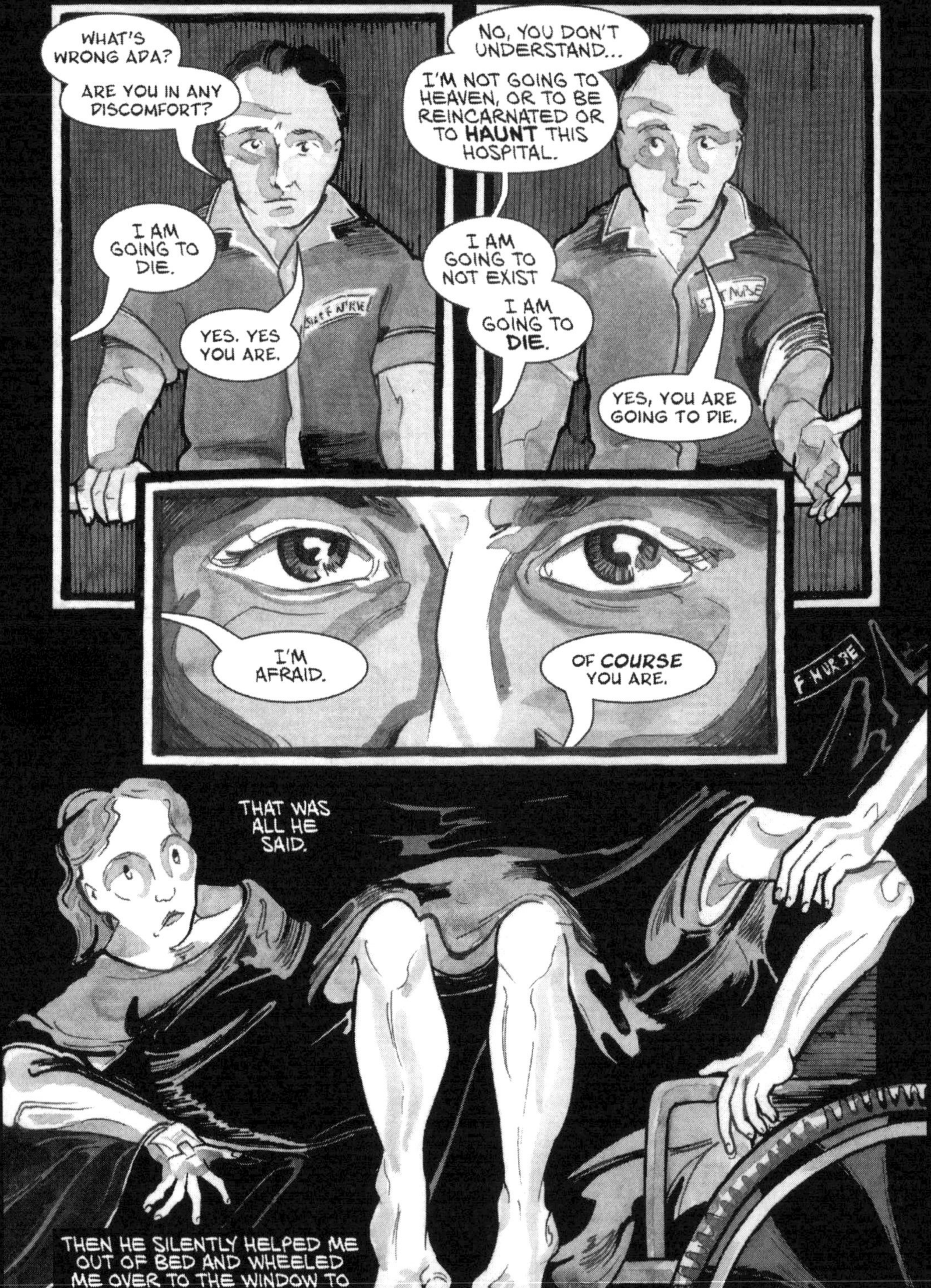
WHAT'S WRONG ADA?
ARE YOU IN ANY DISCOMFORT?
I AM GOING TO DIE.
YES. YES YOU ARE.
NO, YOU DON'T UNDERSTAND...
I'M NOT GOING TO HEAVEN, OR TO BE REINCARNATED OR TO **HAUNT** THIS HOSPITAL.
I AM GOING TO NOT EXIST
I AM GOING TO **DIE**.
YES, YOU ARE GOING TO DIE.
I'M AFRAID.
OF **COURSE** YOU ARE.
THAT WAS ALL HE SAID.
THEN HE SILENTLY HELPED ME OUT OF BED AND WHEELED ME OVER TO THE WINDOW TO WATCH THE DAWN.

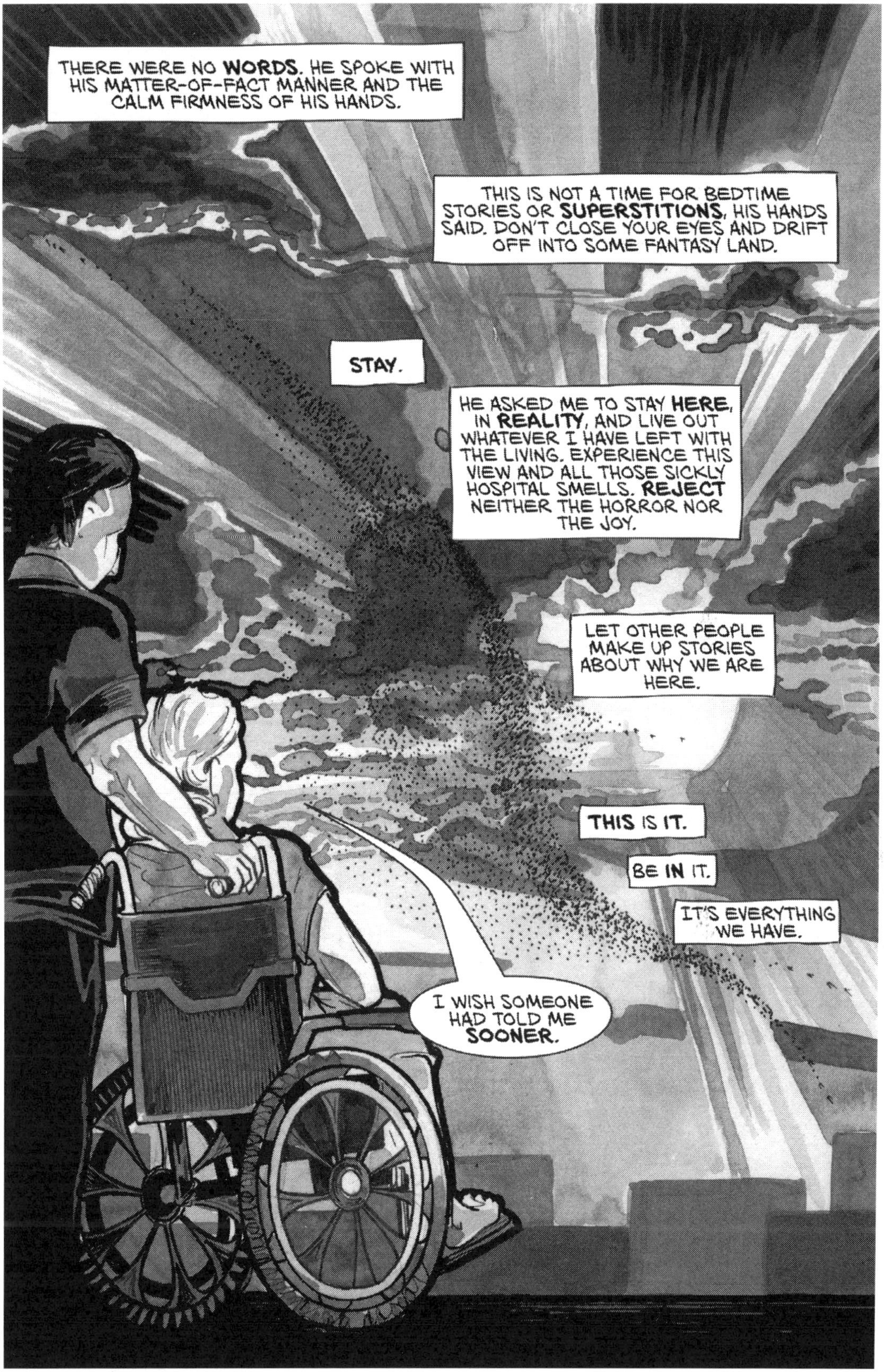
THERE WERE NO WORDS. HE SPOKE WITH HIS MATTER-OF-FACT MANNER AND THE CALM FIRMNESS OF HIS HANDS.
THIS IS NOT A TIME FOR BEDTIME STORIES OR SUPERSTITIONS, HIS HANDS SAID. DON'T CLOSE YOUR EYES AND DRIFT OFF INTO SOME FANTASY LAND.
STAY.
HE ASKED ME TO STAY HERE, IN REALITY, AND LIVE OUT WHATEVER I HAVE LEFT WITH THE LIVING. EXPERIENCE THIS VIEW AND ALL THOSE SICKLY HOSPITAL SMELLS. REJECT NEITHER THE HORROR NOR THE JOY.
LET OTHER PEOPLE MAKE UP STORIES ABOUT WHY WE ARE HERE.
THIS IS IT.
BE IN IT.
IT'S EVERYTHING WE HAVE.
I WISH SOMEONE HAD TOLD ME SOONER.

My family has a tradition of reading a poem at funerals. It's called *Death Is Nothing At All*, by Henry-Scott Holland. It goes like this:

> *What is this death but a negligible accident?*
> *Why should I be out of mind*
> *Because I am out of sight?*
> *I am but waiting for you*
> *For an interval*
> *Somewhere very near*
> *Just round the corner*
> *All is well.*

It never seemed ironic to me that we were all gathered to acknowledge a loved one's death, celebrate their life and help each other through our grief... and then someone stood up and read us a poem that tells us that the person we've lost is not really gone. We don't hold funerals for people who leave the room; we hold funerals for the dead.

A study of terminally ill cancer patients published in the Journal of the American Medical Association had counterintuitive results. A faith in the afterlife, whether vague like the sentiment expressed in Holland's poem or a more structured set of religious beliefs, is often thought to comfort the dying. Some writers have theorised that religion itself is a product of humanity's desperate desire to deny death. Bill Maher starts his documentary *Religulous* voicing this common sentiment:

> *These questions about what happens when you die... they so freak people out, that they will just make up any story and cling to it.*

So you might expect to find religious people more relaxed and optimistic on their deathbeds than atheists or agnostics. But the study found that patients who reported relying on their religion to cope with their illnesses were more likely to pursue aggressive medical interventions in the last days of their lives. They were not resigned to, or welcoming of, death but fighting it. If religion is a strategy to avoid or deny the reality of death, it seems it's a pretty flawed one.

As an atheist I've always had sympathy for people who cling to faith at the hardest time of their life, when they or a loved one is dying. But if, as the results of the JAMA study suggest, at the end of their lives people find their faith insufficient to comfort them or feel it faltering, then what can we offer them other than holding their hands?

We can offer our presence and our sincerity and be brave enough to hear them tell us they are frightened. They may have to face death alone but they do not need their final confrontation to be ignored or diminished. In her book *Comforting Thoughts About Death That Have Nothing to do with God*, Greta Christina refuses to concede the ground of death and grieving to the religious:

> *Here's the thing you have to remember about religious beliefs in an afterlife: They're only comforting if you don't examine them.*

She suggests some humanist perspectives that may not seem as comforting but hold up to rigorous examination.

When I began to find the Holland poem ironic, I rushed into the literary comfort of Dylan Thomas who urges us:

> *Do not go gentle into that good night.*
> *Rage, rage against the dying of the light.*

I'm not sure if the 'rage' still resonates with me, but the passion does. I hope that my last few days are spent wringing every last drop of experience out of my consciousness. Because if we accept that death is real, then the only response is to live, even when our bodies are deteriorating, right up to the edge of our existence.

More information, discussion and links at
doubtcomic.com/dying-of-the-light

UNREAL CITY

The London Underground, London, England

EVENING STANDARD TUESDAY 1 AUGUST 2016

Commuters' late n
an urban fox on t

MARCH BANFORD

They're invaded London's gardens and even homes – now it seems that urban foxes are taking over the Tube.

Nurse practitioner Billy Gates was travelling on the underground late last night when a fox suddenly appeared in her train carriage and approached her where she was seated.

"I was not so shocked to see the fox, but I was surprised when he began speaking to me" said the thirty-two year old. "He initially seemed quite convincing, but after a short conversation veered into nihilistic postmodern philosophy."

MAYORAL ELECTIONS

A spokesperson for Transport for London said: "the foxes that make their way down into the underground system tend to be disproportionately grim characters" – "not all foxes," he said, "so pessimistic".

£25

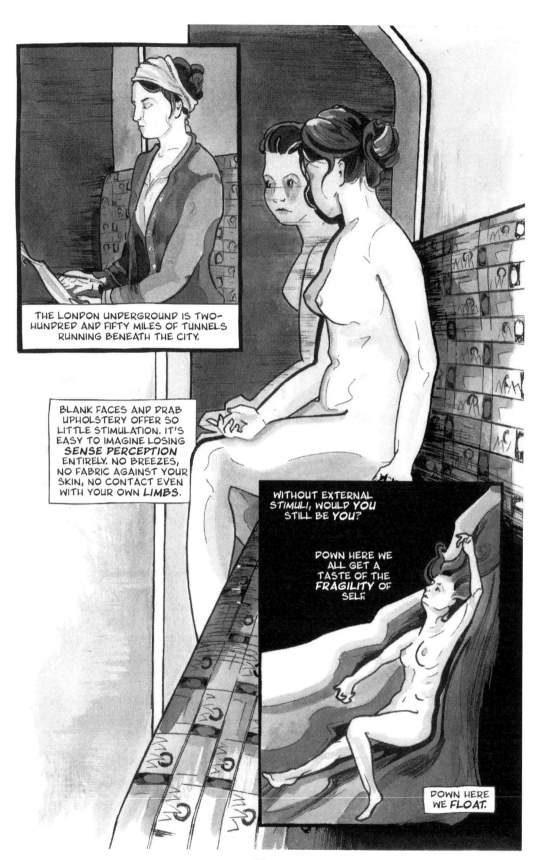

THE LONDON UNDERGROUND IS TWO-HUNDRED AND FIFTY MILES OF TUNNELS RUNNING BENEATH THE CITY.

BLANK FACES AND DRAB UPHOLSTERY OFFER SO LITTLE STIMULATION. IT'S EASY TO IMAGINE LOSING *SENSE PERCEPTION* ENTIRELY. NO BREEZES, NO FABRIC AGAINST YOUR SKIN, NO CONTACT EVEN WITH YOUR OWN *LIMBS*.

WITHOUT EXTERNAL STIMULI, WOULD *YOU* STILL BE *YOU*?

DOWN HERE WE ALL GET A TASTE OF THE *FRAGILITY* OF SELF.

DOWN HERE WE *FLOAT*.

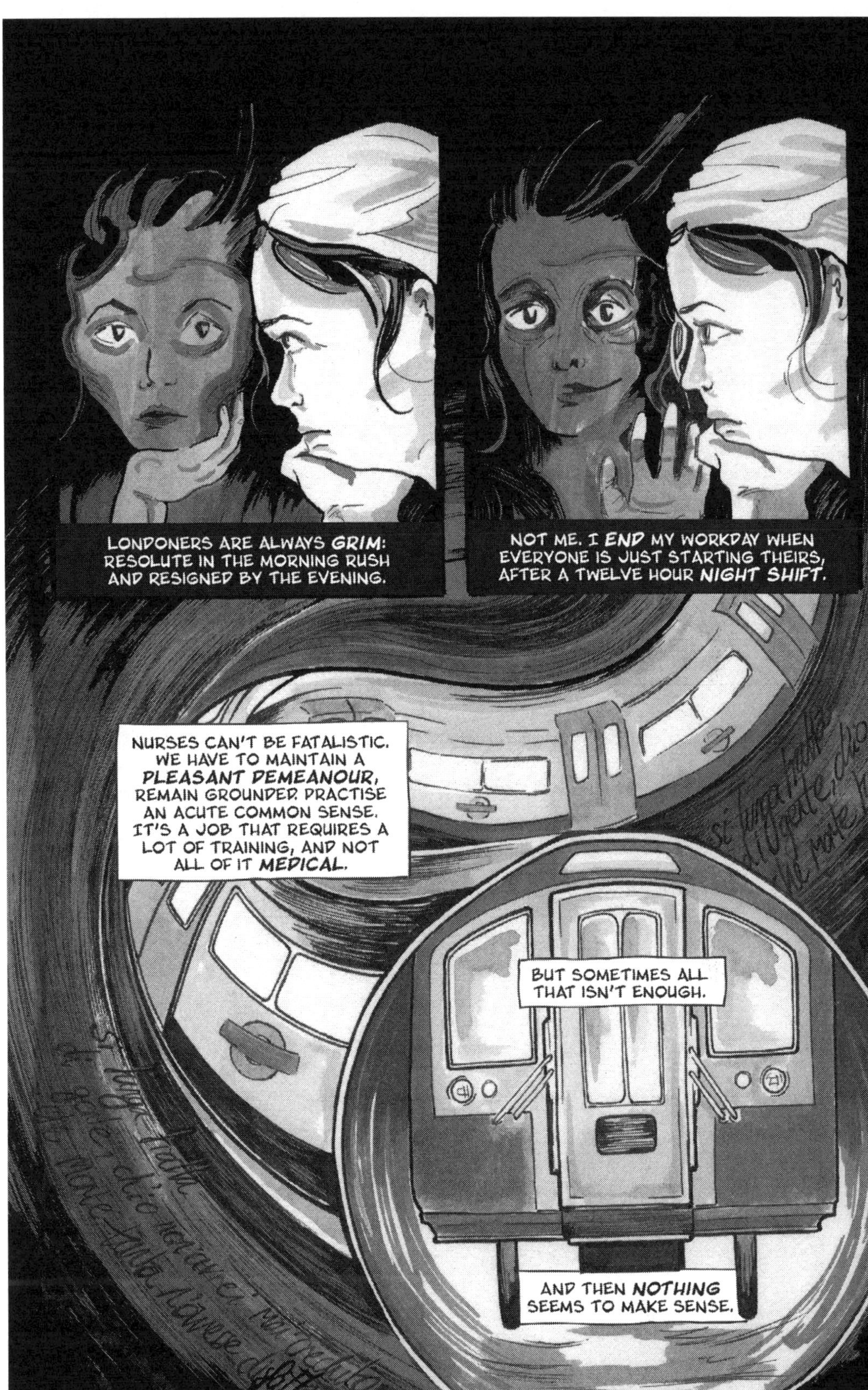
LONDONERS ARE ALWAYS GRIM: RESOLUTE IN THE MORNING RUSH AND RESIGNED BY THE EVENING.
NOT ME. I END MY WORKDAY WHEN EVERYONE IS JUST STARTING THEIRS, AFTER A TWELVE HOUR NIGHT SHIFT.
NURSES CAN'T BE FATALISTIC. WE HAVE TO MAINTAIN A PLEASANT DEMEANOUR, REMAIN GROUNDED, PRACTISE AN ACUTE COMMON SENSE. IT'S A JOB THAT REQUIRES A LOT OF TRAINING, AND NOT ALL OF IT MEDICAL.
BUT SOMETIMES ALL THAT ISN'T ENOUGH.
AND THEN NOTHING SEEMS TO MAKE SENSE.

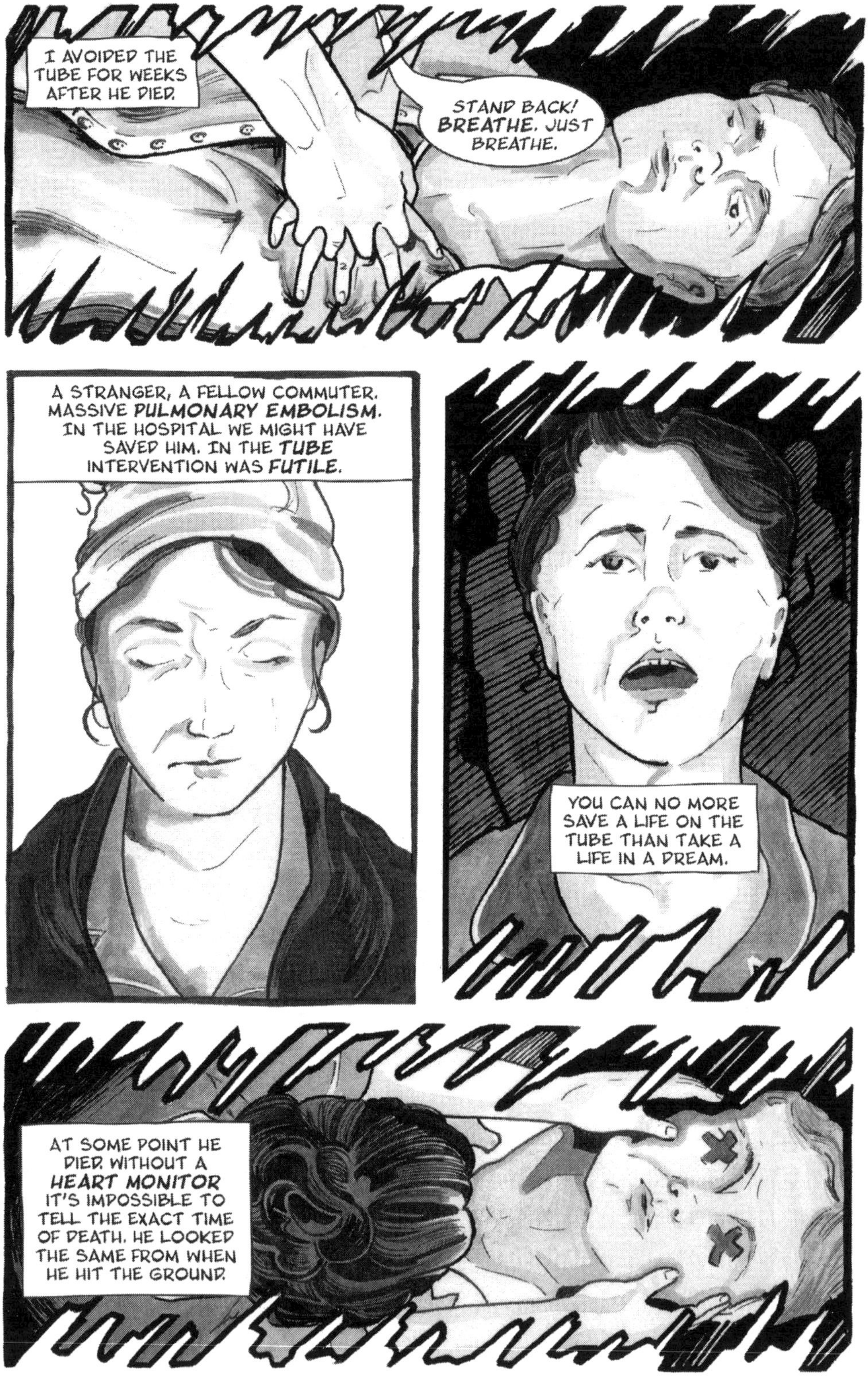
I AVOIDED THE TUBE FOR WEEKS AFTER HE DIED.
STAND BACK! BREATHE. JUST BREATHE.
A STRANGER, A FELLOW COMMUTER. MASSIVE PULMONARY EMBOLISM. IN THE HOSPITAL WE MIGHT HAVE SAVED HIM. IN THE TUBE INTERVENTION WAS FUTILE.
YOU CAN NO MORE SAVE A LIFE ON THE TUBE THAN TAKE A LIFE IN A DREAM.
AT SOME POINT HE DIED. WITHOUT A HEART MONITOR IT'S IMPOSSIBLE TO TELL THE EXACT TIME OF DEATH. HE LOOKED THE SAME FROM WHEN HE HIT THE GROUND.

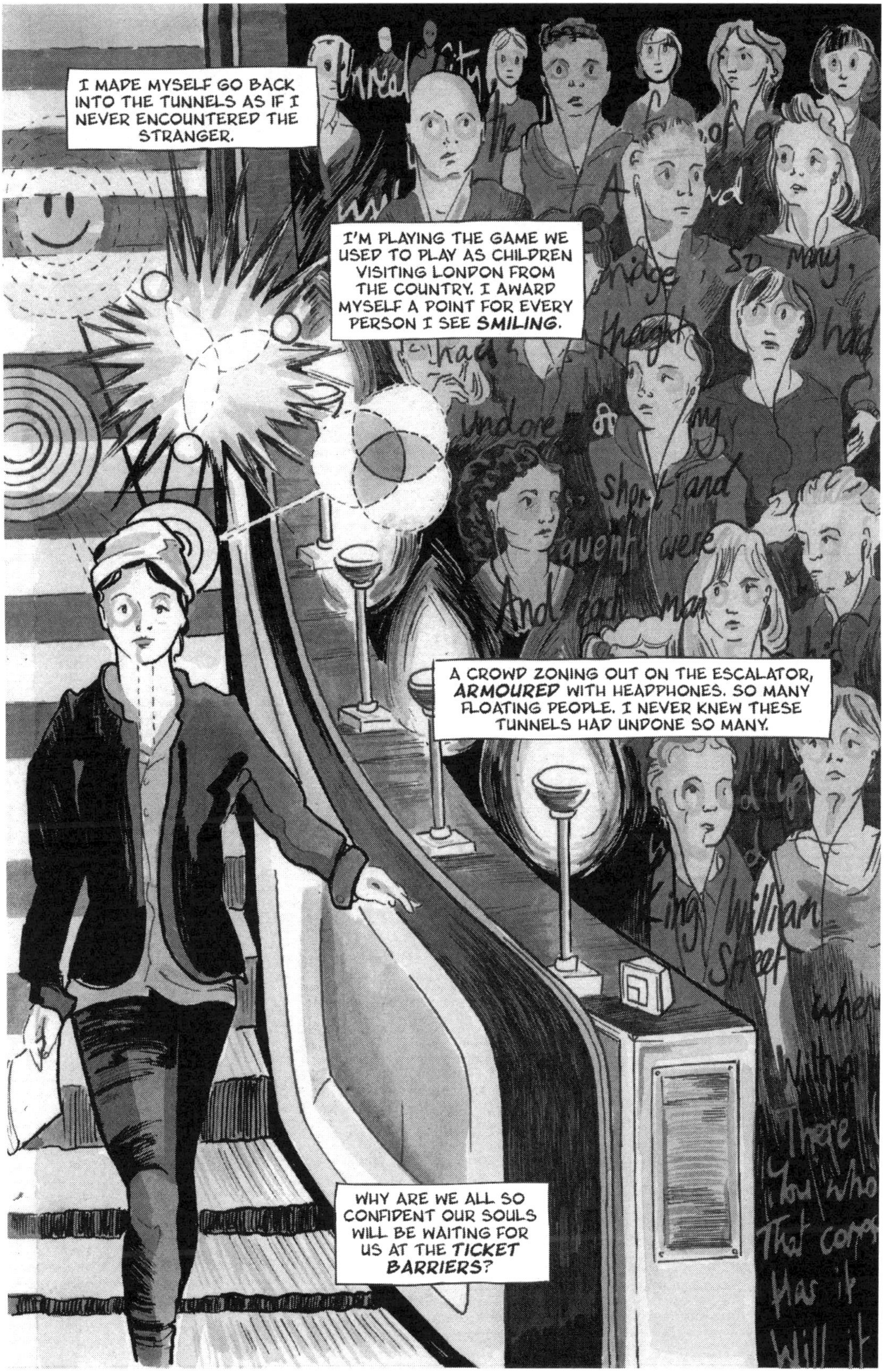
I MADE MYSELF GO BACK INTO THE TUNNELS AS IF I NEVER ENCOUNTERED THE STRANGER.
I'M PLAYING THE GAME WE USED TO PLAY AS CHILDREN VISITING LONDON FROM THE COUNTRY. I AWARD MYSELF A POINT FOR EVERY PERSON I SEE SMILING.
A CROWD ZONING OUT ON THE ESCALATOR, ARMOURED WITH HEADPHONES. SO MANY FLOATING PEOPLE. I NEVER KNEW THESE TUNNELS HAD UNDONE SO MANY.
WHY ARE WE ALL SO CONFIDENT OUR SOULS WILL BE WAITING FOR US AT THE TICKET BARRIERS?

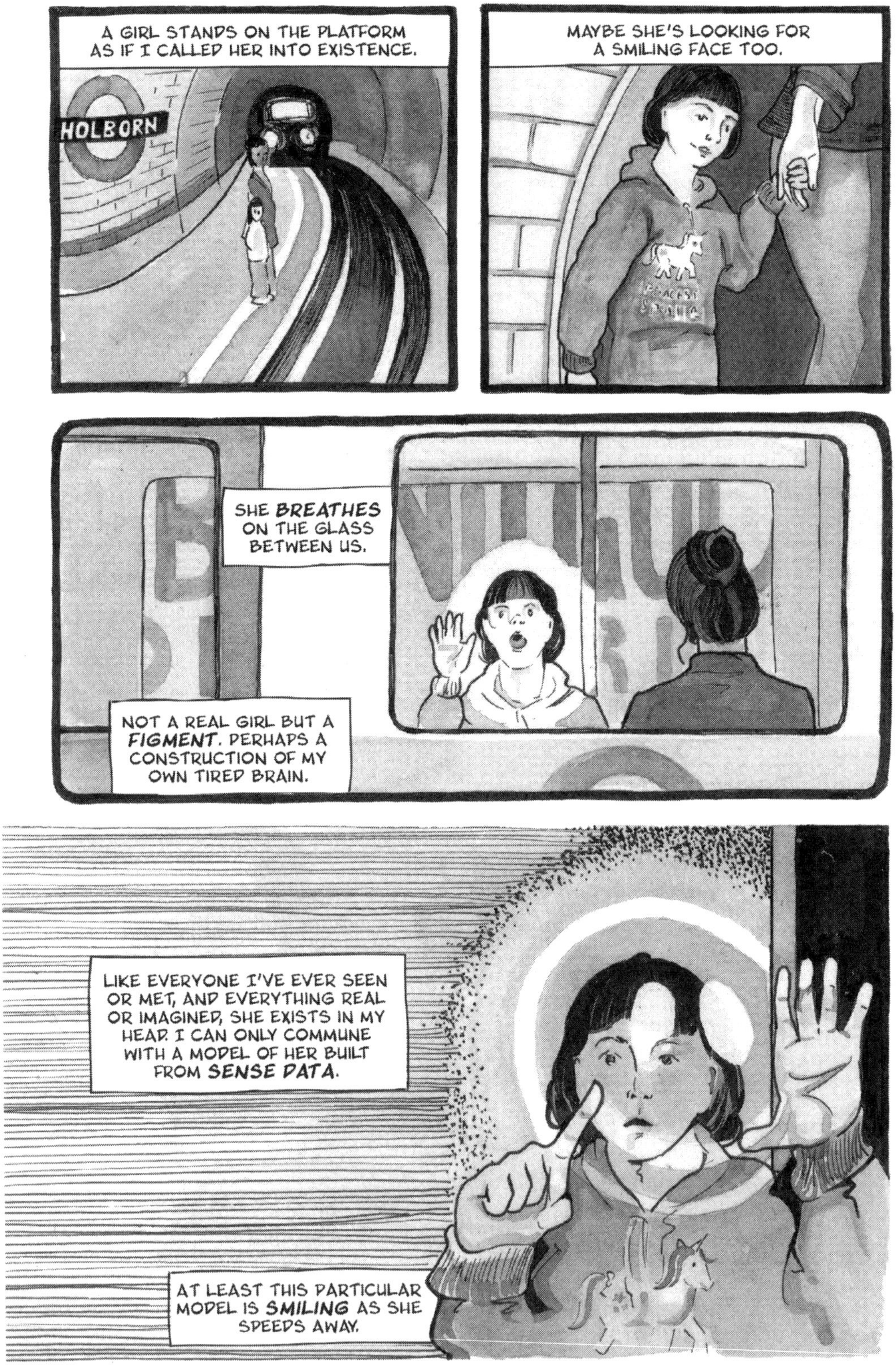
A GIRL STANDS ON THE PLATFORM AS IF I CALLED HER INTO EXISTENCE.
HOLBORN
MAYBE SHE'S LOOKING FOR A SMILING FACE TOO.
SHE **BREATHES** ON THE GLASS BETWEEN US.
NOT A REAL GIRL BUT A **FIGMENT**. PERHAPS A CONSTRUCTION OF MY OWN TIRED BRAIN.
LIKE EVERYONE I'VE EVER SEEN OR MET, AND EVERYTHING REAL OR IMAGINED, SHE EXISTS IN MY HEAD. I CAN ONLY COMMUNE WITH A MODEL OF HER BUILT FROM **SENSE DATA**.
AT LEAST THIS PARTICULAR MODEL IS **SMILING** AS SHE SPEEDS AWAY.

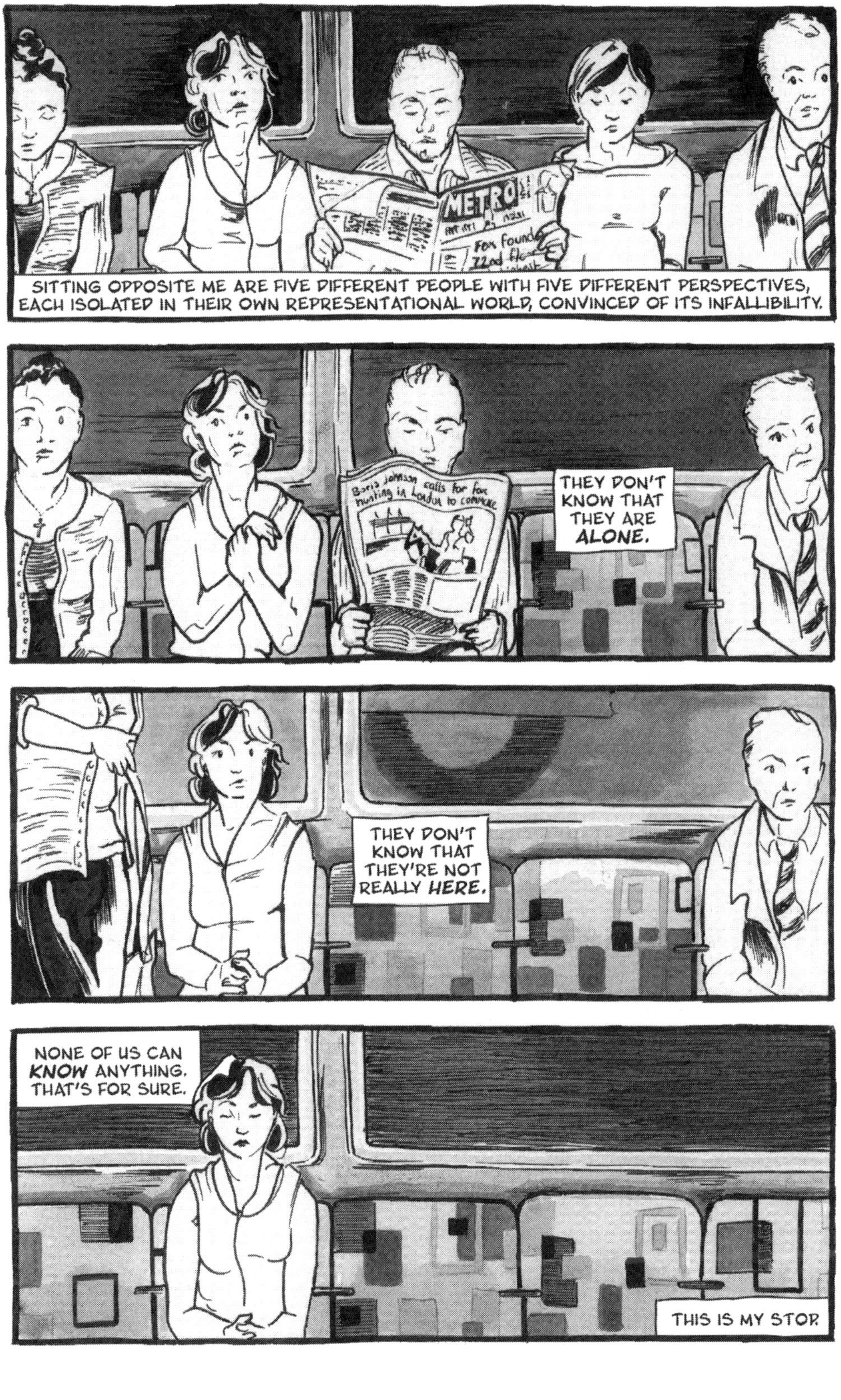
SITTING OPPOSITE ME ARE FIVE DIFFERENT PEOPLE WITH FIVE DIFFERENT PERSPECTIVES, EACH ISOLATED IN THEIR OWN REPRESENTATIONAL WORLD, CONVINCED OF ITS INFALLIBILITY.
METRO
Boris Johnson calls for fox hunting in London to commence
THEY DON'T KNOW THAT THEY ARE *ALONE.*
THEY DON'T KNOW THAT THEY'RE NOT REALLY *HERE.*
NONE OF US CAN *KNOW* ANYTHING. THAT'S FOR SURE.
THIS IS MY STOR

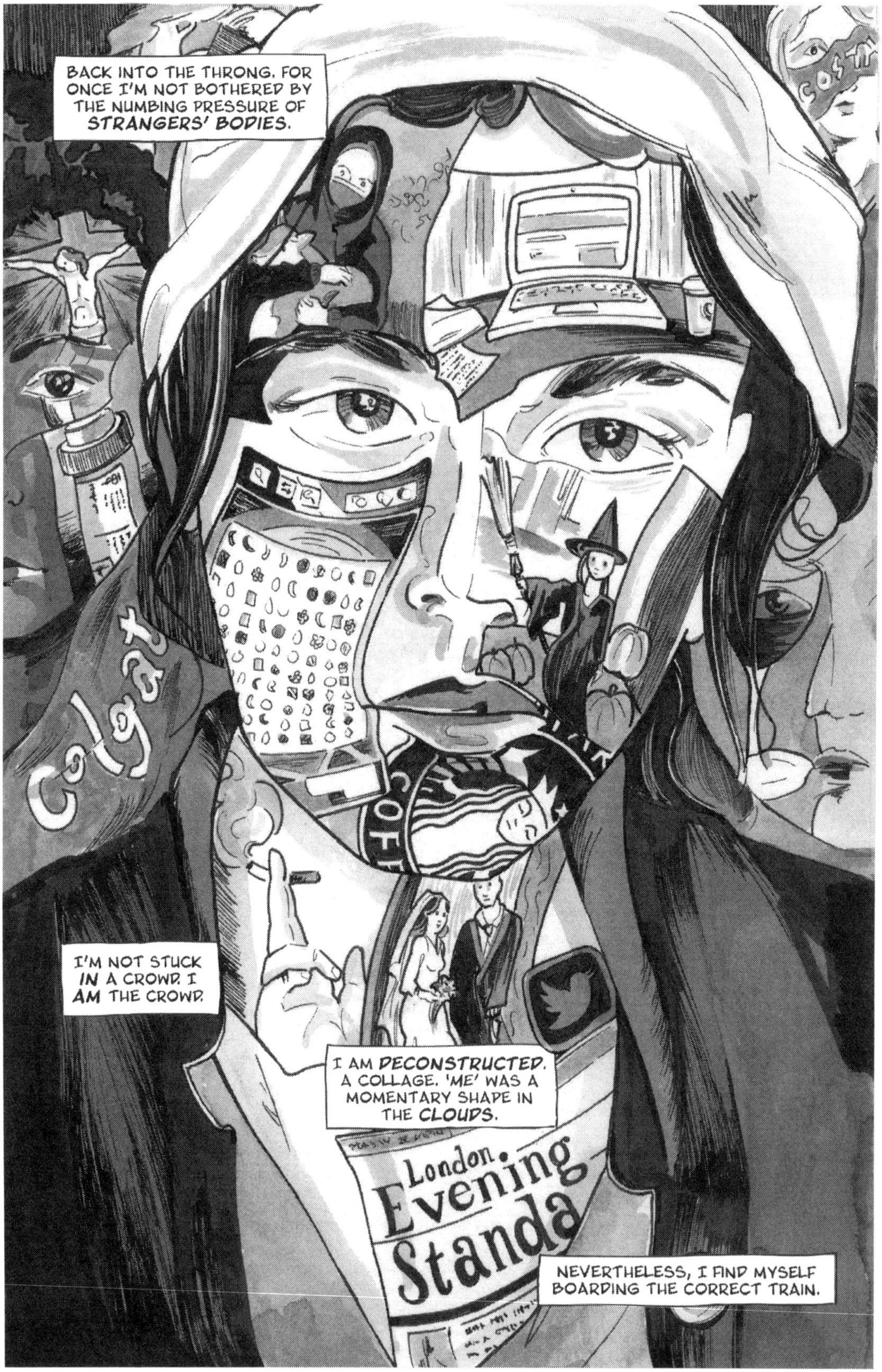
BACK INTO THE THRONG. FOR ONCE I'M NOT BOTHERED BY THE NUMBING PRESSURE OF STRANGERS' BODIES.
I'M NOT STUCK IN A CROWD. I AM THE CROWD.
I AM DECONSTRUCTED. A COLLAGE. 'ME' WAS A MOMENTARY SHAPE IN THE CLOUDS.
London Evening Standa
NEVERTHELESS, I FIND MYSELF BOARDING THE CORRECT TRAIN.

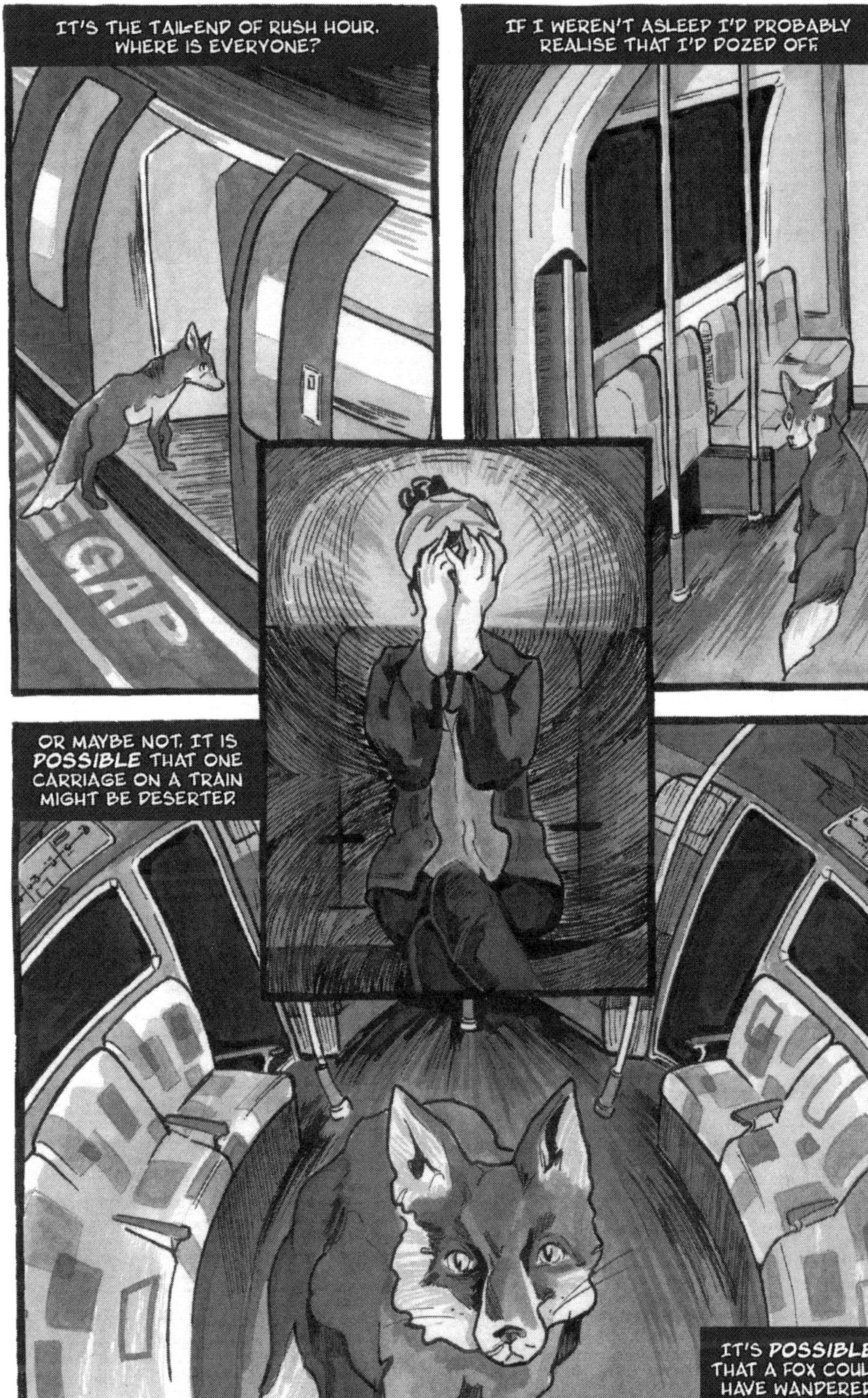
IT'S THE TAIL-END OF RUSH HOUR. WHERE IS EVERYONE?
IF I WEREN'T ASLEEP I'D PROBABLY REALISE THAT I'D DOZED OFF.
OR MAYBE NOT, IT IS POSSIBLE THAT ONE CARRIAGE ON A TRAIN MIGHT BE DESERTED.
IT'S POSSIBLE THAT A FOX COULD HAVE WANDERED DOWN HERE.

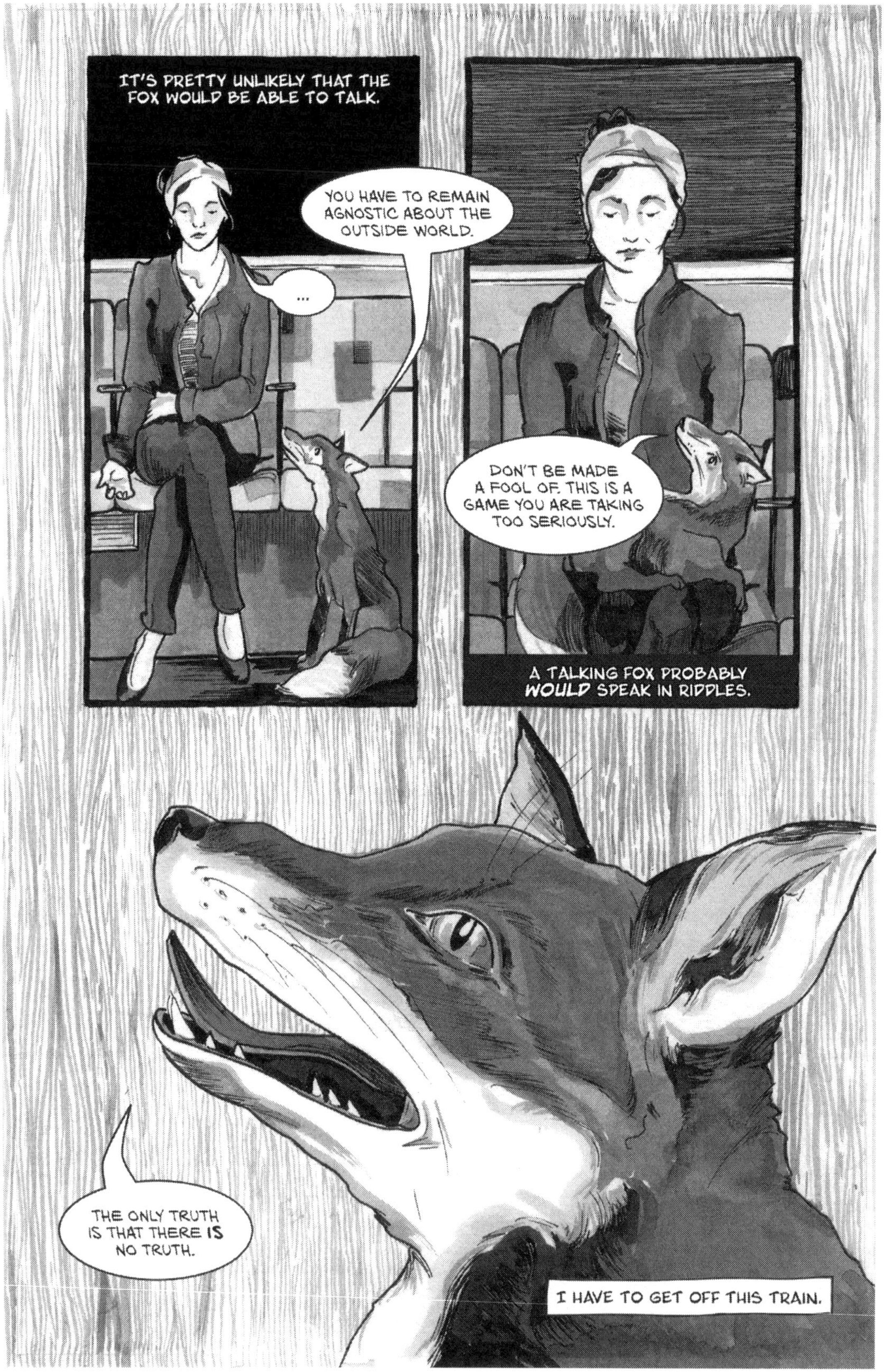
IT'S PRETTY UNLIKELY THAT THE FOX WOULD BE ABLE TO TALK.
YOU HAVE TO REMAIN AGNOSTIC ABOUT THE OUTSIDE WORLD.
...
DON'T BE MADE A FOOL OF. THIS IS A GAME YOU ARE TAKING TOO SERIOUSLY.
A TALKING FOX PROBABLY **WOULD** SPEAK IN RIDDLES.
THE ONLY TRUTH IS THAT THERE **IS** NO TRUTH.
I HAVE TO GET OFF THIS TRAIN.

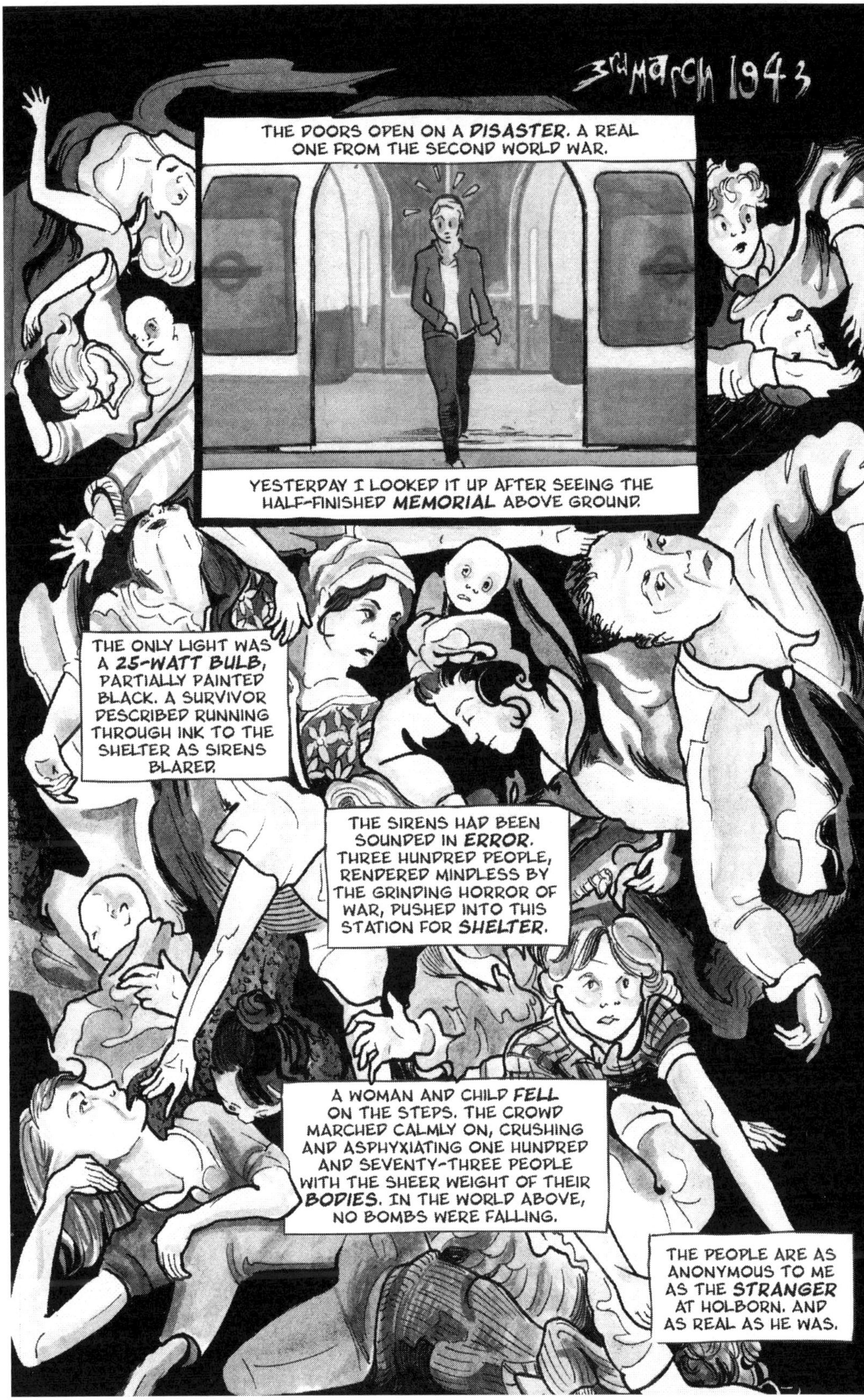
3rd March 1943
THE DOORS OPEN ON A DISASTER. A REAL ONE FROM THE SECOND WORLD WAR.
YESTERDAY I LOOKED IT UP AFTER SEEING THE HALF-FINISHED MEMORIAL ABOVE GROUND.
THE ONLY LIGHT WAS A 25-WATT BULB, PARTIALLY PAINTED BLACK. A SURVIVOR DESCRIBED RUNNING THROUGH INK TO THE SHELTER AS SIRENS BLARED.
THE SIRENS HAD BEEN SOUNDED IN ERROR. THREE HUNDRED PEOPLE, RENDERED MINDLESS BY THE GRINDING HORROR OF WAR, PUSHED INTO THIS STATION FOR SHELTER.
A WOMAN AND CHILD FELL ON THE STEPS. THE CROWD MARCHED CALMLY ON, CRUSHING AND ASPHYXIATING ONE HUNDRED AND SEVENTY-THREE PEOPLE WITH THE SHEER WEIGHT OF THEIR BODIES. IN THE WORLD ABOVE, NO BOMBS WERE FALLING.
THE PEOPLE ARE AS ANONYMOUS TO ME AS THE STRANGER AT HOLBORN. AND AS REAL AS HE WAS.

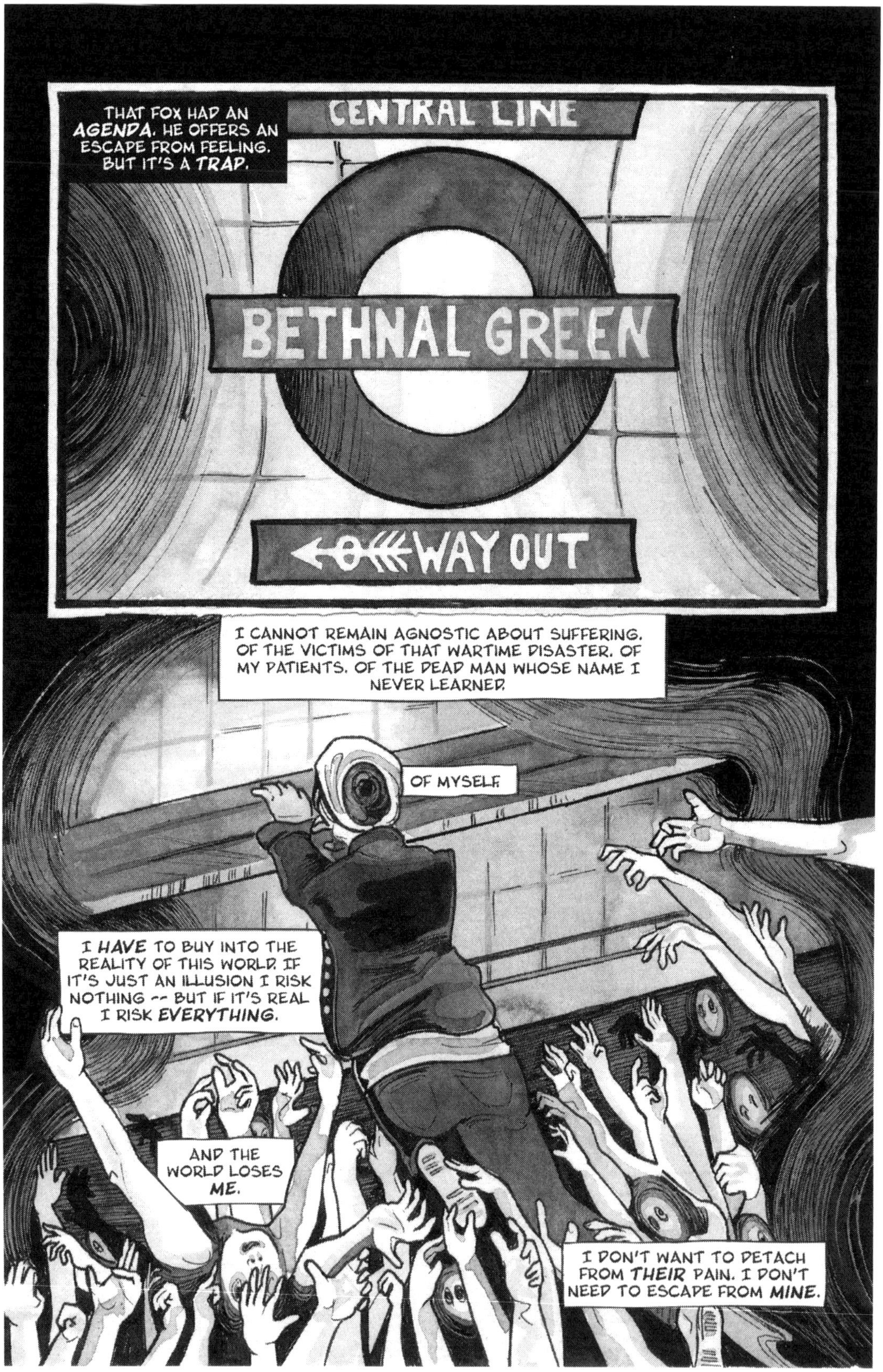
THAT FOX HAD AN AGENDA. HE OFFERS AN ESCAPE FROM FEELING. BUT IT'S A TRAP.
CENTRAL LINE
BETHNAL GREEN
WAY OUT
I CANNOT REMAIN AGNOSTIC ABOUT SUFFERING. OF THE VICTIMS OF THAT WARTIME DISASTER. OF MY PATIENTS. OF THE DEAD MAN WHOSE NAME I NEVER LEARNED.
OF MYSELF.
I HAVE TO BUY INTO THE REALITY OF THIS WORLD. IF IT'S JUST AN ILLUSION I RISK NOTHING -- BUT IF IT'S REAL I RISK EVERYTHING.
AND THE WORLD LOSES ME.
I DON'T WANT TO DETACH FROM THEIR PAIN. I DON'T NEED TO ESCAPE FROM MINE.

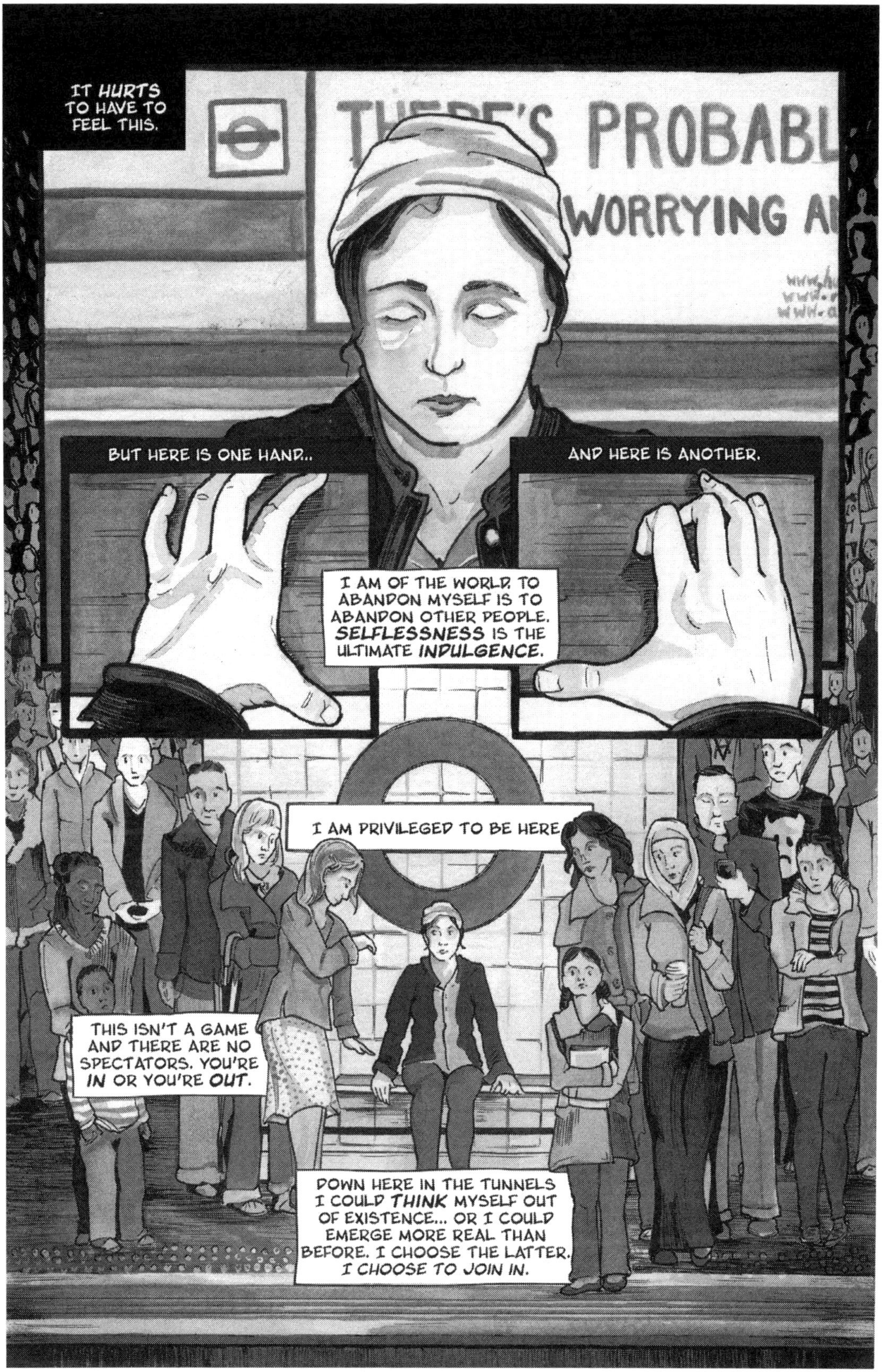
IT HURTS TO HAVE TO FEEL THIS.
THERE'S PROBABL
WORRYING A
BUT HERE IS ONE HAND...
AND HERE IS ANOTHER.
I AM OF THE WORLD. TO ABANDON MYSELF IS TO ABANDON OTHER PEOPLE. SELFLESSNESS IS THE ULTIMATE INDULGENCE.
I AM PRIVILEGED TO BE HERE.
THIS ISN'T A GAME AND THERE ARE NO SPECTATORS. YOU'RE IN OR YOU'RE OUT.
DOWN HERE IN THE TUNNELS I COULD THINK MYSELF OUT OF EXISTENCE... OR I COULD EMERGE MORE REAL THAN BEFORE. I CHOOSE THE LATTER. I CHOOSE TO JOIN IN.

EVERY STORY IN THIS BOOK HAS BEEN ABOUT DOUBT. While many religions and cultures celebrate the certainty of their faith traditions, I think it's important to celebrate doubt. Doubt is a hard sell, especially in a world which praises decisiveness and resolution, but getting comfortable with not knowing is essential if you want to live in reality. Before you can learn anything about the world you have to admit that you don't know everything – and before you admit that you have to formulate a method of 'knowing' that is based on what little you do know.

One thing we do know is that we are capable of thoughts. Our simplest thoughts are sense perceptions which describe the physical world we live in. When postmodern philosophers question the reality of the world we perceive, they are creating a false dichotomy. The inner world of our mind is dependent on the physical reality of our brains, and our brains are as much a part of the physical world as any other part of our bodies. The external world is a necessary precondition to the internal world of thoughts in which we live. To question the existence of the external world is to question the existence of our own bodies, our own brains.

Maybe this seems hypocritical. I am championing doubt but dismissing a profound existential doubt that underlies all of our assumptions. But the type of doubt I respect is a disciplined, humble inquiry that I expect will eventually lead to realisation – not a formless, perpetual deconstruction that only leads to, albeit sometimes cheerful, nihilism.

The doubt I advocate depends on the acceptance of certain propositions; a network of premises that support each other. I propose that I am real, that other people are real too, and the world we live in is best understood by the tools of reason and evidence. Why reason and evidence? Because they work. Anything we've ever learned was informed exclusively by the careful observation of the natural world. Any advance we've made in making the world a more comfortable place to live in, we predicated on the idea that things exist. If you think the world is real, and the beings that populate it matter, then reason and evidence are the best tools we have to make things that feed them, entertain them, and reduce their suffering.

Imagine we're playing a board game. The nature of the game is that the rulebook is revealed page by page as the game progresses. Have you ever played a game with someone who refuses to read the rules? Or who knows what the rules say, but cheats at every opportunity? How about someone who refuses to acknowledge the existence of the rules at all? Well you have now; they're playing the game with us. They declare that rules cannot exist, and they pick up the wrong pieces and move them arbitrarily. On your turn they say 'who cares? It's only a game'. When you read the rules aloud they calmly inform you that what you have said is a matter of opinion. Then on their turn they tell you that games don't exist anyway, so what does any of this matter?

It's not just a metaphor. We really are playing that game. The board is the entire physical universe, and the rule book is the catalogue of all the reasonable observations, models and predictions ever made. Despite the stakes, there are real people in the real world who deny its existence, who hold to the refrain: 'who cares? It's only a game'.

I care. I don't really want to play with people who say they don't.

We need each other desperately, and doubting our beliefs and the beliefs of those around us is critical – but doubting our own existence or the existences of others is unproductive and harmful. We get lost in tunnels of meaningless rhetoric, and lose sight of what's important: the world we are building together.

More information, discussion and links at doubtcomic.com/unreal-city

PRIVILEGED TO BE

ओ मणिपद्मे हूं *(Om mani padme hum)*: An ancient Sanskrit mantra.

FMRI: Functional Magnetic Resonance Imaging; a medical procedure used to measure brain activity.

Gautama: The historical Buddha.

Sangha: The Pali word for 'religious community' used by Buddhists.

AN OCEANIC FEELING

E! Fyle: 'Hey! Boy'. (Greek)

Malakas: A very general expletive. (Greek)

Kani putsokrio: 'It's fucking cold'. (Greek)

MAYFLY

Arré: Hey! (Hindi)

Brahma: One of the three primary Hindu Gods.

Holi: Hindu spring festival.

Jalebi: A kind of deep fried sweet pastry.

Vishnu: One of the three primary Hindu Gods.

BETWEEN WORLDS

Anata: Literally 'you'. Used as term of endearment in Japanese.

Moshi Moshi: Japanese telephone greeting used to mean 'Hello'.

AS ABOVE SO BELOW

Besom: The old english word for broomstick used by some Wiccans.

Reiki: A form of supernatural energy healing.

Skyclad: From the Jain concept of *Digambara* (literally 'sky-clad'); used to mean ritual nudity.

INDONESIAN PUNK ROCK

Distro: Independent media distributors and, in Indonesia's punk scene, informal clubs (an abbreviation of 'distribution source').

Fitna: Sedition (Arabic).

Haram: Forbidden (Arabic).

Hijab: A veil that covers head and chest, often worn by Muslim women.

Maghrib: Evening prayer (Arabic).

Qanun Jinayat: Islamic Criminal Code Bylaw.

Sharia: Islamic Law.

Yogya: Yogyakarta, a city in Java, Indonesia.

CHAKRAS DON'T SPIN

Chakras: Centres of supernatural power in the human body.

Chi: (sometimes *Qi*) The Chinese word for a supernatural energy force.

Namaste: 'I bow to the divine in you'; used in greetings and farewells in India, Nepal and your local yoga studio.

Surya Namaskara (Sun Salutation): Common sequence of yoga postures.

SNAKE OIL SHAMAN

Dinges: Something whose name is unknown or forgotten; thingumabobs.

Kasie: Abbreviated from 'location', meaning a township (or shanty town) surrounding an urban centre.

Lesofe: The word for people with albinism in Sesotho.

Mampara: Idiot

Muti: 'Medicine' performed by a witchdoctor.

Ngaka: Witchdoctor (Sesotho).

Nyaope: A street drug, the components of which are debated but which is agreed to be dangerous and addictive.

Shame: General friendly term used to express sympathy, agreement, sorrow or excitement.

Shrik: Fright (from Afrikaans *geshrik*).

Tokoloshe: Monster from Zulu folklore.

DYING OF THE LIGHT

Murmuration: A flock of starlings flying at dawn or dusk in cold weather in stunning formations.

UNREAL CITY

Tube: The London Underground.

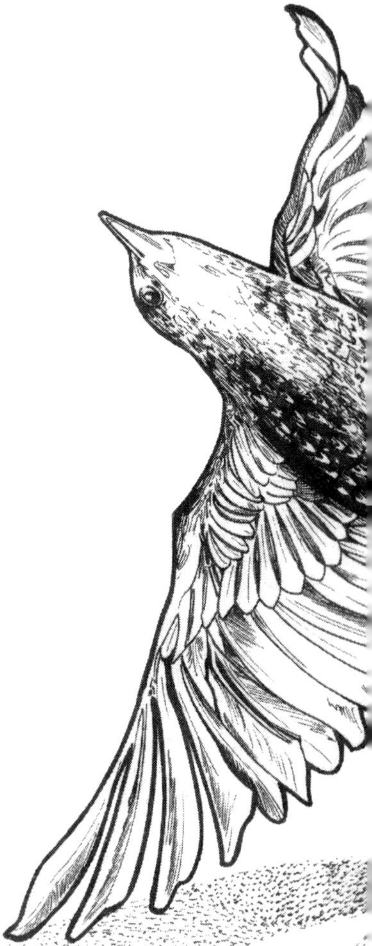

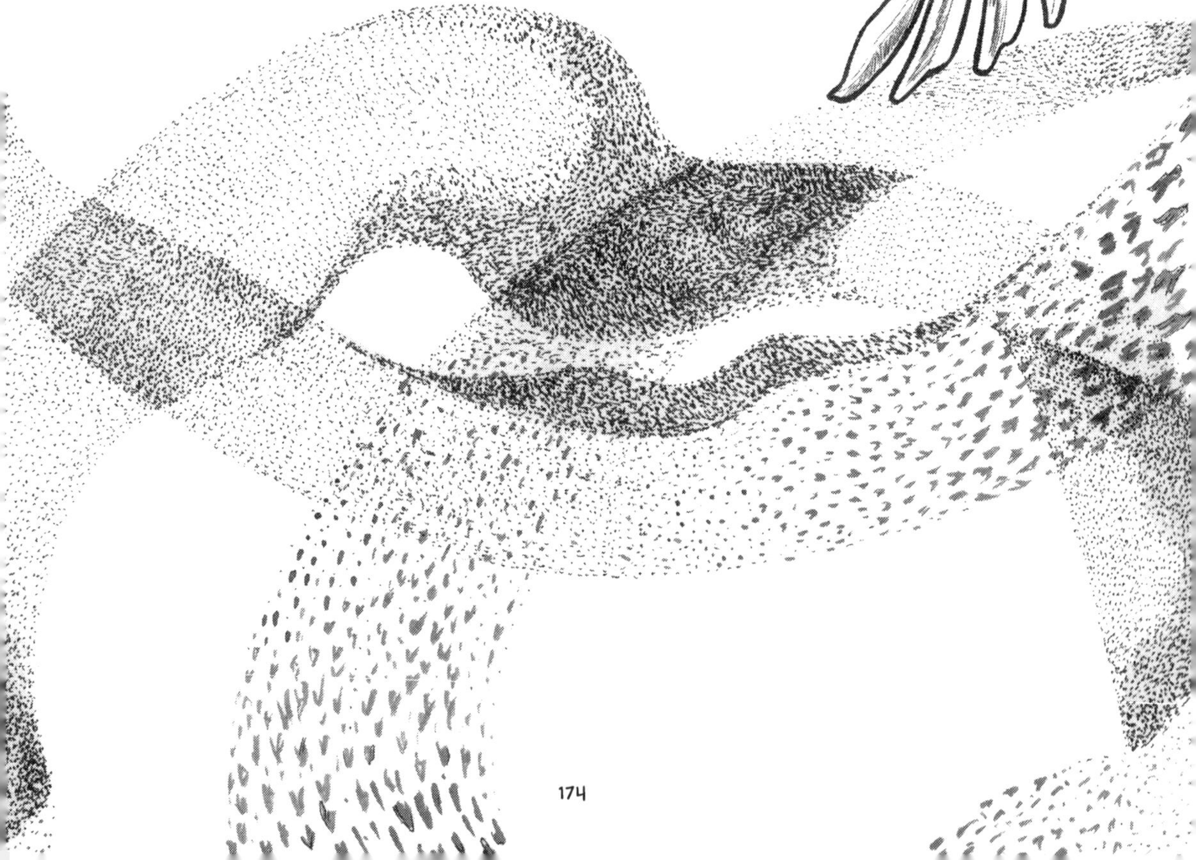

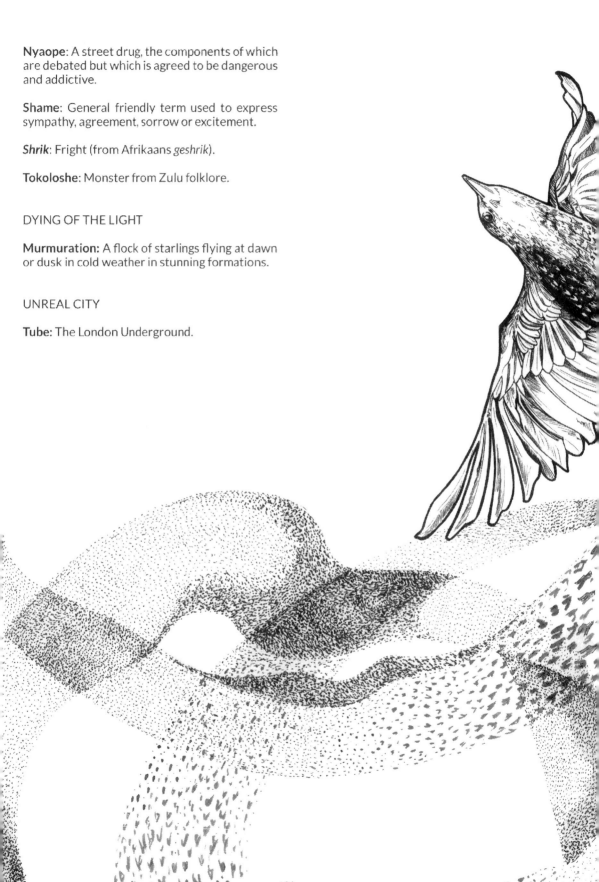

PRIVILEGED TO BE

Batchelor, S. (2010) *Confession of a Buddhist atheist*. New York: Random House Publishing Group.

Bhikkhu, T. (1994) *Kalama Sutta: to the Kalamas*. Available at: http://www.accesstoinsight.org/tipitaka/an/an03/an03.065.than.html (Accessed: 28 August 2016).

Tavris, C. and Aronson, E. (2013) *Mistakes were made (but not by me): Why we justify foolish beliefs, bad decisions and hurtful acts*. 2nd edn. London, United Kingdom: Pinter & Martin.

BORN OF WATER

Beebe, J. (no date) *Internet encyclopedia of philosophy*. Available at: http://iep.utm.edu/evil-log (Accessed: 28 August 2016).

Davis, J. (2002) *Spotlight church abuse report: Church allowed abuse by priest for years - the Boston globe*. Available at: http://www.bostonglobe.com/news/special-reports/2002/01/06/church-allowed-abuse-priest-for-years/cSHfGkTIrAT25qKGvBuDNM/story.html (Accessed: 28 August 2016).

Did the problem of evil make you leave Christianity? • /r/exchristian (2016) Available at: https://www.reddit.com/r/exchristian/comments/48f5mm/did_the_problem_of_evil_make_you_leave/ (Accessed: 28 August 2016).

Fake Buddha quotes (2016) Available at: http://fakebuddhaquotes.com/ (Accessed: 28 August 2016).

Paul, G. (2009) *Theodicy's problem: A statistical look at the holocaust of the children, and the implications of natural evil for free will and best of all possible worlds hypothesis*. Available at: http://gspaulscienceofreligion.com/gsptecharticles.html (Accessed: 28 August 2016).

The Holy Bible: English standard version, containing the old and new testaments (2011) Wheaton, IL: Crossway Bibles.

Wright, B.R.E., Giovanelli, D., Dolan, E.G., Edwards, M.E. and Simkins, R.A. (2011) 'Explaining deconversion from Christianity: A study of online narratives', Creighton Digital Repository, 13.

AN OCEANIC FEELING

The Smashing Pumpkins (1995) *Bullet with Butterfly Wings*.

NASA science (2015) *Dark energy, dark matter*. Available at: http://science.nasa.gov/astrophysics/focus-areas/what-is-dark-energy (Accessed: 28 August 2016).

darknlooking (2007) *Carl Sagan - pale blue dot*. Available at: http://youtube.com/watch?v=p86BPM1GV8M (Accessed: 28 August 2016).

Novella, S. (2009) *Chopra mangles quantum mechanics – again*. Available at: http://theness.com/neurologicablog/index.php/chopra-mangles-quantum-mechanics-again (Accessed 28 August 2016).

MAYFLY

Bhagavatapurana, P. (1976) *Srimad-Bhagavatam: Canto 7: The science of god*. Veda Base.

Lakshmi, R. (2013) *India is taking acid attacks more seriously*. Available at: http://theguardian.com/world/2013/aug/27/india-acid-attack-campaign-harassment (Accessed: 28 August 2016).

Samata: Keeping girls in secondary school (2016) Available at:http://strive.lshtm.ac.uk/projects/samata-keeping-girls-secondary-school (Accessed: 28 August 2016).

UNITING TO COMBAT ACID ATTACKS (2016) Available at: http://asfi.in/ (Accessed: 28 August 2016).

PILLOW TALK

Boghossian, P.G. and Shermer, M. (2013) *A manual for creating atheists*. New York, NY, United States: Pitchstone Publishing.

Boghossian, P.G. (2012) *'Faith: Pretending to know things you don't know' by Dr. Peter Boghossian*. Available at: http://youtube.com/watch?v=qp4WUFXvCFQ (Accessed: 28 August 2016).

Leeuwen, N.V. (no date) *Religious credence is not factual belief*. Available at:

http://philpapers.org/archive/VANRCI.pdf (Accessed: 28 August 2016).

Online K.J.B. (2016) *HEBREWS 11: 1 KJV 'now faith is the substance of things hoped for, the evidence of things not seen.'* Available at: http://kingjamesbibleonline.org/Hebrews-11-1 (Accessed: 28 August 2016).

BETWEEN WORLDS

Dvorsky, G. (2014) *George Takei describes his experience in a Japanese internment camp.* Available at: http://io9.gizmodo.com/george-takei-describes-his-experience-in-a-japanese-int-15333589-84 (Accessed: 28 August 2016).

Museum, J.A.N., Niiya, B., Inouye, D.K. and Okihiro, G.Y. (2006) *Encyclopedia of Japanese American history: An A-to-Z reference from 1868 to the present.* 2nd edn. New York, NY: Facts on File.

AS ABOVE, SO BELOW

Gardner, G.B.B., Murray, M. and Harrow, J. (2004) *Witchcraft today.* 50th edn. New York, NY: Kensington Publishing.

Hutton, R. (1999) *The triumph of the moon: A history of modern pagan witchcraft.* Oxford: Oxford University Press.

Murray, M.A. and Runciman, S. (1996) *The witch-cult in western Europe.* New York: Barnes & Noble Books.

St Mark's Highcliffe, Christchurch, Dorset - church of England (2014) Available at: http://stmarkshighcliffe.org.uk/ (Accessed: 28 August 2016). *Hutton describes much of the known life of Dorothy Clutterbuck in The Triumph of the Moon. With the information Hutton supplied and the help of a church administrator I found the graveyard where Dorothy Clutterbuck is thought to be buried at St Marks Highcliffe, and found the grave she erected upon the death of her husband in 1939.*

INDONESIAN PUNK ROCK

Abbott, R. (2014) *Time to stop criminalizing beliefs in Indonesia.* Available at: http://jakartaglobe.beritasatu.com/opinion/time-stop-criminalizing-beliefs-indonesia/ (Accessed: 28 August 2016).

Abshar-Abdalla, U. (no date) *Informasi Beragam*

Islam. Available at: http://islamlib.com/ (Accessed 28 August 2016). *Jaringan Islam Liberal is a forum for discussing the liberalisation of Islam in Indonesia.*

Atheist Alliance (2016) Available at: http://atheistalliance.org/ (Accessed: 28 August 2016). *The Atheist Alliance offer information on how to support atheists worldwide.*

VICE (2016) *Punk vs. Sharia.* Available at: http://vice.com/en_uk/video/punk-vs-sharia (Accessed: 28 August 2016).

The logo of the metalcore band Avenged Sevenfold (no date) Available at: upload.wikimedia.org/wikipedia/commons/e/e4/Deathbat-avengedsevenfold001.JPG (Accessed: 28 August 2016).

Thomson, M. (2015) *Is Indonesia winning its fight against Islamic extremism?* Available at: http://bbc.co.uk/news/magazine-35055487 (Accessed: 28 August 2016).

CHAKRAS DON'T SPIN

Burkeman, O. (2011) *This column will change your life: The just world bias.* Available at: http://theguardian.com/lifeandstyle/2011/nov/11/oliver-burkeman-just-world-bias (Accessed: 28 August 2016).

Farley, T. (no date) *What's the harm?* Available at: http://whatstheharm.net (Accessed: 28 August 2016). *Documents the people who have been driven into debt, refused proven medical treatment, ingested poison or undergone dangerous treatments and died as a result of using CAM.*

Hall, H. (no date) *Science Based Medicine.* Available at: http://youtube.com/playlist?list=PL8MfjLNsf_miVcNu6eJMNigAMNwQkk_B9 (Accessed: 28 August 2016). *Harriet Hall's ten lecture course, available for free on YouTube, is the best introduction to Complimentary and Alternative medicine that I have come across.*

Lerner, M.J. (1980) *The belief in a just world: A fundamental delusion.* New York: Kluwer Academic/Plenum Publishers.

stormmovie (2011) *Tim Minchin's 'Storm: The animated movie'.* Available at: http://youtube.com/watch?v=HhGuXCuDb1U (Accessed: 28 August 2016).

SNAKE OIL SHAMAN

Albinism Society of South Africa (no date) Available at: http://albinism.org.za/ (Accessed: 28 August 2016). The *Albinism Society of South Africa works to support people with albinism and educate the public about albinism. Part of their work is dispelling myths about people with albinism such as the insidious idea that 'when people with albinism die, they simply vanish'.*

Engstrand-Neacsu, A. and Wynter, A. (2009) *Through albino eyes.* Available at: http://www.ifrc.org/Global/Publications/general/177800-Albinos-Report-EN.pdf (Accessed: 28 August 2016).

Fellows, S. (2009) *Trafficking body parts in Mozambique and South Africa.* Available at: http://www.iese.ac.mz/lib/PPI/IESE-PPI/pastas/governacao/justica/artigos_cientificos_imprensa/trafficking_body_africa.pdf (Accessed: 28 August 2016).

HINARI (2000) 'The Durban declaration', Nature, 406(6791), pp. 15–16. doi: 10.1038/35017662.

Igwe, leo (no date) *A manifesto for a skeptical Africa.* Available at: http://instituteforscienceandhumanvalues.com/pdf/1891-leo-igwe.pdf (Accessed: 28 August 2016).

Specter, M. (2016) *The Denialists.* Available at:http://newyorker.com/magazine/2007/03/12/the-denialists (Accessed: 28 August 2016).

DYING OF THE LIGHT

Religulous (2009) Directed by Larry Charles.

Christina, G. (2015) *Comforting thoughts about death that have nothing to do with God.* United States: Pitchstone Publishing.

Holland, H.S. (1910) *The king of terrors.* Available at: http://en.wikisource.org/wiki/The_King_of_Terrors (Accessed: 28 August 2016).

Phelps, A., Maciejewski, P., Nilsson, M., Balboni, T., Wright, A., Paulk, M., Trice, E., Schrag, D., Peteet, J., Block, S. and Prigerson, H. (2009) 'Religious coping and use of intensive life-prolonging care near death in patients with advanced cancer', JAMA., 301(11), pp. 1140–7.

Thomas, D. (1951) *Do not go gentle into that good night.* Available at: http://poets.org/poetsorg/poem/do-not-go-gentle-good-night.

UNREAL CITY

Butler, C. (2002) *Postmodernism: A very short introduction.* London: Oxford University Press, USA.

Eagleton, T. (1996) *The illusions of postmodernism.* Cambridge, MA: Blackwell Publishers.

Eliot, T.S. (2016) *The waste land.* Available at: http://poetryfoundation.org/poems-and-poets/poems/detail/47311 (Accessed: 28 August 2016).

Moore, G. (no date) *Proof of an External World.* Available at: http://selfpace.uconn.edu/class/ana/MooreProof.pdf (Accessed: 28 August 2016).

Sokal, A. and Bricmont, J. (2003) *Intellectual impostures: Postmodern philosophers' abuse of science.* London: Economist Books.

Made in the USA
Middletown, DE
29 November 2017